DREAMS OF MOD

Psychoanalysis, Literatur

Laura Marcus is one of the leading literary critics of modernist literature and culture. *Dreams of Modernity: Psychoanalysis, Literature, Cinema* covers the period from around 1880 to 1930, when modernity as a form of social and cultural life fed into the beginnings of modernism as a cultural form. Railways, cinema, psychoanalysis and the literature of detection – and their impact on modern sensibility – are four of the chief subjects explored. Marcus also explores gender and sexuality in the period, and the work of modernist women writers, including H.D., Dorothy Richardson and Virginia Woolf. The overriding themes of this work bear on the understanding of the early twentieth century as a transitional age, raising the question of how 'the moderns' understood the conditions of their own modernity.

LAURA MARCUS is Goldsmiths' Professor of English at the University of Oxford, where she is a Fellow of New College. She is the author of *Auto/biographical Discourses: Theory, Criticism, Practice*: *Virginia Woolf: Writers and Their Works* and *The Tenth Muse: Writing about Cinema in the Modernist Period*. She has also coedited *Close Up 1927–1933: Cinema and Modernism* and *The Cambridge History of Twentieth-Century English Literature*.

DREAMS OF MODERNITY

Psychoanalysis, Literature, Cinema

LAURA MARCUS

University of Oxford

CAMBRIDGE
UNIVERSITY PRESS

CAMBRIDGE
UNIVERSITY PRESS

32 Avenue of the Americas, New York, NY 10013-2473, USA

Cambridge University Press is part of the University of Cambridge.

It furthers the University's mission by disseminating knowledge in the pursuit of
education, learning, and research at the highest international levels of excellence.

www.cambridge.org
Information on this title: www.cambridge.org/9781107622951

© Laura Marcus 2014

First published 2014

Printed in Great Britain by Clays Ltd, St Ives plc

A catalog record for this publication is available from the British Library.

Library of Congress Cataloging in Publication Data
Marcus, Laura.
Dreams of modernity : psychoanalysis, literature, cinema / Laura Marcus.
pages cm
ISBN 978-1-107-04496-8 (hardback)
1. Civilization, Modern. 2. Literature and society. 3. Psychoanalysis
and culture. 4. Modernism (Literature) 5. Motion pictures. I. Title.
CB358.M3645 2014
909.8–dc23 2014018138

ISBN 978-1-107-04496-8 Hardback
ISBN 978-1-107-62295-1 Paperback

For Isobel Armstrong

Contents

Acknowledgements

I am grateful for permission to reproduce the cover image: L. Mercier, 'Accident gare de l'Ouest, le 22 octobre 1895' (Musée d'Orsay, Paris).

Parts of a number of these chapters have appeared in the following publications, and I am grateful for permission to reprint.

Part of Chapter 1 appeared as my 'Introduction' to *The Lodger*, pp. ix–xxv (Oxford: Oxford University Press, 1996). Chapters 2 and 3 contain material from 'Oedipus Express: Trains, 'Trauma and Detective Fiction', in *The Art of Detective Fiction*, eds. Warren Chernaik, Martin Swales and Robert Vilain (London: Macmillan, 2000), pp. 201–221, reprinted in *New Formations* 41, Autumn 2000, pp. 173–188 (Lawrence and Wishart), and also from 'Psychoanalytic Training: Freud and the Railways', in *The Railway and Modernity: Time, Space and the Machine Ensemble*, eds. Matthew Beaumont and Michael Freeman (Oxford: Peter Lang, 2007), pp. 155–176. Chapter 4 appeared in *19: Interdisciplinary Studies in the Long Nineteenth Century*, 17, 2013, pp. 1–13, available at: http://www.19.bbk.ac.uk/index.php/19/issue/view/84. Part of Chapter 5 was published in *Modernist Cultures*, Vol. 5, No. 1, 2010, pp. 30–46 (Edinburgh University Press). Chapter 6 appeared in *The New Woman in Fiction and in Fact*, eds. A. Richardson and C. Willis (London: Macmillan, 2000), pp. 136–149; Chapter 7 in *Mapping Lives: The Uses of Biography*, eds. Peter France and William St Clair (British Academy/Oxford University Press, 2002), pp. 193–218; Chapter 8 in *History and Psyche*, eds. Sally Alexander and Barbara Taylor (Basingstoke: Palgrave Macmillan, 2012), pp. 105–128. An early version of Chapter 9 was published in *Psychoanalysis and History*, Vol. 3, No. 1, 2001, pp. 51–68, and reprinted in *The Dreams of Interpretation: A Century Down the Royal Road*, eds. Catherine Liu, John Mowitt, Thomas Pepper and Jakki Spicer (Minnesota: University of Minnesota Press, 2007), pp. 197–214. Chapter 10 appeared in *Pilgrimages: Journal of Dorothy Richardson Studies*, Vol. 1, No. 1, 2008, pp. 50–73; Chapter 11 in *Journal of the Short Story in English*, Spring 2008, 153–169 (Presses Universitaires d'Angers); and

Chapter 12 in *Contemporary Woolf/Woolf contemporaine*, eds. Claire Davison-Pégon and Anne-Marie Smith-Di Biasio (Montpellier: Presses Universitaires de la Méditerranée, 2014), pp. 15–32.

It would be impossible to name and thank all those who have contributed to the research, writing and publication of these essays. I would, however, like to express my gratitude to Ray Ryan at Cambridge University Press for commissioning this volume and for his interest in my work; to the anonymous readers; and to all those at the Press who were involved in its production. Friends and colleagues at the University of Oxford have been valued interlocutors in recent years. I would particularly like to thank David Bradshaw, Michèle Mendelssohn, Ankhi Mukherjee and Kirsten Shepherd-Barr: collaborations with them on other projects, different from but bearing on the preoccupations of this collection, have been immensely rewarding and enjoyable. So, too, are ongoing projects on Dorothy Richardson, with Deborah Longworth, Scott McCracken and Joanne Winning, and on Virginia Woolf's short stories, with Jane Goldman, Bryony Randall and Susan Sellers.

Rebecca Roach gave essential help in the preparation of the final typescript of *Dreams of Modernity*, with her usual efficiency and good cheer. William Outhwaite has helped at every stage, and is my 'without whom'. This book is for him, for Daniel Outhwaite, and for my dear friend Isobel Armstrong.

Introduction

The essays in this volume cover the period from about 1880 to 1930, during which modernity as a form of social and cultural life feeds into the beginnings of modernism as a cultural form. What has been called 'the new modernist studies' has essentially been concerned with locating modernism, now defined more broadly than in the past, in relation to other aspects of the culture of modernity. The journal *Modernism/Modernity*, established in 1994 and now the official journal of the Modernist Studies Association, originally announced its aim as being to 'convey some sense of the grand ambition and scope of artists and intellectuals of the first half of this century'.[1] It currently describes itself as 'Concentrating on the period extending roughly from 1860 to the present', and the journal covers a very wide range of themes in the literary and cultural spheres.

In their recent discussions of 'the new modernist studies', Douglas Mao and Rebecca Walkowitz have emphasized the 'expansion' of the field.[2] While they stress the global dimension of expansion, there are also other dimensions which should be considered. One is temporal, in that 'the new modernist studies' is more open to the prehistory of modernism in the late nineteenth century. More importantly, perhaps, there is also an intrinsic dimension which recognizes something like the same duality which Baudelaire had identified in modernity: the combination of solidity and fragmentation which enables us to use the term 'modernist' both for a high-rise building and for Joyce's prose. Some of the essays in this volume are explicitly concerned with the modernist writing and culture of the early twentieth century; others with longer-term affinities and continuities. As Michael Levenson has suggested, 'The agon of modernism was not a collision between novelty and tradition but a *contest of novelties*, a struggle to define the trajectory of the new.'[3]

The questions raised by what has rather misleadingly been called 'the modernity thesis' in relation to early cinema have a more general application.[4] There is a perceived tension in contemporary modernist studies

I

between approaches which stress the context of social and cultural modernity, opening up questions of gender and globality, and those which focus on the specifically aesthetic dimension of modernism.[5] I would suggest, by contrast, that we need to transcend the sharp opposition that is sometimes presented between a culturalist and a more formalist approach to modernism. An instance of their connectedness is indicated by Hugh Kenner, in *The Mechanic Muse*: 'In the twentieth century, said T.S. Eliot, the internal combustion engine altered people's perception of rhythm: little had been pervasively rhythmic save one's own heart, one's lungs, the waves, and horses' hooves.'[6] Rhythm is both a formal dimension of poetics and is shaped by cultural circumstances and change. Language, experience, culture and technology are not independent of each other, but are profoundly interrelated.

Railways, cinema, psychoanalysis and the literature of detection – four of the key themes of the essays in this volume – lead us from the nineteenth into the early twentieth century. Railways and other modern forms of transport are not intrinsically modernist, but they have been an important inspiration for modernist cultural forms and movements, and there are continuities to be traced between the early responses to rail travel and the automobile and later modernist celebrations of them. Mark Seltzer, in his *Bodies and Machines*, examined, through American naturalist fiction, 'the radical entanglement of relations of meanings and relations of force . . . and the radical entanglement of writing, bodies and mechanics'. He referred not only to the more generalized model of thermodynamics but specifically to the railway itself, as 'the centering nineteenth-century model . . . of the principle of locomotion', and of the mechanisms of relays, exchanges, couplings and cross-points between, for example, the natural and the technological, 'passion and mechanism', bodies and machines.[7] In such accounts, the railway train becomes an icon of mobility. It is, as Nicholas Daly has shown, a central element in sensation fiction, and it continues to be so in the detective fiction that followed.[8] The railway acts as an embodiment of both the progressive and the destructive aspects of industrialism, and as a powerful motor by means of which the nineteenth century is driven into the twentieth. There has been something of a shift of emphasis from the economic and social history of the train to its phenomenology – from the fact of rapid motion to the ways in which it is experienced – but there is also a growing interest in the forms of connectivity, across nations and empires, tracked by the railways.

In 1858 Marx wrote in the *Grundrisse* that 'the means of communication and transport [enable] the annihilation of space by time',[9] and their interrelations have rightly been seen as a central aspect of culture at the turn of the century, notably by Stephen Kern.[10] Discussion of a number of phenomena in the late nineteenth and early twentieth centuries – dreaming, early cinema, transport, telepathy, telegraphy – define their significance as an annihilation of space *and* time. In the first decades of the twentieth century, the distortion of space–time relations was given an aesthetic twist by futurists and others. Léger, for example, pointed to the impact of the visual experience of rapid motion on 'the condensation of the modern picture, its variety, its breaking up of forms ... It is certain that the evolution of means of locomotion, and their speed, have something to do with the new way of seeing.'[11] Aldous Huxley famously claimed that speed, and in particular fast driving, was the only new pleasure invented by modernity.[12] The impact was not just visual: Freud suggested a link 'between railway-travel and sexuality ... clearly derived from the pleasurable character of the sensations of movement',[13] and more recently (and as I discuss in Chapter 2), Sylvie Nysembaum has suggested that this rhythmic motion blurs the boundaries between human and machine.[14]

The period 1880–1930 has been described by Hugh Kenner, glossing Richard Cork's book on Vorticism (and in the process transforming what Cork called the first into the second), as 'the second machine age', and it is true that this was the time when, for example, machine transport became for the first time a central feature of the modern city.[15] The year 1895 has particular significance, marking both one starting point for the history of cinema (if this to be dated from the occasion of the first public exhibition of the Lumière brothers' film) and a spectacular railway accident at the Gare Montparnasse in Paris. The story of early cinema-goers becoming terrified by a film of the arrival of a train at the station at La Ciotat, though it may be exaggerated, links the two forms through affect as well as temporal coincidence.[16] The year 1895 is also of key importance in the early history of psychoanalysis, with (as I discuss in Chapter 9) Freud dating his discovery of the unconscious to that year.

Freud's analysis of dreams, published at the end of 1899, was, he thought, 'the most valuable of all the discoveries it has been my good fortune to make'[17] and 'the royal road to a knowledge of the unconscious activities of the mind'.[18] For Walter Benjamin, dreams are intimately linked to history and utopia: 'the history of the dream remains to be written ... Dreaming has a share in history.'[19] In his *Arcades* project he repeatedly quoted Michelet's remark in an essay of 1839 that 'Each epoch dreams the one to follow, creates it in dreaming.'[20] The arcades are a kind of dreamscape, and historiography as he practised it is a form of dream interpretation and one oriented to the future: 'Every epoch, in fact, not only dreams the one to follow but, in thus dreaming, precipitates its awakening.'[21]

Early reflection on cinema focused substantially on the parallels between dreams and films, even if the Freudian 'screen memory' was a sometimes misunderstood translation of Freud's motif of concealment (*Deckerinnerung*). The interiority of dreams has found conceptual and experiential parallels in the often private character of cinema spectatorship and in railway travel, in which the scenery passes by as if projected onto the train window.[22] Both in the cinema and from the train, there is an element of voyeurism – even perhaps *in* the train, as when Freud speculates that as a two-year-old he saw his mother naked on a night train: the founding moment of his discovery of the Oedipus complex, as he would later theorize it. The interrelation between railways and detective fiction concerns not just plots shaped by new possibilities of mobility but also, as Walter Benjamin noted, by the particular suitability of this form of fiction as reading matter on a train journey. For Benjamin, even in 1930, a railway journey was capable of reawakening the fear experienced by nineteenth-century travellers: an anxiety which could be countered by reading literature which aroused another form of fear.[23]

The literary detective was, Ronald Thomas has suggested, 'arguably the most significant and enduring contribution to the history of English literature made during the Victorian era', but the theme of unmasking and detection, as the Marxist philosopher Ernst Bloch noted, has a much wider prominence, for example in Ibsen's dramas or the work of Poe.[24] It is also central to Freud, whose 'analytical research . . . is no longer informed by cool dissection but by a vigilance typical of the detective. The conviction that, the more neatly the mask conceals, the less salutary that which goes on behind it, gives rise to a deep suspicion of draperies and facades.'[25] Siegfried Kracauer, too, analysed detective fiction at length in 1925, against the background of what in 1963 he called 'the ornament of the mass'.[26] The analysis and decipherment of hieroglyphics was also a recurrent motif in early cinema criticism and in analyses of modern forms of advertising, where it becomes closely linked to both the spectacle and the visual sign-systems of modern urban culture.[27]

Recent cultural theorists have pursued the connections between detection and psychoanalysis – twin sciences of evidence-gathering and of the reconstruction or deduction of the whole from the part. Both, as Carlo Ginzburg argued in his essay 'Clues: Roots of an Evidential Paradigm', are semiotic sciences, methods of reading and interpreting signs.[28] Ginzburg turns to a passage in Freud's 'The Moses of Michelangelo', the essay in which Freud reconstructs a history from a detail and a gesture, deciphers the enigmatic knot in Moses' beard and the position of his index finger, and attempts to transmute the frozen moment of statuary into motion, narrative and temporality. In the essay Freud compared the technique of psychoanalysis with the methods of Giovanni Morelli, an art connoisseur who attributed authorship and detected fakes by diverting attention:

> from the general impression and main features of a picture, and by laying stress on the significance of minor details, of things like the drawing of a fingernail, of the lobe of an ear, of halos and such unconsidered trifles which the copyist neglects to imitate and yet which every artist executes in his own characteristic way ... It seems to me that his method of inquiry is closely related to the technique of psychoanalysis. It, too, is accustomed to divine secret and concealed things from despised or unnoticed features, from the rubbish-heap, as it were, of our observations.[29]

The motif of detection and unmasking was also crucial to the 'new biography' of the early twentieth century, whose novelty has not been sufficiently recognized in discussions of literary modernism. This reworking of the biographical form – pursued more or less independently by Lytton Strachey in Britain, André Maurois in France, Emil Ludwig in Germany and Gamaliel Bradford in North America – was accompanied by a mass of commentary on the genre, written by both its practitioners and its critics. The new biography combined a debunking approach, particularly strong in Strachey, and a 'scientific' emphasis with a painterly focus on revelatory or exemplary detail rather than chronological narrative: the biographer, in Ludwig's understanding, as a portraitist. Moreover, 'Pictures', Ludwig asserts, 'those silent betrayals, provide the biographer with material as valuable as letters, memoirs, speeches, conversations ... or as handwriting. For this reason, a biography without a picture of its subject is impossible'.[30]

In the words of the early twentieth-century American biographer (or, in his phrase, 'psychographer') Gamaliel Bradford: 'If you know what to look for, minor, insignificant actions tell you much, perhaps more than greater, more deliberate deeds, because there is less thought or care for concealment.'[31] Biographical discourse, then, would seem to share a focus on detail and a model of decipherment with the sciences of detection and psychoanalysis. This connection was noted by Freud himself when he wrote to Ernest Jones about the 'slippery ground' of psychobiography: 'It is the danger inherent in our method of concluding from faint traces, exploiting trifling signs. The same as in criminal cases, where the murderer has forgotten to relinquish his *carte de visite* and full address on the *Tatort*.'[32]

A number of critics in the early to mid-twentieth century set up a stark contrast between modernism and detective fiction, but Ginzburg has pointed to the emergence of an 'epistemological paradigm' in the late nineteenth century, tracing links between Galton, Giovanni Morelli, and Freud, and there is certainly an affinity between certain modes of modernist literature and the detective genre. This connection has recently been explored in suggestive ways by Vicki Mahaffey, who links the focus on 'interpretative authority' (that of the detective and the reader) in the Sherlock Holmes stories with the modernist difficulty of Joyce's *Dubliners*, arguing that in both sets of narrative there is a strategy of 'analysing "backwards" from what is observed'.[33] *Dubliners*, she argues, 'is a series of detective stories, but they significantly lack a detective . . . It is up to the reader to detect, by "reasoning backwards" from each collection of facts and observations, what must have happened.'

'The original social content of the detective story was the obliteration of the individual's traces in the big-city crowd', Walter Benjamin wrote in his study of Charles Baudelaire, *The Paris of the Second Empire in Baudelaire*.[34] He explored the centrality of this motif in Edgar Allan Poe's 'The Mystery of Marie Roget' and in 'The Man of the Crowd', which, in his account of the significance of photography both for criminology and for the emergence of detective fiction, Benjamin describes as 'something like the X-ray picture of a detective story'.[35] The city was one of the crucial links, and most often the site, in which modernist culture emerged out of turn-of-the-century modernity. There are significant connections between urban experience and narrative and poetic forms, including the ways in which features associated with literary modernism – the use of stream-of-consciousness techniques, fluid characterizations, explorations of mobility and experiments with temporality – are linked to urban consciousness. Virginia Woolf wrote in a diary entry in 1924:

> One of these days I will write about London & how it takes up the private life & carries it on, without any effort. Faces passing lift up my mind; prevent it from settling, as it does in the stillness at Rodmell. . . . But my mind is full of The Hours [the work which became *Mrs Dalloway*] . . . And I like London for writing it, partly because, as I say, life upholds one . . . to see human beings freely and quickly is an infinite gain to me.[36]

The links between cinema and city as dimensions of modernity are also of central importance to an understanding of modernist culture, with its tropes of movement and dynamism: the connections are explored in my chapter in this volume on the films of the 1920s known as 'city symphonies' (Chapter 5).

One of the most fundamental processes involved here is the way in which the visual metaphors which had pervaded modern literature become, in a sense, literalized as visual media become more prominent. Photography and film had a profound impact upon the visual arts, displacing, for example, the value of artistic realism. The technology to which Benjamin pointed most emphatically, in his 1936 essay 'The Work of Art in the Age of Mechanical Reproducibility', was film. In their power to extend human vision (in what Sigmund Freud understood to be a form of prosthesis) or to penetrate more deeply into reality than could the human eye (as Benjamin has it), the technologies of the visual also exposed the human eye's frailties, partialities and limitations.

In his introduction to *Signatures of the Visible*, Fredric Jameson wrote that the experiences of cinema and cinema-going might underlie the thought and writing of the twentieth century in ways we have not yet understood. Jameson instanced Jean-Paul Sartre's claim for his own theory of 'contingency', 'derived from the experience of film, and in particular from the mystery of the difference between the image and the world outside',[37] and asks whether this might not be true even for artists and writers who have less obvious connections to film and to movie-going. 'Did human nature', Jameson asks, 'change on or about December 28, 1895? Or was some cinematographic dimension of human reality always there somewhere in prehistoric life, waiting to find its actualization in a certain high-technical civilization? (and thereby now allowing us to reread and rewrite the past now filmically and as the philosophy of the visual)?'[38] The emergence of these issues alongside the new medium is in part because film seemed, to its first viewers, to be a reproduction or doubling of the world itself – 'a recreation of the world in its own image', in André Bazin's words[39] – and thus engendered models or 'film fables' (to borrow the title of Jacques Rancière's 2001 book) of origin and evolution. I addressed these issues in detail in my book *The Tenth Muse: Writing about Cinema in the Modernist Period*.[40]

The conscious concern of literary writers and other cultural producers in this period with cinema, psychoanalysis and transport varies in degree, but these and other aspects of this central period of modernity formed a background and sometimes (as in the case of writers whom I have not had sufficient space to discuss in this volume, including Elizabeth Bowen, Jean Rhys and Katherine Mansfield) a foreground to their work.[41] Affinities and cross-currents between the cultural phenomena of the period run through and between the essays in this book. They focus more often on modernity than on modernism, narrowly defined, but they nonetheless address their complex interrelations, pointing to the emergence of modernism in the crucial decades spanning what remains, a century later, the definitive *fin de siècle*.

The temporal complexities of narrative are a central theme, taking up the ways that forms of 'reasoning backwards' (as an aspect of the hermeneutic culture of the turn of the century, evidenced in the interpretative drive of detective fiction, with its intense focus on the legibility of the detail) co-exist with the modes of 'dreaming forward' explored by Walter Benjamin. Such temporal reversals and inversions are a significant dimension of the reshaping of time and space, to be found not only in the speed of railway travel but also in the juxtapositions and inversions common to dreams and cinema. A related thread in this volume is the topic of asychronicity or a doubled time-frame. It connects the novelist Marie Belloc Lowndes's early twentieth-century reinscriptions of an episode of late nineteenth-century danger; Freud and Breuer's patient's '*double conscience*' and Freud's concept of the way in which the new always leads back to the old; and Benjamin's account of nineteenth-century fears which are reawakened in the transport of the twentieth century. This strand also emerges in discussions of the temporal preoccupations of women modernist writers, for whom the connections between past, present and future are particularly charged. Dorothy Richardson's novel sequence *Pilgrimage* is an archive of the self – the writing, begun in 1915, of a young woman's life in the last decades of the nineteenth century and the first years of the twentieth – and a project in which Richardson seeks to recapture past presents. In the work of Virginia Woolf, models of continuity and of the depth and complexity of present time, 'backed' as it is by the past, carry as much, or more, weight as those of modernist or avant-garde 'rupture'. Woolf's capturing of a Victorian scene 'through the telescope' (the topic of my penultimate chapter) becomes emblematic of the relationship between spatial and temporal distance and proximity which has guided many of my readings.

The first chapter in the volume, '*The Lodger*', explores a defining episode in late nineteenth-century British culture: the series of murders of women in London in 1888 held to have been committed by the figure who came to be known as 'Jack the Ripper'. The chapter starts from the depiction of the murders in the terms of fiction, with associations at the time drawn between Whitechapel's 'murder mystery' and works by Edgar Allan Poe and Robert Louis Stevenson. Both Poe's detective Dupin and Arthur Conan Doyle's Sherlock Holmes have the power to read bodies like texts, a capacity made very literal in Poe's 'The Murders in the Rue Morgue', in which Dupin first reads about the mutilated bodies of the women in the newspaper accounts of the murders which detail the physician's official examination of the corpses. The hermeneutic understanding of the performances and representations of murder is clearly central to the nineteenth century and beyond; it has become combined with the perception, deeply influenced by the work of Michel Foucault, of the nineteenth century as a culture of surveillance, and one in which the work of detection is most prevalent where it is most invisible or, perhaps, most dispersed. 'We are all on the private detective lay now', as the journalist George Sims put it in 1888. The chapter traces a number of the journalistic, literary and cinematic/filmic representations of the 'Ripper' crimes, focusing on *The Lodger*, the novel published in 1913 by the Edwardian writer Marie Belloc Lowndes, which was the inspiration for Hitchcock's 1926 film of the same title.

The railway and train travel is the subject of the next two chapters. Chapter 2, 'Oedipus Express', examines the centrality of the railways to psychoanalytic thought. It explores the ways in which some of Freud's most fundamental concepts were influenced by nineteenth-century accounts of 'railway shock' and 'railway spine', as diseases of modern life, and charts the recurrence of metaphors and dreams of the railway in Freud's writings and in the dreams and symptoms of his patients. The genesis of Chapter 3, 'Railway Reading', is Walter Benjamin's 1930 article, 'Kriminalromane, auf Reisen' ['Detective Novels, on Journeys'] and its claim that 'Travel reading is as closely linked to railway travel as is the time spent in stations.'[42] Matthew Arnold wrote, in a critical account of railway reading, of 'the tawdry novels which flare in the book-shelves of our railway stations'; the image of a flaring or firing up makes an implicit connection between trains and novels that the chapter pursues through discussion of nineteenth- and early twentieth-century sensation and detective fiction.

The psychology of the turn of the century was strongly focused on concepts of 'attention' and 'distraction', and the models of consciousness which these terms imply became central to modernist literature and thought. In Chapter 4, '"From Autumn to Spring, Aesthetics Change": Modernity's Visual Displays', I explore the ways in which models of 'attention', drawn in part from the work of the nineteenth-century psychologist Théodule Ribot, shaped theories of 'attraction', advertising, film spectatorship and the pictorial 'language' of modernity. The work of the German-born philosopher and psychologist Hugo Münsterberg ties these strands together in particularly significant ways. Münsterberg, who left his post at the University of Freiburg in the 1890s in order to take up a position in William James's psychological laboratory at Harvard, where Gertrude Stein became one of his students, was a polymath. His researches, theoretical and applied, reached into many corners of modern life: crime and detection (he invented the lie-detector test), industrial efficiency, transport (he created a prototype for a simulated driving apparatus), visual psychology and optics, and film (his 1916 study *'The Photoplay: A Psychological Study'* is a foundational work of film aesthetics). The chapter discusses Münsterberg in tandem with the American poet and early writer on film Vachel Lindsay, showing how the work of these two individuals, with their radically different backgrounds and experiences, came together in their writings on modern visuality and, in particular, on the cinema. Modernism's 'visual turn' is indeed a connecting thread of the essays in this volume, as is the correlation of late nineteenth- and early twentieth-century literature's models of (in Fredric Jameson's phrase) 'presented vision' with the visual and optical technologies of the same period, in particular the new medium of film.

Chapter 5, '"A Hymn to Movement": The "City Symphony" of the 1920s and 1930s', continues the focus on cinema, exploring the cluster of city films made in the US and Europe in the first decades of the twentieth century. It examines the films in relation to the one-day novels of the same period, notably Joyce's *Ulysses* and Woolf's *Mrs Dalloway*, and discusses the centrality of 'modernist dailiness' in relation to the urbanism which provides the strongest conjunction between cultural modernity and literary modernism. The incidence of literary and filmic 'city symphonies' in this period also points up, in highly significant ways, the connections and contestations between literature and film.

Chapter 6, 'Staging the "Private Theatre": Gender and the Auto-erotics of Reverie', takes the theatrical metaphor of its title from one of psychoanalysis's early patients, 'Anna O', whose case history is included in Freud and Breuer's *Studies in Hysteria*, a key text of 1895. The 'private theatre' is the sphere of fantasy, reverie and 'systematic day-dreaming' which becomes intimately linked to literary fiction-making. The chapter explores the relationship between fantasy and writing, in the stories of Freud's patients and in the work of women writers at the turn of the century, opening up the question of the New Woman as a figure of, and for, modernity. It also addresses the issue of the 'interiority' of the New Woman, and the contrasting images of the auto-eroticism attached to this figure (in the writings of the sexologist and psychologist Havelock Ellis and others) as a question of internal fantasy or external stimulation, 'fiction' or 'friction'; an aspect of the uncertain relationship between the inner and the outer that shaped much turn-of-the-century thought. The drive to inwardness was defined in the 1880s by Max Nordau as 'ego-mania', and the critique of modernist literature's engagement with interiority and the play of consciousness continued to shape literary theory into the twentieth century.

The psychoanalytic case history, Michael Levenson has argued, offers 'a new metaphysics of character. Character is the precipitate of fantasies, desires, and dreads; it is an overlay of past and present; it possesses an inexhaustible convergence of meanings.'[43] Chapter 7 explores a literary form, the 'new biography', which took on a close and complex relationship to the case history in the early decades of the twentieth century and which was also part of the new focus on, and understanding of, character (both literary and psychological) at this time. 'On or about December 1910 human character changed', Virginia Woolf famously, and perhaps facetiously, asserted.[44] Her wording is significant: she does not refer, as might be expected, to 'human nature', but uses a term, as I discuss in my final chapter, with connections to text and writing ('character' derives from the Greek *kharattein*, to engrave). Chapter 7 examines the centrality of the 'new biography' to literature and culture in the 1920s and 1930s, arguing that it should be seen as a central dimension of literary and cultural modernism. It further notes the importance of biography to psychoanalysis at the turn of the century: 'We must take hold of biography', Freud wrote to Jung in 1909, in the context of his explorations of Leonardo da Vinci.[45]

Chapter 8 pursues the topic of psychoanalysis, this time in the context of British encounters with European psychoanalytic culture between the wars. The 'European Witnesses' of my title include Alix Strachey (who was analysed by Karl Abraham and Freud, and became, with her husband James Strachey, the foremost English translator of Freud's works), and Bryher and H.D. H.D.'s analysis in Vienna in the 1930s, described in her memoir *Tribute to Freud*, took place during a period in which, in psycho-analytic circles, there was ferment around the question of female sexuality. It was also a time of political turmoil, as the National Socialists began to take over the city. The chapter examines the topic of inner and outer realities, explored in the volume in its various manifestations, through the relation-ship between psyche and polis in the Europe of the 1920s and 1930s.

H.D. is also a significant figure in Chapter 9, 'Dreaming and Cinematographic Consciousness'. Turning back to 1895, as the founda-tional year for both psychoanalysis and cinema, the chapter follows through the connections between dreaming and cinema over the following decades. It discusses this interrelationship in the work and thought of, amongst other psychoanalytic figures, Hanns Sachs: one of Freud's closest colleagues, the analyst of both Bryher and H.D., and a central figure in the Berlin film culture of the 1920s to which Bryher, in particular, became so fully committed. The final section of the essay looks at H.D.'s film-acting and her writings on cinema in relation to her accounts of her analytic sessions with Freud, pointing up the centrality of film to her representations of memory, dreaming and visionary experience.

Dream-life is the central theme of Chapter 10, which explores the question of 'lucid' or 'directed' dreaming in the nineteenth and twentieth centuries, in the context of a history of writing about dreams, and of dreaming as a project. The chapter takes up a topic examined in a number of the essays in this volume: that of the interplay between the still and the moving image in dreams, which took on a particular significance in relation to the histories of photography and cinema. In nineteenth-century contexts, the connection also bears on the prehistory of the cinema, the history of optical technologies such as the magic lantern and the zoetrope, and the motion-studies of the period, including the photographic work of Étienne-Jules Marey and Eadweard Muybridge. The topic of 'directed dreaming' is also addressed in this chapter in relation to Dorothy Richardson's *Pilgrimage*.

Modernist women's writing is the topic of the final two chapters of the volume, which discuss aspects of Virginia Woolf's short stories, fiction and essays. Chapter 11, 'In the circle of the lens', examines a short story, 'The Telescope Story', which Woolf wrote and rewrote in many versions. It explores the different drafts of the story in relation to scene-making, optics and memory. The final chapter, 'Virginia Woolf and the Art of the Novel', turns to Woolf's essays on fiction in the context of the development of novel criticism in the early twentieth century. It focuses on Woolf's, and her contemporaries', constructions of literary history in relation to linear and synchronic models of the novel, as a 'new' genre, and the various responses to views of its 'development'. These issues bear, in significant ways, on the understanding of the early twentieth century as a 'transitional' age, opening up the question, central to this collection as a whole, of how 'the moderns' understood the conditions of their own 'present day' and their own modernity.

Notes

1 Lawrence Rainey and Robert von Hallberg, 'Editorial/Introduction', *Modernism/ Modernity* 1.1 (1994), 1.
2 Douglas Mao and Rebecca Walkowitz, 'The New Modernist Studies', 123. 3, 2008, pp. 737–748.
3 Michael Levenson, *Modernism* (New Haven: Yale University Press, 2011), p. 5 (emphasis in the original). See also Jean-Michel Rabaté, *1913. The Cradle of Modernism* (Malden, MA and Oxford: Blackwell, 2007), especially pp. 3–5.

4 For a critique of this concept, see Tom Gunning, 'Modernity and Cinema: A Culture of Shocks and Flows', in Murray Pomerance (ed.), *Cinema and Modernity* (New Brunswick, NJ: Rutgers University Press, 2006), pp. 297–315.

5 See, for example, Charles Altieri (2012) 'Afterword. How the "New Modernist Studies" Fails the Old Modernism', *Textual Practice*, 26:4, 763–782. Also Marjorie Levinson, 'What Is New Formalism?, *PMLA* 122, 2, March 2007, 558–569.

6 Hugh Kenner, *The Mechanic Muse* (Oxford and New York: Oxford University Press, 1987), p. 9.

7 Mark Seltzer, *Bodies and Machines* (New York and London: Routledge, 1992).

8 Seltzer, *Bodies and Machines*.

9 Karl Marx, *Grundrisse: Foundations of the Critique of Political Economy* (Harmondsworth: Penguin, 1973), p. 538.

10 Stephen Kern, *The Culture of Time and Space 1880–1918* (Cambridge, Mass: Harvard University Press, 1983).

11 Fernand Léger, 'Contemporary Achievements in Painting' (1914), in Edward F. Fry (ed.), *Cubism* (London: Thames and Hudson, 1966), p. 135; cited in Andrew Thacker, *Moving Through Modernity. Space and Geography in Modernism* (Manchester: Manchester University Press, 2003), pp. 7–8. Léger nearly abandoned painting for cinema, and co-directed *Ballet Mécanique* (1924).

12 See Enda Duffy, *The Speed Handbook. Velocity, Pleasure, Modernism* (Durham, NC: Duke University Press, 2009), p. 1.

13 Freud, *Three Essays on Sexuality*, in The Standard Edition of the Complete Psychological Works of Sigmund Freud (London: The Hogarth Press and the Institute of Psycho-Analysis, 1953), trans. James Strachey, vol. 7, pp. 201–202.

14 Sylvie Nysembaum, 'Une pensée qui va et vient,' quoted in J.-B. Pontalis, *Ce temps qui ne passe pas, suivi de Le Compartiment de chemin de fer* (Paris: Gallimard, 1997), p. 154.

15 Hugh Kenner, *The Mechanic Muse*.

16 See Stephen Bottomore, 'The Panicking Audience? Early Cinema and the Train Effect', *Historical Journal of Film, Radio and Television* 19.2 1999, 177–216; Tom Gunning, 'The Cinema of Attractions: Early Film, Its Spectator and the Avant-Garde', in Thomas Elsaesser (ed.) *Early Film: Space, Frame, Narrative* (London: British Film Institute, 1990), pp. 56–62; and Martin Loiperdinger, 'Lumière's Arrival of the Train: Cinema's Founding Myth', *The Moving Image* 4.1, Spring 2004, 89–113. See also Annemone Ligensa and Klaus Kreimeier (eds.), *Film 1900: Technology, Perception, Culture* (New Barnet: John Libbey, 2009), for a critical discussion of the relation between cinema and modernity around this time.

17 Sigmund Freud, *The Interpretation of Dreams* (First Part) (1900), *Standard Edition*, vol. 4 (1953), p. xxxii.

18 Freud, *The Interpretation of Dreams* (Second Part) (1900), *Standard Edition*, vol. 5 (1953), p. 608.

19 Walter Benjamin, *The Arcades Project*, trans. Howard Eiland and Kevin McLaughlin (Cambridge, Mass: Harvard University Press, 1999), p. 4.

20 Walter Benjamin, 'Dream Kitsch', in *Selected Writings, Vol. 2, 1927–1934*, translated by Rodney Livingstone (Cambridge, Mass: Harvard University Press, 1999), p. 3.

21 Benjamin, *The Arcades Project*, p. 898.

22 See Michel de Certeau, 'Railway Navigation and Incarceration', in *The Practice of Everyday Life* (Berkeley: University of California Press), pp. 111–114.

23 See Walter Benjamin, 'Kriminalromane, auf Reisen', *Gesammelte Schriften* IV. 1 (Frankfurt: Suhrkamp, 1989), pp. 381–382. Benjamin's own outline for a detective novel is in *Gesammelte Schriften* VII. 2, pp. 845–851.

24 Ernst Bloch, 'A Philosophical View of the Detective Novel' (1965), trans. Jack Zipes and F. Mecklenburg, in Ernst Bloch, *Literary Essays*, trans. Andrew Juron and others (Stanford University Press 1998), pp. 209–227.

25 Op. cit., p. 218.

26 The book with this title was republished in a fuller version in 1977 and in English translation in 1995 (*The Mass Ornament: Weimar Essays*, Harvard University Press). See also Kracauer, *Der Detektiv-Roman: Ein philosophischer Traktat. Schriften* 1 (Frankfurt: Suhrkamp, 1971), pp. 103–204. Also David Frisby, 'Walter Benjamin and Detection', *German Politics and Society* 32, Summer 1994, pp. 89–106, and 'Between the Spheres: Siegfried Kracauer and the Detective Novel', *Theory, Culture and Society* 9, 2, 1992, 1–22.

27 See my discussion in *The Tenth Muse*; also 'Hieroglyphics in Motion: Representing Ancient Egypt and the Middle East in Film Theory and Criticism of the Silent Period', in Pantelis Michaelakis and Maria Wyke (eds.), *The Ancient World in Silent Cinema* (Cambridge: Cambridge University Press 2013), pp. 74–90, and Chapter 4 in this volume.

28 Carlo Ginzburg, 'Clues: Roots of an Evidential Paradigm', in *Myths, Emblems, Clues*, translated by John and Anne C. Tedeschi (London: Hutchinson Radius, 1986), pp. 96–125.

29 Freud, 'The Moses of Michelangelo' (1914), *Standard Edition* vol. XIII, pp. 209–238, p. 222.

30 Emil Ludwig, *Genius and Character* (London: Jonathan Cape, 1927), p. 136.

31 Gamaliel Bradford, *Bare Souls* (New York and London: Harper, 1924), p. 3.

32 Letter from Freud to Ernest Jones, 7 February 1921, quoted in Ronald Clark, *Freud: The Man and the Cause* (London: Weidenfeld and Nicolson, 1980), p. 361.

33 Vicky Mahaffey, *Modernist Literature: Challenging Fictions* (Oxford: Blackwell, 2007), p. 80.

34 *The Paris of the Second Empire in Baudelaire*, in *Walter Benjamin's Selected Writings Vol. 4 1938–40*, pp. 3–92, translated by Edmund Jephcott et al. (Cambridge, MA: Harvard University Press, 2003), p. 23.

35 Ibid., p. 27.

36 *The Diary of Virginia Woolf, Vol. 2 1920–24* (May 26th, 1924), edited by Anne Olivier Bell (Harmondsworth: Penguin, 1981), p. 301.

37 Fredric Jameson, *Signatures of the Visible* (London: Routledge, 1990), p.7.

38 Ibid., p. 5.

39 André Bazin, *What Is Cinema? Vol. 1*, translated by Hugh Gray (Berkeley, CA: University of California Press, 1967), p. 21.

40 Published by Oxford University Press, 2007. See also my essay 'Modernism and Visual Culture', in Jean-Michel Rabaté (ed.), *A Handbook of Modernism Studies* (Blackwell 2013), pp. 239–254.

41 For an outstanding recent exploration of early twentieth-century literature and technology, see David Trotter, *Literature in the First Media Age: Britain Between the Wars* (Cambridge, MA: Harvard University Press, 2013).

42 *Gesammelte Schriften* Bd 4.1 (Frankfurt: Suhrkamp, 1972), pp. 381–383, here p. 382.

43 Levenson, *Modernism*, p. 83.

44 'Character in Fiction' (1924), in *The Essays of Virginia Woolf*, vol. 3, edited by Andrew McNeillie (London: Hogarth Press, 1988), pp. 420–438, p. 421.

45 *The Freud/Jung Letters,* ed. William McGuire (Harmondsworth: Penguin, 1991).

CHAPTER I

The Lodger

In an essay published in the mid-1980s, Christopher Frayling wrote that '"Jack the Ripper" remains the elusive figure he always was: a space in the files, an *absence* which has been given a name by "an enterprising journalist", and a character by successive writers, reporters and members of the reading public.'[1] Books on the series of murders of prostitutes in the autumn and winter of 1888 in the Whitechapel district of East London by an unknown figure who has been turned by popular legend into 'Jack the Ripper' have proliferated in recent decades. There have been continual attempts to solve the crimes and name the killer – as in the crime writer Patricia Cornwell's exhaustive endeavours to prove that Jack the Ripper was the painter Walter Sickert – as well as a series of critical and cultural studies.[2]

In reconsidering Jack the Ripper in this chapter, I look at some of the representations, early and recent, that have grown out of the Ripper murders of 1888, and examine the fascination with this particular moment of Victorian crime. I explore one text in detail: Marie Belloc Lowndes's novel of 1913, *The Lodger*, which merits renewed attention for several reasons.[3] It is to this fictionalized version of the Ripper murders that a number of film directors turned, as I discuss at the close of the chapter, including Alfred Hitchcock, John Brahm and Maurice Elvey. The novel not only produces its own version of the Ripper narrative but is a form of metanarrative, embedding already existing accounts within itself. It is, moreover, one of the very few representations of the murders to have been written by a woman, and it gives a central place to a woman's response – that of the landlady, Mrs Bunting – in whose house the Ripper figure lodges, and about whom she remains silent, despite her suspicions.

The community of Ripperologists, with their journal, elegantly titled *Ripperana*, is overwhelmingly male. It is indeed a community, with each new study of the murders, usually claiming evidence for a new suspect or suspects, containing extensive acknowledgements to other works in the field, though also expressing contempt for those whose claims to have uncovered new suspects are revealed, or are held, to be 'hoaxes'. It is interesting that such distinctions between truth and falsehood, authentic and inauthentic knowledges, can be so firmly upheld in a field near entirely composed of legend, fiction and fantasy.

It was acknowledged from the start that fictionality was the only means by which the murders could be represented. A *New York Times* article of 4 September 1888 ran as follows:

> Whitechapel has a murder mystery which transcends anything known in the annals of the horrible. It is Poe's *Murders in the Rue Morgue* and *The Mystery of Marie Roget* rolled into one story. It is nothing less than a midnight murderer, whose step is noiseless, whose strike is deadly, and whose cunning is so great that he leaves no trace whatsoever of his work and no clue to his identity . . . This man is called 'Leather Apron' and nobody knows him by any other name. He is a character halfway between Dickens's Quilp and Poe's Baboon.[4]

A week later, a columnist for the same newspaper wrote, 'What adds to the weird effect [the murders] exert on the London mind is the fact that they occur while everybody is talking about Mansfield's "Jekyll and Hyde" at the Lyceum.'[5] The Jekyll and Hyde analogy was drawn by W.T. Stead, in an editorial in *The Pall Mall Gazette* for 8 September 1888, in which he wrote of the weakness of the civilized restraints which

> keep the Mr Hyde of humanity from assuming visible shape among us. There seems to be a tolerably realistic impersonation of Mr Hyde at large in Whitechapel. The Savage of Civilization whom we are raising by the hundred thousand in our slums is quite as capable of bathing his hands in blood as any Sioux who ever scalped a foe. But we should not be surprised if the murderer in the present case should not turn out to be slum bred.[6]

The Ripper became linked to Hyde not only through his seeming powers of shape-changing, his silent disappearances into the London night, but through the degenerationist narratives which had come to dominate concepts of crime and criminality by the 1880s. These then gathered up earlier cultural and literary representations of murder, so that 'Poe's baboon' – in fact an orang-utan, who is the perpetrator of the violent murders in Edgar Allen Poe's *Murders in the Rue Morgue* – was linked to the concept of the 'savage within' and of the criminal type as an evolutionary throwback. Such constructions reinforced the representation of the slum areas of London as 'Darkest England', to be equated with (to borrow Joseph Conrad's phrase) 'the dark places of the Earth',[7] and of the prostitute as its lowest form of life.

The play of Robert Louis Stevenson's novel was running in London during the 'autumn of terror' of 1888, but was taken off in response to the murders. 'Leather Apron' became 'Jack the Ripper' at the end of September 1888, when a letter signed with this soubriquet was posted to the Central News Agency and sent on to Scotland Yard. As a number of commentators have suggested, the name undoubtedly played the most crucial role in the continued fascination with the murders and their perpetrator, while the 'birth' of Jack the Ripper inaugurated modern concepts of sexual crime and serial killing.

The Ripper letters, hoaxes or not, spawned hundreds of imitations and the field was opened to graphologists as well as to Scotland Yard detectives. Leaping ahead by a century, we find both professions involved in the 'discovery' and publication in 1993 of *The Diary of Jack the Ripper*, subtitled 'The Discovery, the Investigation, the Authentication'.[8] The diary was purported to be that of the Liverpool cotton merchant James Maybrick, whose wife Florence was tried for his murder by poisoning in 1889. Philip Sugden, the author of *The Complete History of Jack the Ripper*, called it 'an impudent fake', full of erroneous details about the murders that were published in the Victorian press and subsequently repeated: the handwriting, moreover, does not match those samples that exist of Maybrick's hand. 'It is astonishing', Sugden wrote, 'how many experts were fooled and allowed their names to be used in the promotional literature. They remain there, preserved like flies in amber, warnings to the complacent and the credulous.'[9] The diary's editors claimed that it was Maybrick's will in Somerset House that was faked, not the diary. As with the published diary's subtitle – 'The Discovery, the Investigation, the Authentication' – detective activity was now centred on graphological and textual clues: handwriting, the age of the paper and the ink. The book came to stand in for the body, and the diary's owner and publishers were engaged in an attempt to prove their property innocent of fraud and guilty of serial murder.

The published volume in fact begins with a body, for the introduction to the diary, written by Shirley Harrison, opens with James Maybrick's post-mortem. An eye-witness to his dissection and disembowelling by doctors is quoted thus:

> There was scarcely anyone present who did not experience an involuntary shudder as the pale, worn features of the dead appeared in the flickering rays of a lamp, held over the grave by one of the medical men . . . As the dissecting knife of Dr Barron pursued its rapid and skilful work there was, however, whenever the wind blew, a slight odour of corruption.[10]

The Gothic elements of this account are obvious, as are the echoes of grave-robbing and dissection, of Burke and Hare. The irony and the narrative that we are being required to see and understand is that this dissection is in some sense part of the 'sequence' or 'serial' that constitutes the Ripper murders, characterized by the mutilation of bodies. Maybrick the murder victim is added to the list of corpses that he himself is held to have opened up, and the 'odour of corruption' becomes that of his murderous deeds as well as of his eviscerated body.

The opening illustrations of the *Diary* volume, like many books on the Ripper murders, give us two 'maps': a map of Whitechapel and the murder sites, and a 'map' of the women's bodies, defined in terms of their missing organs and parts. Immediately following the account of Maybrick's post-mortem is a description of the corpse of Mary Jane Kelly, held to have been the Ripper's fifth and final victim, and the one most savagely mutilated. Presenting the last corpse first contributes to the narrative whereby Maybrick becomes, in a curious way, part of the seriality of the serial killing. At twenty-five years of age, Kelly was 'the youngest of them all' (the other women were in their forties), and the narrative homes in on the female body whose relative youth signals greater desirability and which presented the most horrifying spectacle:

> It was naked, apart from a skimpy shift. There had been a determined effort to sever the head. The stomach was ripped wide open. The nose, breasts and ears were sliced off, and skin torn from the face and thighs was lying beside the raw body. The kidneys, liver and other organs were placed around the corpse, whose eyes were wide open, staring, terrified, from a mangled, featureless face.[11]

One of the ways in which Shirley Harrison sought to confirm the identity of Maybrick as the Ripper is through his mark on or around his victims' bodies. Presumably because there was not much left of Mary Kelly on which to make a mark, we are asked to read the letters FM – the initials of Florence Maybrick, whom the husband is killing in surrogate – on the wall immediately above Kelly's body. Catherine Eddowes, by contrast, has an 'inverted V' cut into each cheek: 'At the time reports referred to triangular flaps. No one spotted that together they formed an "M" – the "M" that was by now his calling card, the "M" of Maybrick.'[12] In a volume whose credibility rests on textual verification, the women's bodies, dead for a century, are 'read' for the murderer's mark and signature. Harrison also makes much of the chalked writing found on the tenement wall at the site of Catherine Eddowes's murder, which read either 'The Juwes are the men who will not be blamed

for nothing' or 'The Juwes are not the men who will be blamed for nothing'
(the writing was effaced on the orders of Metropolitan Police Commissioner
Sir Charles Warren, who feared increased violence against Jews, and the
transcriptions of the message were not exact). Many commentators on the
Ripper murders turn at this point to a discussion of the intense anti-Semitic
feeling in the East End at the time, and the construction of the unknown
murderer as a Jew.[13] Harrison has a different agenda: 'The bizarre spelling of
"Juwes", with its five letters, significant "e" and inverted "m", strongly suggests
that Maybrick was willing to risk writing "James" on the wall, in a form that
could be read as "Juwes".'[14] Maybrick is thus held to have inscribed himself in
coded form at every step of the way, while the sixty or so pages of the diary are
represented as a final, undistorted writing of the truth.

Inscriptions, including the mark and the map, are central to accounts and
images of the Ripper murders, representations of the 'signature' style of
murder or mutilation which has become one of the conventional formulae
for serial killing. Inscriptions appear, for example, in Hitchcock's silent film
The Lodger, in which we see the lodger drawing triangles on the map of
London which he uses to trace the murderer's route and the points between
the murders, a diagram or mark associated with that of the Avenger (the
Ripper figure), who leaves a kind of 'calling card' on his victims' bodies in
the shape of a bottomless triangle or 'A'. The triangle is also linked with the
heart shape which Joe the police detective – in love with Daisy, the landlady's daughter – cuts out of pastry and tears in two to indicate a broken
heart, the cutting and tearing presenting disturbing echoes of other forms of
mutilation.

Perhaps every reconstruction of the Ripper murders entails an attempt to
create a whole story out of the bits and pieces: hence the significance of the
murders as a sequence. Every item in the cases – a bit of blood-stained apron
or the writing on the wall – has been subjected to the most intense scrutiny
and required to act as some kind of sign. The paucity of 'evidence' leads to a
piling up of parts and pieces. The following quote is from Donald
Rumbelow's *The Complete Jack the Ripper* and describes the discovery of
Catherine Eddowes's body:

> She was lying on her back, with her left leg extended and her right leg bent.
> Her throat had been cut and she had been horribly mutilated ...
> Examination of her clothes showed that some of the cuts had been made
> through the clothing ... The remaining clothes included a black cloth jacket
> with imitation fur edging; a grey stiff petticoat; a man's white vest; no
> drawers or stays; brown ribbed stockings which had been mended with
> white thread and a pair of men's boots the right one of which had been

repaired with red thread. Her black straw bonnet, trimmed with black beads and green and black velvet, was still tied to the back of her head.

In her pockets was everything she owned; this included two small blue bed ticking bags, two short black clay pipes, one tin box containing sugar and another tea, one piece of flannel and six pieces of soap, a small tooth comb, a blunt white bone handle table knife together with a metal teaspoon, a red cigarette case with white metal fitting, an empty tin match box, a piece of red flannel containing pins and needles, a ball of hemp, a piece of old white apron, a portion of a pair of spectacles, and two handkerchiefs, one with a red border.[15]

There is social and historical significance, and pathos, in this list of 'everything she owned'. The adjacency of the list of objects carried to the description of the body, a moment present in almost all Ripperology, suggest another impulse, however. It is as if there is some sort of exchange – interchangeability or inversion, to borrow the term so central to the account of Maybrick's 'mark' on the bodies of his victims – between what should be within the body, its internal parts and organs, and the bits and pieces outside it, in its pockets. Christopher Frayling notes that 'speculations about the contents of Mary Kelly's room have long ago reached the stage where it would be impossible to fit all her possessions into room 13, which was less than twelve feet square'.[16] Mary Kelly's body was almost entirely eviscerated, and the piling up of objects around her becomes a way of representing this. It may also be significant that she was the only one of the murder victims to be killed in a room, rather than a courtyard, passage or stairwell, and evidence at the time suggested that her killer spent some two hours working on her body after murdering her. The filling up of her room with imaginary objects may also be a way of negotiating the relationship between domestic – or, at least, interior – space, 'public' women, and what had come to be perceived as 'sexual' and essentially urban crime.

These questions of interior and exterior worlds, rooms and streets, open up the issue of the relationship between the 'street murders' of the Ripper crimes and the staging of the nineteenth-century detective novel in the bourgeois *intérieur*. As Walter Benjamin wrote, in his *One-Way Street*:

> The furniture style of the second half of the nineteenth century has received its only adequate description, and analysis, in a certain type of detective novel at the dynamic center of which stands the horror of apartments. The arrangement of the furniture is at the same time the site plan of deadly traps, and the suite of rooms prescribes the path of the fleeing victim.[17]

One would be spoilt for choice for examples to illustrate Benjamin's point, but we might turn to the detective novel to which he alludes, Anna

Katherine Green's *The Leavenworth Case*, published in 1878. A wealthy old man is discovered dead at his library table: the coroner asks the deceased's secretary what was on the table and receives the answer: 'The usual properties, sir, books, paper, a pen with the ink dried on it, besides the decanter and the wine-glass from which he drank the night before.'[18] These 'properties' are indeed props in the theatricalized mise-en-scène; sometimes, as in the case of the decanter and the wine-glass, they are also clues. As Jean-Michel Rabaté notes: 'Murder is productive violence in so far as it appears inseparable from a certain set-up, a staging of details that add up to create a whole scene.'[19] The 'props' or 'properties' attest to the whole drama of property, the inheritance plots that almost invariably drive such fictions. In the transposition to street murder, and to the other end of the class and social spectrum, as in the Ripper murders, objects – the 'everything she owned' – retain vestiges, for the amateur or professional sleuth, of the 'aura' of bourgeois props or properties. The map of the bourgeois house is likewise transmuted into the map of the streets. As Iain Sinclair puts it, in his *White Chappell, Scarlet Tracings*: 'The zone was gradually defined, the labyrinth penetrated. It was given limits by the victims of the Ripper: the Roebuck and Brady Street to the East, Mitre Square to the West, the Minories to the South, the North largely unvisited.'[20]

When the novelist Marie Belloc Lowndes turned to the Ripper murders for the short story she published in *McClure's Magazine* in 1911 (which became the basis for her 1913 novel *The Lodger*), she shifted the focus almost entirely to the private and domestic sphere. *The Lodger* is the central example of what Tom Cullen has called 'the favourite Ripper myth . . . a fiendish killer harboured in the bosom of an ordinary family'.[21] Belloc Lowndes's concern is with the private house and not the public streets. Her strategy with the Jack the Ripper murders is to focus not on the female victims, nor on the psychology of the murderer, but on the woman who shields him, the landlady desperate for respectability, an ordinary person caught up in extraordinary circumstances.

Marie Belloc Lowndes's literary career had started in the late 1880s. At the age of twenty-one she had published her first book, *The Life and Letters of Charlotte Elizabeth, Princess Palatine*, and had begun to work as a journalist on periodicals and newspapers, specializing in sketches of literary figures and articles on French literature and culture. The daughter of the journalist, writer and campaigner for women's rights Bessie Rayner Parkes and a French lawyer, Louis Belloc, Marie Belloc Lowndes (she married the journalist and writer Frederic Lowndes in 1896) had influential connections in French and English literary and social circles. She had determined on writing as a profession, but originally had fiction rather than journalism as her goal. She achieved some early success with short stories, published in various periodicals, and began to publish novels in the first decade of the century. Her first novels were, in her words, 'studies of character, rather than studies of crime',[22] and it was not until she began to turn to fictional advantage her life-long interest in criminal cases, particularly the murders that so fascinated Victorian and Edwardian society, that her popularity as a writer grew. Ernest Hemingway, in his autobiography, recalled that Gertrude Stein had recommended Marie Belloc Lowndes's novels to him:

> Miss Stein loaned me *The Lodger*, that marvelous story of Jack the Ripper, and another book about murder at a place outside Paris that could only be Enghien-les-Bains [*The Chink in the Armour*]. They were both splendid after-work books, the people credible and the action and the terror never false.[23]

During her long writing life, Marie Belloc Lowndes wrote a number of novels based on true crimes, including *The Chink in the Armour* (1912), based on the Gould murder at Monte Carlo; *What Really Happened* (1926), based on the Florence Bravo case of 1876; *Letty Lynton* (1931), a fictionalization of the Madeleine Smith murder case of 1857; and *Lizzie Borden: A Study in Conjecture* (1939), in which she assumes without question Lizzie Borden's guilt in the murder of her father and stepmother (Borden was in fact acquitted of the murders) and sets out to find a motive. Her interest here, as in *Letty Lynton*, is in the psychology of the woman murderer, and in both cases she represents women who, in the words of a contemporary reviewer, are 'of no character rather than evil character'.[24] The most striking aspect of *Lizzie Borden: A Study in Conjecture* is not, in fact, the portrait of Lizzie, but the depiction of domestic space in the novel. The unhappy family members – and the family structure of father, daughter and stepmother repeats that in *The Lodger* – turn themselves or are turned into prisoners inside their home. Belloc Lowndes presents a household in which entrances and connecting doors are locked, but in which family secrets can be heard through the walls.

The basis for *The Lodger* is clearly of a different order to the crimes of passion and greed that informed Belloc Lowndes's other novels based on historical criminal cases. In her diary entry for 9 March 1923, Belloc Lowndes wrote of the inception of her most famous novel:

> The story of *The Lodger* is curious and may be worth putting down, if only because it may encourage some fellow author long after I am dead. *The Lodger* was written by me as a short story after I heard a man telling a woman at a dinner party that his mother had had a butler and a cook who married

and kept lodgers. They were convinced that Jack the Ripper had spent a
night under their roof. When W.L. Courtney, the then literary editor of *The
Daily Telegraph*, in order to please a close friend of mine, commissioned a
novel from me (I then never having written a novel for serial publication)
I remembered *The Lodger*. I sent him the story and he agreed that it should
be expanded. This was a piece of great good fortune for me, and would
certainly not have been the case among any subsequent editors of my work.
      As soon as the serial began appearing – it was I believe the first serial story
published by *The Daily Telegraph* – I began receiving letters from all parts of
the world, from people who kept lodgings or had kept lodgings.[25]

Belloc Lowndes turned the butler and the cook into Mr and Mrs Bunting,
former butler and former lady's maid. The lodger comes to stay for consid-
erably longer than a night. The Buntings' concealment, even from each other,
of their suspicion of their lodger is motivated by the emphasis, at the novel's
opening, on the penury into which they have fallen and the desperation of
their need for money – a desperation which buys their silence. In the first
scene of the novel, the Buntings' resources are almost exhausted, and Ellen
Bunting has succumbed to despair, when 'a loud, tremulous, uncertain
double knock' sounds on the front door, announcing the arrival of a man
seeking lodgings, who, 'odd as he looked, was a gentleman': 'It seemed to
good to be true, this sudden coming of a possible lodger and of a lodger who
spoke in the pleasant, courteous way and voice which recalled to the poor
woman her happy, far-off days of youth and of security.'[26]

The drama of class is played out to a far greater extent between the
Buntings and their 'gentleman' lodger than between the Avenger and his
victims, to whom the novel pays almost as little attention as Mrs Bunting –
at least until she attends the inquest on the murdered women. It is in part
the class relationship between the Buntings – in particular Mrs Bunting –
and the lodger that secures their silence and protection: his money (ultimately revealed to have been stolen from the asylum in which he was
incarcerated and from which he has escaped) saves them from destitution.
The Buntings are, moreover, tolerant of the 'eccentricity'[27] of their lodger,
for which they have reassuring precedents after a lifetime of domestic service
and which becomes a form of talisman, used to guard them against a more
dangerous knowledge. Mrs Bunting's sense of what is owing to a 'gentleman' also increasingly leads to her determination to protect her lodger –
from the law and from himself.

The themes of service and servitude are central to the novel. It hints that
the servant classes who turn their backs on the protection afforded by
domestic employment open themselves up to the dangers of poverty and,

more dramatically, to the visitation of evil. The ostensible basis of *The Lodger* – the anecdote recounted at a dinner party of a cook and a butler who set up their own establishment, open their doors to lodgers and unwittingly let in Jack the Ripper – is laden with class assumptions. No longer protected by a 'situation', the Buntings must take their chances with the readers of the sign 'APARTMENTS' above the door. The traditional role of the butler is to guard the threshold of the house and to protect the inner sanctum, but for the ex-servants who let in lodgers the boundaries between inside and outside are no longer secured but crossed – as they also are by the cries of the newspaper boys who bring the appalling murders into the home. Mrs Bunting's response to such transgressions of boundaries and spaces is to attempt to 'lock in', and thus to both guard and make safe, the danger that has entered from outside. Trying to prevent the lodger, Mr Sleuth, from going out into the fog to commit the deed which she now suspects him to be planning:

> She moved back, still holding the tray, and stood between the door and her lodger, as if she meant to bar his way – to erect between Mr Sleuth and the dark, foggy world outside a living barrier.[28]

The Lodger is set almost entirely within the Buntings' home, with some important exceptions. The novel, like the short story, draws to its climax in Madame Tussaud's. It adds to the short story two new scenes: the visit of Mr Bunting and his daughter Daisy to the Black Museum at Scotland Yard, guests of Joe Chandler, the young police detective who is on the 'Avenger' case, and Mrs Bunting's solitary and secret outing to the inquest on the Avenger's victims. The action is thus divided almost entirely between the house and the sites of law, policing and criminality – the Black Museum, with its 'relics' of infamous nineteenth-century murderers, the Coroner's Court and Madame Tussaud's.[29] Belloc Lowndes depicts a society saturated by crime and detection: even the lodger's name, Mr Sleuth, gives him an ironic association with the forces of law and order. Joe Chandler, the detective, is in part introduced into the novel (he does not appear in the short story) to provide romantic interest (he and Daisy become engaged during the course of the novel), and to bring 'insider' knowledge of the Avenger's crimes (although Mrs Bunting in fact knows far more than he does). He also represents a law that comes knocking and, like the lodger, cannot be kept out.

Belloc Lowndes's account of her novel's inception is in many ways, but not altogether, revealing. She says nothing of the fact that she had made her entry into journalism in the winter of 1888, when the Ripper terror was still at its height. W.T. Stead, to whom she was introduced by Cardinal Manning, offered her work on the *Pall Mall Gazette*, which he edited between 1883 and 1889. The *Gazette*, an evening paper, gave the Whitechapel murders substantial coverage, turning the news accounts of the morning papers into copy as commentary and, increasingly, using the murders to criticize the organization of the Metropolitan Police and to campaign for housing and other reforms in the East End. The murders also became central to the circulation wars between the newspapers, with papers vying for the most sensational accounts.

By the late 1880s, Stead was the leading figure of Victorian investigative journalism. In 1885, he had authored a series of articles in the *Pall Mall Gazette* on the evils of child prostitution, subsequently published as 'The Maiden Tribute of Modern Babylon', that had scandalized, and titillated, British readers. He was a key agent in bringing about the downfall of Sir Charles Dilke, the Radical politician who became involved in sexual scandal, with whom Belloc Lowndes remained fascinated throughout her life. Stead's journalistic preoccupations, as Judith Walkowitz has argued, contributed to the location of Jack the Ripper in a nexus of late Victorian 'sexual danger' and 'sexual crime'.[30]

The Lodger, although written a quarter of a century after the Whitechapel murders, gives remarkably close versions of the newspaper debates of the time, down to the correspondence over the use of bloodhounds to track the killer. Belloc Lowndes very effectively represents the role of newspapers in orchestrating the panic around the murders and the impact of newspaper reports on her characters' perceptions of the killer. She reproduces the voices of many of the influential popular commentators of the period and their pet theories as to the identity of Jack the Ripper. In a key scene, Daisy reads aloud from the letters page of a daily newspaper; Mrs Bunting's horror at the suggestion that the Avenger might be a West-End gentleman is of course motivated by her growing awareness of her lodger's identity, but also echoes the broader social horror produced by this theory at the time of the Ripper's crimes.

Belloc Lowndes not only focuses on the Buntings' increasingly fearful readings of newspaper accounts of the murders, but depicts the way in which news is made. Reporters and journalists are significant figures in the novel. A newspaper column read by Mrs Bunting closes with these words: 'Tomorrow I hope to give an account of the impression made on me by the inquest, and by any statements made during its course.'[31] She determines to attend the inquest on two of the murder victims. Outside the court she picks out 'a famous journalist, whose shrewd, animated face was familiar to her owing to the fact that it was widely advertised in connection with a preparation for the hair'.[32] The reference is to George R. Sims, a journalist, novelist and crime writer whose newspaper columns over more than twenty years referred, or referred back, to the Ripper murders, many of them written for the *Sunday Referee* under the pen-name 'Dagonet'.[33] In the first years of the twentieth century, Belloc Lowndes and Sims worked together on *Living London*, a collection of illustrated articles on aspects of London life.[34]

Sims offered speculations about the Ripper, many of which still retain currency and which almost certainly informed *The Lodger*. Sims insisted that there were no more than five 'Ripper' murders, and that they were the work of a single killer, whose style of murder he refers to as his 'hand-writing';[35] he also argued that the murders ended in 1888 because the Ripper drowned himself – the closure which Belloc Lowndes used for her short story. He believed the Ripper to have been a doctor, either liberated or escaped from a lunatic asylum. He emphasizes that the murderer, after committing his 'maniacal deeds', walked through the public streets and into a home in which he slept, ate, changed his linen, kept his clothes, lived his life. He told his own 'Jack the Ripper as lodger' story, writing on 25 February 1911:

> Three years ago, when the discussions as to Jack's identity cropped up again in the press, I wrote again on the subject. Soon afterwards a lady called upon me late one night. She came to tell me that the Whitechapel fiend had lodged in her house. On the night of the double murder he came in at two in the morning. The next day her husband, going into the lodger's room after he had left it, saw a black bag, and on opening it discovered a long, sharp knife, and two bloodstained cuffs. The lodger was a medical man, an American. The next day he paid his rent, took his luggage, and left.[36]

Sims also provided highly satirical accounts of the frenzy and fascination produced by the Ripper murders in the late 1880s. Whitechapel was 'remarkably lively', he commented on 21 October 1888, packed with 'private detectives and amateur policemen'. 'Everybody is on the private detective lay now', he had written on 7 October 1888:

> In the railway, on the tram, in the omnibus, at the restaurant, in the street, everybody looks at everybody else, and wonders if the other man is the Blanca Cappella Assassino. Several people have looked at me lately in a way I don't like, and the other evening, in Oxford-street, a bloodhound, followed by Sir Charles Warren and Mr Matthews, came and walked around me, and growled, and evidently had doubts about my moral character.[37]

Underlying Sims's witty journalistic performances is the perception that his interest in the Ripper murders might shade into a more dangerous form of identification. 'Dagonet' was indeed named as a suspect, when his portrait, reproduced on the jacket of a book he had written, was pointed out to the authorities as a likeness of a Ripper suspect: 'The thought that came like a bolt from the blue and nearly stunned me was that I myself, *moi-même, moi qui vous parle*, was the person suspected by the police of being *Jack L'Éventreur*.'[38] The Jekyll and Hyde motif returns in the shape of a doubling between journalist and murderer. Recalling the events in 1904, Sims continued to assert his physical likeness to the Ripper (basing this in part on the appearance of the drowned man whom Sims always held had, in late 1888, been identified by the police as Jack the Ripper): 'The danger of being the double of such a man was great.'[39] There seems to have been a prevalent masculine fear, or fantasy, of possessing a fatal likeness to Jack the Ripper; one which might well explain the responses of a figure such as Walter Sickert, who was clearly fascinated by the performances and spectacle of the murders and would subsequently depict a version of their horrors in his Camden Town Murder paintings of 1908.

Throughout all of George Sims's writing on the Ripper, but particularly marked during the period of the murders, was a form of rivalry between the journalist used to the attention of his readers and the monster or madman who threatened to usurp this attention: 'It is possible that there may be human beings so depraved in their tastes that they would rather read about Jack the Ripper than "DAGONET".'[40] For Dagonet to be mistaken for Jack the Ripper was one way of resolving the competition. Belloc Lowndes's representation of Sims, the face of the hair tonic advertisement, surrounded by professional men might well be a comment on journalism as a male club. Mrs Bunting is invisible to the confident and successful men at the inquest, but it is she who possesses the knowledge they seek, and who hears a piece of crucial evidence from a witness whose age and lack of authority – Belloc Lowndes names him 'Mr Cannot' – puts him outside their circle of interest.

Both Stead and Sims inform Belloc Lowndes's representations, but there is a further Victorian commentator whose theories are echoed strongly in *The Lodger*. In a letter to *The Times* of 12 September 1888, Dr Lyttleton Forbes Winslow, lunacy doctor or 'alienist' and former asylum operator, put forward the theory that the murderer was of 'the upper class of society' and that 'the murders were committed by a lunatic lately discharged from some asylum, or by one who has escaped'.[41] Winslow subsequently came to hold the view that the murders were committed by a homicidal lunatic driven by a religious monomania, who 'laboured under the morbid belief that he had a destiny in the world to fulfil; and that he had chosen a certain class of society [prostitutes] to vent his vengeance on'.[42]

These words are taken from Forbes Winslow's memoirs, *Recollections of Forty Years*, published in 1910. Here Winslow gives detailed accounts of the criminal cases in which he acted as medical expert or expert witness, many of them cases where criminal responsibility was at issue, or in which he took up cudgels in a personal capacity against legal process and on behalf of defendants. He was involved, or involved himself, in the most notorious of Victorian murder cases, among them the Bravo and the Maybrick cases, both of which involved wives accused of poisoning their husbands. In her diary for 1912, Belloc Lowndes recorded her dinner party conversations with Lord Moulton and with the Prime Minister, Mr Asquith, on the topic of crime and the Bravo case in particular; Mr Asquith 'thinks Mrs Bravo was guilty, which I do not'.[43] It seems highly probable that Belloc Lowndes, with her intense interest in Victorian 'true crimes' and in the details of trials and inquests, often incorporated into her novels, would have read Winslow's *Recollections* in 1910 and that his lengthy account of the Whitechapel murders and his theories of Jack the Ripper's identity influenced her in the writing of *The Lodger*.

Winslow represented himself as a crucial actor in the Ripper investigations: 'I became more than a builder of scientific theories – I found myself pursuing clues and searching for facts to prove my scientific deductions. I was at once a medical theorist and a practical detective.'[44] Frequenting the sites of the crimes to the point where he himself became a suspect, Winslow saw himself as a far more likely captor of the murderer than the detectives of Scotland Yard. Pitting medical expertise against the law, Winslow at one point wrote to Sir Charles Warren, head of the Metropolitan Police, suggesting that the police should be supplanted by 'attendants experienced in dealing with lunatics placed about Whitechapel', perhaps disguised as female prostitutes, who would be in a position to know whether 'anyone was of unsound mind or not'.[45] His pet plan, however, was to catch the murderer in his own trap by humouring his ideas. To this end, he proposed, an advertisement should be placed in the newspapers as follows: 'A gentleman who is strongly opposed to the presence of fallen women in the streets of London would like to co-operate with someone with a view to their suppression.' Detectives would then be on hand at the place of appointment. To Winslow's chagrin and annoyance, Scotland Yard 'refused to entertain the idea'.[46]

Winslow's triumph, as he perceived it, came several months after what is generally agreed to have been the fifth and last 'Ripper' murder: the

appalling mutilation of Mary Jane Kelly on 9 November 1888. Winslow
located the murder of Alice McKenzie on 17 July 1889 as part of the series,
explaining the gap as a 'lucid interval' in the mind of a lunatic and holding
to his theory that 'the assassin was a well-to-do man suffering from religious
mania'.[47] He claimed that on 30 August 1889, a woman informant told him
of several suspicious incidents relating to the murder on 17 July. A man seen
washing blood off his hands was followed to a lodging-house; when the
house was searched, the man had gone, but the landlord with whom he had
lodged during the previous year gave Winslow vital information:

> He said that in April 1888 a gentlemanly-looking man called in answer to an
> advertisement. He engaged a large bed-sitting-room in his house, and said
> that he was over on business, and might stay a few months or perhaps a year.
> Before he came there he told them that he had occupied rooms in the
> neighbourhood of St. Paul's Cathedral.
>   The proprietor and his wife noticed that whenever he went out of doors he
> wore a different suit of clothes from that which he wore the day before, and
> would often change them three or four times a day. He had eight or nine
> suits of clothes and the same number of hats. He kept very late hours, and
> whenever he returned home his entry was quite noiseless. In his room were
> three pairs of rubbers coming high over the ankles, one pair of which he
> always used when going out at night . . .
>   While he was in the lodging-house he was regarded by all as a person of
> unsound mind. He would frequently suddenly break out into remarks
> expressing his disgust at the number of fallen women in the streets. He
> would sometimes talk for hours with the proprietor of the lodging-house,
> giving his views upon the subject of immorality. During his leisure time he
> would often fill up fifty or sixty sheets of foolscap, writing upon religious
> matters connected with morality. These he would sometimes read to the
> proprietor, who told me they were very violent in tone and expressed bitter
> hatred of dissolute women.[48]

Winslow took this information, along with a pair of the purportedly blood-
stained galoshes (it has been suggested that upon inspection the blood
turned out to be mud), to the police, but Scotland Yard were apparently
unimpressed. The exasperated Winslow then published his 'conclusions' in
the London edition of the *New York Herald*, after which, he claimed, the
murders ceased.[49]

   The Lodger builds an image of 'the Avenger' from details very similar to
those in Winslow's account – religious obsession, hatred of women, days
spent writing Biblical commentary, silent nocturnal exits and entrances. A
further detail, the lodger's burning of his clothes, which plays such a significant part in the novel, echoes another 'Jack the Ripper as lodger' narrative, that

offered by Walter Sickert, Patricia Cornwell's 'suspect' in recent years.[50]
Sickert, it would seem, was fond of recounting a story in which, as a young
man, he had taken a room in a London suburb a few years after the murders,
in a house looked after by an elderly couple. The woman told him that the
previous occupant of the room, a young and gentle veterinary student, had
been 'Jack the Ripper'. Sickert's account of her story was recorded by Osbert
Sitwell, in his introduction to *A Free House!*, an anthology of Sickert's writings:

> His landlord and landlady would hear him come in about six in the morning;
> and then walk about in his room for an hour or two, until the first edition of
> the morning paper was on sale, when he would creep lightly downstairs and
> run to the corner to buy one. Quietly he would return and go to bed; but an
> hour later, when the old man called him, he would notice, by the traces in the
> fireplace, that his lodger had burnt the suit he had been wearing the previous
> evening. For the rest of the day the millions of people in London would be
> discussing the terrible new murder ... Only the student seemed never to
> mention them:...[51]

The student was removed from London by his family, after which the
murders stopped. He died three months later.

In Sickert's anecdote, the lodger's landlord and landlady were held back
from warning the police by their inability to believe 'that this gentle, ailing,
silent youth should be responsible for such crimes'. What perplexed
Victorian commentators, and underlies the representation of the murderer
in Belloc Lowndes's novel, is the question of how the Ripper must have
appeared when not engaged in his vicious acts. An irony with which Belloc
Lowndes plays is that the Avenger, guilty by inference of fearsome butchery,
is also the Mr Sleuth who refuses to eat 'flesh meat'.[52]

One account of the juxtaposition of bestial violence and gentlemanly
behaviour was the Dr Jekyll and Mr Hyde motif. I referred earlier to
W.T. Stead's account of the weakness of the civilized restraints which 'keep
the Mr Hyde of humanity from assuming visible shape among us. There
certainly seems to be a tolerably realistic impersonification of Mr Hyde at
large in Whitechapel.'[53] *The Lodger* introduces the Jekyll and Hyde theme in
the form of the newspaper letter read out by Daisy, and it is echoed at the end
of the novel when the lodger believes himself to have been betrayed by Mrs
Bunting: 'There came a terrible change over his pale, narrow face; it became
discomposed, livid with rage and terror.'[54] The themes of doubling, splitting
and dual personality are also expressed in Ellen Bunting's efforts to keep Mr
Sleuth and the Avenger uncoupled in her thoughts, as well as in her hope that
the Avenger's acts are the product of a temporary aberration and that,
'vengeance' complete, he will return to normality.

The broader theme of insanity was central to Dr Winslow's concerns. He undoubtedly had professional, and at one point financial, interests in endorsing committals to asylums rather than to penal institutions or the gallows. His readiness to commit individuals who exhibited a hint of 'eccentricity' (a term much employed by the Buntings of their lodger to reassure themselves of his harmlessness but which, for a number of nineteenth-century psychologists, betokened the early stages of insanity) makes alarming reading, but the result of these interests was often a leniency in relation to the question of criminal responsibility.[55] Issues of insanity and criminality are taken up a number of times in *The Lodger*. The following conversation occurs when Mr Bunting, as yet innocent of his wife's suspicions of their lodger, is, as usual, discussing the Avenger with Joe Chandler:

> 'Then it's your idea that he's not responsible for the wicked things he does?' Mrs Bunting raised her head, and looked over at Chandler with eager, anxious eyes.
>
> 'I'd be sorry to think he wasn't responsible enough to hang!', said Chandler deliberately. 'After all the trouble he's been giving us, too!'
>
> 'Hanging'd be too good for that chap,' said Bunting.
>
> 'Not if he's not responsible,' said his wife sharply. 'I never heard of anything so cruel – that I never did! If the man's a madman, he ought to be in an asylum – that's where he ought to be.'
>
> 'Hark to her now!' Bunting looked at his Ellen with amusement. 'Contrary isn't the word for her! But there, I've noticed the last few days that she seemed to be taking that monster's part. That's what comes of being a born total abstainer.'[56]

Belloc Lowndes's exploration of the relationship between Ellen Bunting and Mr Sleuth/the Avenger is the central aspect of the novel, and is very much her own contribution to the narratives that circulated about Jack the Ripper. At certain moments, the identification between Mrs Bunting and Mr Sleuth seems almost complete:

> To her sharpened, suffering senses her house had become a citadel which must be defended; aye, even if the besiegers were a mighty horde *with right on their side*. And she was always expecting that first single spy who would herald the battalion against whom her only weapon would be her woman's wit and cunning.[57]

'It is round the reason for Mrs Bunting's silence that Mrs Lowndes has written this remarkable book', a contemporary reviewer wrote.[58] In one of the most striking passages in the novel, Belloc Lowndes offers an explanation for Mrs Bunting's failure to give Mr Sleuth up to the police:

> In the long history of crime it has very, very seldom happened that a woman has betrayed one who has taken refuge with her. The timorous and cautious woman has not infrequently hunted a human being fleeing his pursuer from her door, but she has not revealed the fact that he was ever there. In fact, it may also be said that such betrayal has never taken place unless the betrayer has been actuated by love of gain, or by a longing for revenge. So far, perhaps because she is subject rather than citizen, her duty as a component part of civilised society weighs but lightly on woman's shoulders.[59]

A number of contemporary reviewers quoted this passage, and at least two of them placed it in the context of current debates about women's suffrage. A reviewer for the *Westminster Gazette* wrote that 'Mrs Belloc-Lowndes is almost persuaded into a side-track on the Franchise question',[60] though the *Times Literary Supplement* reviewer held that women's protective instinct 'cannot be explained away by the suggestion that it may be due to all lack of the sense of citizenship, and "The Lodger" is not a tract in favour of diluting the franchise'.[61] Certainly, the emphasis in the novel on women's 'natural' desire to build and protect their 'nests' does not suggest a radical feminism. Yet Belloc Lowndes does imply that women's exclusion from civic life may weaken their concepts of 'good citizenship' and make them sympathetic to other outsiders, criminals included. She also departs from conventional narratives of femininity in her focus on, and interest in, the psychology and experience of the respectable, almost Puritanical, woman in late middle-age (who, we are told, was brought up in London's Foundling Hospital) and not her young and pretty stepdaughter. 'Mr Sleuth won't hurt Daisy, bless you! Much more likely to hurt me', Mrs Bunting tells her husband, after the denouement in which Mr Sleuth mistakenly comes to believe that she has betrayed him to the police.[62] The *Punch* reviewer of 1913 saw this as a definite drawback to the novel's interest: 'Had *Daisy* been a victim I would gladly have assisted in her matrimonial affairs; but she was never within a mile of it.'[63] The subsequent films based on *The Lodger* create narrative suspense by hinting at Daisy's likeness to the murderer's youthful, 'flighty' victims. Belloc Lowndes is much more faithful to historical record in representing the Avenger's victims not as girls but as women, working-class wives and mothers whose 'downfall' was drink and for whom Mrs Bunting feels little sympathy, though Belloc Lowndes goes no further in her suggestion that they are prostitutes or, in the terms of Victorian society, 'unfortunates'.

The novel also turns Mrs Bunting into rather more of a detective figure than Joe, the police detective. Where Joe remains wholly uninterested in the identity of the Buntings' lodger, Mrs Bunting searches for clues, investigating the contents of cupboards and the ashes in the stove. Her aim, however, is not to uncover and reveal the mystery, but to know the lineaments of the secret she is keeping. The Buntings, the novel suggests, have the victims' blood on their hands. Towards the end of the novel, Mr Bunting, up to this point ignorant of the lodger's suspicious activities, encounters Mr Sleuth returning to the house late at night and accidentally brushes against the lodger's coat. He finds that his hand is streaked with blood, but he washes it off and, like his wife, remains silent. Mrs Bunting, who begins to suspect Mr Sleuth from an early point in the story, has previously colluded with him when she takes his money for the use of her stove, ostensibly for an 'experiment' – in reality, as she suspects, to burn his clothing: 'As she walked down the stairs, the winter sun, a scarlet ball hanging in the smoky sky, glinted in on Mr Sleuth's landlady, and threw blood-red gleams, or so it seemed to her, on the piece of gold she was holding in her hand.'[64] And yet Belloc Lowndes does not appear to hold her characters to blame for their silence, bred as it is by their poverty, their desire for respectability, their fear of ostracism, their respect for 'gentlemen' and, overwhelmingly in Mrs Bunting's case, by her pity for her lodger, to whom she imputes a loneliness and an outsider status that is also her own.

Maurice Yacowar, in a discussion of Alfred Hitchcock's *The Lodger* (1926), the silent film version of the novel, refers to Belloc Lowndes's text and to the way in which Mrs Bunting 'drifts into a sentimental, selfish complicity with the killer, finally allowing him freedom to pursue his murders elsewhere'.[65] This account omits the torture of Mrs Bunting's predicament, but Belloc Lowndes was certainly playing a difficult game in constructing her Jack the Ripper persona as a figure of pity and even sympathy. Mrs Bunting's point of view so dominates the novel, despite Belloc Lowndes's emphasis on the limitations of her understanding, that there is little room for readerly distance from her perspectives. The novel's attraction for film-makers – in addition to Hitchcock's version, there were three more, including John Brahm's fine film of 1944[66] – lay in part in its dramatic and cinematic qualities, including the striking moments when the lodger turns the pictures of women in his sitting-room round to face the wall – 'these women's eyes followed me about'[67] – and Mrs Bunting's awareness of Mr Sleuth pacing overhead.[68] It was also an attractive source because of its central protagonist's sympathy for the Avenger figure.

Both Hitchcock and Brahm work with this sympathy, and while they also use it to depart significantly from the novel, the themes of division and doubling opened up by Belloc Lowndes are, in particular, central to Hitchcock's film. At the end of his film version, Hitchcock reveals the lodger, played by Ivor Novello, to be innocent: he is in pursuit of the real Avenger who, it would seem, killed his sister. The film viewer is made doubly and paradoxically guilty: for suspecting an innocent man and for having sympathized with him while suspecting him. William Rothman (who sees the character's innocence as, to a degree, contestable) argues that the lodger is himself a divided figure – 'He is the Avenger's innocent, righteous enemy, but he is also the Avenger's vengeful double'[69] – and the splitting and doubling of his presentation operates at every level of the film. In his first appearance he is framed in the doorway of the Buntings' lodgings house in a shot which owes a direct debt to German Expressionist cinema, in particular F.W. Murnau's vampire film *Nosferatu*, which Hitchcock had seen in 1922. As Richard Allen suggests, 'the Hitchcock romance is defined by the way in which the encounter with a dark self-annihilating desire is promised in and through conventional appearances that appear to negate it'.[70]

Allen terms the double aspect of romance and irony in Hitchcock 'metaskepticism', arguing that in the film *The Lodger* it 'sustains our uncertainty about the Lodger's motivation'.[71] Belloc Lowndes does not produce any uncertainty in relation to Mr Sleuth's identity as 'the Avenger' (by contrast with the early stage version of the novel, *Who Is He?*, in which the lodger is found to be innocent, and which appears to have been Hitchcock's introduction to the story). Nonetheless, the metafictional dimensions of her novel (in relation to cultural representations and interpretations of the events of 1887), in addition to the troubled identification between her central characters, find new forms in Hitchcock's complex, ambivalent and, in many ways, self-consciously 'modernist' adaptation.[72] Moreover, the novel's focus on the newspaper reports, the inquest, and the workings of public opinion are supplemented in the film by Hitchcock's focus on spectatorship, voyeurism, sexuality and the visual arena of modernity – a strategy he repeated when he transmuted the setting of Verloc's seedy bookshop in Joseph Conrad's *The Secret Agent* into a cinema in the film *Sabotage*. At the opening and close of Hitchcock's *The Lodger* we see the flashing words 'Tonight "Golden Curls"', a neon advertisement for a stage-show of that title. The legend is both a sinister light-writing with the appearance of a warning from the Avenger to his blonde victims, and an inscription of, to borrow Siegfried Kracauer's words, the 'drizzle poured out by economic life [which] becomes images of stars in a strange sky':[73] the 'hieroglyphic' of a culture of advertising and urban spectacle which, as I discuss in Chapter 4, is closely identified with film in the first decades of the twentieth century.

In John Brahm's film, the lodger is found to be guilty, and ends by drowning himself, as does Mr Sleuth in Belloc Lowndes's short story version.[74] Yet his actions are motivated by a 'righteous' desire for vengeance; his brother had been ruined by a woman. The first supposedly 'factual' history of the Jack the Ripper murders was Leonard Matters's somewhat improbable reconstruction of the events of 1888, *The Mystery of Jack the Ripper*, published in 1929. In Matters's version, the Ripper is a Harley Street surgeon, Dr Stanley, whose beloved son contracts syphilis from a prostitute called Marie Jeannette Kelly. When his son dies, the father swears to avenge his son's death. He tracks her through Whitechapel, despatching five other women along the way. Matters's narrative shares with those of Hitchcock and Brahm – and, to an extent, Belloc Lowndes – a play on the concept of vengeance; this is most prominent in Hitchcock's film, in which the lodger is an avenger but not 'the Avenger'. Belloc Lowndes's version differs from the other three, however, in its avoidance of the revenge narrative, located, as in all good melodramas, in the structures of the family – sister, brother, son – and, in the case of Matters's and Brahm's versions, endorsing an extreme hostility to women. Belloc Lowndes refuses to explain away the murders through family romances, and retains the essential unknowability of the Avenger/Ripper, an unknowability that has inspired so many attempts to pin down his identity: 'Mrs Bunting always visioned the Avenger as a black shadow in the centre of a bright, blinding light – but the shadow had no form or definite substance. Sometimes he looked like one thing, sometimes like another'.[75]

The Lodger is not only a fictionalized version of the Ripper murders, but a history of the way in which the fictions surrounding the murders came into being, in large part as the creation of the new journalism of the late nineteenth century. The tension between the private sphere of the home and the public sphere of legal institutions, which also contains the journalists who form public opinion, is a tension between the singular history and the sphere of competing narratives and theories. *The Lodger*, I would argue, reflected in a far more complex and interesting way on the processes whereby the events of 1888 became one of the dominant cultural narratives of modernity than the greater part of the 'Ripperology' that came after it.

Notes

1 Christopher Frayling, 'The House That Jack Built', in *Rape*, eds. Sylvana Tomaselli and Roy Porter (Oxford: Basil Blackwell, 1986), pp. 174–215, p.214.
2 Studies exploring the identity of Jack the Ripper and giving accounts of the murders include Robin Odell, *Jack the Ripper in Fact and Fiction* (London: Harrap, 1965), Tom Cullen, *Autumn of Terror* (London: Bodley Head, 1965), Stephen Knight, *Jack the Ripper: The Final Solution* (London: Harrap, 1976),

Donald Rumbelow, *The Complete Jack the Ripper* (London: W.H. Allen, 1981) and Paul Begg, *Jack the Ripper: The Uncensored* Facts (London: Robson, 1988). Recent cultural studies approaches include Judith Walkowitz's chapter on 'Jack the Ripper', in her *City of Dreadful Delight: Narratives of Sexual Danger in Late-Victorian Britain* (Chicago: Chicago University Press, 1992), L. Perry Curtis, *Jack the Ripper and the London Press* (Newhaven and London: Yale University Press, 2001), *Jack the Ripper: Media, Culture, History*, eds. Alexandra Warwick and Martin Willis (Manchester: Manchester University Press, 2007) and *Jack the Ripper and the East End*, ed. Alex Werner (London: Chatto and Windus, with the Museum of Docklands and the Museum of London, 2008).

3 Marie Belloc Lowndes, *The Lodger* (1913) (Oxford: Oxford University Press, 1996).
4 *New York Times* (4 September 1888).
5 *New York Times*, 11 September 1888.
6 W. T. Stead, *The Pall Mall Gazette*, 8 September 1888, p. 1.
7 Joseph Conrad, *Heart of Darkness*, in Joseph Conrad, *Youth: A Narrative and Two Other Stories* (Edinburgh and London: John Grant, 1925), pp. 45–162, p. 48.
8 *The Diary of Jack the Ripper: The Discovery, the Investigation, the Authentication, the Debate*, narrative by Shirley Harrison (London: Smith Gryphon, 1993).
9 Philip Sugden, *The Complete History of Jack the Ripper* (London: Robinson Publishing, 1994), p. 8.
10 *The Diary of Jack the Ripper*, p. 2.
11 Ibid., p. 3.
12 Ibid., p. 76.
13 See Sander Gilman, '"Who kills whores?" "I do," says Jack: race and gender in Victorian London', in Warwick and Willis, *Jack the Ripper: Media, Culture, History*, pp. 215–228.
14 Ibid., p. 81.
15 Donald Rumbelow, *The Complete Jack the Ripper* (New York: Little Brown and Co, 1975), p. 64.
16 Frayling, 'The House That Jack Built', p. 185.
17 Walter Benjamin, *Selected Writings*, vol. 1 (Cambridge, MA: Harvard University Press, 1996), p. 446.
18 Anna Katherine Green, *The Leavenworth Case* (London: Ward, Lock and Co., 1878), p. 21.
19 Jean-Michel Rabaté, *Given: 1° Art 2° Crime: Murder and Mass Culture* (Eastbourne: Sussex University Press, 2007), p. 80.
20 Iain Sinclair, *White Chappell, Scarlet Tracings* (London: Granta, 2001), p. 27.
21 Tom Cullen, *Autumn of Terror* (London: Bodley Head, 1965), p. 247.
22 Marie Belloc Lowndes, *Diaries and Letters of Marie Belloc Lowndes, 1911–1947*, edited by Susan Lowndes (London: Chatto and Windus, 1971), p. 19.
23 Ernest Hemingway, *A Moveable Feast* (London: Cape, 1964), p. 29.
24 *Times Literary Supplement* (12 February 1931), p. 1.
25 Lowndes, *Diaries and Letters of Marie Belloc Lowndes 1911–47*, p. 97.
26 Marie Belloc Lowndes, *The Lodger* (1913), ed. Laura Marcus (Oxford: Oxford University Press, 1996), pp. 12, 13.

27 Ibid., p. 17.

28 Ibid., p. 97.

29 Belloc Lowndes pays scrupulous attention to factual detail in her account of the exhibits held in the Black Museum, but the scene also suggests that she was not unduly concerned about the dating of her novel in relation to the Whitechapel murders. The Metropolitan Police did not begin their move to New Scotland Yard until 1890, two years after the Ripper murders.

30 Walkowitz, *City of Dreadful Delight*, especially chapter 7.

31 Belloc Lowndes, *The Lodger*, p. 127.

32 Ibid., p. 136. Sims marketed a hair oil, 'Tatcho', which was sold as a cure for baldness.

33 Sims, *Sunday Referee*, 1888–1917.

34 *Living London*, ed. George Sims, 3. Vols. (London: Cassell, 1901–1903).

35 Ibid., 22 September 1907.

36 *Living London*.

37 *Living London*.

38 Ibid., 1 March 1891.

39 Ibid., 31 July 1904

40 Ibid., 7 October 1888.

41 Dr Lyttleton Forbes Winslow, Letter to the Editor, *The Times* (12 September 1888), p. 6.

42 Lyttleton Forbes Winslow, *Recollections of Forty Years* (London: John Ousley, 1910).

43 Belloc Lowndes, *Diaries and Letters*, p. 41.

44 Winslow, *Recollections*, p. 251.

45 Ibid., pp. 256–257.

46 Ibid.

47 Ibid.

48 Ibid., p. 270.

49 Ibid.

50 Stephen Knight, in *Jack the Ripper: The Final Solution* (London: Harrap, 1976), argued that the Whitechapel murders were part of an elaborate conspiracy to cover up the sexual misdemeanours of members of the Royal Family, and that Walter Sickert was one of the murderers. Knight further argues that the fifth victim, Mary or Marie Kelly, was the *intended* final victim: 'these were no random victims, perpetrated by a sexual lunatic, but the systematic elimination of specific targets'. It seems that so-called Ripperologists, including the earliest, Leonard Matters, discussed in this chapter, are unable to accept the randomness of serial killings, and thus construct from the series a connective narrative and *telos*.

In 1990 Jean Overton Fuller published *Sickert and the Ripper Crimes* (Oxford: Mandrake, 2001). Fuller's theory that Walter Sickert was Jack the Ripper is based on a claim, attributed to Sickert's friend Florence Pash, that Sickert had seen the bodies of all the victims. Patricia Cornwell's *Portrait of a Killer: Jack the Ripper – Case Closed* (London: Sphere, 2003) seeks to 'close' the case with her 'identification' of Sickert as the murderer.

51 *Walter Richard Sickert, A Free House: Or the Artist as Craftsman*, ed. Osbert Sitwell (London: Macmillan, 1947), p. xxxix.

52 Belloc Lowndes, *The Lodger*, p. 20.

53 *Pall Mall Gazette*, 8 September 1888 (editorial).

54 Belloc Lowndes, *The Lodger*, p. 195.

55 Forbes Winslow wrote: 'If anyone who has been in a normal condition suddenly becomes in state which people call eccentric, that is insanity'. *Recollections of Forty Years*, p. 242.

56 Belloc Lowndes, *The Lodger*, p. 84.

57 Belloc Lowndes, *The Lodger*, p. 77.

58 *The Bystander* (17 September 1913).

59 Belloc Lowndes, *The Lodger*, p. 98.

60 *The Westminster Gazette* (6 September 1913), p. 13.

61 *Times Literary Supplement* (4 September 1913), p. 364.

62 Belloc Lowndes, *The Lodger*, p. 200.

63 *Punch, or the London Charivari* (17 September 1913), p. 258.

64 Belloc Lowndes, *The Lodger*, p. 118.

65 Maurice Yacowar, *Hitchcock's British Films* (Hamden, CT: Archon, 1977), p. 32.

66 *The Lodger: A Story of the London Fog*, directed by Alfred Hitchcock (London: Gainsborough Pictures, 1926); *The Lodger* (alternative title *The Phantom Fiend*), directed by Maurice Elvey (London: Twickenham Film Studios, 1932); *The Lodger*, directed by John Brahm (Los Angeles: Twentieth-Century Fox, 1944); *The Man in the Attic*, directed by Hugo Fregonese (Los Angeles: Twentieth-Century Fox/Panoramic Productions, 1953); *The Lodger*, directed by David Ondaatje (U.S., Stage 6 Films, 2009); television version of the novel: *The Lodger*, directed by Don Leaver, Armchair Mystery Theatre (New York: ABC TV, 1965).

   Marie Belloc Lowndes's novel was early made into a stage-play, entitled *Who Is He?*, written by H.A. Vachell, which ran for a few months at the Haymarket theatre from the end of 1915. There was also an opera of *The Lodger* composed by Phyllis Tate, produced in 1960.

67 Belloc Lowndes, *The Lodger*, p. 24.

68 Belloc Lowndes's emphasis on Mrs Bunting's anxious attention to Mr Sleuth's footsteps in the room overhead inspired one of the most famous shots in cinema history: Hitchcock's use of the glass ceiling, through which the soles of the lodger's shoes are visible as he paces back and forth over the family's head.

69 William Rothman, *Hitchcock: the Murderous Gaze* (Cambridge, MA: Harvard University Press, 1982), p. 47.

70 Richard Allen, 'Hitchcock, or the Pleasures of Metaskepticism', in *Alfred Hitchcock: Centenary Essays*, eds. Richard Allen and S. Ishii-Gonzales (London: BFI Publishing, 1999), pp. 221–238, p. 224.

71 This is discussed by Charles Barr, in his English Hitchcock. The stage play was probably the version of the story that Hitchcock first encountered. Barr has reconstructed the play's loose adaptation of the novel from contemporary reviews. 'The play was evidently more of a comedy than a thriller, playing on the

exaggerated build-up of suspicion against the lodger. "When he is arrested by the police it is time to be serious. So he is revealed as a distinguished young nobleman, who had hidden himself in the ground-floor lodgings after being heartlessly jilted" (*The Times*, 10th December 1915). Stannard [Hitchcock's screenwriter] and Hitchcock took from the play his innocence and his aristocratic status, but darkened his motivation, and in general stayed closer to the novel's tone' (Barr, *English Hitchcock* (Moffat: Cameron and Hollis, 1999), p. 218).

72 The film's modernism emerges not only in its deployment of the techniques of Expressionist cinema, but in aspects such as Hitchcock's use of E. McKnight Kauffer's graphic designs for the film's intertitles.

73 Siegfried Kracauer, 'Lichtreklame' ['Neon Advertising'], in *Schriften: Aufsätze 1927–1931* (Frankfurt am Main: Suhrkamp Verlag, 1990), p. 19. [My translation].

74 In the short story, the lodger is found drowned in the Regent's Canal, presumably a suicide; in the novel he disappears, and the 'Avenger' murders cease 'as suddenly and mysteriously as they had begun' (p. 202). In both cases, the discovery of a knife and 'a half-worn pair of rubber-soled shoes' buried in Regent's Park, made known to the police but not revealed in the press, implies that the police knew more of the identity of the murderer that they were prepared to reveal (p. 202).

75 Belloc Lowndes, *The Lodger*, p. 90.

CHAPTER 2

Oedipus Express
Psychoanalysis and the Railways

In the cultural narratives of the railway in the nineteenth and early twentieth centuries, the categories of shock and trauma – which were often differentiated, though not in consistent ways – were central.[1] Freud's *Three Essays on the Theory of Sexuality* contain a striking example of the swerve from the anticipated account of the railway as a vehicle for smooth linear progress to a model which emphasizes 'mechanical agitation of the body'.[2] Although Freud's account described a very specific historical trajectory – railway travel arouses sexual impulses in the male child which are subsequently repressed and re-emerge as railway anxiety – the model of shock (here 'mechanical agitation') is not only inseparable from the discourses of the railway, but emerges at a number of historical junctures. These include the 1860s, when 'railway shock' was extensively conceptualized and when the discourse of fictional 'sensation' reached its height; the 1890s, when the nineteenth-century obsession with nerves and nervousness met the languages of degeneration; the 1920s, when Freud, Benjamin and others most substantially theorized the concept of 'shock'; and the present day, when we retrace a certain history of modernity as a history of shock, fragmentation, dispersal, heterogeneity.

The following text was published in 1884:

> The man, for the time being, becomes a part of the machine in which he has placed himself, being jarred by the self-same movement, and receiving impressions upon nerves of skin and muscle which are none the less real because they are unconsciously inflicted.[3]

These lines, published in 1884, are, as Wolfgang Schivelbusch's study suggests, indicative of the concern in the last decades of the nineteenth century with the effects of rail travel on passengers and railway personnel. The terms of the quotation construct a striking logic of equivalence: man and machine are 'jarred by the self-same movement'. If, to take up Schivelbusch's arguments, the railway destroyed the mimetic relationship between preindustrial transport and natural phenomena in its felt 'annihilation of time and space', mimesis insistently returns in the equivalence between, and perceived interchangeability of, human and machine organisms.

The railway, Schivelbusch argues throughout his study, effected the most profound of revolutions in the nineteenth century, confronting the bourgeois traveller with the industrial process. The history of such conceptual and perceptual rupture is not only a history of progress but also of shock and trauma. These last terms are themselves reinvented, or come into being, to describe the effects of industrialized modernity, and the disasters of the industrial 'accident', on the human organism, whether the effects are somatic or psychological. The anxieties attached to the railway are at least fourfold, though they may be temporally staged, with one replacing (though not entirely effacing) the other: the initial difficulty of adjustment to mechanized travel and new temporal–spatial relations; the fear of the railway accident; anxiety attaching to the specific architecture of trains, with their isolated and corridor-less compartments; and concern over the effects of mechanized motion on the human nervous system, a concern which becomes increasingly insistent in the later nineteenth century in both medico-legal and psychological discourses.

The 1860s saw a proliferation of medical literature on the manifestations of railway-related fear and nervous disorder. The vibrations to which travellers were subjected caused, it was believed, nervous, muscular and mental exhaustion. In 1892, Max Nordau wrote in his highly influential work *Degeneration* [*Entartung*]: 'Even the little shocks of railway travelling, not perceived by the consciousness ... cost our brains wear and tear'. He added that the so-called railway neuroses were:

> Exclusively a consequence of the present condition of civilized life ... the terms 'railway-spine' and 'railway-brain,' which the English and American pathologists have given to certain states of these organs, show that they recognise them as due partly to the effects of railway accidents, partly to the constant vibrations undergone in railway travelling.[4]

The concept of railway shock became prevalent in medico-legal thinking from the 1860s onwards. One of its most influential theorists was John Erichsen, a Professor of Surgery concerned with spinal injuries from accidents. They occur, he wrote, 'in none more frequently or with greater severity than in those which are sustained by persons who have been subjected to the violent shock of railway collision ... consequent on the extension of railway traffic'.[5] Erichsen's location of a set of symptoms with a pathological cause was subsequently superseded by a focus on psychological factors, especially fright, in railway accidents and a concept of nervous shock, a traumatization of the victim without there being discernible physical injury. Herbert Page, a surgeon for the London and Northwest Railway, focused on 'the profound impression upon the nervous system' in railway accidents, at times 'sufficient to produce shock, or even death itself'.[6] The perception of railway danger is certainly sustained (if not produced) in the medico-legal discourse of this time, which must insist upon the unique nature of the railway's power and effects in order to justify a specific pathology of the railway accident.

The shift in the latter decades of the nineteenth century from 'railway spine' to 'traumatic neurosis' is a crucial episode in the history of psycho-analysis and its theorizations of trauma and hysteria. Jean-Martin Charcot, who exerted such an important influence on Freud's early writings, used Page's tentative suggestions that hysterical phenomena, including a form of 'psychical automatism', might result from railway injuries, to argue the case for 'male hysteria', which he opposed to 'neuraesthenia'.[7] Hermann Oppenheim, writing in Germany, used the railway accident to theorize 'traumatic neurosis', emphasizing that symptoms may arise some time after the event,[8] while Page noted that collapse from bodily injury, coincident with the injury itself, served to protect the accident victim from the 'prolonged and delayed manifestations of mental shock'.

Psychoanalysis could indeed be said to draw its most fundamental concepts from the supposed effects of railway travel and railway accidents. In a slightly different logic and narrative, the railway becomes the symbol (rather than the generator) of what Ian Hacking calls the 'psychologization of trauma' – the shift from *soma* to *psyche* which is central in Freudian psychoanalysis's account of itself.[9] The shift from *soma* to *psyche* at the same time suggests an equivalence between material and psychic life, as the railway accident comes to stand for traumas brought about by modernity and its new technologies, the forces of civilization and industrialization. In the early twentieth century and in Freud's work of the 1920s, in particular *Beyond the Pleasure Principle*, the theory of shock (which Walter Benjamin was to use in his theories of modern structures of perception) re-emerges in the concept of shell-shock and war neurosis, the successors to 'railway shock'. As Ernst Bloch was to write: 'the modern war machine recalls the hellish face of the first locomotive'.[10]

From his first writings onwards Freud had articulated the uncertain relationship between 'neuroses arising from trauma' ('railway spine') and hysteria. On the one hand, the 'railway accident' is central to the concept of 'hysterical conversion': 'During the days following a railway accident, for instance', Freud wrote in *Studies on Hysteria*, 'the subject will live through his frightful experiences again both in sleeping and waking, and always with the renewed affect of fright, till at last, after this period of "psychical working out" or of "incubation", conversion into a somatic phenomenon takes place'.[11] On the other hand, 'railway shock' comes to function as an exception to the rule that neuroses have their roots in childhood. It thus operates as a 'disruption' to psychoanalysis's most fundamental principle – that 'hysterics' suffer from reminiscences.

The complexities of Freud's models of shock and trauma, and the ambiguous relationship between the physiological and the psychological, are indicated by Jean Laplanche and J.-B. Pontalis in *The Language of Psychoanalysis*, when they assert that psychoanalysis, in adopting the term 'trauma', 'carries the three ideas implicit in it over on to the psychical level: the idea of a violent shock, the idea of a wound and the idea of consequences affecting the whole organization'.[12] In their entry on 'traumatic neurosis', Laplanche and Pontalis stress the two senses in which this term is used: one emerging from 'the surgical notion of trauma' and possibly involving 'manifest lesions of the nervous tissue' and a second sense where 'the notion is metaphorically transposed to the mental sphere'. To this extent, an understanding of a conceptual transition from *soma to psyche* needs to be qualified by an acknowledgement of the continued interplay between them.

Freud's biographers have wanted to locate an intimate – and indeed founding – relationship between the railways and the founder of psycho-analysis. Marthe Robert speaks of Freud's 'profound travel phobia which could be cured only by analysis'.[13] Ernest Jones notes that Freud's *Reisefieber* (anxiety at departing on a journey) was cured by analysis but left its legacy in the form of a lasting anxiety about missing trains.[14] 'Freud was always a good deal ahead of the schedule and had to wait at the station for an hour or so', Hanns Sachs writes.[15] This behaviour, or neurosis, was not specific to Freud. The particular anxiety about *missing* trains was understood in the early decades of train travel as a response to the rigid structures of a newly instituted 'railway time'. An article in the *Journal of Public Health* in 1855 (referenced by Schivelbusch) described the psychic strain caused by the fear of missing the train: 'The causes of the evil are not to be found in the noise, vibration, and speed of the railway carriage ... but in the excitement, anxiety and nervous shock consequent on the frequent efforts to catch the *last* express; to be in time for the fearfully punctual train.'[16] While Freud acknowledged his obsessive relationship to the schedule to be a form of travel anxiety, he also, in *The Interpretation of Dreams* (1900), suggested that dreams of missing a train are in fact dreams of consolation for another kind of anxiety felt in sleep – the fear of dying: '"Departing" on a journey is one of the commonest and best authenticated symbols of death. These dreams say in a consoling way: "Don't worry, you won't die (depart)."' The difficulty of understanding such dreams 'is due to the fact that the feeling of anxiety is attached precisely to the expression of consolation'.[17]

Two train journeys taken by Freud and his family in his very early childhood become founding narratives of psychoanalysis. The first is the journey from Freiberg, the town of Freud's birth, to Leipzig, on which, passing through Breslau, he saw gas lamps burning and believed he was in Hell. His self-analysis, the 'inner work', undertaken some forty years later, revealed to him a fear of the loss of his mother, caught up with the actual loss of his birthplace. The second train journey was occasioned by the family's move from Leipzig to Vienna, later in the same year. Writing to his close friend and colleague Wilhelm Fliess in 1897, during the period in which he was most fully immersed in his 'self-analysis', and was corresponding with Fliess on an almost daily basis, Freud observed: 'between the ages of 2 and 2 and a half, my libido was stirred up towards *matrem*, namely on the occasion of a journey with her from Leipzig to Vienna, during which we must have spent the night together and I must have had an opportunity to see her *nudam*'.[18] This 'memory' (which Freud clearly presents as a reconstruction of events) founds the theory of the Oedipus complex and thus, in more than one way, the railway journey 'founds' psychoanalysis. In addition, it might be noted that Freud and Fliess travelled to see each other by some of the train routes Freud had taken as a child, while the topic of Freud's railway phobia or travel anxiety comes up time and again in Freud's letters to Fliess, as a sign of his friend's intimate knowledge of him: 'You yourself have seen my travel anxiety at its height', he wrote, towards the close of the letter in which he imagined the childhood journey from Leipzig to Vienna.[19]

In this chapter I take this narrative in a number of directions. The first is part of a story of railway travel in late nineteenth-century Europe as migration and as exile. As Diane O'Donoghue and others have suggested, rail travel for Freud was inseparable from childhood experiences of loss and dislocation.[20] In his 1899 essay 'Screen Memories', Freud produced a brief case history – in fact a thinly disguised autobiographical account – in which he wrote of the 'catastrophe' – his father's business failure – which had necessitated the departure from Freiberg to Leipzig and then to Vienna.[21] Ernest Jones, in his biography of Freud, writes that: 'In the forties the new Northern Railway from Vienna had bypassed Freiberg, dislocating trade there and leading to considerable unemployment.'[22] We know, from *The Interpretation of Dreams* and other autobiographically informed writings, the extent to which scenes of failure and humiliation arose for Freud in connection with his father, Jacob Freud, and in particular with his inferior cultural status as a Jew. The railway, as O'Donoghue notes, 'bypassed not only Freiberg, but also his father, thus reiterating the belief that missing the train could, indeed, court disaster'.[23]

There is also a broader history here of economic migration, closely tied to the experience of European Jews in the late nineteenth and early twentieth centuries, and of the railway as the locus of nationalist and anti-Semitic politics. As John Schad notes, the father of Georg von Schönerer, who organized the radical German nationalists in the 1880s and led them into extreme anti-Semitism, was Matthias Schönerer, who built Austria's first railway in 1828 (drawn by horses), and, after studying railway engineering in the United States, returned to Vienna with the first steam locomotive, the Philadelphia.[24] Matthias Schönerer worked with the great Jewish financial houses of his day – those of the Rothschilds and of Baron Simon Sina – and in 1834 he was called upon by the Rothschilds to determine whether they should power their proposed *Nordbahn* (the Northern Railway) by horse or by steam. It was this railroad that the son, Georg von Schönerer, made the focus of his anti-Semitic nationalization crusade in 1884, in what Carl Schorske calls a belated Oedipal rebellion.[25] Making 'Northern Railway Jews' one of the main targets of his political diatribes, Georg von Schönerer was committed to getting Jews out of, and off, the railway.

Freud's accounts of his experiences of anti-Semitism run throughout his theoretical and personal writings, and a number of them are connected to both railway travel and the relationship with the father. In 1885, Freud travelled on a train between Dresden and Leipzig. He opened a window in the train compartment and, as he reported in a letter to his then fiancée, Martha Bernays, 'became embroiled in an argument with fellow passengers who wanted it closed':

> While the discussion ensued and the man said he was prepared to open a ventilation slip instead of the window, there came a shout from the background: 'He's a dirty Jew!' and with this the whole situation took on a different colour. My first opponent also turned anti-Semitic and declared: 'We Christians consider other people; you'd better think less of your precious self,' etc. and muttering abuses befitting his education, my second opponent announced that he was going to climb over the seats to show me, etc. I was quite prepared to kill him but he did not step up.[26]

In his analysis of his 'Count Thun' dream in *The Interpretation of Dreams*, Freud referred to 'a recollection of a piece of anti-semitic provocation during a railway journey in the lovely Saxon countryside' which was almost certainly the experience he had described to Martha Bernays.[27] The 'Count Thun' dream, which Freud called 'A Revolutionary Dream', was itself a 'railway dream', dreamed in the corridor-less compartment of a sleeper train and structured around the spaces of railway compartments and railway stations. While waiting, in waking life, for his train the evening before, Freud had seen on the railway platform the Austrian politician Count Thun, who was travelling for an audience with the emperor; the Count had waved aside the ticket inspector 'with a curt motion of his hand and without giving any explanation'.[28] A little later Freud saw a government official he knew claiming 'a first-class half-compartment to himself in virtue of his official position'. Freud was not in a position to secure such privileges – he was given a compartment to himself, 'but not in a corridor coach, so that there would be no lavatory available during the night'[29] – and awoke early in the morning 'with a pressing need to micturate', having had the dream he then goes on to recount. Freud's interpretation of the final scene of the dream, in which he had to help a half-blind elderly man to urinate, led him back to his father, and to the reversal of relationships between father and child: 'The older man (clearly my father, since his blindness in one eye referred to his unilateral glaucoma) was now micturating in front of me, just as I had in front of him in my childhood.' The childhood occasion to which Freud was referring had led to his father's pronouncement 'The boy will come to nothing', an assertion that 'must have been a frightful blow to my ambition, for references to this scene are always linked with an enumeration of my achievements and successes, as though I wanted to say: "You see, I *have* come to something."'[30]

The 'piece of anti-semitic provocation' experienced in 1885 and its incorporation into a dream also appear to have been repeated, in a rather different guise, on a journey Freud made along the *Südbahn* railway-line. The dream he had in the compartment was itself of travelling in a train, and in his dream (which begins with his hearing the station announcement '*Hollthurn, "ten minutes" being called out*' – the imaginary name perhaps again recalling Hell [*die Hölle*]) he finds himself 'suddenly in another compartment, in which the upholstery and seats were so narrow that one's back pressed directly against the back of the carriage. I was surprised by this, but I reflected that I MIGHT HAVE CHANGED CARRIAGES WHILE I WAS IN A SLEEPING STATE'.[31] The immediate context for the dream was the response of Freud's fellow travellers in the first-class railway compartment, an aristocratic lady and gentleman who did not seek to disguise their annoyance at his presence:

> The door was shut immediately, and pointed remarks were exchanged between them on the subject of opening windows. They had probably seen that I was longing for some fresh air. It was a hot night and the atmosphere in the completely closed compartment soon became suffocating. My experiences of travelling have taught me that conduct of this ruthless and overbearing kind is a characteristic of people who are travelling on a free or half-price ticket. When the ticket-collector came, and I showed him the ticket I had bought at such expense, there fell from the lady's mouth, in haughty and almost menacing tones, the words: 'My husband has a free pass.'[32]

Railway travel thus becomes inextricably bound up with questions of unearned status and privilege and Freud's exclusion from the world of privilege, even though he is in possession of the first-class ticket which his work and his gifts have secured.

'In my dream', Freud wrote, 'I took fearful vengeance on my disagreeable companions; no one could suspect what insults and humiliations lay concealed behind the broken fragments of the first half of the dream.'[33] In his dream analysis he focused on the second wish to make itself felt in the dream – to change compartments. It was unsurprising, he noted, that he should have wished to replace his travelling companions by more agreeable ones: the curious element of the dream was its insistence on the surprising quality of the change of scene, and its explanation that 'he might have changed carriages while asleep'.

> We know of people who have gone upon railway journeys in a twilight state, without betraying their abnormal conditions by any signs, till at some point in the journey they have suddenly come to themselves completely and been amazed at the gap in their memory. In the dream itself, accordingly, I was declaring myself to be one of these cases of *automatisme ambulatoire*.[34]

Freud's reference here is to *fugeurs* or, in Ian Hacking's phrase, 'mad travellers', who, in the late nineteenth century, became the focus of psychiatric interest in ways which were frequently bound up with theorizations of hysteria. The subjects of this syndrome were held to be driven by an irresistible compulsion to travel, to manifest automatism, and in most cases to be amnesiac about their journeying. Hacking links the figure of the 'mad traveller' to that of 'the Wandering Jew'. He notes that 'Charcot rode high on all three horses, vagrancy, eastern refugees and Jewish mental illness', though he also emphasizes that Charcot did not connect 'ambulatory automatism' (the term Freud quotes directly from Charcot's French) with the Wandering Jew but with the category of the neuraesthenic, theorized by the American neurologist George M. Beard, author of *Nervous Exhaustion*

(*Neuraesthenia*) (1879) and its supplement *American Nervousness: Its Causes and Consequences* (1881).[35]

These contexts undoubtedly informed Freud's dream and its interpretation. He does not make them in any way explicit, however, but proceeds by suggesting that he was copying his neurosis from one of his patients, with whom he had travelled on a night journey a few weeks previously. The patient's parents had both died, and he had begun to suffer from the delusion that he murdered them and from 'severe obsessions'. Incarcerating himself in his house in case he should be the murderer whose crimes were currently being reported in the press, he became struck by the possibility that '*he might have left his house while he was in an unconscious state* and have thus been able to commit the murder without knowing anything about it'.[36] Freud derives the root of his patient's illness from his hostile impulses towards his father, 'dating from his childhood and involving a sexual situation', and suggests that his own dream revealed an identification with the patient and a confession to something analogous. Furthermore:

> The second scene of the dream ended in a somewhat extravagant fantasy that my two elderly travelling companions had treated me in such a standoffish way because my arrival had prevented the affectionate exchanges which they had planned for the night. This phantasy went back, however, to a scene of early childhood in which the child, probably driven by sexual curiosity, had forced his way into his parents' bedroom and been turned out of it by his father's orders.[37]

There is a striking emphasis on reversals and substitutions in Freud's accounts of railway journeys and in the dreams they engendered, to which I will return. For the moment, however, I want to focus on Freud's representation of the Oedipal awakening on the train journey, as a different face of the focus on the Oedipal struggle with the father that informed the dreams I have just been discussing. Tracing the sources of infantile sexuality, in his 'Three Essays on Sexuality' of 1905, Freud wrote of the 'production of sexual excitation by rhythmic mechanical agitation of the body':

> The shaking produced by driving in carriages and later by railway-travel exercises such a fascinating effect upon older children that every boy, at any rate, has at one time or other in his life wanted to be an engine driver or a coachman. It is a puzzling fact that boys take such an extraordinarily intense interest in things connected with railways, and, at the age at which the production of phantasies is most active (shortly before puberty), use those things as the nucleus of a symbolism that is peculiarly sexual. A compulsive link of this kind between railway-travel and sexuality is clearly derived from

the pleasurable character of the sensations of movement. In the event of repression, which turns so many childish preferences into their opposite, these same individuals, when they are adolescents or adults, will react to rocking or swinging with a feeling of nausea, will be terribly exhausted by a railway journey, or will be subject to attacks of anxiety on the journey and will protect themselves against a repetition of the painful experience by a dread of railway-travel.

Here again we must mention the fact, which is not yet understood, that the combination of fright and mechanical agitation produces the severe, hysteriform, traumatic neurosis. It may at least be assumed that these influences, which, when they are of small intensity, become sources of sexual excitation, lead to a profound disorder in the sexual mechanism or chemistry if they operate with exaggerated force.[38]

One of the striking things about this passage is the interplay between the somatic and the psychological, between sensation and symbolization. The last sentence recalls the uncertain relations between 'fright' and physiological damage which arose in nineteenth-century theories of 'railway spine' and 'railway brain'. Freud's account makes the model of shock ('mechanical agitation') both integral to male sexual development and to the discourses of the railway. A more recent commentator, Sylvie Nysembaum, has a similar conception of the train 'as the site of an excitation' for the child, who finds in it a 'fascinating mechanism: the track rods, rigid elements animated by a coming-and-going movement, transformed and transmitted to the wheels' in which 'you feel and hear the rhythm'. This becomes identified with 'the representation of body parts, of the body in action, the repeated and noisy conduct of a sexual scene so engaging that the sight of the rhythm suggests the sound and vice versa'.[39] The animation of the machine blurs the boundaries between human and machine, animate and inanimate, and creates a new relationship between the realms of sight and sound, in which 'rhythm' becomes both rhythmic sound or noise (that produced by the engine and the pleasured body) and the machine/body in motion.

Railway phobia, for Freud, arises as a result of the repression of the pleasures attendant upon 'mechanical agitation' of the body. These terms are threaded through Freud's 'Analysis of a Phobia in a Five-Year-Old Boy' (the case history of 'Little Hans'), published in 1909, in which Freud uses the analysis of a child to demonstrate the Oedipal trajectory, the workings of infantile sexuality, and the paths of association in the development of phobias. Some way into the case history and analysis, which was in large part carried out by Little Hans's father, who reported his findings to Freud throughout the course of the analysis, it is recorded that the child had a phantasy in which a street-boy was riding on a truck. Freud comments:

> It has been noticeable for some time that Hans' imagination was being coloured by images derived from traffic, and was advancing systematically from horses, which draw vehicles, to railways. In the same way a railway-phobia eventually becomes associated with every street-phobia.[40]

This sounds like a curiously general principle, rather than one specific to Little Hans. A footnote to this passage refers us to Freud's summative discussion, in which he argues for the secondary nature of the relation between the anxiety and its objects; the material for the particular disguises adopted by Little Hans's fear, Freud argues, 'was collected from the impressions to which he was all day long exposed owing to the Head Customs House being situated on the opposite side of the street': at this site, Freud tells us, there was 'a loading dock at which carts are driving up all day long'.[41] Yet is also as if there is something much more determinate about a route of association which would take us from horses to railways, from street phobia to railway phobia, one which would describe an historical trajectory from horse to steam power, while at the same time suggesting the ways in which the railway becomes a way of metaphorizing paths of association themselves.

This is made explicit in Freud's case history 'Fragment of an Analysis of a Case of Hysteria [Dora]', in which he wrote of dream interpretation:

> In a line of associations, ambiguous words (or, as we might call them, 'switch-words') act like points at a junction. If the points are switched across from the position in which they appear to lie in the dream, then we find ourselves on another set of rails; and along this second track run the thoughts which we are in search of but still lie concealed behind the dream.[42]

The railway 'points' and 'tracks' become mechanisms to access the latent thoughts behind the manifest dream, while words themselves are seen as the containers of complex and contradictory meanings. The railway is a privileged analogy for unconscious and repressed thoughts, with the 'mental current' indicating the neurological bent of Freud's earlier writings, in which he focused on the distribution of energy or quantity. The train metaphor thus functions as a way of imaging the mental apparatus and its lines of conduction.

Railways and train travel also appear in 'Dora' as 'symbols'. In the second of Dora's dreams, which Freud analyses exhaustively, her father is dead and a letter from her mother tells her she can come home:

> I then went to the station [*Bahnhof*] and asked about a hundred times: 'Where is the station?' I always got the answer 'Five minutes.' I then saw a thick wood before me which I went into, and there I asked a man whom I met. He said to me: 'Two and a half hours more.' He offered to accompany

me. But I refused and I went alone. I saw the station in front of me and could
not reach it. At the same time I had the usual feeling of anxiety that one has
in dreams when one cannot move forward. Then I was at home. I must have
been travelling in the meantime, but I know nothing about that.[43]

Freud's analysis of the dream says nothing about the ways in which temporal
categories ('Five minutes', 'Two and a half hours more') are substituted for
spatial ones ('Where is the station?'), though he was writing in a cultural
context in which it was being claimed that train travel, and industrial
modernity more generally, was precisely an annihilation of space by time.
He does not explore the rendering of the dreamer as a '*fugeur*', the victim
of an '*automatisme ambulatoire*', nor the connections between the sensation
of 'anxiety' surrounding questions of stasis and motion and the question of
'travel anxiety'. He focuses instead on the use of *Bahnhof* [station: literally,
'railway-court'] to represent the female genitals, noting also that 'a "station" is
used for purposes of "*Verkehr*"' [traffic, intercourse, sexual intercourse]. 'This
fact', he wrote in an unelucidated footnote, 'determines the psychical coating
in a number of cases of railway phobia'.[44]

The 'station' and the 'thick wood' were, Freud asserted, 'a symbolic
geography of sex.'[45] The sex is female, as are Freud's representations of
landscape: *The Interpretation of Dreams*, to take a central example, could be
read as a form of navigation or exploration of a woman's body, as Freud
leads the reader through the narrow defiles and wooded promontories that
he also represents as dream symbols for the female form. Some of the
dreams Freud explored reconnect the dreamer to the lost mother: in others
the woman's body signifies the horror of castration and of the female
genitals 'as a wound'. The mother is the terrain – the landscape – through,
towards and away from which the traveller journeys.

This provides one context, at least, for the image of the landscape seen
from the train window in Freud's work and thought. In 1913, Freud wrote
an article called 'On Beginning the Treatment: Further Recommendations
on the Technique of Psychoanalysis', in the form of an address to a patient.
Here he described the technique of free association, though he did not use
this precise term here, enjoining: 'So say whatever goes through your mind.
Act as though, for instance, you were a traveler sitting next to the window of
a railway carriage and describing to someone inside the carriage the changing views which you see outside.'[46] The passage relates in very significant
ways to the question of the new forms of perception and mentation brought
about by the experience of railway travel, including that of the panoramic
perception defined by Dolf Sternberger as 'the tendency to see the discrete

indiscriminately'.[47] The absence of discrimination would map onto the relaying of (apparently) random thoughts and ideas in 'free-association'.

The metaphor echoes one expressed by Freud in a letter to Fliess during the intense period of Freud's self-analysis in 1897. Writing a few days after he had recounted to Fliess the Oedipal import of seeing '*matrem nudam*' on the Leipzig–Vienna journey, Freud wrote:

> I live only for the 'inner work.' I am gripped and pulled through ancient times in quick association of thoughts; my moods change like the landscapes seen by a traveler from a train; and as the great poet [Goethe] using his privilege to ennoble (sublimate) puts it:
>
> > *Und manche liebe Schatten steigen auf:*
> > *Gleich einer alten, halbverklungnen Sage*
> > *Kommt erste Lieb' und Freundschaft mit herauf.*
>
> [And the shades of loved ones appear, and with them, like an old, half-forgotten myth, first love and friendship.][48]

The train-ride is figured in at least two ways in this passage, to describe Freud's journeying through the scenes and episodes of the past. As Bertram Lewin has argued, the first image of the 'inner' work (translated here as 'I am gripped and pulled through ancient times') suggests 'something like a locomotive latching on to cars and hauling them to wherever it is headed'.[49] Here the focus is on the mechanism of the train and its subordination of the subject to the force of its direction. This image is followed closely by one in which the sensations of the self-analyst become analogous to those of the train traveller observing the world – 'the landscape' – through the carriage window. Yet the railway analogy here suggests not the indiscriminate reception of images from outside but, as Bertram Lewin has argued, Freud's expectation that free associations would 'bring back before his inner eye the important scenes of his early life'.[50] The focus, as in the later paper on technique, is on the window of the railway carriage, that windowpane which, so Michel de Certeau has argued in his essay 'Railway Navigation and Incarceration', produces an inversion of the relationship between the inside and the outside.[51] The everyday image of the railway traveller in 'On Beginning the Treatment' is a reworking – in Lewin's term a 'sublimation'[52] – of the more charged image of the letter to Fliess, in which it is the 'inner work' that produces the changing landscape, in an inversion of inner and outer, past and present.

De Certeau defined the experience of 'the railway journey' through the rhetorical structures of paradox and chiasmus, instanced by the inversions of

reason/dream, inside/outside and mobility/immobility, and closely linked
by him to the train's windowpane and the rail: 'The windowpane is what
allows us to see, and the rail, what allows us to *move through*.'[53] Lewin notes
the displacements in Freud's railway metaphors (instanced in the analytic
situation described in 'On Beginning the Treatment') from (latent) inside
to (manifest) outside. He connects these to the dream of one of Freud's
patients, who became known as the 'Wolf-Man'. In the case history, Freud
described the analysand's childhood dream of observing, through a window, a number of white wolves sitting on a tree and looking at him. 'He had
woken up and seen something', Freud comments. 'The attentive looking,
which in the dream was ascribed to the wolves, should rather be shifted on
to him. At a decisive point, therefore, a transposition has taken place.'[54]
Behind the content of the dream, Freud suggests, lies the 'primal scene', the
'*Urszene*', in which the very young child observed the parents' sexual
intercourse.

Here, in Lewin's words, 'the sights depicted in the dream as being outside
the window referred to what went on inside a room'.[55] As in the railway
metaphor, there is an exchange of affect between the space of the inside and
the outside. Events in motion (paradigmatically the parents 'operating'
together in the 'primal scene') are, moreover, remembered by the 'Wolf-
Man' as 'stills'; 'screen memories', it could be said, 'freeze-frame' the
moving picture. The optical imagery opens up the ways in which panoramic
and cinematographic perception became identified with railway travel, with
the traveller, as Benjamin Gastineau wrote in 1861, 'gazing through the
compartment window at successive scenes'.[56]

We have seen in Freud's thought the ways in which the sexual excitation
produced in the male child by railway travel is connected to the inversions
and exchanges of the properties of animate and inanimate forms, the human
and the mechanical. Such inversions are also central to theorizations of 'the
uncanny', as is the concept of 'the double'. In his 1919 essay 'The Uncanny',
Freud writes in a footnote:

> Since the uncanny effect of a 'double' also belongs to this same group it is
> interesting to observe what the effect is of meeting one's own image unbid-
> den and unexpected. Ernst Mach has related two such observations in his
> *Analyse der Empfindungen* (1900, 3). On the first occasion he was not a little
> startled when he realized that the face before him was his own. The second
> time he formed a very unfavourable opinion about the supposed stranger
> who entered the omnibus, and thought 'What a shabby-looking school-
> master that man is who is getting in!' – I can report a similar adventure. I was
> sitting alone in my *wagon-lit* compartment when a more than usually violent

jolt of the train swung back the door of the adjoining washing-cabinet, and an elderly gentleman in a dressing-gown and a travelling cap came in. I assumed that in leaving the washing-cabinet, which lay between the two compartments, he had taken the wrong direction and come into my compartment by mistake. Jumping up with the intention of putting him right, I at once realized to my dismay that the intruder was nothing but my own reflection in the looking-glass on the open door. I can still recollect that I thoroughly disliked his appearance. Instead, therefore, of being *frightened* by our doubles, both Mach and I simply failed to recognize them as such. Is it not possible, though, that our dislike of them was a vestigial trace of the archaic reaction which feels the 'double' to be something uncanny?[57]

Train travel thus produces a chance encounter with one's own image. This is another version of railway 'shock', in which 'a more than usually violent jolt' results in the appearance of the other, the 'double'. The recognition of this self not only as other but as older – 'an elderly gentleman' – is a kind of momentary death – 'nothing but my own reflection' – so that the self carries on the journey as a revenant.

In 1997 J.-B. Pontalis, co-author of the definitive multilingual dictionary of psychoanalytic terminology, published a series of extracts from memoirs and literary texts, 'The Train Compartment'. The epigraph at the beginning of the collection is from Alain Hervé's *'L'abécédaire de l'ange'*: 'Let us give thanks to the inventor of the compartment, who shut us in his ephemeral enclosures.'[58] The original phrase, *'huis clos'* (literally 'closed doors') has the sense of 'no exit' made famous by the translators of Sartre's play about Hell, but also that of a closed session, *in camera*. In a closed and corridor-less compartment, of course, one was not only constrained to remain until the next stop, but also protected from external intrusion. The analytic session, too, is supposed to continue until its allotted stopping time, but also to be uninterrupted. In one of the essays that accompanies 'The Train Compartment', *'La saison de la psychanalyse'*, Pontalis writes of the peculiar role played by time in psychoanalysis, in which the real time of the analytic hour is filled with the 'past present' of memory, the impulses of the timeless Id described by Freud, and the repetitions of association and transference.[59] Sitting in a train imposes a similar immobility and, as de Certeau also suggests, encourages – or constrains – the mind to wander: this is a different version of 'railway time' to that which, in the nineteenth century, produced such an anxious relationship between subject and schedule, with the ever-present possibility of missing the train.

Pontalis's account at the end of his collection takes us back to Freud's encounter in the railway compartment with his 'double' and to the scene of the psychoanalytic session itself. His fragmentary extracts for the most part concern the real or imagined interactions between passengers so closely thrust together in 'ephemeral enclosures'. He suggests that the 'precursor and model' of the analytic situation is not the hypnotist and illusionist Mesmer's box, but:

> The railway compartment: this compartment which one enters and, after a time, leaves changed, checking that one has not left one's suitcase behind; where, all through the journey, there occur meetings and dreams, giving rise to fantasms and reveries, where at any moment someone may arrive or something may happen, where, even when you think you are alone, there is something of the other.[60]

Notes

1 For a nuanced discussion of these issues, see Tim Armstrong, 'Two Types of Shock in Modernity', *Critical Quarterly* 42:1, 2000, 60–73.

2 Sigmund Freud, 'Three Essays on the Theory of Sexuality' (1905), in *The Standard Edition of the Complete Psychological Works of Sigmund Freud* (Hereafter '*SE*'), edited by James Strachey et al. (London: The Hogarth Press and the Institute of Psychoanalysis, 1953), vol. 7, pp. 201–202.

3 *The Book of Health* (1884), edited by Malcolm Morris. Quoted in Wolfgang Schivelbusch, *The Railway Journey: The Industrialization of Time and Space in the Nineteenth Century* (Munich: Carl Hanser Verlag, 1977; this edition: Leamington Spa: Berg, 1986), p. 113.

4 Max Nordau, *Entartung*, 2 vols (Berlin: Duncker, 1892), translated as *Degeneration* (London: William Heinemann, 1895), p. 41.

5 John Eric Erichsen, *On Railway and Other Injuries of the Nervous System* (London: Walton and Maberley, 1866), p. 2.

6 Herbert W. Page, *Railway Injuries: With Specific Reference to Those of the Back and Nervous System in Their Medico-Legal and Clinical Aspects* (London: Charles Griffin, 1891), p. 28.

7 See Eric Michael Kaplan, 'Trains, Brains and Sprains: Railway-Spine and the Origins of Psychoneuroses', *Bulletin of the History of Medicine* 69, 1995, 387–419.

8 See Hermann Oppenheim, *Diseases of the Nervous System: A Text-Book for Students and Practitioners of Medicine*, translated by Edward E. Mayer (London: Lippincott, 1904), especially pp. 778–794.

9 Ian Hacking, *Rewriting the Soul: Multiple Personality and the Sciences of Memory* (Princeton: Princeton University Press, 1995), especially pp. 183–197. See also E. Fischer-Homberger, *Die traumatische Neurose: Vom somatischen zum sozialen Leiden* (Berne, Stuttgart, Vienna: Hans Huber, 1975).

10 Ernst Bloch, *Spuren* (Frankfurt: Suhrkamp, 1969), p. 161.

11 Breuer and Freud, *Studies in Hysteria* (1895), *SE* 2, p. 213.

12 J. Laplanche and J. B. Pontalis, *The Language of Psycho-Analysis*, translated by Donald Nicholson-Smith (London: Hogarth Press and the Institute of Psychoanalysis, 1993), p. 466.

13 Marthe Robert, *The Psychoanalytic Revolution: Sigmund Freud's Life and Achievement*, translated by Kenneth Morgan (London: George Allen and Unwin, 1966), especially p. 111 and pp. 144–147.

14 Ernest Jones, *The Life and Work of Sigmund Freud, vol. 1, 1856–1900* (New York: Basic Books, 1953), pp. 13, 181, 305–307.

15 Hanns Sachs, *Freud: Master and Friend* (London: Imago Publishing Co., 1945), p. 81.

16 Schivelbusch, *The Railway Journey*, p. 118.

17 Freud, *SE* vol. 5, p. 385.

18 Sigmund Freud, *The Complete Letters of Sigmund Freud to Wilhelm Fliess 1887–1904*, translated by Jeffrey Moussaieff Masson (Cambridge, MA: Harvard University Press, 1985), Letter to Fliess, 3 October 1897, p. 268.

19 Ibid., p. 268.

20 Diane O'Donoghue, 'On the Train(ing),' *Journal for the Psychoanalysis of Culture and Society* 6, no. 3 (Fall 2001): 313–315.

21 Freud, *SE* vol. 3, p. 312.

22 Jones, *The Life and Work of Sigmund Freud*, vol. 1, p. 13.

23 O'Donoghue, p.

24 John Schad, *Queer Fish: Christian Unreason from Darwin to Derrida* (Brighton and Portland: Sussex Academic Press, 2004).

25 Carl E. Schorske, *Fin-de-Siècle Vienna: Politics and Culture* (London: Weidenfeld and Nicolson, 1980), p. 128.

26 Quoted in Frederic Grunfeld, *Prophets without Honour: Freud, Kafka, Einstein and Their World* (New York: Random House, 1979), p. 19.

27 Freud, *The Interpretation of Dreams*, *SE* vol. 4, p. 212.

28 Ibid., p. 208.

29 Ibid., p. 209

30 Ibid. p. 216. Emphasis/italics in original.

31 Freud, *SE* vol. 5, p. 455.

32 Ibid., pp. 456–457.

33 Ibid., p. 457.

34 Ibid., p. 457.

35 Ian Hacking, *Mad Travellers: Reflections on the Reality of Transient Mental Illnesses* (Charlottesville and London: University Press of Virginia, 1998), pp. 119–120.

36 Freud, *SE* vol. 5, p. 458. Emphasis in the original.

37 Ibid., pp. 458–459.

38 Freud, *SE* vol. 7, pp. 201–202.

39 Sylvie Nysembaum, 'Une pensée qui va et vient', quoted in J-B. Pontalis, *Ce temps qui ne passe pas, suivi de Le Compartiment de chemin de fer*' (Paris: Gallimard, 1997), p. 154.

40 Freud, *SE* vol. 10, p. 84.

41 Ibid., p. 125.

42 Freud, *SE* vol.7, p. 65.

43 Ibid., p. 94.

44 Ibid., p. 99.

45 Ibid., p. 99.

46 Freud, *SE* vol. 12, p. 135.

47 Quoted in Schivelbusch, *The Railway Journey*, p. 61.

48 Freud, letter to Fliess, 27 October 1897, in *The Complete Letters of Sigmund Freud to Wilhelm Fliess*, translated and edited by Jeffrey Moussaieff Masson (Cambridge, MA: Harvard University Press, 1985), p. 274.

49 Bertram Lewin, 'The Train Ride: A Study of One of Freud's Figures of Speech', *Psychoanalytic Quarterly* 39 (1970), 73.

50 Ibid., p. 78.

51 Michel de Certeau, 'Railway Navigation and Incarceration', in *The Practice of Everyday Life* (Berkeley: University of California Press, 1984), pp. 111–112.

52 Lewin, 'The Train Ride', p. 86.

53 De Certeau, 'Railway Navigation and Incarceration', p. 119. Emphasis in the original.

54 Freud, *SE* vol. 17, pp. 34–35.

55 Lewin, 'The Train Ride', p. 82.

56 Benjamin Gastineau, 'vie an chemin de fer' (1861), quoted in Schivelbusch, *The Railway Journey*, p. 63.

57 Freud, *SE* vol.17, p. 248.

58 From *La Nouvelle Revue Française*, June 1933. Quoted in Pontalis, *Ce temps qui ne passe pas suivi de Le Compartiment de chemin de fer*, p. 137.

59 Ibid., p. 13.

60 Ibid., p. 199.

CHAPTER 3

Railway Reading

At the close of the twentieth century, it was possible to buy a short thriller or detective story from vending machines in Paris railway and underground stations. A spokeswoman for the publisher, Éditions de la Voûte, said in early 1997: 'The idea is just a rethink of the success of station and airport novels. Since commuter journeys tend to be short, we decided that none of our books should take more than one hour to read.' The novel on offer was changed every week, alternating between a new book and a reprint. The first offering in the Metro-Police series, as it was called, was Gérard Delteil's *Le Nouveau Crime de L'Orient Express*, a new version of Agatha Christie's famous train-crime novel.

Walter Benjamin noted the elective affinity between the railway journey and detective fiction in an article, published in 1930, entitled 'Kriminalromane, auf Reisen' ['Detective Novels, on Journeys'].[1] In this short piece Benjamin (who, like a number of the theorists associated with the Frankfurt School, was fascinated by detective fiction and indeed wrote a synopsis of a detective novel)[2] observed that railway travellers prefer to buy their reading material from station bookstalls, opting for the contingency of what they find there rather than for the certainties of what they might bring from home:

> less out of pleasure in reading than in the dim feeling that they are doing something which pleases the gods of the railway. He [the traveller] knows that the coins which he offers up to this sacrificial column recommend him to the protection of the boiler god which glows through the night, the smoke naiads which play above the train, and the demon who is master over all lullabies. He knows all of them from dreams, but he also knows the succession of mythical trials and dangers which has presented itself to the Zeitgeist as a 'railway journey,' and the unforeseeable flow of spatio-temporal thresholds over which it moves, starting with the famous 'too late' of the person left behind, the original image of everything missed, through to the loneliness of the compartment, the fear of missing the connection and

the grey of the unknown station into which he is riding. Unsuspectingly, he
feels himself drawn into a giants' kingdom and recognises himself to be the
mute witness of the struggle between the gods of the railway and the station.
  Simila similibus. The anaesthetising of one fear by the other is his salvation.
Between the freshly separated pages of the detective novel he seeks the leisured,
almost virginal anxieties which can help him over the archaic anxieties of the
journey.[3]

As he lists the detective novelists the traveller might most wish to read,
Benjamin's main criterion appears to be the fittingness of the detective
story's shape and structure to the rhythms of the journey. One might also
turn, he suggests, to the stories of Gaston Leroux (author of *The Phantom of
the Opera*) for an 'understanding of the future into which one is travelling,
for the unresolved riddles left behind', or to Anna Katherine Green (author
of *The Leavenworth Case*, discussed in my first chapter), whose 'short stories
are just the same length as the Gotthard tunnel and [whose] great novels
Behind Locked Doors, *In the House Next Door*, bloom in the purple-shaded
coupé light like night violets.'[4]

  'So much', Benjamin concludes, 'for what reading offers the traveller. But
what does travelling offer the reader?' 'When else', he asks,

is he [the reader] so involved in reading and can feel his hero's existence so
certainly combined with his own? Is his body not the weaver's shuttle which
follows the rhythm of the wheels in tirelessly shooting through the paper? . . .
People didn't read in post-coaches and they don't read in cars. Travel reading
is as closely linked to railway travel as is the time spent in stations.[5]

  In this chapter, I take up the question of train travel, narrative and reading,
with a particular focus on the affinities between train travel and detective
fiction which are, as Benjamin suggests, multiple. From Benjamin's arguments we can begin to draw out the relationship between railway travel and
the 'railway novel', which arises as a genre in the mid-nineteenth century to
meet – or perhaps to shape – the needs of travellers. This is closely linked to
the reflexive structure of reading about a train journey while journeying on a
train: Benjamin instances Holmes and Watson, in 'the strange familiarity [*das
Unheimlich-Heimliche*] of a dusty second class coupé, both sunk in silence as
passengers, one behind the windshield of a newspaper, the other behind a
curtain of smoke clouds'.[6] This line branches off into the many and various
representations of trains and train journeys in detective fiction, some of which
I discuss in this article. There is also, in Benjamin's account, the relationship
between the movement of the train and the movement of the text from
one place to another, departures and arrivals, the rhythms of the journey and
the rhythms of the narrative. This rhythm combines with the physical

sensations experienced by the train traveller, the movement of the train felt and through the body, producing, in Benjamin's words, not only 'a shudder of tension', but a very particular and very intense kind of identification with the trajectory of the hero's destinies and destinations. Underlying these relationships, though this concept is not present in Benjamin's very brief discussion, is the simultaneity of production and consumption in railway travel, whereby the industrial machinery 'produces' the traveller as both consumer and commodity.[7] Conjoining them is the observance of what Mark Seltzer has described, with reference to the nexus of 'body' and 'machine' in naturalist fiction and in his recent work on serial killing, as a 'logic of equivalence'.[8]

The logic of equivalence (journey/book, body/machine) exists, however, in relation to, and in tension with, the logic of belatedness, the 'missing' of points in space and time on which Benjamin also insists. In his account, the logic of equivalence, of synchronicity and simultaneity, serves to suppress or mask the anxiety of 'everything missed'. Yet the logic of equivalence can also be the logic of violence and of murderous repetition. If, as Seltzer suggests, the logic of equivalence is the driving force behind the naturalist novel of the end of the nineteenth century, the logic of belatedness may be more characteristic of modernism, with, in Thomas Hardy's phrase, its 'ache', its awareness of things 'passing' and, in Freudian terms, its dynamics of deferral and *Nachträglichkeit*. The railroad, Wolfgang Schivelbusch suggests in his brilliant study *The Railway Journey*, 'knows only points of departure and destination'.[9] The spatial dimensions of the present are thus effaced: there is only the past and the future.

Benjamin writes of 'the struggle between the gods of the railway and the station', thus calling attention to a complexity which, as I argue later, is crucial to detective fiction in its relation to trains.[10] 'The railway' is made up of a number of different and disparate structures and mechanisms – engines, carriages, tracks, viaducts, embankments, bridges, tunnels, stations – the links and spaces between which detective fiction and thrillers use to construct plot and narrative movement. In his essay 'Railway Navigation and Incarceration' (touched on in the previous chapter), Michel de Certeau introduces a further element of the railway – the windowpane – and a logic we can add to the logics of equivalence and of belatedness, 'an imperative of separation'.[11] The traveller is, de Certeau writes, 'Immobile inside the train, seeing immobile things slip by', less a reader than a character or 'type':

> Every being is placed there like a piece of printer's type arranged in military order. This order, an organizational system, the quietude of a certain reason,

is the condition of both a railway car's and a text's movement from one place to another ... Between the immobility of the inside and that of the outside a certain *quid pro quo* is introduced, a slender blade that inverts their stability. The chiasm is produced by the windowpane and the rail ... The window-pane is what allows us to *see*, and the rail, what allows us to *move through*. These are two complementary modes of separation. The first creates the spectator's distance: You shall not touch; the more you see, the less you hold ... The second inscribes, indefinitely, the injunction to pass on; ... an imperative of separation which obliges one to pay for an abstract ocular domination of space by leaving behind any proper place, by losing one's footing.[12]

De Certeau argues that 'it is the silence of these things put at a distance, behind the windowpane, which, from a great distance, makes our memories speak or draws out of the shadows the dreams of our secrets'.[13] Benjamin points to 'the succession of mythical trials and dangers which has presented itself to the Zeitgeist as a 'railway journey';[14] de Certeau suggests the relationship between the quotidian or rationalized aspects of the train journey and the train as dream and dream-symbol. He also alludes to the 'railway journey' as an experience which blurs the boundaries between the imaginary and the real.

The paradox, in de Certeau's account, is that the passenger's location in an ordered system leaves him or her free or, perhaps, constrained to dream, in an inversion of reason and dream which is mirrored in the chiasmus of inside/outside and mobility/immobility. At the close of his essay, de Certeau describes the incongruity of the train, the 'immobile machine', in 'the mobile world of the train station'.[15]

In the next section of this chapter, I discuss briefly the significance of the railway accident for the nineteenth-century novel, and in particular sensation fiction, before turning to the ways in which the three logics which I have isolated here – the logics of equivalence, belatedness and separation/inversion – are worked through different kinds of crime and detective fiction. The previous chapter explored the terms of trains and trauma in the nineteenth century, and the development, in psychology and psycho-analysis, of the logics which this chapter traces through fictional forms. Thus the psychological discourse of hysterical identification and 'neuro-mimesis', and the psychical deferral generated by the railway and its accidents, find their counterparts in Walter Benjamin's language of narra-tive identification, simultaneity and temporal 'missing'.

> The exigencies of railway travelling do not allow much time for examining the merits of a book before purchasing it; and keepers of bookstalls, as well as

of refreshment-rooms, find an advantage in offering their customers something hot and strong, something that may catch the eye of the hurried
passenger, and promise temporary excitement to relieve the dulness [*sic*] of
a journey.[16]

'Railway fiction' emerged soon after the growth of the railway system in the
early to mid-nineteenth century; cheap books or 'yellowbacks' were produced to be sold at the railway bookstalls which W.H. Smith inaugurated in
1849. Routledge, with their 'Railway Library', and Chapman and Hall
swiftly entered to compete for the production of cheap editions. The growth
of the railways is thus directly linked to the production of popular literature
with a mass circulation.

Although travel literature and other forms of non-fiction formed an
important part of 'railway literature', a number of publishers had their
greatest successes with modern fiction, including some detective novels
and a substantial number of the 'sensation novels' which are the object of
the critique, quoted above, by H.L. Mansel (a philosopher and theologian,
and Dean of St Paul's from 1868 to his death in 1871). Mary Braddon's first
novels, for example, appeared in yellow-back editions in the 1860s and
1870s. In Richard Altick's account of nineteenth-century reading patterns:
'Every passenger train of the hundreds that roared down the rails in the
course of a single day carried a cargo of readers, their eyes fixed on *Lady
Audley's Secret* or the *Times*.'[17] Altick might or might not have intended a
gendered division of reading here, but the topic opens up the question of the
impact of the railways, which enabled women to travel far more easily and in
far greater numbers than ever before, on the 'feminization' of literature.

Mansel's perception that the function of railway fiction, instanced by
the sensation novel, was to provide 'temporary excitement to relieve the
dulness [*sic*] of a journey' was repeated in discussions of travel throughout
the century. His account of the sensation novel's 'preaching to the nerves'
could be read as a displacement of the nervous shocks produced by railway
travel to railway literature, in which case it comes close to Benjamin's
assertion that the pleasure of the detective novel on the railway journey is
that it provides a substitute anxiety for that produced by the journey itself.
Reading and train travel were linked from the start: in 1830 a *Quarterly
Review* contributor wrote that the railway journey is 'so easy, that a
passenger might read a newspaper with perfect comfort'. Reading on the
train is in this account inseparable from the naturalization of railway travel:
it may only have been possible when the first, intense anxiety about railway
travel had subsided, although, as Schivelbusch argues, the traveller's retreat
into his or her book is also a surrogate activity. It becomes a substitute for an

engagement with the realities of the landscape, from which the train traveller is now alienated as an effect of the speed with which he or she moves through it, and for the communication that no longer took place between travellers in this new form of transport.

In Mansel's 1863 review article on sensation fiction, books, bodies and machines become closely identified. Mansel links sensation novels with industrial processes: 'a commercial atmosphere floats around works of this class, redolent of the manufactory and the shop'.[18] They are condemned not only for their unnatural 'excitement' but also for the speed of their production'. Such novels employ 'rapid and ephemeral methods of awakening the interest of their readers' and 'carry the whole nervous system by steam'.[19] They are limited to contemporary subjects because 'proximity ... is one great element of sensation. It is necessary to be near a mine to be blown up by its explosion; and a tale which aims at electrifying the nerves of the reader is never thoroughly effective unless the scene be laid in our own days and among the people we are in the habit of meeting.'[20] Novels, in this model, sound remarkably like trains, with the difference that in reading 'nervous shock' can become a pleasurable sensation. And although Mansel represents the train journey as dull, the train-book equivalence he constructs suggests that the railway nonetheless continues to be imbued with a high potential for danger.

The railway accident, and trains and train travel more generally, played a crucial part in the themes and structures of the Victorian novel. Charles Dickens' engagements, in particular, with the railways were many and various. They include his representations of speed and locomotion in the sketch 'A Flight' (1851), experienced as at once exhilarating and disorientating, as he narrates an impressionist account of a journey by rail and sea to Paris. 'Railway Dreaming' (1856) opens with a version of the familiar nineteenth-century trope of 'the annihilation of time and space': 'I am never sure of time or place upon a Railroad. I can't read, I can't think, I can't sleep. I can only dream.'[21] The two sketches enact a form of free-associative thinking which connects with the themes of my previous chapter, as well as de Certeau's account of the train traveller and dream-states: 'I take it for granted', Dickens wrote in 'Railway Dreaming', 'I am coming from somewhere, and going somewhere else. I seek to know no more. Why things fly into my head and fly out again, whence they come and why they come, where they go and why they go, I am incapable of considering'.[22] With this loss of identity – 'I know nothing about myself' – the space of fantasy is entered: the narrative details an imagining of a science-fiction Moon-life, as if the self's unmooring from time, place and self-certainty has opened up an alternative universe. Half a century before George Méliès created his trick-film *Voyage à la Lune*, Dickens's train goes to the Moon, and in both 'A Flight' and 'Railway-Dreaming' Dickens depicts the high-speed rail travel of his day as a form of flying or 'taking wing'.[23]

Darker representations of the railway emerged in *Dombey and Son* (1848) and in the short story 'The Signalman', which was composed soon after Dickens's own experience of a railway disaster at Staplehurst, Kent, in June 1865. Throughout *Dombey and Son* the railway is associated with death, as in the description of Dombey's train journey after his son Paul has died: 'The very speed at which the train was whirled along, mocked the swift course of the young life that had been borne away so steadily and so inexorably to its foredoomed end'.[24] This formulation of a death drive, as well as the image of the train's hybrid organic-mechanical monstrosity, culminates in the train accident that kills the villainous Carker, on whom 'the fierce impetuous rush of the steam-train' exerts a combined fear and fascination:

> He heard a shout . . . saw the red eyes, bleared and dim, in the daylight, close upon him – was beaten down, caught up, and whirled away upon a jagged mill, that spun him round and round, and struck him limb from limb, and licked his stream of life up with its fiery heat, and cast his mutilated fragments in the air.[25]

In 'The Signalman', a ghost/sensation story, there is less emphasis on the train's rush and speed – though 'vibration' and 'pulsation' are all-important – and a greater focus on the inhuman 'architecture' of the railway. The story's events are held within the site of the unfortunate signalman's hut, and the spaces, vertical and horizontal, adjacent to it: 'the dismal mouth of the tunnel' and 'the high, wet walls of the cutting'.[26] In *Dombey and Son*, the train devours distances; in 'The Signalman', lives are confined to the narrowest of places, an 'unnatural valley' cut out of the earth. The ghost story works with the technology of communication at a distance: the telegraph and its wires, which the wind makes into a 'wild harp', and which divides sound from sight, and gesture, symbol or code from spoken language. The 'uncanniness' of the story – in which the accidents of the railway are foretold but cannot be averted – resides in the ultimate conjoining of a 'gesticulation' and a warning cry: 'For God's sake, clear the way.'

The railway disaster was also central to the sensation novel, with notable examples in Mrs Henry Wood's *East Lynne* (1861) and Mary Braddon's *John Marchmont's Legacy* (1863), as a device allowing for the exploration, and destabilizing, of identities and of memory and its loss. Wood's plotting uses the railway accident to cut the novel in two, making the second half a punitive (for the heroine) repetition of the first. At the centre of the novel is a railway accident which kills the errant Lady Isabel Vane's illegitimate child and radically disfigures Lady Isabel herself. The rescuers at the scene of the railway accident had left her for dead, but

> the surgeons, on further inspection, had found life in her still shattered frame ... She remained three months in the hospital before she could be removed. The change that had passed over her in those three months was little less than death itself: no one could have recognized in the pale, thin, shattered, crippled invalid, she who had been known as Lady Isabel Vane.[27]

The railway accident 'shatters' and 'disfigures' the human form and face: dissolving identities in an instant. Presumed dead in the accident, Lady Isabel is able to return, unrecognized, to her former home, where she acts as governess to the children she had left behind and witnesses, in agonies of remorse and jealousy, the happiness of her former husband and his new wife. She dies soon after, of consumption and grief.

In Braddon's *John Marchmont's Legacy*, brain fever and amnesia follow a skull fracture sustained by the hero in a railway accident: 'For eleven weeks after that terrible concussion upon the South-Western Railway, Edward Arundel had lain in a state of coma – helpless, mindless; all the story of his life blotted away, and his brain transformed into as blank a page as if he had been an infant lying on his mother's knees.'[28] Braddon's novel, in line with a number of theories of hysteria, represented female pathologies as innate, sexually charged, and perhaps hereditary, while male pathologies were understood as the product of external traumatic forces. Yet the equivalence between machine and body, and the complex question of identification in the discourse of 'sensation' (a relay between nervous systems, as in Mrs Oliphant's famous pronouncement that in the sensation novel 'the reader's nerves are affected like the hero's'[29]) also disturbs the distinction between endogenous and exogenous aetiologies. At the same time, the gender of psychopathology is troubled through the discourses of hysteria, which arose, as I discussed in the previous chapter, in large part out of the study of railway shock.

If the sensation novel drew, literally or figuratively, on the railway accident and the traumas of train travel, what did the railways offer to writers of detective fiction, its generic successor? The standardization of time, which directly resulted from railway travel, is clearly central to a genre dependent on establishing alibis and times of death. The railway timetable becomes the detective and the detective novelist's guide – the text of standardized time. Train travel also comes to represent the combination of rationality and the unknown which corresponds to the play between ratiocination and intuition in the classical detective narrative.

Secondly, the railway created not only the possibility of combining an enclosed space with mobility and changing views, but also new spaces of darkness and isolation: the tunnel (perhaps the bourgeoisie's only experience of a subterranean world familiar to a number of industrial workers) and the corridor-less compartment. Railway detective fiction charts the changing architecture of trains and often based itself on 'true railway crimes', such as the murder in 1881 of Mr Gold, a businessman, shot as the train passed through one tunnel and thrown out of the train in the next. *The Times* reporter concluded that 'the ordinary railway compartment into which English men and women pen themselves off by twos or threes affords facilities to the garotter or the murderer of which we may be thankful that advantage has been so seldom taken'.[30] *Reynolds's Newspaper* also linked this murder with that of a Mr Briggs in 1864, and noted the particular dangers of the closed compartment: 'The man who sits opposite may be a madman or an assassin. The train thunders along, and the roar, deadening all other sounds, conceals a shriek as effectually as the deepest dungeon of the Bastille.'[31]

I return now to my three logics – equivalence, belatedness, separation/inversion – and to their working through in crime and detective fiction. Any discussion of railways and novels must include Émile Zola's *La Bête humaine*, in which murder is modernized as inseparable from machine culture, and accident and psychopathology become indivisible. Roubaud, the deputy stationmaster at Le Havre, discovers that his young wife Séverine has been having a long-standing affair with her godfather President Grandmorin, a former judge who is now on the board of directors of the railway company for which Roubaud works. He murders the President on the train on which they are both travelling, a murder which is glimpsed by Jacques, a train driver tormented by his pathological desire to kill. Jacques sees the murder enacted as he stands at a spot near a railway tunnel:

> The whole line of carriages followed, the little square windows, blindingly light, making a procession of crowded compartments tear by at such a dizzying speed that the eye was not sure whether it had really caught the fleeting visions. And in that precise quarter-second Jacques quite distinctly saw through the window of a brilliantly lit coupe a man holding another man down on the seat and plunging a knife into his throat, while a dark mass, probably a third person, possibly some luggage that had fallen from above, weighed down hard on the kicking legs of the man being murdered.[32]

Finding the body of the President, thrown from the carriage, Jacques's 'itch for murder intensified like a physical lust at the sight of this pathetic corpse'.³³ The tableau he has seen does not fall into place, however, until later in the novel, when he and Séverine have become lovers. She describes the murder to him when they are in bed, revealing that she was the dark mass holding down the President; her body was the medium through which the shock of the stabbing was felt. 'I didn't see anything', she tells Jacques, 'but felt it all, the impact of the knife in his neck, the long tremor of the body, and death in three hiccuping gasps, like the spring of a clock breaking ... Oh, I can still feel a sort of echo of his death-struggle in my own limbs.'³⁴ It is not the sight of murder but its physiological sensations – its shock effects – that excite Jacques so intensely; after her confession 'they possessed each other ... with the same agonizing pleasure as beasts disembowelling each other in mating'.³⁵

Throughout the novel Zola represents the connection between mechanical agitation and sexual arousal which Freud and Karl Abraham were later to theorize for psychoanalysis, as well as the ways in which the murderer represents his own death through the death of another. The train itself becomes the focal point of the interchange between the ostensibly disparate systems of machines and bodies: the collapse of the distinction also collapses the distinction between desire and the desire to destroy. Jacques finally murders Séverine, 'the same kind of stab as for President Grandmorin, in the same place, with the same savagery. At that moment the Paris express dashed past, so noisy and fast that the floor shook, and she was dead as if this storm had struck her down.'³⁶ The repetition of the act – 'the same kind of stab ... in the same place, with the same savagery' – is a reinscription on the body and in the writing of the novel itself. Repetitive murder, of the kind that obsesses Jacques, is, as Seltzer notes, defined in the conjunction of compulsive sexualized violence on the one hand and technological system, schedule and routine, such as the railway is governed by, on the other.³⁷

Zola's narrative is itself obsessively and repetitively punctuated by railway murders and disasters. In addition to the murder on the train, the novel describes a perilous journey through a snowstorm, in the aftermath of which Flore, also in love with Jacques, resolves to kill Jacques and Séverine. She effects a railway disaster by drawing a horse-drawn cart in front of their train; she then commits suicide in a railway tunnel. At the close of the novel, Jacques and his assistant fight to the death under the train they are driving. The runaway train speeds towards the future and towards destruction with a cargo of soldiers bound for the Franco-Prussian wars; their bodies will presumably be broken and fragmented by one of two technologies of modernity: the war machine or the railway.

My next example, in which I locate what I have called the logic of belatedness, is a reworking of Zola's novel in which equivalence and simultaneity are rejected in favour of various forms of 'missing'. Georges Simenon's *l'homme qui regardait passer les trains* ['The Man Who Watched the Trains Go By'] is the story of Kees Popinga, a middle-aged Dutch bourgeois who, on discovering that his employer's business has collapsed and that his career has been founded on sand, suddenly abandons family life, takes a train to Amsterdam, murders his employer's mistress when she refuses his advances, and escapes to Paris. Simenon uses the image of passing trains to suggest the potential for sexual violence always present in Popinga and his murderous innocence:

> And if, in introspective mood, he had set himself to discover if there were a streak of wildness latent in his mental make-up, nothing is less likely than that he would have thought of a certain queer, half-guilty feeling that crept over him whenever he saw a train go by – especially a night-train, with all its blinds down, rife with mystery.[38]

The most evocative image of the thriller genre – the night train, 'with all its blinds down' – thus becomes, in Simenon's crime novel, the figure of (male sexual) fantasy and unacknowledged desire itself: for Popinga, the 'dimmed lights and close-drawn blinds' of night expresses are linked with the shadows on the blinds on Groningen's one 'gay house'. On the run after committing murder, Popinga hides out next to a marshalling yard. The movement of the trains at night retroactively produces the desire for a prostitute with whom he has recently spent a chaste night: 'before getting into bed, [he] gazed for several minutes at the glimmering expanse of railway lines, red and green lights, a long, black goods-train rumbling by. His thoughts kept harking back to Jeanne, and now he found a curious pleasure in picturing amorous contacts which, when they were available, he had foregone.'[39]

Popinga's former conventionality is imaged through the mores of railway travel: 'On railway journeys I had to pretend to read a book or look out of the window, instead of showing any interest in those around me, and to wear gloves, uncomfortable as they might be – because it's the right thing to do when travelling.'[40] Trains arouse desire: the conventions of travelling demand its repression and its sublimation through reading or looking through the glass at the world outside. This becomes the equivalent to wearing gloves, in its buffering effects and its refusal to engage with the dangerous proximity between bodies in a railway carriage or the fascination of looking from railway corridor into compartment. A similar tension exists between the train's transgressive properties – its movements through the night, 'the rhythmic panting of engines',[41] and its crossing of borders – and the routinized spatio-temporal world of railway travel, mirrored in the obsessive calculations and grids – maps, chess-games, accounting – which preoccupy Popinga, managing clerk turned murderer. At the close of the novel, Popinga attempts suicide by lying across a railway-track: he is caught and arrested, 'clad only in his overcoat': 'In the course of the night he was roused and made to put on a ticket-collector's uniform which was much too small for him.'[42]

Simenon's reworking of Zola's novel splits the machine–body complex. Popinga's desire, aroused by the sight and sound of the trains in the shunting yard, is too late, a connection missed. Popinga even 'misses' his own death, lying across the wrong line:

> With a rattle and a roar the light bore down on him, and the roar swelled to such a din as he had never heard in his life before, so tremendous that he almost fancied he was dead already.
>
> But presently there came a sound of voices, followed by an eerie silence. Only then he realized that the train had stopped, on the other line, and saw two men climbing down from the engine, and carriage windows being let down.[43]

By placing Popinga on the wrong track, the narrative prevents body and machine from meeting and constructs an alternative nemesis, with Popinga incarcerated in an asylum.

In coming to our third 'logic' – the imperative of separation/inversion – we encounter, in another term of de Certeau's, the 'spatializing frenzy' of the detective novel.[44] The space of the tunnel, as we have seen, is the most consistent nexus of narrative activity and anxiety; subterranean and viewless, it is frequently figured as the site of lawlessness and of action without witness. In the history of railway construction, tunnels accounted for the largest number of fatalities and injuries amongst workers. They were also the most frequent sites of railway 'accidents', thus threatening not just the working class but also the travelling middle classes. The spaces of anxiety from the start, it would seem as if fear of injury or death from the railway accident commuted itself, or began to run concurrently with, fear of injury or death, or loss to property or propriety, at the hands of one's *compagnons de route*. Certainly, it is the latter or later anxiety which motivates the narratives of railway detective fiction.

The journey through the tunnel precludes the view from the outside in and the inside out. The spatial structures of the closed compartment and the corridor-less train create mysteries dependent less on sight and sightlessness than on the seemingly inexplicable movement of people or objects into and out of an enclosed space which moves through space and time at an unprecedented rate. The virtual interchangeability of bodies, living and dead, and luggage (particularly boxes of various kinds – jewel boxes, despatch boxes) in railway detective fiction plots suggests something of the felt commodification of persons on the railway. It is a reminder of John Ruskin's complaint that the railway journey 'transmutes a man from traveller into a living parcel', ticketed and despatched from one place to another: 'For the time', Ruskin adds, 'he has parted with the nobler characteristics of his humanity for the sake of a planetary power of locomotion'.[45]

Sherlock Holmes is, as Benjamin suggests, closely identified with the railway; yet – despite the fact that at least two thirds of the Sherlock Holmes stories contain train journeys, and that Holmes is a figure shot through with nervous sensations – Conan Doyle rarely makes the railway the site of crime. The railway journey tends to be used, as Benjamin suggests, to mark narrative duration and movement, or as a narrative space in which Holmes can impart to Watson the contexts of crimes on outward journeys and their solutions on return. Holmes' famous comment that it is the country rather than the city in which criminality flourishes is made on a train journey, the view out of the window allowing for a kind of inversion – in this case of the traditional city/country divide.[46]

For one among numerous examples of 'closed carriage mysteries' we could turn to Conan Doyle's 'The Story of the Man with the Watches' (not a Holmes story).[47] Here the closed compartment mystery substitutes one form of 'crossing' for another, hypothesizing a movement between parallel trains, the traversal of separate spaces, in order to reveal that the 'crossing' was in fact sexual, the murdered man having entered the carriage as a woman. The movement from one train to another could not have occurred because the two trains do not in fact run in parallel or at the same speed; the explanation is thus not that of the straight lines of the railway, but of the confusion of sexual 'deviance' or 'inversion'. Doyle, in this story, explicitly turns his back on the view into the train carriage from a train passing alongside. It is, however, central to railway detective fiction, most famously, perhaps, in Agatha Christie's *The 4.50 from Paddington*. The fleeting landscape is transformed by the violent act into a tableau, perceptible only as a result of the pure contingency of being at a particular point at a specific time, as Mrs McGillicuddy, travelling on a train on her way to stay with her

friend Jane Marple, sees a woman strangled in a compartment of a train
running parallel to her own:[48]

> At the moment when the two trains gave the illusion of being stationary, a
> blind in one of the carriages flew up with a snap. Mrs McGillicuddy looked
> into the lighted first-class carriage that was only a few feet away.
>
> Then she drew her breath in with a gasp and half-rose to her feet.
>
> Standing with his back to the window and to her was a man. His hands
> were round the throat of a woman who faced him, and he was slowly,
> remorselessly strangling her. Her eyes were starting from their sockets, her
> face was purple and congested. As Mrs McGillicuddy watched, fascinated,
> the end came; the body went limp and crumpled in the man's hands.
>
> At the same moment, Mrs McGillicuddy's train slowed down again and
> the other began to gain speed. It passed forward and a moment or two later it
> had vanished from sight.
>
> Almost automatically Mrs McGillicuddy's hand went up to the commu-
> nication cord, then paused, irresolute. After all, what use would it be ringing
> the cord of the train in which *she* was travelling? The horror of what she had
> seen at such close quarters, and the unusual circumstances, made her feel
> paralysed. *Some* immediate action was necessary – but what?[49]

The transformation of the 'flying countryside', as seen from the train
window, into the interior space, as seen from the parallel railway compartment, inaugurates the plot: a bourgeois family drama situated in a country
house which is encircled by the railway. The intimacy of Mrs McGillicuddy's
view from one compartment into another (what allows her, in de Certeau's
terms, 'to see') rests on 'the illusion of being stationary', in the same way that
she is drawn to pull the communication cord by the momentary illusion that
the proximity of the two trains in space and time is equivalent to an identity
of their systems. The logic of separation here runs alongside, or perhaps gives
way to, a logic of equivalence, as Miss Marple brings about a resolution of the
mystery (a mystery which is initially that of a murder without a body): first by
repeating the course of the train journey herself and finally by forcing the
murderer into a repetition of his murderous gestures:

> [Miss Marple] gave a sudden gasp and began to choke. 'A fish bone', she
> gasped out, 'in my throat.' . . . Mrs McGillicuddy gave a sudden gasp as her
> eyes fell on the tableau in front of her, Miss Marple leaning back and the
> doctor holding her throat and tilting up her head.
>
> 'But that's *him*', cried Mrs McGillicuddy. 'That's the man in the train . . . '[50]

Ethel Lena White's *The Lady Vanishes* (better known through Hitchcock's
film version) is a train mystery which largely excludes the outside, a Balkan
landscape, making its substitutions within and between train compartments.

Thus Iris Carr is alerted to the disappearance of Miss Froy, the English spinster who has befriended her, when her seat becomes and remains empty; she is confirmed in her belief in a conspiracy when Miss Froy's place in the compartment is taken by a woman wearing her clothes. Miss Froy is, in fact, lying heavily bandaged and under guard in the next-door compartment, disguised by her abductors as a maimed accident victim.

Iris, herself the recent recipient of a blow to the head, cannot be entirely sure of what she knows and sees; the reality of Miss Froy's existence is secured for Iris by the sight of her name written on a pane of glass. In White's novel, the glass separates the compartment from the corridor: Iris and Miss Froy occupy corner rather than window seats. Hitchcock, in his 1938 film *The Lady Vanishes*, transferred the signature from the corridor glass to the train window, adding for good measure a label from the packet of tea ('Harriman's Herbal Tea') preferred by Miss Froy. The train window – the windowpane which connects, separates and inverts inside and outside – becomes the site on which identity is both secured and effaced, as signature and label respectively are revealed and vanish, adhere and are whirled away. With a knowing gesture to Freudian psychology, the film script plays with the concept of 'substitution' as both an unconscious mental act and as a villainous ploy: 'We believe there's been a substitution, doctor', Iris and her one ally on the train declare. There is even an allusion to the name of Freud himself: 'Froy – it rhymes with joy', proclaims the young-old English spinster, as she spells out her curious name on the windowpane of the restaurant car.

My final example of the logic of separation/inversion is Patricia Highsmith's *Strangers on a Train*. Here one train traveller finds not only that he has swapped stories with a fellow traveller, but that he is expected to swap murders. 'We murder for each other, see? I kill your wife and you kill my father! We meet on the train, see, and nobody knows we know each other! Perfect alibis!' The psychopathic Bruno kills Guy's estranged wife and then demands of Guy that he kill Bruno's hated father. The structure is 'criss-cross', as Bruno reiterates in Hitchcock's film version of the novel, or, in the terms of de Certeau's account of railway travel, 'chiasmic'. Here the structures of exchange become caught up in a logic as murderous as that of the equivalence and compulsion to repeat which drives the characters in Zola's novel.

In the 1930s, Benjamin's account of railway anxiety is anachronistic – and deliberately so. Representing the anxieties of the journey in 'mythic' form, he condenses the cultural history of a century in its movement from wonder and fear of the new technology of rail travel to its 'naturalization', embodied in the traveller who reads during the journey. But Benjamin leaves open, or opens up, the space of anxiety – a subliminal anxiety, which he terms 'mythic', specific to the technologies of travel and always capable of being reawakened. It is appropriate, then, that on the journey the traveller should turn to the 'mythic' literature of nineteenth-century detective writing, a genre near-contemporaneous with the expansion of the railways and railway travel. And yet Benjamin's account is also fitted to his own times. It was film, including that of Hitchcock, which would reinvent both the railway journey and detective narrative for the twentieth century while, in the 1930s, new anxieties and dangers would emerge as trains criss-crossed Europe's increasingly fraught borders.

Notes

1 Walter Benjamin, 'Kriminalromane, auf Reisen', *Gesammelte Schriften*, edited by Rolf Tiedemann et al., 7 vols. (Frankfurt: Suhrkamp, 1974–1989), 4.1, pp. 381–382. Translations from Benjamin are my own.

2 Benjamin's outline for a detective novel is published in *Gesammelte Schriften*, 2.2, pp. 845–851. See also Ernst Bloch, 'A Philosophical View of the Detective Novel' (1965), in *The Utopian Function of Art and Literature: Selected Essays*, translated by Jack Zipes and F. Mecklenburg (Cambridge, Mass: MIT Press, 1988), pp. 245–264, and Siegfried Kracauer, *Der Detektiv-Roman: Ein philosophicher Traktat*, vol. 1 of *Werke*, edited by Inka Mülder-Bach and Ingrid Belke (Frankfurt: Suhrkamp, 1971), pp. 103–204. For further discussion of Frankfurt School theorists and their interest in detective fiction, see David Frisby, 'Walter Benjamin and Detection', *German Politics and Society*, 32 (Summer 1994), 89–106, and 'Between the Spheres: Siegfried Kracauer and the Detective Novel', *Theory, Culture and Society* 9, no. 2 (1992): 1–22.

3 Benjamin, 'Kriminalromane', p. 381.

4 Ibid., p. 382.

5 Ibid., p. 382.

6 Ibid., p. 382.

7 Ernst Bloch claims, in a discussion of the first locomotive, that 'the crises of accidents (of unmastered things) are more long-lasting and deep-seated than the crises of the economy (of unmastered commodities)': Ernst Bloch, *Spuren* (1959), in Bloch, *Gesamtausgabe* 1 (Frankfurt: Suhrkamp, 1988), pp. 160–161.

8 Mark Seltzer, *Bodies and Machines* (New York and London: Routledge, 1992), and *Serial Killers* (New York and London: Routledge, 1988).

9 Schivelbusch, *The Railway Journey*, p. 38.

10 Benjamin, 'Kriminalromane', p. 382.

11 Michel de Certeau, 'Railway Navigation and Incarceration', in *The Practice of Everyday Life* translated by Steven Rendall (Berkeley: University of California Press, 1984), pp. 111–114, 112.

12 Ibid., pp. 111–112.
13 Ibid., p. 112.
14 Benjamin, 'Kriminalromane', p. 381.
15 Ibid., p. 114.
16 H. L. Mansel, 'Sensation Fiction', *Quarterly Review*, 113 (1863), 481–514, 485.
17 Richard Altick, *The English Common Reader* (Chicago: University of Chicago Press, 1957), p. 89.
18 Mansel, 'Sensation Fiction', p. 483.
19 Ibid., p. 487.
20 Ibid., pp. 488–489.
21 Charles Dickens, 'Railway Dreaming', *Household Words*, vol. XIII, no. 320, 10 May 1856 (385–388), 385.
22 Ibid., 385.
23 Dickens, 'A Flight'.
24 Charles Dickens, *Dombey and Son*.
25 Ibid.
26 Charles Dickens, 'Mugby Junction: No. 1 Branch Line. The Signalman', in *Selected Short Fiction*, ed. Deborah Thomas (Harmondsworth: Penguin, 1976).
27 Mrs Henry Wood, *East Lynne* (London: Dent, 1994), 327.
28 Mary Elizabeth Braddon, *John Marchmont's Legacy*, 25. For an interesting discussion of the novel in relation to Victorian psychology and psychiatry, see Sally Shuttleworth, 'Preaching to the Nerves', in *A Question of Identity: Women, Science and Literature*, edited by Marina Benjamin (New Brunswick, NJ: Rutgers University Press, 1993), especially pp. 214–220.
29 Margaret Oliphant, 'Sensation Novels', *Blackwood's*, vol. 91, May 1862, 572.
30 *The Times* (London), 7 July 1881, p. 9.
31 *Reynold's Newspaper*, 3 July 1881.
32 Émile Zola, *La Bête Humaine*, translated by Leonard Tancock (Harmondsworth: Penguin, 1977), p. 70.
33 Ibid., p. 73.
34 Ibid., pp. 231–232.
35 Ibid., pp. 234–235.
36 Ibid., p. 331.
37 Mark Seltzer, 'Serial Killers (II): The Pathological Public Sphere', *Critical Inquiry* 22 (Autumn 1995), 122.
38 Georges Simenon, *The Man Who Watched the Trains Go By*, translated by Stuart Gilbert (London: Pan, 1948), p. 5.
39 Ibid., p. 82.
40 Ibid., p. 129.
41 Ibid., p. 86.
42 Ibid., p. 186.
43 Ibid., p. 185.
44 Michel de Certeau, 'Spatial Stories', in *The Practice of Everyday Life*, pp. 115–130, 118.

45 John Ruskin, *The Seven Lamps of Architecture* (London: Routledge, 1907), p. 125.

46 Arthur Conan Doyle, 'The Adventure of the Copper Beeches', in *The Penguin Complete Sherlock Holmes* (Harmondsworth: Penguin, 1981), pp. 316–332, 322–323.

47 Arthur Conan Doyle, 'The Story of the Man with the Watches', *Strand*, August 1898, 175–185.

48 Agatha Christie, *4.50 From Paddington* (1957) (London: Pan, 1974).

49 Ibid., pp. 7–8.

50 Ibid., p. 215.

CHAPTER 4

'From Autumn to Spring, Aesthetics Change'
Modernity's Visual Displays

In this chapter, I explore the topic of new visualities and new visual spaces at the turn of the nineteenth and twentieth centuries, through questions of advertisement, spectatorship, display and the pictorial 'language' of modernity. In recent decades, there has been significant critical discussion of, on the one hand, literature and advertising and, on the other, literature and cinema. There has been little exploration, however, of the ways in which these three terms – literature, advertising, cinema – might function together. Yet it is certainly the case that many of the early twentieth-century literary texts which are most fully in dialogue with the medium of film are also those which are most directly engaged with the visual and verbal dimensions of advertising culture. Central examples from British, Irish and American fiction include Joyce's *Ulysses*, Woolf's *Mrs Dalloway*, John Dos Passos's *Manhattan Transfer*, Scott Fitzgerald's *The Great Gatsby* and Jean Rhys's *Good Morning Midnight*.

The connection between film and advertising in these texts is suggested, or secured, in a number of ways: through the representation of the shop or display window as a kind of screen; through the depiction of the mobile spectator in the urban sphere, caught by what he or she sees in passing and, in texts such as Dos Passos's, having a new subjectivity or identity modelled upon it; through a focus on gesture and physiognomy; through various forms of projection, as in the aeroplane episode in *Mrs Dalloway*, in which advertising letters are written on the sky; through the construction of 'a new alphabet', comprised of both words and images; and through a focus on fashion, as in *Ulysses*, in which, as Jennifer Wicke has argued in her important study *Advertising Fictions*, fashion becomes 'a kind of compact with modernity'.[1] *Ulysses* is indeed the text in which modernist literature intersects with the culture of advertising most completely and most radically. The discourses of advertising both compose and flow through the inner and outer worlds of Leopold Bloom, an advertising canvasser, shaping sound, vision and, above all, language.

While these connections underlie my thinking about the culture of modernity, I have chosen in this chapter to focus not on literary texts, but on that early twentieth-century film theory which has connections to theories of advertising. Central texts in this context include the American poet and artist Vachel Lindsay's *The Art of the Moving Image* (1915/1922) and his *The Progress and Poetry of the Movies*, written in 1922 but unpublished in his lifetime, as well as the psychologist Hugo Münsterberg's *The Art of the Photoplay* (1916). The chapter closes with a brief discussion from a different cultural context – the Polish/French film theorist and director Jean Epstein's early writings on literature and cinema.

Vachel Lindsay will be a familiar name to those with an interest in early writings on cinema. Lindsay, an artist and poet, published *The Art of the Moving Picture* in 1915 (a revised version was published in 1922). The book can claim the status of the first English-language book of film theory or film aesthetics. Writing against the view that film was closest as an art to stage drama, Lindsay emphasized its relation to art and the art gallery and with sculpture. His central preoccupation was with the 'hieroglyphic' dimensions of silent film, which led him in two, interconnected dimensions. Firstly, film was to be understood as a 'hieroglyphic' language, a 'new universal alphabet',[2] 'a moving picture Esperanto'.[3] Movies, in their pictorialism, are, Lindsay wrote,

> as revolutionary in their own age as the invention of Hieroglyphics was to the cave-man. And they can be built up into a great pictorial art. The Egyptian tomb-painting was literally nothing but enlarged Hieroglyphics. We now have Hieroglyphics in motion – and they can be made as lovely as the Egyptian if we once understand what we are doing.

It would profit any photoplay man', Lindsay wrote, 'to study to think like the Egyptians, the great picture-writing people.[4] Lindsay claimed that he found the decipherment of hieroglyphics 'extraordinarily easy' (though significant doubt was later cast on his ability to interpret them) 'because I have analyzed so many hundreds of photoplay films'.[5] *The Book of the Dead* (the most significant collection of ancient Egyptian funerary texts), to which Lindsay repeatedly returned, 'is certainly the great motion picture I ever attended'.[6] Not only film, but modern American civilization in its entirety is to be linked to ancient Egyptian culture. 'American civilization', Lindsay writes, 'grows more hieroglyphic every day. The cartoons of Darling, the advertisements in the back of the magazines and on the billboards and in the street-cars, the acres of photographs in the Sunday newspapers, make us into a hieroglyphic civilization far nearer to Egypt than to England'.[7]

Lindsay's hieroglyphic preoccupations place him in a tradition of philosophical and cultural theorizing, from the writings of the American transcendentalists (for whom hieroglyphics represented a unity of word and image and a form of occulted knowledge) through to Jean Epstein's references to film as Egyptian hieroglyphics and Sergei Eisenstein's writings on the filmic ideogram, and extending further to writers of the Frankfurt School, notably Siegfried Kracauer and Theodor Adorno, with their interest in 'mass-cultural hieroglyphics'.

Lindsay, for all his eccentricities, was, I would argue, producing a significant form of cultural commentary or cultural critique. The critique is heightened in *The Progress and Poetry of the Movies*, in which Lindsay wrote of American modernity, with its 'extreme fanaticism in the worship of raw light and raw action'. He argued that:

> Action and speed and blazing light must alternate with moments of mellowness and rest. Even between each heart-beat, there is a split-second of absolute rest, which the American spirit would deny. It is the American idea to destroy that split-second of rest, which is between every heart-beat . . . No one to whom the moon is sufficiently dear will permit his nerves to be chopped into little pieces 1/16 of an inch long, and no longer, nor his time chopped into little pieces 1/16 of a second long, and no longer.[8]

This image was taken up later in Lindsay's manuscript in a brief discussion of Chaplin's artistry, located in his films' 'intimate passages, some of them not longer than the split second between every heart-beat, but long enough to give the touch of eternity in time, the hint of moonlight interrupting broad sunlight'.[9] The heart-beat was a way of giving human measure to mechanized modern time, including the factory-time of a society dominated by Taylorist and Fordist models of 'scientific management', with its automatization of the human body and its energies, and to cinematic time (projection at 1/16 of a second). For Lindsay, film was both continuous with the world of 'action and speed and blazing light' and resistant to it, in its imagined creation of 'rests' or intervals, whose identity overlapped with that of the passages through which 'beauty' could be 'glimpsed'.

His account finds an echo in the writings on photography of Walter Benjamin and Roland Barthes, in which the medium's 'aura' was perceived to diminish as the duration of exposure time decreased and photography became increasingly instantaneous. There are also connections to the late twentieth-century writings of Paul Virilio, in which the contrast between modernity and postmodernity is often predicated on the idea that the greater the speed of the image, the more absolute the loss of a contextualized time, and in which we find a nostalgia for a slower speed of projection/representation. The destruction of human consciousness, Virilio suggests, comes with the closure of the interval, temporal and spatial, between the representation and what it records.[10]

The claims for film 'beauty' in Lindsay's writings, as in Hugo Münsterberg's, were to some extent linked to the granting of a high-art status to film. Nonetheless, it would seem that for Lindsay, in particular, 'beauty' was also credited with the 'social task' of giving human measure to modern time, and of penetrating the seductive surfaces of modernity. In *The Progress and Poetry of the Movies*, the 'glimpse'[11] (of beauty) was contrasted, though the distinction was not absolute, with the 'magical glitter' that created a continuum between the film, the plate glass windows of commodity culture and the glass architecture of the modern city:

> Now this impression of looking into a crystal, which gives a magical glitter to everything within it, is the impression a true movie should convey . . . The first story of the principal streets is becoming all glass. It is not the glass itself that is desirable in the eyes of the American. It is the film of light upon the surface of the glass which has become his luxury . . . We have come to a time when we are slaves indeed to this glamor. There is many a gigantic shop which owes its influence to the elimination of all but the transfiguring glassy surface between the customer and the goods displayed. . . . This madness of the crystalline is getting to be more and more a habit of the American eye.[12]

While 'the glimpse' and 'glitter' are both forms of 'beauty', the former was not held to be collusive with a commodified modern time and modern vision. In this sense the 'glimpse of beauty' in the film could be said to anticipate some of the perceived functions of a montage aesthetic, which disrupts surfaces (through fragmentation, collision or the creation of new conceptual relationships) and 'awakens' the spectator.

For Hugo Münsterberg, as for so many writers on film in its first decades, cinema was 'a new art . . . A new form still undeveloped and hardly understood.'[13] 'For the first time', Münsterberg writes, 'the psychologist can observe the starting of a new aesthetic development, a new form of true beauty in the turmoil of a technical age, created by its very nature and yet more than any other art destined to overcome outer nature by the free and joyful play of the mind'.[14]

Münsterberg published his account of the 'new art' of the film, *The Photoplay: A Psychological Study*, in 1916, the year of his death. It was written during the summer of 1915, when Münsterberg's personal and professional situation, as a patriotic German living in the US, was becoming increasingly untenable. Münsterberg was, he wrote, a very recent convert to film: on going to the cinema for the first time in 1914,

'I recognized at once that here marvellous possibilities were open, and I began to explore with eagerness the world which was new to me.'[15] While he represented his 'conversion' to moving pictures as being of recent date, the preoccupations he brought to his writings about film were not. He had left Germany for the US in 1892 when William James invited him to take charge of the psychological laboratory at Harvard (where his students included the young Gertrude Stein) and was centrally concerned with the psychology of vision and perception, though his extensive publications also included work on aesthetics, American culture, the 'applied psychology' of law, advertising, industry and 'scientific management'. *The Photoplay* drew on a number of his long-standing interests: optical technologies and the physiology and psychology of perception; the philosophy of attention; the relationship between 'inner' and 'outer' realities; a neo-Kantian 'aesthetic of isolation'; and an affirmation of eternal and absolute values in art.

His study of film is divided into two major parts – 'The Psychology of the Photoplay' and 'The Aesthetics of the Photoplay' – which follow on from introductory chapters on its outer and inner development. In the 'Psychology' section of the study, Münsterberg devoted separate chapters to 'Depth and Movement', 'Attention', 'Memory and Imagination', and 'Emotions', the categories closely following the chapter titles of William James's *The Principles of Psychology*. In *The Photoplay*, Münsterberg's interests lay in 'the mental processes which this specific form of artistic endeavour produces in us', and he was particularly concerned with the ways in which we invest the film with a depth and movement which it does not itself possess: 'we create the depth and the continuity through our mental mechanism'.[16] In Münsterberg's argument, we give more than we receive, and film spectatorship entails an encounter between an abundance of inner processes and 'the world of impressions'.

The concept of 'attention' is defined by Münsterberg as the most central of all the internal functions that create the meaning of the world around us. The world of impressions is a 'chaos' given order and meaning by our acts of attention, both 'voluntary' and 'involuntary'. A fundamental tenet of *The Photoplay* is that the close-up defines the art of the film – it is the point at which film leaves all stage-craft behind. For Münsterberg it can be identified with the mental act of attention – the close-up is indeed the 'projection' or 'objectivation' of 'the mental act of attention': 'Whenever our attention becomes focused on a special feature, the surrounding adjusts itself, eliminates everything in which we are not interested and by the close-up heightens the vividness of that on which our mind is concentrated.'[17]

The issue of the film close-up is overdetermined in Münsterberg's study, as it is in the writings of the film theorist and film-maker Jean Epstein, whose writings on cinema in the 1920s and 1930s established many of the central terms for film aesthetics. The close-up is firmly connected, for Münsterberg, with the philosophy and psychology of attention of the late nineteenth and early twentieth centuries, including the work of Théodule Ribot. Ribot's 'The Psychology of Attention' (translated into English in 1890), defines 'attention' (in its two forms – spontaneous and voluntary) as 'an exceptional, abnormal state, which cannot last a long time, for the reason that it is in contradiction to the basic condition of psychic life; namely, change'.[18] Attention is, Ribot argues, a form of inhibition. Jonathan Crary has suggested, in his study *Suspensions of Perception*, that 'attention becomes a fundamentally new object within the modernization of subjectivity',[19] and that the problem of *attention* becomes a fundamental issue in the late nineteenth century, directly related

> to the emergence of a social, urban, psychic and industrial field increasingly saturated with sensory input [and one in which the constituent elements of perceptual experience would be identified as 'mobility, novelty and distraction'[20]]. Inattention ... began to be treated as a danger and a serious problem ... It is possible to see one crucial aspect of modernity as an ongoing crisis of attentiveness.[21]

The work of the psychologists of attention, including Ribot, was drawn on extensively by the psychologists of advertising in the early twentieth century: the American William Dill Scott is the central figure here. Scott, writing in his 1908 study *The Psychology of Advertising*, wrote that 'one aim of every advertisement is to attract attention. Therefore the entire problem of attention is one of importance to the advertiser, and an understanding of it is necessary for its wisest application as well as for a correct understanding of advertising'.[22] The experiments Scott describes include tests on the relative efficacy of repetition and novelty, and the ways in which attention is attracted by features including the size of the advertisement and the size and font of its lettering.

'Attention' also becomes a key term, if a somewhat conceptually reduced one, in an early work on cinema advertising: Ernest Dench's 1916 handbook for 'the modern business man', *Advertising by Motion Pictures*. 'It will probably seem rather strange to you', Dench writes in his Introduction, 'that an invention like the cinematograph, which has achieved widespread fame as a form of entertainment, can perform the functions of advertising, but it is nonetheless a fact'.[23] His discussions of the most efficacious forms of film advertising bear in interesting ways on perceptions of cinema more broadly at this time, as in his argument that 'when adopting motion-picture advertising, everything has to be visualized by means of animated photographs, so, therefore, the appeal is presented through the eye. As for the printed word, this takes a back seat.'[24] This insistence on the essentially visual and pictorial qualities of cinema is at one with Lindsay's arguments, while Dench also makes very direct allusion to the significance of silent film as a 'universal language' in the contexts of the low levels of verbal literacy among working people and of the immigrant culture of the early twentieth century in the US: 'If you overload your films with titles, you will befog a good number of foreigners who have not been long enough in our country to master the English language, so that their probable patronage is lost just because the international language of the film has been abused.'[25] Used strategically, however, the cinema provides the most effective context for the advertiser, because it has an audience

> already waiting to be tackled. Their attention is literally glued to the screen. No matter what species of film you adopt to get over your arguments, then the spectators will give it the self-same attention. They can not do otherwise, since only one thing appears on the screen at the same time, and the hall is too dark for them to do anything else.[26]

Münsterberg, whose book on film appeared in the same year as Dench's handbook, used advertising and the lure of the shop window as direct analogies to the close-up in the cinema, showing how 'attraction' could shape 'attention':

> As we are passing along the street we see something in the shop window and as soon as it stirs up our interest, our body adjusts itself, we stop, we fixate it, we get more of the detail in it, the lines become sharper, and while it impresses us more vividly than before, the street around us has lost its vividness and clearness.'[27]

He had focused on the psychology of advertising in his earlier texts, including *Psychology and Industrial Efficiency* (1913) and on the ways in which advertising succeeds, or fails, by its appeals to memory and attention.

Film and the urban scene are also brought together in the laboratory experiments Münsterberg described in his 1913 study *Psychology and Industrial Efficiency*, designed to reduce the number of accidents on the electric railway by testing the motormen's responsive speeds and the quality of their attention to 'the quickly changing panorama of the streets'.[28] Underlying his analysis of film was undoubtedly an interest in the ways in which film motion and cinematic spectatorship might aid the eye of the viewer in the organization – spatial and perceptual – of 'the chaos of experience', 'training' the eye and the mind to deal with the rapid, visually oriented tasks demanded by modern industry and commerce and essential for the successful management of modern life, with its unprecedented motion and speed. Yet a neo-Kantian 'aesthetic of isolation' continued to lie at the heart of Münsterberg's theories of art – in which he sought to include film. It is possible that Münsterberg perceived film as the means by which the tensions between his psychophysical preoccupations – central to his engagement with the new forms of mental and physical life demanded by modern industrial society – and his idealist aesthetics could finally be resolved. Film was indeed to be a 'new form of true beauty in the turmoil of a modern age'.[29]

It was not a role he had been prepared to grant to the realm of advertising, and despite the connections Münsterberg draws between the advertisement (or the shop window) and the film, he was adamant that an advertisement should not aim for beauty:

> It is surely a mistake to believe that pure beauty best fulfils the function of the advertisement ... The very meaning of beauty lies in its self-completeness. The beautiful picture rests in itself and does not point beyond itself ... If the [advertising] display is to serve economic interests, every line and every curve, every form and every color, must be subordinated to the task of leading to a practical resolution, and to an action, and yet this is exactly the opposite of the meaning of art ... The aesthetic forms are adjusted to the main aesthetic aim, the inhibition of practical desires. The display must be pleasant, tasteful, harmonious, and suggestive, but should not be beautiful, if it is to fulfil its purpose in the fullest sense ... This of course stands in no contradiction to the requirement that the advertised article should be made to appear as beautiful as possible.[30]

There are clear tensions here, which indicate something of the ways in which the entry of advertising and cinema into the literary and visual spheres was disrupting traditional aesthetic categories. In *The Photoplay*, we see Münsterberg attempting to 'frame' this new art in traditional aesthetic contexts which it continually seems to elude or disrupt.

'To picture emotions must be the central aim of the photoplay', Münsterberg wrote, and he represented this picturing through the power of the close-up to enlarge the 'emotional action of the face to sharpest relief', or 'a play of the hands in which anger and rage or tender love or jealousy speak in unmistakeable language'.[31] This is the language of 'gestures, actions, and facial play', and Münsterberg provides an account of a physiognomic basis for filmic expression which would be powerfully developed in the writings of, amongst others, Jean Epstein and Béla Balázs. I have noted some of the striking connections between Münsterberg's and

Epstein's film theories, including their essentially physiognomic account of film representation, their concepts of film as the drama of physiology and motion, and their intense focus on the filmic close-up.

Yet Epstein, unlike Münsterberg, had little commitment, in his early writings at least, to the eternal values of art. 'The film, like contemporary literature, hastens unstable metamorphoses', Epstein wrote: 'From autumn to spring, aesthetics change.'[32] These words come from his 1921 book, *La Poésie d'aujourd'hui*, a text which T.S. Eliot read and admired, and on which he commented in his 1921 essay on 'The Metaphysical Poets'. Epstein's argument, in this essay or letter (the book was written for his friend Blaise Cendrars), on 'Le cinéma et les lettres modernes', was that both modern literature and cinema were linked by their opposition to theatre (by which Epstein meant classical French theatre). In the theatre, he argued, the actor is drowned under verbiage, whereas on the cinema screen we are given the extraordinary drama of human movement and the human face.

'Cinema and the new approach to literature', Epstein declared, need to support one another by superimposing their aesthetics.[33] These aesthetics, as he enumerated them, included 'the aesthetic of proximity', instanced in 'the succession of details with which modern authors have replaced narrative development and first close-ups generally attributed to [D.W.] Griffith, and which create a "theatre of flesh".'[34]

Epstein also defined 'an aesthetic of suggestion' – 'One no longer tells, one shows' – and 'an aesthetic of succession'. In cinema and literature, 'everything moves': 'A rush of details constitutes a poem; and the editing of a film gradually intertwines and combines shots … The physiological utopia of seeing things "together" is replaced by an approximation: seeing them quickly.' Related to this is what he terms 'an aesthetic of mental quickness'.[35] It is possible, Epstein suggested, that in the course of a life, and in successive generations, a human being could develop speed of thought. Not all human beings, he asserted, think at the same speed. The slowness of Italian films, he argued (in a reference, perhaps, to the 'Italian Diva' films which flourished between 1910 and 1920, in which the movement of the film was the drawn-out enactment of the diva's postures, poses and attitudes), was a result of the slowness of thought of the Italian brain:

> That which mysteriously interests and deceives the Italian spectator, we, the French, catch onto in a matter of seconds. For this and many other reasons there will never be an international cinema for the elite.[36]

Films shown quickly, Epstein argued, lead us to think quickly: perhaps a form of education:

This speed of thought which the cinema records and measures, and which in part explains the aesthetic of suggestion and succession, can also be found in literature. In the *Illuminations* of Rimbaud, or in the *Dix-Neuf Poèmes Élastiques* of Blaise Cendrars, there is one image a second, whereas in Marinetti we are given barely one image in five seconds.[37]

Epstein further delineated 'an aesthetic of sensuality' (not sentimentality) and 'an aesthetic of metaphors'.[38] Here he drew a connection between screen images and poetic metaphor. 'Within five years, he wrote, people will be writing cinematographic poems: 150 metres on film with a string of 100 images that minds will follow.'[39] Finally, he outlined 'a momentary aesthetic'. Forget Racine, Epstein argues, for at least 300 years, after which 'a new audience will rediscover him':

> The written word always ages, but more or less rapidly . . . This is not intended as a criticism . . . One style doesn't suffice for a whole generation. In the last twenty years the path of beauty has reached a new turning point . . . Like contemporary literature, film hastens volatile metamorphoses. From autumn to spring, aesthetics change. One speaks of eternal canons of beauty whereas two successive catalogues from Bon Marché give the lie to this nonsense. Nothing appeals to our sensuality with as keen a sense of the times and as fine an ability to adapt as fashion. From here, film adopts some of the same magnetic charms, and it is such a faithful image of our childlike infatuations that, five years later, it is only suitable for the fairground lantern'.[40]

Epstein's image of film's transience was also articulated in 1924, in rather more melancholy terms, by the film director René Clair, who wrote that

> Cinema lives under the sign of relativity. Its makers, its actors, the films themselves and the ideas that inspired them, pass quickly. It looks almost as though the cinematograph, that apparatus designed to capture the transient moments of life, has thrown out a challenge to time, and that time is taking a terrible revenge by speeding up its effects on everything pertaining to the cinema.[41]

For Siegfried Kracauer and Walter Benjamin, photography and film were also bound to time and to the transience of fashion:

> The photograph becomes a ghost because the costumed mannequin was once alive . . . This terrible association which persists in the photograph evokes a shudder [also] evoked in drastic fashion by the pre-World War One films screened in the avant-garde 'Studio des Ursulines' in Paris – film images that show how the features stored in the memory image are embedded in a reality which has long since disappeared.[42]

For Kracauer, the shudder induced by the photograph and the film is that of lost time, the divorce between present reality and the temporalities of the memory images we carry with us. Epstein, by contrast, celebrated cinema, contemporary writing and fashion/advertising as a drama or adventure of transience and change, an 'unstable metamorphosis' which stages a constant becoming and which was part of, in Jacques Rancière's words, 'the great ode to energy that his epoch sung and illustrated in myriad ways'.[43]

Notes

1 J. Wicke, 'Joyce and consumer culture', in *The Cambridge Companion to James Joyce*, edited by Derek Attridge (Cambridge University Press, 2004), pp. 234–253, here p. 247. Cambridge Collections Online. Cambridge University Press. Accessed 15 May 2012. http://cco.cambridge.org/extract?id=ccol0521837103_ CCOL0521837103_root.

2 V. Lindsay, *The Art of the Moving Picture* (New York: The Modern Library, 2000), p. 118.

3 Ibid., p. 119.

4 Letter to George Brett, cited in *Letters of Vachel Lindsay*, edited by Marc Chénetier (New York: Burt Franklin, 1979), p. 121.

5 *The Art of the Moving Picture*, p. 117.

6 *The Art of the Moving Picture*, p. 13

7 *The Art of the Moving Picture*, p. 14

8 *The Progress and Poetry of the Movies. A Second Book of Film Criticism by Vachel Lindsay*, edited by Myron Lounsbury (Lanham: The Scarecrow Press, 1995), pp. 187–188.

9 Ibid., 271.

10 P. Virilio, *The Aesthetics of Appearance*, translated by Philip Beitchman (New York: Semiotext(e), 1991), p. 104.

11 *The Progress and Poetry of the Movies*, p. 317.

12 *The Progress and Poetry of the Movies*, p. 326.

13 Hugo Münsterberg, *Hugo Münsterberg on Film*, edited by Allan Langdale (London: Routledge, 2002), p. 160.

13 Ibid., p. 31.

14 Münsterberg, *Hugo Münsterberg on Film*, p. 160.

15 Ibid., p. 172.

16 Ibid., p. 78.

17 Ibid., p. 87–88.

18 Théodule Ribot, *The Psychology of Attention* (Chicago: Open Court, 1890), p. 8.

19 J. Crary, *Suspensions of Perception* (Cambridge, MA: MIT Press, 1999), p. 17.

20 Ibid., p. 30.

21 Ibid., pp. 13–14.

22 W. D. Scott, *The Psychology of Advertising* (London: Pitman, 1913), chapter 2.

23 E. Dench, *Advertising by Motion Pictures* (Cincinatti: Standard Publishing Company, 1916), p. 8.

24 Ibid., p. 11.

25 Ibid., pp. 12–13.

26 Ibid., pp. 86–87.

27 Münsterberg, *Hugo Münsterberg on Film*, p. 86.

28 Hugo Münsterberg, *Psychology and Industrial Efficiency* (London: Constable, 1913), p. 66.

29 Münsterberg, *Hugo Münsterberg on Film*, p. 160.

30 Ibid., pp. 272–273.

31 Münsterberg, *Hugo Münsterberg on Film*, p. 99.

32 J. Epstein, *La Poésie d'aujourd'hui* (Paris: Éditions de la Sirène, 1921), p. 179. See Epstein, 'Cinema and Modern Literature', translated by Audrey Brunetaux and Sarah Keller, in *Jean Epstein: Critical Essays and New Translations*, edited by Sarah Keller and Jason N. Paul (Amsterdam: Amsterdam University Press, 2012), pp. 271–276, here p. 276.

33 Ibid., p. 170; trans. p. 272.

34 Ibid., p. 171; trans. p. 272.

35 Ibid., p. 173; trans. p. 273.

36 Ibid.; trans. p. 273–274.

37 Ibid., p. 173–175.

38 Ibid.; trans. 274.

39 Ibid., pp. 175–177; trans. pp. 275–276.

40 Ibid., pp. 178–180; trans. pp. 275–276.

41 René Clair, *Reflections on the Cinema*, translated by Vera Traill (London: William Kimber, 1953), p. 59.

42 Siegried Kracauer, 'Photography', *The Mass Ornament: Weimar Essays*, edited by Thomas Y. Levin (Cambridge, MA: Harvard University Press, 1995), p. 56.

43 Jacques Rancière, 'Prologue: A Thwarted Fable', in *Film Fables*, translated by Emiliano Battista (Oxford : Berg, 2006), pp. 1–12, here pp. 3–4.

CHAPTER 5

'A Hymn to Movement'
The 'City Symphony' of the 1920s and 1930s

The 'city symphonies' of my title refer primarily to a cluster of films made in the US and Europe in the 1920s and into the 1930s. The best known, and most frequently imitated, is Walter Ruttmann's *Berlin: Symphony of a Great City* of 1926. Other 'city symphonies' of this period include Alberto Cavalcanti's *Rien que les heures* (1926), Dziga-Vertov's *Man with a Movie Camera* (1929), Joris Ivens' *Regen* ['Rain'] (1929) and Jean Vigo's *A Propos de Nice* (1930). The earliest of the city symphonies was Charles Sheeler and Paul Strand's *Manhatta* of 1921, which appears to have had a significant influence on the European city symphonies and city films of the later 1920s, as well as on less well-known US avant-garde films, including Jay Leyda's *A Bronx Morning* and Herman Weinberg's *City Symphony* and *Autumn Fire*. City and cinema have, of course, been inextricably linked from the very first films onwards. The avant-garde city films of the 1920s show the influence of early urban panoramic films and city actualities, and they are part of the complex history whereby film-makers in the 1920s sought to renew the medium – and to turn away from commercial and narrative cinema – by returning to cinema's origins in the documenting of reality, but with the particular twist given by the perspectives and angles of modernism.

The 'city symphonies' of Sheeler and Strand, Ruttmann, Cavalcanti, and Dziga-Vertov follow the course of a day in the life of the city. Like the one-day novels of the period, they open up the question of 'modernist dailiness': the preoccupation with everyday life is combined with the intimation that much greater spans of time and culture are condensed within the diurnal round. Space and time relations – and duration and the passing of time – are some of the central preoccupations of the films, frequently underlain by the perception that 'plot' and 'story' must be excluded in order for time and space to become apparent. *Rien que les Heures*, for example, opens with a seeming rejection of narrative: the introductory title reads: 'This film contains no story. It is just a sequence of impressions on the passage of time.' These silent films (some of them in fact made in the early years of the sound era, so that their silence exists in the face of the possibility of sound) often include images of dance and music, including orchestration. Their symphonic dimensions are also structural – they are often divided into movements which correspond to parts of the day – and rhythmic.

Rhythm was indeed placed at the heart of writing about film in the 1920s, in which it was frequently conceptualized in relation to filmic 'city symphonies', and in opposition to the relentless linear drive of plot and narrative. As Graham Greene wrote:

> There must be rhythm in films – rhythms of time and of space . . . The wave of rhythm must be planned, as it was planned in *Berlin*, to afford variety without breaking the continuity. Variety has hitherto been sought in a multitude of plots. How small is the variety in treatment is only realized when the camera for a moment turns from the restless race of actions to poetry, perhaps, an emptyroom, sun-drenched, barred with cool shadows. There is the tip of the rhythmic wave, perhaps of photographic art, and it should break, not once when it is too late to revive the battered eyesight, but at regular intervals – like the recurrence of the great ninth wave, which leaves its spray the farthest up the shore.[1]

The distinction between the linear and the cyclical, only suggested in Greene's analysis, would be fully developed by Henri Lefebvre in his work on 'rhythmanalysis', in which he pointed to the differences and relationships between 'cyclical repetition and the linear repetitive', natural time and social time, which he also renders as the distinction between 'rhythmed times and the times of brutal repetitions'.[2] The representation of repetitive labour in the filmic city symphonies rarely functions (or rarely functions unambiguously) as critique: there is more frequently an absorption in, and an identification with, the energies of the city as machine. Nonetheless, almost all the city films suggest that the beginning of the day (Lefebvre's 'the return of a cycle') serves as a necessary renewal or 'recommencement'. In their habitual openings with the dawn, with a time that is not yet the time of routine, city symphonies will, moreover, represent a world which is not yet seen by the city's human inhabitants: its emptiness becomes that of a first dawn. Such depictions are also a revelation of cinema's powers to present the world in our absence from it.

The emergence and the passing of daily time in the city symphonies is marked, time and again, by the depiction of the hours marked on clock faces. For Lefebvre, the clock conjoins 'cyclical repetition and the linear repetitive': 'The circular course of the hands on (traditional) clock faces and watches is accompanied by a linear tick-tock. And it is their relation that enables or rather constitutes the measure of time (which is to say, of rhythms).'[3]

In Virginia Woolf's writings on the city we find an anticipation of Lefebvre's 'rhythmanalytical' discussions, though the distinction she would draw in *Orlando* (and, less explicitly, throughout her writing) between 'time on the clock' and 'time in the mind' is closer to the thought of Bergson, for whom cyclical or deep time and linear time existed in separate streams.[4] For Woolf's representation of 'rhythm' and its centrality we should turn to one of her first essays, 'Street Music', published in the *National Review* in 1905. In this early piece, she discussed the question of the public nuisance which street musicians (instanced here by German bands and Italian organ-grinders, placed in opposition to 'the British public') were held to present to the 'candid dwellers in most London squares', and the scorn with which 'the artist of the streets' treated such judgements: 'the vagrant musician is if anything on the increase'.[5] While the street musician's accomplishment might be in question, Woolf suggested, the effort of human beings 'to express the music that is in them is not': 'it is not unreasonable to suppose that the men and women who scrape for the harmonies that never come while the traffic goes thundering by have as great a possession, though fated never to impart it, as the masters whose facile eloquence enchants thousands to listen'.[6]

The essay is in part a meditation on the place and public perception of the (male) artist in contemporary British society. Art is mistrusted, Woolf argued, because it is held 'to be unmanly to give expression to the thoughts and emotions which the arts express and which it should be the endeavour of the good citizen to repress'.[7] Society does its best to contain its artist figures by domesticating them. The successful artist is such a domesticated figure and is treated with the highest respect. On the other side is the artist as pagan, and the musician is the least tamed, and hence most dangerous, of all: 'music incites within us something that is wild and inhuman like itself'.[8]

This something, Woolf suggests, is 'rhythm', and the conventions of taught music are attempts to repress it: 'The whole of rhythm and harmony have been pressed, like dried flowers, into the neatly divided scales, the tones and semitones of the pianoforte'.[9] The sense of rhythm, she argues, precedes a sensitivity to 'music proper', and she invokes 'savages who have none of the arts of civilisation':

> The beat of rhythm is akin to the beat of the pulse in the body; and thus though many are deaf to tune hardly any one is so coarsely organised as not to hear the rhythm of its own heart in words and music and movement. [. . .]

> The strange sight of a room full of civilised people moving in rhythmic motion at the command of a band of musicians is one to which we have grown accustomed, but it may be that one day it will suggest the vast possibilities that lie within the power of rhythm, and the whole of our life will be revolutionised as it was when man first realised the power of steam. The barrel-organ, for instance, by reason of its crude and emphatic rhythm, sets all the legs of the passers by walking in time; a band in the centre of the wild discord of cabs and carriages would be more effectual than any policeman; not only cabman but horse would find himself constrained to keep time in the dance, and to follow whatever measure of trot or canter the trumpets dictated . . . And when the sense of rhythm was thoroughly alive in every mind we should if I mistake not, notice a great improvement not only in the ordering of all the affairs of daily life, but also in the art of writing, which is nearly allied to the art of music, and is chiefly degenerate because it has forgotten its allegiance. We should invent – or rather remember – the innumerable metres which have so long outraged, and which would restore both prose and poetry to the harmonies that the ancients heard and observed.[10]

The passage, and the essay as a whole, chimes with many of those perceptions of art that we now define as 'modernist': the 'primitivism' of the appeal to the savage within; the suggestion that all art aspires to the condition of music; the breaking down of the distinction between the dancer and the dance. We can also make a more specific link between this early essay and Woolf's 1926 essay 'The Cinema'. This later essay begins and ends with the image of the primitive – 'the savages of the twentieth century watching the pictures', who are separated by no great distance 'from those bright-eyed naked men who knocked two bars of iron together and heard in that clangour a foretaste of the music of Mozart'.[11] The image is one familiar from accounts of the birth of poetry: T.S. Eliot's 'Poetry begins, I dare say, with a savage beating a drum in the jungle' is just one example among many.[12] The cinema, Woolf concludes, has, however, been born the wrong end first:

> The mechanical skill is far in advance of the art to be expressed. It is as if the savage tribe instead of finding two bars of iron to play with had found scattering the sea shore fiddles, flutes, saxophones, grand pianos by Erard and Bechstein, and had begun with incredible energy but without knowing a note of music to hammer and thump upon them all at the same time.[13]

Woolf's imagery here was in fact a familiar one in the film criticism and film aesthetics of the 1920s. It lay at the heart of the view that film's mechanical skill had militated against its artistic growth. The machine aesthetic, and the celebration of the machine, was of course central to avant-garde and experimental cinema and to film criticism and theory in the first decades of the century. Yet claims made for film as an art form were often dependent on the suppression of cinema's mechanical and techno-logical dimensions and on attempts (discursive and conceptual) to construct for the medium an 'organic' birth and identity, frequently resting on its perceived ability to renew the representation of life itself. The focus on 'rhythm' in much early writing about cinema was an aspect of a vitalism, strongly influenced by Bergsonian philosophy, which served to militate further against the concept of film as mere mechanism.

In 'The Cinema' Woolf suggests that 'the art of the cinema is about to be brought to birth':

> Watching crowds, watching the chaos of the streets in the lazy way in which faculties detached from use watch and wait, it seems sometimes as if movements and colours, shapes and sounds had come together and waited for someone to seize them and convert their energy into art; then, uncaught, they disperse and fly asunder again. At the cinema for a moment through the mists of irrelevant emotions, through the thick counterpane of immense dexterity and enormous efficiency one has glimpses of something vital within.[14]

I have elsewhere related the accidental shadow on the screen (which Woolf placed at the heart of her meditations on film's future and potential as an art) to this 'something vital within'.[15] It is a tadpole-shaped form which appears on the screen as she watches *The Cabinet of Dr Caligari*, and it could be seen as protozoic – or protoplasmic (Sergei Eisenstein's word for ani-mated drawing) – and thus as a life-form which might engender and birth a 'new' cinema. This might either be conceived as cinema liberated from its mechanical origins or, perhaps more interestingly, as a confounding of the distinction between the organic and the mechanical.

What, though, of the image of the city and its streets and crowds which Woolf also seems to be making central to her imaginings of a future cinema? 'We get intimations only in the chaos of the streets, perhaps, when some momentary assembly of colour, sound, movement, suggests that here is a scene waiting a new art to be transfixed'.[16] It was to *Orlando* that Raymond Williams turned when, in *The Country and the City*, he offered a brief but suggestive account of the relationships between mod-ernism, urban experience, and cinema. Writing of the passage in which Orlando, now living in the present day, motors out of London and has her identity 'entirely disassembled' – 'it is an open question in what sense Orlando can be said to have existed at the present moment' – Williams commented:

This fragmentary experience – now accelerated by 'motoring fast' – has remained a perceptual condition. It is deeply related to several characteristic forms of modern imagery, most evident in painting and especially in film which as a medium contains much of its intrinsic movement. There is indeed a direct relation between the motion picture, especially in its development in cutting and montage, and the characteristic movement of an observer in the close and miscellaneous environment of the streets . . . This experience of urban movement has been used . . . to express a gamut of feelings from despair to delight.[17]

Glossing this passage in his introduction to Williams' posthumously published collection of essays *The Politics of Modernism*, Tony Pinkney commented on the ways in which

it is the essence of film to have no essence, to be uniquely responsive as a medium to the disorientating ephemerality of the modern city . . . if film is the definitive Modernist mode, then Modernism can now be located . . . in the *intermediate zone* of urban experience . . . in a 'structure of feeling' that has not yet assumed the relatively formalized shape of aesthetic doctrine or political act.[18]

The concept of Modernism's location in the 'intermediate zone' of urban experience chimes with Woolf's complex sense that a future cinema might move to seize the sense-impressions of the city at the moment of their fleeting unity, but in such a way as to capture their energies without thereby petrifying them: 'to catch them', as Woolf wrote in another context, 'before they become "works of art"'.[19]

Woolf's invocation of the urban scene in 'The Cinema' returns the essay to the imagery of 'Street Music', written some twenty years earlier, and to 'rhythm' as the 'something vital within'. In the earlier essay, street music (including that of the street or barrel organ, whose music-making is mechanically driven) seems to possess the power to orchestrate the 'wild discord' of crowds and traffic: now this becomes the potential of the cinema, once it discovers or recovers its vitalism, 'the kick of life'. Music, film and urban modernity come together, then, in this imagining of a 'city symphony', governed by the power of rhythm which is akin, as Woolf suggests in 'Street Music', to the human heartbeat.

We are reminded of *Mrs Dalloway* at this point: 'In people's eyes, in the swing, tramp and trudge; in the bellow and the uproar; the carriages, motor cars, omnibuses, vans, sandwich men shuffling and swinging; brass bands; barrel organs; in the triumph and the jingle and the strange high singing of some aeroplane overhead was what she lived; life; London; this moment of June'.[20] In the novel, there is a 'pulse' or heartbeat of the city as well as of its inhabitants – 'The throb of the motor-car sounded like a pulse irregularly drumming through an entire body.'[21] The heart, the heartbeat – associated throughout the novel with Clarissa Dalloway, whose heart is weak – is a pulse which throughout is the novel contrasted with the chime of Big Ben as it sounds the hours. Many critics have identified *Mrs Dalloway* and Joyce's *Ulysses* as the exemplars of the literary city symphony of the 1920s: one-day novels of the city, taking us from the beginning of the day to its end.[22] As Ann Banfield has noted, 'the great modern novels of multiple viewpoints and moments set them ticking in the geography of the modern city . . . The crowded urban spaces become the obvious correlative of the multiplications of points of space-time in constant motion; the slowness of time Proust claims that the novel speeds up is there accelerated and made visible'.[23] For Paul Ricoeur, writing on *Mrs Dalloway* in *Time and Narrative*, what is significant is the relation that characters establish with the markers or measurers of time.[24] 'In the streets', Banfield writes, 'the private worlds are in motion relative to one another. It is a postrelativity world: each has its own clock, keeping its own time'.[25] Experienced time is also slowed down by the magnification of its smallest units: the day, the moment. 'Arrested moments punctuate the novels of the city', though this is not an escape from time: 'modernist time passes through arrested moments'.[26]

Time, and the marking of time, was at the heart of Woolf's conception of *Mrs Dalloway*. The first draft, 'The Hours', used the structure of the hours to measure out the day in very precise terms. In early notes she wrote: 'Hours: 10.11.12.1.2.3.4.5.6.7.8.9.10.11.12.1.2. Eleven o'clock strikes. This is the aeroplane hour, wh. Covers both Septimus and Rezia in Regent's Park & Clarissas reflections which lead to 12 o'clock: interview with special-ist.'[27] The revised novel played down the hours and loosened the tight chronological structure, though 11 a.m. remains a central temporal juncture in this text, and one in which time seems to stand still (a reference, almost certainly, in this post-WW1 text, to the commemoration of Armistice Day from 1919 onwards: at 11 o'clock on the 11th day of the 11th month, there was a two-minute silence and a cessation of activity).

While we associate literature structured around diurnal time and the city with modernist aesthetics, it has a significant, though largely forgotten, precedent in a work by the Victorian journalist George Augustus Sala, *Twice Round the Clock: Or the Hours of the Day and Night in London*. This was first published in serial form in 1858 – each weekly instalment being devoted to one of the hours – and as a book in 1859. Sala begins the day – a day in June – at 4 a.m. in Billingsgate fish market – 'Simply because four a.m. is in reality the first hour of the working London day. The giant is wide awake at midnight; he sinks into a fitful slumber about two in the morning: short is his rest, for at four he is up again and at work, the busiest bee in the world's hive' – and closes it the following morning with the hour of 3 a.m., a masked ball and the police station.[28] Through the course of the twenty-four hours Sala leads the reader to markets, London institutions (*The Times* newspaper offices, banks, the law-courts, Parliament), to public spaces (clubs, shops, theatres, railway stations, parks) and into domestic homes and streets, where the organ-grinders and ragged musicians gather to produce their cacophonous 'street music'.

In the opening sections, or 'hours', Sala describes a form of 'city symphony', beginning his first hour (4 a.m.) with the different pitches of London's church bells, sounding out the hour, moving at 5 a.m. to the publication of *The Times* newspaper: 'It is a pulsation of London's mighty heart, that should not be neglected',[29] and has a louder 'bell' than all the others: 'For though the sides of the bell are only paper, the clapper is the great public tongue; the booming sound that fills the city every morning, and, to use the words of Mr Walter Whitman, "utters its barbaric youp over the house-tops of creation," is the great Public Voice.'[30]

This is the city of commerce, the money economy (in Simmel's phrase), display, public opinion, locomotion and 'great piles of printed paper', organized by and within diurnal time. The forward momentum of Sala's text is that of the movement of the hours and the accumulated energies of the day. Yet it is striking that, in his 8 a.m. chapter ('St James's Park and The Mall'), Sala is drawn to the pull of past time, conjuring up 'ghosts' and 'footstep memories'. Two cities, London and Paris, are, he claims, 'so haunted by impalpable ghosts of the traces of famous deeds, that locomotion, to one of my temperament, becomes a task very slow, if not painfully difficult, of accomplishment'.[31] 'Locomotion' here refers not only to the act of walking, but also to narrative digression and progression.

As his 'hours' proceed, Sala as narrator and guide takes on the identity of, in his term, 'a chronological Asmodeus'.[32] Asmodeus, a demon figure in early Biblical and mythological representations, and frequently defined as the demon of 'lust', became in later representations a more benign and satirical figure, amongst whose powers was the ability to lift the roofs off houses in order to reveal the private lives therein. Sala defines the complexities of his own role in this way:

> How can I hope, I reiterate, to give you anything like a complete picture of the doings in London while still the clock goes round? I might take one house and unroof it, one street and unpave it, one man and disclose to you the secrets of twenty-four hours of his daily and nightly life; but it is London,

in its entirety, that I have presumed to 'time' – forgetting, oh! egregious and insistent! – that every minute over which the clock hand passes is as the shake of a wrist applied to a kaleidoscope, and that the whole aspect of the city changes with as magical rapidity.[33]

For the 'chronological Asmodeus', the passing of time turns the urban 'panorama' into a 'kaleidoscope': time alters the face of the city from moment to moment, and it is this temporal shifting as well as the spatial city that Sala must attempt to depict in words. Sala had, in his Preface (an address to Augustus Mayhew), rejected the idea of writing from a single vantage point:

> I brooded fitfully over the scheme [of his hours] for many months. At first I proposed to take my stand (in imagination) at King Charles's Statue, Charing Cross, and describe the Life revolving round me during the twenty-four hours; but I should have trenched upon sameness by confinement to singularity; and I chose at last all London as the theme of description.[34]

The Asmodeus figure would be taken up in early accounts of the cinema, most strikingly in Hugo von Hoffmansthal's 1922 essay 'Ersatz für die Träume', translated into English as 'A Substitute for Dreams' in 1924.[35] Hoffmansthal suggests that in the dreams of those whose restricted lives otherwise provided little in the way of imaginative resources: 'Everything was charged with meaning [in dreams]; the dark room behind the cellar stairs, an old barrel in the courtyard half-full of rain water, the lumber chest, the door to the store-room, the garrett-door, or that to the neighbour's house through which someone came'. Now:

> The old-lumber chest, with its magical contents, is once again thrown open – through the motion-picture. The motion-picture reveals all that was before mysteriously hidden: it shows what was behind the impenetrable cold façade of people's houses; doors fly open, and we see the homes of the rich, the young girl's room, the lobbies of hotels; we peer into the robber's den and into the secret workroom of the alchemist. The motion-picture is like the aerial journey with Asmodeus, who took off the roofs of houses and revealed men's secrets. But there is something more than the mere satisfaction of oft-disappointed curiosity: a secret instinct is appeased, an instinct familiar to the dreamer of dreams. Dreams are facts, and with the endless spectacle of the motion-picture there is mingled a pleasant sort of self-deception; the fleeting shadows are like the ebb and flow of life, they are indeed the ebbs and flows of innumerable existences.

The filmic city symphonies of the 1920s and 1930s largely eschew individual narratives in order to render the city as protagonist, but they also hint at 'the ebbs and flows of innumerable existences' or, in Sala's words, at 'the thousand little dramas' that take place at each moment, or hour, of the day.

The incidence of literary and filmic 'city symphonies' has been an important factor in making the connections between literature and cinema in the modernist period. *Mrs Dalloway* and *Ulysses*, when set alongside the seminal film in this context, Walter Ruttmann's *Berlin: Symphony of a City* of 1926, seem to produce representations which cut across the divide between the two media: the movement of litter, of yesterday's daily newspaper, along the empty streets; the intimation (as in Vertov's *Man with a Movie Camera*) that the city in the early morning might function as an image of the unconscious, and that the relationship between sleep and waking might correlate to the interplay between stasis and motion in the film medium; the charting of the city's awakening into life – blinds and doors opening; the movement of travel and transport around the city; the use of the reflective surfaces of the modern city (glass culture, display windows, the cinema itself) to mirror and to double the perceiving subject; the rhythmic orchestration of motion into pattern. For Alfred Döblin, author of *Berlin Alexanderplatz*, Joyce's *Ulysses* had shown the extent to which cinema had

> penetrated the sphere of literature; newspapers must become the most important, most broadly disseminated form of written testimony, everybody's daily bread. To the experiential image of a person today also belongs the streets, the scenes changing by the second, the signboards, automobile traffic . . . A part of today's image is the disconnectedness of his activity, of his existence as such, the fleeting quality, the restlessness.[36]

In this account, modernist literature now contained – had been penetrated by – cinematic vision, which Döblin defines – without using the term – through a model of 'montage'. Modernist writers indeed recognized an affinity between their projects and that of Ruttmann's film. When the question of filming *Ulysses* arose, the two possible directors named by Joyce were Ruttmann and Eisenstein. Ezra Pound, writing in the fourth and final issue of his short-lived journal *The Exile* in 1928, observed that:

> Perhaps art is healthiest when anonymous, at any rate I can not remember the names of the artists, but in the Grossstadt Symphony we have at last a film that will take serious aesthetic criticism: one that is in the movement, and that should flatten out the opposition (to Joyce, to me, to Rodker's Adolphe) with steam-rolling ease and commodity, not of course that the authors intended it.[37]

As Pound praises *Berlin* he criticizes 'that mixed bag "La Roue"', Abel Gance's film which is both a celebration of the machine – the train – and a narrative drama: 'In La Roue the money-grabbers ruined a noble effort, inserting a punk sentimental plot and I hope they lost heavily on it'. *Caligari* is, for Pound, beneath contempt: 'one of the most craven hypocrisies of our time'. Against that 'mixed bag' *La Roue*, Pound sets the 'machine film, the "abstract" or Gestalt film', and he did in fact have some involvement in the making of the Fernand Léger/Dudley Murphy film *Ballet mécanique*.

The 'city symphony', then, becomes allied to the machine and abstract film (represented most strongly in Dadaist cinema). Underlying Pound's judgements is the distinction between 'abstract' and 'empathetic' art theorized by the art historian Wilhelm Worringer, mediated to the artists and writers associated with the Imagist and Vorticist movements in the 1910s by T.E. Hulme. For Hulme, 'abstraction' (which Worringer identified with the art of Africa, Egypt and China) was exemplified in the geometric art of his avant-garde contemporaries, and contrasted with an 'empathetic' humanist art, associated with the Renaissance, which Hulme believed had been superseded. Ruttmann's films prior to *Berlin* had indeed included a number of abstract films, and the making of the city film points to the ways in which experimental and avant-garde cinema became allied with, or transmuted into, documentary cinema in the 1920s and 1930s.

Pound perceived the 'city symphony' to be 'in the movement' – the modernist literary movement he represents by the names of Joyce, John Rodker and himself. It was 'punk sentimental plot' that he repudiated in *La Roue*, and that he would have identified with the particular models of the literary on which he was also turning his back. But we might think more broadly of the alliances and contestations between film and literature in this period, and of the ways in which they coalesce and part company in the 'city symphony'. Dziga-Vertov's city film *Man with a Movie Camera* proudly announces itself as a film without intertitles – that is, as a film free of 'literary' influence, though Dziga-Vertov would elsewhere acknowledge the profound impact of Mayakovsky's poetry on his film-making. Freedom from the literary would almost certainly mean freedom from 'plot' (as Pound defines it) and from 'character': Pound was drawn to the anonymity of Ruttmann's *Berlin*, in which human figures are significant to the extent to which they participate in the events that mark the day and the passing of daily time in the city. The city is indeed, as has often been remarked, the film's protagonist.

The values Pound expressed were also made explicit in a discussion by Elliot Paul and Robert Sage in the 'little magazine' *transition* – 'Artistic Improvements of the Cinema' – in which they wrote of Alberto Cavalcanti's 'city symphony' *Rien que les Heures*:

In his *Rien que les Heures*, Cavalcanti made a commendable effort to get away from the ancient hero-and-heroine tangle by composing a series of views of a city at successive hours of the day from dawn until late at night. The 'plot' was merely the cycle of the day, the characters were the persons or scenes most representative of each hour, the 'style' was the artistic personal touch which unmistakably accompanies the arrangement and photography of each picture by this producer. If the structure faltered, it was through the momentary introduction of an orthodox plot towards the middle.

Although not complete satisfactory, *Rien que les Heures* was a preliminary demonstration that the cinema is capable of being under no obligations to literature, drama or painting, a fact more perfectly proved by Cavalcanti's two succeeding films. [*La P'tite Lilie* and *En Rade*].

The degree to which a picture is true or false cinema is in approximate proportion to the number of subtitles which have to be used.[38]

The perceived symbiosis between city and cinema would, from this perspective, appear to exclude literature – and, more broadly, the established arts. The 'city symphony' would seem to correspond to an ideal of art which has not been reified into 'the work of art' – it retains the freedom of, in Bergsonian terms, 'becoming'. Louis Delluc, in an article on 'Beauty in the Cinema' published in 1917, wrote of cinema's power 'to provide us with impressions of evanescent eternal beauty, since it alone offers us the spectacle of nature and sometimes even the spectacle of real human activity'.[39] It is in this sense that the 'documentary' dimensions of the city films (and the term 'documentary' is said to have been first used by the Scottish documentary film-maker and producer John Grierson, writing in 1926 of Robert Flaherty's *Moana*) could coalesce with cinematic avant-gardism.

For Joris Ivens, writing in 1921, 'the documentary film is the only means that remains for the avant-garde filmmaker to stand up to the film industry'.[40] Grierson emphasized the connections between the 'city symphony' and the 'field of realism', identifying Cavalcanti's *Rien que les Heures* as the first of the city symphonies, and noting the ways in which Ruttmann

carried on the idea in a still more whirling round of day and night in *Berlin*. No film has been more influential, more imitated. Symphonies of cities have been sprouting ever since, each with its crescendo of dawn and coming-awake and workers' processions, its morning traffic and machinery, its lunch-time contrasts of rich and poor, its afternoon lull, its evening denouement in sky-sign and night club.[41]

Grierson became increasingly critical of what he perceived as the formalism and the absence of social and political content in the 'city symphonies' (a view later echoed in Kracauer's account of *Berlin* in *From Caligari to*

Hitler), but he nonetheless maintained that *Berlin* 'had at least the effect of turning the tide of abstraction in the German cinema and bringing it back to earth. It initiated the tradition of realism which produced such admirable films as *Mutter Krausen* and *Kameradschaft*, and it set a mark for amateurs the world over.'[42] We should also note that the 'city symphony' played a crucial role as an orchestration of, and advertisement for, the burgeoning independent film cultures and film networks in cities across Europe – an imbrication of metropolitan life, modernist cultures and cinematicity.

In order to explore these issues further, I turn now to a more detailed discussion of two city films from the 1920s – one from the beginning of the decade and one from its end. The films, and their critical reception, open up something of the significance of the city symphony in the construction of the relationship between the arts that the new medium of film had brought into sharp new focus.

Charles Sheeler and Paul Strand's *Manhatta*, made in 1920–1921 and premiered on 24 July 1921 at the Rialto Theater in New York City (under the title *New York the Magnificent*) is held to be the first significant American avant-garde film. Strand and Sheeler were at this time amateur film-makers, being photographers first and foremost. *Manhatta* was to be Sheeler's only film, whereas Strand became increasingly involved in cinematography, though he is undoubtedly best known for his photographic work. The film was shot from rooftops and streets in Lower Manhattan and shows the influence of Alfred Stieglitz's New York photographs of the 1910s, in addition to remaking images from some of Strand's own early photographs, such as his 'Wall Street' (1915). The interplay between photography and cinematography is clear; more ambiguous is the intention underlying the use of lines from Walt Whitman's poems in the film. Most of the intertitles were taken from Whitman's poetry, though not all from his 'Mannahatta' (1860), as the film's title would suggest. They are drawn from 'A Broadway Pageant' (1860), 'From Noon to Starry Night: Mannahatta', and 'Crossing Brooklyn Ferry' (1856).

The seven-minute film follows the course of a day, from morning to evening, in line with the 'day in the life of a city' theme that characterizes filmic and literary city symphonies in the 1920s. Its four movements – which could be thought of as 'symphonic' – show, as Jan-Christopher Horak notes, a doubling of images, 'positioning the subject first on one side and then on the opposite side, inscribing the landscapes as the viewer/camera, both subject and object'.[43] In Horak's reading of the film, the final imagery of natural elements – river, clouds and sun – rather than of cityscape position the viewing subject in a transcendental reality which is inscribed in the previous intertitle, taken from 'Crossing Brooklyn Ferry': 'Gorgeous clouds of sunset! Drench with your splendour me or the men and women generations after me.' The use of Whitman's poetry is held by Horak to confirm the transcendental view of the city as a natural phenomenon, which ultimately resolves the tensions in the film between its romanticism and its modernism, the latter inhering in the use of multiple, reflexive points of view, fragmentation, and extreme camera angles. In a different reading of *Manhatta*, which perceives it as more modernist than romantic or transcendentalist, Juan Suarez describes the film as a 'complex cultural artifact', 'at once a documentary, a critical statement about modernity, an aestheticist exploration of patterns, shapes, movements and rhythms, and a visual counterpart of the descriptions of metropolitan modernity produced by contemporary sociologists, architects and planners'.[44] Similarly, and contra the terms of Grierson's argument, it could be argued that the significance of *Berlin* and of the city symphonies which followed it is not that they demonstrate a movement from abstraction to realism, but that they bring these different modes into new conjunctions.

The role of Whitman's poetry in *Manhatta* is complex and overdetermined. The lines function as intertitles of a kind with which audiences would have been familiar from narrative cinema, raising the question of whether they are intended to provide a form of narrative structure to the film. There is also a sense in which the imagery serves to provide a visual counterpart to, or even an 'illustration' of, the verbal imagery: the verbal thus seems to take on a primacy here, apparently at odds with the anti-literary bent of the avant-garde, but also opening up the complexities of word-image relations in this period, and the very etymology of photography as 'words of light'. We might think in this context of one of Strand's best-known early photographs, of a blind woman begging, in which the verbal sign, 'Blind', plays such a powerful role in this most paradoxical of portraits, with its representation of the seer and the (apparently) unseeing.

It may well be that, as Horak suggests, the choice of Whitman's verse was part of the film's attempt to create a specifically American perspective and aesthetic, and to project a homogeneous, non-conflictual model of the city as melting-pot. There is more to say, however, about the significance of Whitman in relation to film and film aesthetics in its first decades. His poetics lay at the heart of D.W. Griffith's *Intolerance*: the shot of 'The Woman Who Rocks the Cradle', drawn from the first line of Whitman's poem 'Sea-Drift' ('Out of the cradle endlessly rocking'), punctuates the film and, repeated as it is numerous times across it, draws the four different strands of the narrative together. For the poet and film theorist Vachel

Lindsay the cradle shot was 'the key hieroglyphic' of the film, a 'picture-word' in the 'universal alphabet' of the cinema.[45] The film hieroglyphic conjoins word and image, creating, as Miriam Hansen has argued, 'a reading space' in Griffith's film which acts as 'a training ground of hiero-glyphical signification and interpretation'.[46] For Lindsay, film would be able to realize what poetry had initiated but not fulfilled: the visualization of Whitmanian 'moods' and principles through the new medium of universal literacy. As he wrote in his 1915 (revised 1922) study *The Art of the Moving Picture*:

> We must have Whitmanesque scenarios, based on moods akin to that of the poem By Blue Ontario's Shore. The possibility of showing the entire American population its own face in the Mirror Screen has at last come. Whitman brought the idea of democracy to our sophisticated literati, but did not persuade the democracy itself to read his democratic poems. Sooner or later the kinetoscope will do what he could not, bring the nobler side of the equality idea to the people who are so crassly equal.[47]

There are also formal correlatives between Whitman's poetry and cinema. Like film, the Whitmanian mode is metonymic and sequential. Whitman, Lawrence Goldstein writes, contained and ordered 'the prolific spectacle of commodified objects and behaviours by means of his catologs and the inspired sequencing of his discrete impressions'.[48] In *Manhatta* the coherence of the film's discrete impressions is brought about by the doubling of images between opening and closure (which also speak of the shape of the day – the journey out and the journey home). A form of coherence is also provided by the use of Whitman's poetry (though it is significant that the film-makers fragment the verse, taking lines from different poems and adding lines which are not identifiably those of Whitman). For Peter Brooker, 'Whitman's subjects are amassed in the cosmic net of his ego, his lists like snapshots of Manhattan assembled in a mighty photograph album with headlining cap-tion and wrap-around voice over'.[49] Brooker also notes, however, the ways in which Whitman's characteristic lists follow 'the upward movement of the camera eye or of an elevator, as he versifies the perceptual shift associated with the breathtaking, celestial reach of the next century's skyscrapers'.[50] The Whitmanian dream of American literature was, in Goldstein's account, that 'space might replace time, the linkages between place and place   railways, canals, telegraph lines, bridges – might usurp the time cycles of events as principal facts of everyday consciousness'.[51]

Pursuing these lines of argument, we might suggest that the film *Manhatta* illustrates not so much the discrete lines of poetry (themselves fragments of larger wholes composed of sequences of fragments), but

Whitman's 'proto-cinematic' vision, in which verbal sequences are them-selves ways of seeing. Instead of excluding 'literature', *Manhatta* presents it in terms of the movement – historical, perceptual – towards the new medium of film.

Manhatta, Juan Suarez writes, 'pulsates with possibility: it anticipates a story without actually producing one'.[52] This statement chimes with my earlier discussion of the 'intermediate zone' of film and urban modernity. As I have noted, Strand and Sheeler's film was not only the earliest of the avant-garde city films, but also a major structural influence on the city symphonies and city films that proliferated throughout the 1920s and into the 1930s. It should be said, though, that few (if any) of these films exclude the human countenance and human and social relations within the city as rigorously as *Manhatta*, and all of them function without intertitles.

The Dutch documentary film director Joris Ivens' *Regen* ['Rain'] of 1929 represents a rain-shower in a city whose identity is not marked by graphic signs, though we might recognize it as Amsterdam. The time-passage of the film (which was in fact made over a number of months) is the duration of the shower; diurnal time is here condensed into a single incident. The equivalent of the dawn and the emergence of the day in many of the other 'city symphonies' becomes, in Ivens' film, the space–time of the city just before it rains: the city knows it is raining (the raindrops meet the waters of the canal) before the human subject in the film, who puts out his hand to confirm what we, and the city, already know. The movement of the film is along the lines of the vertical and the horizontal: the rain comes down and umbrellas go up; we see the city through the window of a tram as it moves along the wet streets. The rain acts as a reflector or mirror, creating a doubled city. The film also intimates that there is a question of quantity or number in the city: we begin with the single drops before the downpour, and this in turn becomes an issue of individual and group or mass among the city's inhabitants.

Béla Balázs, in his *Theory of the Film* (which gathered together material he had written and published in German in the 1920s) described *Rain* as an 'impressionist film' which captures

> visual impressions – not bound into unity by any conception of time and space ... not what rain really is, but what it looks like when a soft spring rain drips off leaves, the surface of a pond gets gooseflesh from the rain, a solitary raindrop hesitatingly gropes its way down a window-pane, or the wet pavement reflects the life of a city. We get a hundred visual impres-sions, but never the things themselves; nor do these interest us in such films. All we want to see are the individual, intimate, surprising optical

effects. Not the things but these their pictures constitute our experience and we do not think of any objects outside the impression. There are in fact no concrete objects behind such pictures, which are images, not reproductions.[53]

Gilles Deleuze developed this argument in his category of 'any-space-whatever': 'it is rain as affect', he wrote, 'pure power or quality'.[54]

Balázs' argument defined Ivens' film against the terms of realism. His concern was to render *Regen* as an 'absolute film' and to suggest, moreover, that the terms of reality and copy had been reversed within it: 'the rain-pictures of Ivens could not be seen by anyone else in any rain; at most he could recognize them after seeing the Ivens picture and after his eyes had been sufficiently trained by them'.[55] The filmic world, in this account, has primacy over the 'real' world: the city film will train the spectator's eyes to see the impressions that cinema alone has brought into being. The account is a contentious one – Ivens was, after all, committed to documentary film as a conjoining of realism and avant-gardism – and it does not, perhaps, take into account the ways in which Ivens used the doubled world brought into being by the effects of rain on the reflective surfaces of the city as an analogue for cinema's own doubling of the world. Nonetheless, it suggests the extent to which the city film – and the city/cine poem – became the nodal point for arguments about filmic ontology and the nature of the real.

The relationships of music and of poetry to the film return us, in closing, both to the question of rhythm in film and to the film/literature dynamic. The director and film theorist Germaine Dulac wrote of Ivens' earlier documentary film *The Bridge* that it was 'a moving symphony, with harmonies, chords, grouped in several rhythms . . . For me Joris Ivens, the man who orchestrated everything, is one of the visual musicians of the future'.[56] This perception of the symphonic as contained within Ivens' (silent) films relates in interesting and complex ways to the attraction of *Regen* for composers. The composer Lou Lichtfeld produced a score for the 1931 version of the 1929 silent film. Later Hanns Eisler wrote a score for the film entitled 'Fourteen Ways to Describe Rain' (in honour of Arnold Schönberg's seventieth birthday). The analysis of Ivens' *Regen* and the composition for the film were at the heart of the project undertaken by Adorno and Eisler in their exile in America, after Eisler had been awarded a grant by the Rockefeller Foundation for a research project on music in films, which also resulted in the book by Adorno and Eisler, *Composing for the Films*. The authors write in their study: 'a slow tempo was out of place in the newly composed music to Joris Ivens' *Rain*, not because it was necessary to illustrate the falling of the rain, but because the music's task was to push forward this plot-less and therefore static motion picture'.[57] Their account of the film as 'static' is, however, disputable – *Rain*, like *The Bridge*, could be seen as a film in and about movement. Their comment also raises questions about the perceived relationship between 'plot' and 'movement', which could be contrasted with the perception (held by a number of the writers discussed earlier) that it was only in the absence of 'plot' that 'rhythm' could emerge.

In his introduction to a recent edition of Adorno and Eisler's study, Graham McCann writes of *Regen*: 'Numerous visual effects of rain had been filmed by Ivens as symbols of sorrow. Eisler composed music, in the form of variations for quintet, which he felt best captured the expressive possibilities of these images.'[58] The assertion that the film expresses 'symbols of sorrow', for which McCann offers no evidence, has been repeated in the claim (apparently based on a comment made by Ivens) that a primary influence on *Regen* were lines by Paul Verlaine: '*Il pleure dans mon Coeur, comme il pleut sur la ville*' ('There is weeping in my heart, like the rain falling on the city'). In this account of the derivation of the film, 'literature' – in the shape of the symbolist poem – is both origin and an absent presence in the film. Alternatively, we could see the absence of writing, of markers of the 'literary' (by contrast with *Manhatta*), as part of Ivens' attempt to forge a singular and autonomous language for the cinema. In this model, the city and the cinema become so fully symbiotic that they are, in fact, able to tell each other's stories.

Notes

1 Graham Greene, 'A Film Technique: Rhythms of Time and Space', *The Times*, 12 June 1928. Reprinted in *Mornings in the Dark: A Graham Greene Film Reader*, edited by David Parkinson (Harmondsworth: Penguin, 1995), p. 392.

2 Henri Lefebvre, *Rhythmanalysis: Space, Time and Everyday Life*, translated by Stuart Elden and Gerald Moore (London: Continuum 2004), pp. 8; 73.

3 Lefebvre, *Rhythmanalysis*, p. 8.

4 Virginia Woolf, *Orlando* (1928) (Oxford: Oxford University Press, 1992), p. 95.

5 Virginia Woolf, 'Street Music' (1905), *The Essays of Virginia Woolf*, Volume 1: 1904–1912, edited by Andrew McNeillie (London: The Hogarth Press, 1986), p. 27.

6 Woolf, 'Street Music', p. 28.

7 Ibid., p. 28.

8 Ibid., p. 29.

9 Ibid., p. 30.

10 Woolf, 'Street Music', pp. 30–31.

11 Woolf, 'The Cinema' (1926), *The Essays of Virginia Woolf*, Volume 4: 1925–1928, edited by Andrew McNeillie (London: The Hogarth Press, 1994), p. 348.

12 T. S. Eliot, *The Use of Poetry and the Use of Criticism* (London: Faber and Faber 1933, p. 155).

13 Woolf, 'The Cinema', pp. 352–353.

14 Woolf, 'The Cinema', p. 352.

15 See Laura Marcus, *The Tenth Muse: Writing about Cinema in the Modernist Period* (Oxford: Oxford University Press, 2007), pp. 123–124.

16 Woolf, 'The Cinema'. Variant edition, *Essays* Volume 4, p. 595.

17 Raymond Williams, *The Country and the City* (1973) (London: The Hogarth Press, 1993), p. 242.

18 Raymond Williams, *The Politics of Modernism: Against the New Conformists*, edited by Tony Pinkney (London: Verso, 1989), p. 11.

19 Virginia Woolf, *The Diary of Virginia Woolf*, edited by Anne Olivier Bell. Volume 3: 1925–30 (Harmondsworth: Penguin, 1982), p. 102.

20 Virginia Woolf, *Mrs Dalloway* (1925) (Oxford: Oxford University Press, 2000), p. 4.

21 Woolf, *Mrs Dalloway*, pp. 12–13.

22 See, for example, James Donald, *Imagining the Modern City* (London: Athlone, and Minneapolis, University of Minnesota Press, 1999) and Keith Williams, 'Symphonies of the Big City: Modernism, Cinema and Urban Modernity', in Paul Edwards (ed.), *The Great London Vortex: Modernist Literature and Art* (Bath: Sulis Press, 2003), pp. 31–50.

23 Ann Banfield, 'Remembrance and Tense Past', in *The Cambridge Companion to the Modernist Novel*, edited by Morag Shiach (Cambridge: Cambridge University Press, 2007), p. 53–54.

24 Paul Ricoeur, *Time and Narrative* Volume 2, translated Kathleen McLaughlin and David Pellauer (Chicago: University of Chicago Press, 1985), p. 105.

25 Banfield, 'Remembrance and Tense Past', p. 55.

26 Banfield, 'Remembrance and Tense Past', p. 57.

27 Virginia Woolf, *The Hours: The British Museum Manuscript of Mrs Dalloway*, edited by Helen M. Wussow (New York: Pace University Press, 2010), p. 416.

28 George Augustus Sala, *Twice around the Clock or the Hours of the Day and Night in London* (1859) (Leicester: Leicester University Press, 1971), p. 11.

29 Ibid., p. 25.

30 Ibid., p. 26.

31 Ibid., p. 67.

32 Ibid., p. 49.

33 Ibid., p. 50.

34 Ibid., x.

35 Hugo von Hoffmansthal, 'The Substitute for Dreams', trans. Lance W. Garner, in *German Essays on Film*, edited by. Richard W. McCormich and Alison Guenther-Pal (New York: Continuum, 2004), pp. 52–56.

36 Alfred Döblin, '*Ulysses* by Joyce' (1928), reprinted in *The Weimar Republic Sourcebook*, edited by Anton Kaes, Martin Jay and Edward Dimendberg (Berkeley and Los Angeles: University of California Press, 1994), p. 514.

37 'The Editor' [Ezra Pound], *The Exile*, No. 4, 1928, p. 114 (New York: Johnson Reprint Corporation, 1967).

38 Elliot Paul and Robert Sage, 'Artistic Improvements of the Cinema', *transition* 10, January 1928, p. 132 (New York: Kraus Reprint Corporation, 1967).

39 Louis Delluc, 'Beauty in the Cinema' (1917), translated and reprinted in *French Film Theory and Criticism*, Volume 1, 1907–1929, edited by Richard Abel (Princeton, NJ: Princeton University Press, 1988), p. 137.

40 Joris Ivens, quoted in Malte Hagener, *Moving Forward, Looking Back: The European Avant-Garde and the Invention of Film Culture, 1919–1939* (Amsterdam: Amsterdam University Press, 2007), p. 52.

41 John Grierson, 'The Course of Realism', in *Grierson on Documentary*, edited by Forsyth Hardy (London: Faber 1966), p. 76.

42 Grierson, *Grierson on Documentary*, p. 76.

43 Jan-Christopher Horak, 'Paul Strand and Charles Sheeler's *Manhatta*', in Jan-Christopher Horak (ed.) *Lovers of Cinema: The First American Avant-garde 1919–1945* (Madison, Wisconsin: University of Wisconsin Press, 1995), p. 282.

44 Juan Suarez, 'City Space, Technology, Popular Culture: The Modernism of Paul Strand and Charles Sheeler's *Manhatta*', *Journal of American Studies* 36 (2002) 1, 88.

45 Vachel Lindsay, 'Photoplay Progress', *The New Republic* 10, no. 20 (February 17, 1917), 76.

46 Miriam Hansen, 'The Hieroglyph and the Whore: D.W. Griffith's *Intolerance*', *South Atlantic Quarterly* 88 (Spring 1989), 361–392. Hansen develops these arguments throughout her study *Babel and Babylon: Spectatorship in American Silent Film* (Cambridge, Mass: Harvard University Press, 1991).

47 Vachel Lindsay, *The Art of the Moving Picture* (1915/1922) (New York: Random House, 2000), pp. 57–58.

48 Lawrence Goldstein, *The American Poet at the Movies: A Critical History* (Ann Arbor: University of Michigan Press, 1995), p. 32.

49 Peter Brooker, *New York Fictions: Modernity, Postmodernism, the New Modern* (Harlow, Essex: Longman, 1996), p. 34.

50 Ibid., p. 35.

51 Goldstein, *The American Poet at the Movies*, p. 33.

52 Suarez, 'City Space, Technology, Popular Culture', p. 100.

53 Béla Balázs, *Theory of the Film*, translated by Edith Bone (London: Dennis Dobson, 1951), p. 176.

54 Gilles Deleuze, *Cinema 1, The Movement Image*, translated by Hugh Tomlinson and Barbara Habberjam (Minneapolis: University of Minnesota Press, 1986), p. 110.

55 Ibid., p. 175.

56 Germaine Dulac, 'Holland and the Visual Ideal', in *Monde*, 12 January 1929. Cited in Ed Hughes, 'Film Sound, Music and the Art of Silence', in

Nicky Losseff and Jenny Doctor (eds.), *Silence, Music, Silent Music* (London: Ashgate, 2007), p. 91.

57 Theodor Adorno and Hanns Eisler, *Composing for the Films* (1947) (London: Athlone, 1994), p. 101.

58 Graham McCann, 'Introduction', in *Composing for the Films* (1994), p. xxxii.

CHAPTER 6

Staging the 'Private Theatre'
Gender and the Auto-Erotics of Reverie

> The young woman who writes and the young man who writes are alike dissatisfied; but the woman writes in order to have something, the young man in order to be relieved of something.
>
> (Laura Marholm, The Psychology of Women)[1]

The phrase 'private theatre' comes from Freud and Breuer's *Studies in Hysteria* (1895), in which it is used by one of Breuer's women patients, Bertha Pappenheim, known as 'Anna O':

> This girl, who was bubbling over with intellectual vitality, led an extremely monotonous existence in her puritanically-minded family. She embellished her life in a manner which probably influenced her decisively in the direction of her illness, by indulging in systematic day-dreaming, which she described as her 'private theatre.' While everyone thought she was attending, she was living through fairy-tales in her imagination, but she was always on the spot when she was spoken to, so that no one was aware of it. She pursued this activity almost continuously while she was engaged on her household duties, which she discharged unexceptionally . . . this habitual day-dreaming while she was well passed over into illness without a break.[2]

One of the tasks Breuer and Freud set themselves in *Studies on Hysteria* was to demonstrate that the roots of hysteria lie 'in an excess rather than a defect'.[3] According to Breuer's 'energetic' model of mental and 'nervous' life, affect or excitation liberated by active mental work is also used up by this work. In states of abstraction and dreaminess, on the other hand, 'intercerebral excitation sinks below its clear waking level', a state which passes over into sleep. If, in this 'state of absorption', 'a group of affectively coloured ideas is active', it is put at 'the disposal of abnormal functioning, such as conversion [hysteria]'. While Anna O's 'private theatre' is at one moment seen as an aspect of a creative and active imagination, in which 'energetic mental work is carried on', at the next it becomes identified with 'habitual reverie', the first step towards 'pathogenic auto-hypnosis'.[4] This double perspective indicates a more general uncertainty as to the normality or abnormality of creativity and imaginative life. This issue was explored in the numerous studies of genius, creativity and pathology at the turn of the century, as well as in psychoanalytic debates and writings, the best known of which is Freud's essay 'Creative Writers and Day-Dreaming' (1907).

Hysteria and feminism were, a number of recent critics have argued, two sides of the same coin – two forms of nineteenth-century protest against women's lack of freedom and self-determination. Time and again in the early case histories of psychoanalysis we find references to the woman patient's confinement in the home – often confinement to the sick-room of one or other parent. Their attempts to develop lives and careers outside the domestic sphere – often through classes and lectures of various kinds – are almost uniformly thwarted by illness, either their own or that of family members.

For Breuer, 'being in love' and 'sick-nursing' (the latter almost always the province of the unmarried daughter of the house) are the 'two great pathogenic factors' leading to hysteria:

> neither 'absence of mind' during energetic work nor unemotional twilight states are pathogenic; on the other hand, reveries that are filled with emotion and states of fatigue arising from protracted affects *are* pathogenic. The broodings of a care-ridden man, the anxiety of a person watching at the sick-bed of someone dear to him, the day-dreams of a lover – these are states of this second kind. Concentration on the affective group of ideas begins by producing 'absence of mind.' The flow of ideas grows gradually slower and at last almost stagnates; but the affective idea and its affect remain active, and so consequently does the great quantity of excitation which is not being used up functionally ... This is the way in which pathogenic auto-hypnosis would seem to come about in some people – by affect being introduced into a habitual reverie.[5]

Throughout *Studies on Hysteria* we find an ambivalence towards reverie and the 'private theatre'. On the one hand, there is perceived to be a continuity between daydreaming and hysterical illness, and a concern that the doubling effected by daydreaming – the fact of living simultaneously in real and phantasy worlds – results in a pathological state of 'double consciousness' (*double conscience*). Anna O, Breuer writes, 'was in the habit, while she was in perfect health, of allowing trains of imaginative ideas to pass through her mind during her ordinary occupations. While she was in a state that favoured auto-hypnosis, the affect of anxiety entered her reverie and created a hypnoid state for which she had amnesia'.[6] On the other hand, Anna O's ability to create a 'private theatre', and to construct and narrate 'stories', is also seen to have played a part in her cure. Symptoms and affects can be 'removed' precisely because Anna O is capable of recounting her stories, 'which acted as a psychic stimulus' and so brought about 'release and relief'.[7]

At the close of *Studies in Hysteria*, Breuer explores the workings of 'double consciousness', 'the habitual co-existence of two heterogeneous trains of ideas'. He suggests that it is women's conventional tasks, 'monotonous, simple and uninteresting occupation[s]', that lead to habitual reverie. Daydreaming is also linked to suggestibility by literary products: 'an interesting set of ideas, derived for instance from books or plays, forces itself upon the subject's attention and intrudes into his thoughts'.[8] Breuer implies not only a link between femininity and reading, but an understanding of daydreams as inhabited by literary forms of representation and 'ready-made phantasies'. Freud, as Jean Laplanche and J.-B. Pontalis write, 'always held the model fantasy to be the reverie, that form of novelette, both stereotyped and infinitely variable, which the subject composes and relates to himself in a waking state'.[9] Breuer makes the link between reverie and fiction in *Studies in Hysteria* through repeated references to the 'scenes' and 'book[s] of pictures' of the patients' memories and reminiscences. This bears in particularly complex ways on the case of Anna O, whose illness and cure were so intricately bound up with daydreaming, story-telling and, ultimately, story-writing.

To alleviate the monotony of her life, Anna O, prior to her illness, indulged in 'systematic day-dreaming'. When, following her father's illness and death, she became ill herself, her 'psychical disturbance' manifested itself not only in somatic symptoms, but also in the presence of 'two entirely distinct states of consciousness ... which alternated very frequently and without warning and which became more and more differentiated in the course of the illness'.[10] The only relief from the hallucinatory '*absences*' she suffered in one state of consciousness was obtained by narration during the states of auto-hypnosis which succeeded them. As Breuer notes, the daily pattern of her mental states was a version of the schedule established during the period in which she was nursing her father. Moreover, the stories Anna O was able to tell often took as their 'starting-point or central situation ... a girl anxiously sitting by a sick-bed'. 'The stories were always sad', Breuer notes, 'and some of them were charming, in the style of Hans Andersen's *Picture Book without Pictures*, and, indeed, they were probably constructed on this model'.[11]

These stories became an essential part of the 'talking-cure', as 'Anna O' entitled the analytic procedure, although the deterioration in her mental condition for a time transmuted her evening narratives from 'more or less freely-created poetical compositions . . . into a string of frightful and terri-fying hallucinations'.[12] Moreover, for almost a year, she re-lived, during her hypnotic states, the events of the year preceding the one in which she was in fact historically situated, each day narrating the events of the day exactly one year previously, as if her consciousness were shaped by the temporality and form of a diary. (The veracity of her memories was in fact checked against the diary her mother had kept of the events of the previous year.) Breuer refers to his evening visits to his patient, during which he 'relieved her of the whole stock of imaginative products which she had accumulated since my last visit. It was essential that this should be effected completely if good results were to follow'.[13]

But Bertha Pappenheim also found other ways of 'discharging' her imaginative life. She had written down the 'sad' and 'charming' stories she had composed while under Breuer's treatment, and at the end of 1882, while she was still ill but no longer seeing Breuer, she read some of her own fairy tales to her cousin, Anna Ettlinger, who encouraged her literary work. In the later 1880s, she anonymously published a first collection entitled *Little Stories for Children*; a second collection of stories appeared in 1890. In 1899, she published a play, *Frauenrecht* ['A Woman's Right'] and a translation of Mary Wollstonecraft's *Vindication of the Rights of Women*. In 1900, the first of her polemical articles was published. Although she continued to produce literary works, she became increas-ingly involved in political and social work, becoming a central figure in the Jewish women's movement in Germany, and a founder, in 1904, of the League of Jewish Women.

These later aspects of Bertha Pappenheim's experience do not enter into Breuer's case study of the hysteric 'Anna O', whose clinical biography closes abruptly in the early 1880s. There was thus no occasion for Breuer to explore the paths Bertha Pappenheim's life had taken, nor the relationship between the 'stories' elaborated during her illness and those that she produced for publication, an issue which would have borne interestingly on those ques-tions of creativity and psychopathology that so absorbed psychoanalysis in the first decades of the twentieth century.

It is striking that at least two of Freud's closest women followers and collaborators – Lou Andreas-Salomé (1861–1937) and Freud's daughter Anna – were concerned, in their earliest contributions to psychoanalytic debate, with questions of daydreaming, auto-eroticism and narcissism. Both Anna Freud and Andreas-Salomé took the daydreamer as their self-definition, describing their childhood and adolescent years as bound into a continuous process of story-telling, of auto-narration, which, as

Lisa Appignanesi and John Forrester note, culminated in detailed written histories of their invented worlds.[14]

In her autobiography, Lou Andreas-Salomé wrote of a childhood 'full of lonely reverie', and repeatedly returned, in her autobiographical and fictional texts, to the ways in which much of her childhood was spent in the creation of an imagined world, peopled by characters whose faces she had seen in passing, and whose lives she invented on the basis of these glimpses in the streets or through windows. (This form of fiction-making is strikingly echoed in Virginia Woolf's essay 'Street Haunting', in which Woolf likens the act of reading to the social relations that characterize the modern city: 'one is forced to glimpse and nod and move on after a moment of talk, a flash of under-standing, as, in the street outside, one catches a word in passing and from a chance phrase fabricates a lifetime'.[15]) As Angela Livingstone writes: 'Lou was ... always to see herself as engaged in a special kind of egoistic and proto-artistic activity, the half-inventing of a better-shaped world from the actual world's transitory and disorderly data; the half-transforming into something of her own everything that was prescribed and alien.'[16]

Anna Freud's first professional paper, 'Beating Fantasies and Daydreams' (1922),[17] was written and delivered following her reading and translation of the Dutch psychologist Varendonck's *The Psychology of Day-Dreams*, a work modelled on *The Interpretation of Dreams*, in which Varendonck uses his own daydreams as material.[18] Her paper also took up some of the issues explored in Freud's 'Creative Writers and Day-Dreaming' (1908), and was a direct response to his essay 'A Child Is Being Beaten' (1919), in which he explores a beating phantasy common to his patients which, in Anna Freud's words, 'is discharged in an act of pleasurable autoerotic gratification'. Freud argues that the phantasy – a scenario which can be expressed in the sentence 'a child is being beaten' – goes through different stages of development and syntax, but that the wish underlying all its stages could be articulated as 'My father loves only me', a wish expressed in the language of the anal-sadistic organization as an act of beating. Anna Freud's essay was also profoundly influenced by her discussions with Salomé, whose thinking and writing at this time were centred on fantasies, daydreams and anal eroticism.

In 'A Child Is Being Beaten', Freud refers to four male and two female patients or analysands for whom this phantasy was significant. One of the female cases was almost certainly Anna Freud. (We can leave aside the complexities of a situation in which the analysand reveals the desire *for* her father to the analyst who *is* her father.) In her essay, Anna Freud quotes Freud's brief account of two female cases, for whom 'an elaborate structure of day-dreams ... had grown up over the masochistic beating fantasy ...

mak[ing] possible a feeling of satisfied excitation, even though the mastur-batory act was refrained from'.[19] 'I have been able to find one daydream', Anna Freud writes, 'which seemed especially well suited to illustrate this brief remark ... formed by a girl of about fifteen'. The girl was in fact herself, though this is never acknowledged: she writes as if she were producing the case history of a patient. The occlusion of first by third person narrative both suggests the structures of primal fantasies (as in 'A Child Is Being Beaten'), which are not, to borrow Laplanche's and Pontalis's phrase, 'weighted by the ego', and a more defensive reversal of subject positions.

Anna Freud recounts in some detail a structure whereby the daydreamer struggles over some years to 'retain the [beating] fantasy as a source of pleasure and, at the same time, to give up the sexual gratification which could not be reconciled with the demands of her ego'.[20] The beating fantasy became less frequent as the guilt with which it was associated led increas-ingly to unpleasure rather than pleasure. At about the same time, when the girl was aged somewhere between eight and ten, she 'initiated a new kind of fantasy activity which she herself called "nice stories" in contrast to the ugly beating fantasies ... it was inconceivable that a figure playing a part in a nice story could even appear in the beating scene'. The 'nice stories', she writes, 'deserve to be called "continued stories" in view of the constancy of the acting figures and the entire general setting'.[21] The most significant of these 'continued daydreams' was triggered by the girl's reading, in her fourteenth or fifteenth year, of 'a boy's storybook' which contained a short story set in the Middle Ages. (Anna Freud uses the fact of the boy's story to make the case for 'bisexuality' rather than a 'masculinity complex'.) The girl took possession of the figures and 'further spun out the tale, just as if it had been her own spontaneous fantasy product'. In her story, a fifteen-year-old noble youth (the age of the daydreamer) is captured by a knight who holds him prisoner, alternately threatening and nurturing him during the long impris-onment: 'All this takes place in vividly animated and dramatically moving scenes', Anna Freud writes, barely concealing her pride in her own creation.

Analysis revealed to the daydreamer what the reader of the essay by now realizes: that the masturbatory beating phantasies and the 'nice stories' are far from distinct. Both revolve around the interplay between a strong and weak person, and both enact scenarios of punishment and humiliation, although 'the nice stories admit the occurrence of unexpected affectionate scenes precisely at the point where the beating phantasy depicts the act of chastisement ... While the beating fantasy ... represents a return of the repressed, the nice stories on the other hand represent its sublimation.'[22]

The essay thus establishes the mutual dependence of beating fantasies and daydreams (nice stories). A coda recounts the 'development and fate of one of these continued day-dreams. Several years after the story of the knight first emerged, the girl put it in writing'. But 'while the actual writing was done in a state of happy excitement, similar to the state of daydreaming, the finished story does not elicit any such excitement'. There is also a 'renunciation of the daydreamlike pleasure gain at specific climaxes', Anna Freud writes. The written story spreads the load of pleasure over the whole, rather than concentrating it into 'a single great climax at the end of the written tale'. Moreover, the act of writing is seen as a defence against 'excessive preoccupation'. An exorcism of obsession: 'The daydream of the knight was in fact finished, as far as she was concerned, after it had been written down.' This is, then, a 'full discharge' which will not be followed by further releases of 'accumulated excitement'.

The essay closes with the claim that the shift from fantasy and daydream to writing was 'an important developmental step: the transformation of an autistic into a social activity'.[23] The dangerous pleasures of private fantasy are thus transmuted into the aesthetic and ambitious strivings of the author: 'For the better she succeeds in the presentation of her material, the greater will be the effect on others and therefore also her own indirect pleasure gain'.[24] The final part of the essay thus enacts the 'sublimation' it describes, seeking to end the dangerous circulation of the fantasy material it has brought to the surface and preventing, as it were, this particular nice story – the birth of the author as social subject – from collapsing back into ugly fantasy. What the essay cannot explore is its own status as an autobiographical text disguised as a scientific document, or the pleasures attendant upon the redescription of the fantasy materials it simultaneously hoards and discharges.

I have turned to Anna Freud's 1922 essay because it so fully opens up the topic of daydreaming, fantasy, auto-eroticism and literary product. I now want to return to the *fin de siècle* and, in passing, to Lou Andreas-Salomé's Russian-born contemporary, the painter Marie Bashkirtseff (1859–1884), who died in Paris of tuberculosis at the age of twenty-five, and whose journals caused a sensation when they were published (albeit in expurgated form) in France in 1887, and in England and America in 1890. Hugh Stutfield, writing in *Blackwood's* in 1897, described Bashkirtseff's journal as 'a kind of secret Bible' in which 'the tired and discontented women of the time [. . .] read a few sentences every morning, or at night before going to sleep'.[25] It would seem that the journals fill the transitional and transgressive space between sleeping and waking.

Bashkirtseff became a significant representative figure of *fin de siècle* femininity, perceived, like Lou Andreas-Salomé, as a type of 'modern woman'. Stutfield links her with George Egerton, castigating both for their introspection and 'morbid ego-mania' – 'the literature of hysteria'. Bashkirtseff was destroyed, Stutfield has it, by her own ambition and by her nervous disposition, which is also the destructive temper of her times. Moreover, she reveals her 'inner life' in her journals, those documents which, as the private become public, are both retentive and confessional – and which, *pace* Laura Marholm, could be said to stem from the desire both to have something and to be relieved of something. The journals are, in addition, the writings of adolescence, frequently perceived as the age of reverie. According to G. Stanley Hall, whose monumental study of adolescence appeared in 1904, 'Inner absorption and reverie is one marked characteristic of this age of transition'; 'Puberty is the birthplace of the imagination. This has its morning twilight in reverie.'[26]

Adolescence, I would suggest, is also one of the ages of the New Woman. The New Woman, like the adolescent, is frequently figured as a transitional figure. Ambiguously sexual, poised between worlds, the adolescent and the New Woman stand at the dawn of a new age – in a period, moreover, in which the individual's life-span and the century's age are each other's favourite analogies. In other, non-progressivist models, women remain adolescents throughout their lives, existing almost permanently, in Stanley Hall's words, 'in what is really a suppressed semi-erotic state'.[27]

Adolescence, Julia Kristeva has argued, figures interiority for modernity: '"psychic interiority" is a creation that affirms itself magnificently in the nineteenth-century psychological novel ... the adolescent character serves as a standard of measure within this involution of baroque man, who is neither within nor without, into nineteenth-century psychological man'.[28] I now wish to turn to the question of interiority and the New Woman, by way of Havelock Ellis and his account of 'Auto-Erotism', the term he coined and discusses at length in his *Studies in the Psychology of Sex*. Ellis writes:

> It was the wish to group together all the far-flung manifestations of the inner irresistible process of sexual activity that underlay my own conception of *auto-erotism*, or the spontaneous erotic impulse which arises from the organism apart from all definite external stimulation, to be manifested, or it may be transformed, in mere solitary physical sex activity, in dreams of the night, in day-dreams, in shapes of literature and art, in symptoms of nervous disorder such as some forms of hysteria, and even in the most exalted phases of mystical devotion.[29]

Ellis adds that: 'the conditions of modern civilization render auto-erotism a matter of increasing social significance. As our marriage-rate declines, and as illicit sexual relationships continue to be openly discouraged, it is absolutely inevitable that auto-erotic phenomena of one kind or another . . . should increase among us both in amount and intensity.'[30]

Let other pens dwell on the more recherché forms of 'auto-erotism' explored by Ellis. We will, however, pause briefly to consider the bicycle, the vehicle of the New Woman, and its role 'in exciting auto-erotic manifestations'. Ellis suggests that 'Sexual irritation may . . . be produced by the bicycle in women', though he takes issue with the view upheld by 'most medical authorities on cycling', 'that when cycling leads to sexual excitement the fault lies more with the woman than with the machine'. There may or may not have been a sexual charge attached to popular representations of the New Woman on her bicycle. What interests me in Ellis's account are the contrasting images of auto-eroticism as *external* or (as in the production of daydreams) as *internal* stimulation: the distinction between 'auto-erotism', we could say, as *friction* or as *fiction*.

The friction/fiction divide is one, I would suggest, that informs twentieth-century debates over female sexuality as clitoral or as vaginal – the former characterized (as in the Freudian analyst Marie Bonaparte's account) as external and masculine-identified, the latter as internal and properly feminine.[31] Freud's accounts of female development chart the shift from the clitoris to the vagina as the site of pleasure. In this model, 'becoming a woman' entails an interiorization of sensation and sexuality. The friction/fiction distinction would also seem to be an aspect of the dual image of the New Woman. While in popular representations she is often figured as aggressively seeking stimuli in the outer world (movement, experience, education), there is another image of the New Woman as dreamer, turned inward to sensation and feeling.

In Ellis's account, the external, or 'voluntary mechanical', production of sexual excitement is contrasted with 'spontaneous' sexual emotion:

> Schrenck-Notzing knows a lady who is spontaneously sexually excited on hearing music or seeing pictures without anything lascivious in them; she knows nothing of sexual relationships. Another lady is sexually excited on seeing beautiful and natural scenes, like the sea; sexual ideas are mixed up in her mind with these things, and the contemplation of a specially strong and sympathetic man brings the orgasm on in about a minute. Both these ladies 'masturbate' in the streets, restaurants, railways, theatres, without anyone perceiving it.[32]

As in much turn-of-the-century sexological material on auto-eroticism and masturbation, as well as in the literary texts of the period, there is a particular fascination with the production of private dreams in public places. While for Ellis these ladies manifest an eroticism which shades into 'hyperaesthetic weakness', the phenomenon is also closely allied to 'that form of auto-erotism . . . associated with revery, or day-dreaming'.[33] Ellis footnotes several psychological studies of reverie and daydreaming, particularly focused on adolescents and young women, including research into the 'continued story', 'an imagined narrative, more or less peculiar to the individual, by whom it is cherished with fondness. . . . . The growth of the story is favoured by solitude, and lying in bed before going to sleep is the time specially sacred to its cultivation'.[34] We have seen the representation of the 'continued story' in Anna Freud's account – a form of narrative which could be traced through from Jane Eyre, with her 'tale that was never ended', to the uses of 'feminine' forms of stream of consciousness and interior monologue in modernist fiction.

The most significant elements of Ellis's discussion of 'Auto-Erotism' in the present context are the connections he makes between sexuality, dreams, daydreams and art, and the intensity of his focus on the 'spontaneous erotic impulse which arises from the organism apart from all definite external stimulation'. The biologistic context for this claim is Ellis's understanding of 'internal secretions' as the key to sexual identity: 'a woman is a woman because of her internal secretions'.[35] The point of stressing the absence of 'definite external stimulation' in the arousal of erotic impulses is to drive sexuality into (or to construct it out of) the interior, to introject it. As Freud notes, in his *Three Essays on the Theory of Sexuality*, the essential feature of the term 'auto-erotism' for Ellis is that it describes 'an excitation which is not provoked from outside but arises internally'.[36]

Ellis's biologistic account of the 'inner foci' and 'intimate recesses' of the body is inseparable from models of sexuality, identity and aesthetics as profoundly interiorized and subjectivist. This drive to inwardness (characterized by Max Nordau, in the most negative account of *fin de siècle* subjectivism, as 'ego-mania'[37]) is also manifest in much of the writing by and about women at the turn of the century. For Salomé, women are characterized by a narcissism which represents not an absence of relationship to an external world, but a feminine self-sufficiency and completeness; she also observed that Narcissus' mirror was a pool, and thus not a man-made and bounded artefact, but a part of the natural world with which the subject merges.[38] Laura Marholm characterized George Egerton as 'a subject without an object',[39] and the emphasis of theorists such as Stanley Hall

and Marholm is on what women generate from within. For these conserva-
tive thinkers, education, as I've suggested, is represented as an irrelevant
external stimulus – as a kind of 'friction' – diverting women from their true
role and destiny in motherhood.

The writers we label New Women novelists responded in diverse ways to
this interiorization, though there is a shared link between constructions of
female inwardness and representations of daydream, fantasy and reverie.
George Egerton, for example, hollows out the space of women's interiority
through fantasy in 'A Cross Line', though the modern woman's desire to
become, in Marholm's phrase, 'a substance in herself' has turned into *having*
'a substance in herself' by the end of the story, when Egerton's heroine
realizes she is pregnant.[40]

The passage from reverie and daydreaming to writing is represented in
detail in Sarah Grand's *The Beth Book*. The novel (which could be seen as a
rewriting of *Madame Bovary*) constructs a moral chart of good and bad
fantasizing. Bereft of the 'wholesome companionship of boy and girl' and of
'the rational plans and pursuits she had been accustomed to make and to
carry out with the boys', the young Beth has 'nothing to substitute but
dreams; and on these she lived, finding an idle distraction in them, until the
habit grew disproportionate, and began to threaten the fine balance of her
other faculties . . . . To fill up her empty days, she surrounded herself with a
story, among the crowding incidents of which she lived, whatever she might
be doing.'[41]

After her marriage to a boorish doctor, Beth finds herself without peace
or privacy until she discovers a 'secret chamber' in the attic of the house her
husband is renting:

> Everything about her [in this room] was curiously familiar, and her first
> impression was that she had been here before. On the other hand, she could
> hardly believe in the reality of what she saw, she thought she must be
> dreaming, for here was exactly what she had been pining for most in the
> whole wide world of late, a sacred spot, sacred to herself, where she would be
> safe from intrusion.[42]

In this sacred and secret spot, she begins first to read – biographies and
autobiographies and the lives of authors, not the three-volume novels
favoured by her husband: 'Her mind, which had run riot, fancy-fed with
languourous dreams in the days when it was unoccupied and undisciplined,
came steadily more and more under control, and grew gradually stronger as
she exercised it' – and then to write. Leaving her husband, she exchanges her
secret chamber for an attic room in London, writes and publishes a novel,

but finally abandons fiction-making for a life of 'active service' and public oratory.

The Beth Book thus follows the path delineated by Bertha Pappenheim, representing the passage from reverie and daydreaming to writing and from thence to political/social activism. Yet to read the psychoanalytic and literary texts of the period associatively is to find Grand's trajectory from reverie/reading to writing to being-in-the-world troubled by the circularities of the hoardings and discharges of, to take the most striking example, Anna Freud's narrative of fantasy and its renunciation. The exit from the private theatre could be read as another wishful staging, while daydreaming continues to function both as a guilty secret pleasure and as the site of women's resistance, transgression and autonomy.

The most complex issue is that of the uses of dream, daydream and fantasy in turn-of-the-century writing to explore sexual and gendered identities, confusions and reversals, including cross-dressing. 'For the first time I had a daydream or a story with a female main person in my head', Anna Freud wrote to Lou Andreas-Salomé in 1922 – a 'nice story', perhaps, of 'proper' feminine identification which also suggests, by contrast, those spaces in which women (and men) are other than, and others to, themselves.

Notes

1 Laura Marholm, *The Psychology of Woman*, translated by Georgia A. Etchison (London: Grant Richards, 1899), p. 54.
2 Sigmund Freud, *Standard Edition* (London: Hogarth Press, vol. 2, 1955), p. 22.
3 Ibid., p.240.
4 Ibid., p. 296.
5 Ibid.
6 Ibid., p. 314.
7 Quotations from the case history compiled by Joseph Breuer, and the report of her treatment in Bellevue Sanatorium, Appendix D23 in Albrecht Hirschmuller, *The Life and Work of Josef Breuer*, revised edn. (New York: New York University Press), pp. 282–283.
8 Freud and Breuer, *Studies in Hysteria*, p. 83.
9 Jean Laplanche and Jean-Bertrand Pontalis, 'Fantasy and the Origins of Sexuality', reprinted in *Formations of Fantasy*, edited by Victor Burgin et al. (London: Methuen, 1986), pp. 5–27, 22.
10 Freud and Breuer, *Studies in Hysteria*, p. 76.
11 Ibid., p. 82.
12 Ibid., p. 29.
13 Ibid., p. 86.

14 Lisa Appignanesi and John Forrester, *Freud's Women* (London: Weidenfeld and Nicolson, 1992), p. 243.

15 Virginia Woolf, 'Street Haunting: A London Adventure', in *The Essays of Virginia Woolf*, vol. 4, edited by Andrew McNeillie (London: Hogarth, 1994), pp. 480–491.

16 Angela Livingstone, *Lou Andreas-Salomé* (London: Gordon Fraser, 1984), p. 21.

17 Anna Freud, 'Beating Fantasies and Daydreams' (1922). Revised version, in *Introduction to Psychoanalysis: Lectures for Child Analysts and Teachers 1922–1935* (London: Hogarth Press, 1974), pp. 137–157.

18 J. Varendonck, *The Psychology of Day-Dreams* (London: George Allen and Unwin, 1921).

19 Anna Freud, 'Beating Fantasies and Daydreams', p. 138.

20 Ibid.

21 Ibid., p. 144.

22 Ibid., pp. 152–153.

23 Ibid., p. 157.

24 Ibid., p. 157.

25 Hugh Stutfield, 'The Psychology of Feminism', *Blackwoods*, 161 (January 1897), 104–117, 109.

26 G. Stanley Hall, *Adolescence: its Psychology* (1904) (New York and London: D. Appleton and Co., 1925), p. 313.

27 Ibid., pp. 572, 578.

28 Julia Kristeva, 'The Adolescent Novel', in *Abjection, Melancholia and Love*, edited by John Fletcher and Andrew Benjamin (London: Routledge, 1991), p. 14. See also Mary Jacobus' superb essay, 'Narcissa's Gaze: Berthe Morisot and the Filial Mirror', in *First Things: the Maternal Imaginary in Literature, Art, and Psychoanalysis* (New York and London: Routledge, 1995), pp. 269–296.

29 Havelock Ellis, 'Auto-Erotism', in *Studies in the Psychology of Sex*, vol. 1, 3rd edn. (Philadelphia: F.A. Davis, 1920). pp. 161–283.

30 Ibid., p. 164.

31 See Marie Bonaparte, *Female Sexuality* (1949), translated by John Rodker (New York: Grove Press, 1962).

32 Ellis, 'Auto-Erotism', pp. 183–184.

33 Ibid., p. 184.

34 Ibid., p. 185.

35 Havelock Ellis, *Man and Woman*, 5th edn. (London: Walter Scott Publishing, nd), pp. vi–vii.

36 Sigmund Freud, *Three Essays on the Theory of Sexuality*, SE vol. 7, p. 181, n. 2. For psychoanalysis, by contrast, 'the essential point is not the genesis of the excitation, but the question of its relation to an object'.

37 See Max Nordau, *Degeneration* (London: William Heinemann, 1895), especially pp. 241–265.

38 See especially 'The Dual Orientation of Narcissism' (translation by S. Leavy of 'Narzissmus als Doppelrichtung' (1921)), *Psychoanalytic Quarterly* 31, nos. 1–2 (1962): 1–30.

39 Laura Marholm, *Modern Women* (London: John Lane, 1896), p. 80.

40 George Egerton, 'A Cross Line', in *Keynotes* (London: John Lane, 1894), pp. 1–36.

41 Sarah Grand, *The Beth Book* (1897) (London: Virago, 1980), p. 264.

42 Ibid., p. 347.

The Newness of the 'New Biography'
Biographical Theory and Practice in the Early Twentieth Century

The dominance of modernist and avant-garde literature in the first decades of the twentieth century has directed attention away from certain texts and genres. Biography is a prime example of this process. While numerous histories of the biographical genre do exist, few critics have attempted to situate early twentieth-century biography in the broader literary and cultural arena.[1] Those who focus on modernist experimentation rarely consider the ways in which biographers approached the new aesthetics, or address the extraordinary popularity and perceived significance of the genre in the period of 'high modernism'. Yet the marked increase in the popularity of biography during this period – the 1920s and 1930s particularly – was closely connected to the new forms of, and experiments with, the genre. 'It is the day of the biographer', Hesketh Pearson wrote in 1930.[2] The rise in popularity of biographies was linked to the perception that biography had been reinvented for the twentieth century, requiring a new level of critical self-awareness.

David Cecil, for example, writing in 1936, called biography 'the only new form' of modern literature.[3] Its newness and its success were due, he suggested, to the fact that it was the genre most congenial to the 'scientific' modern age, and the one most allied to modern psychology and the study of 'human character'. Biography is, he argued, on the side of science on the one hand, while, on the other, biographers approach their subjects with newly aesthetic aims, taking advantage of a 'literary' space made available by the mutual lack of sympathy between literature (particularly poetry) and scientific modernity. Cecil's argument is clearly flawed (there is no evidence that poets and novelists in the 1920s and 1930s felt peculiarly threatened by science, and indeed many embraced its terms), but it is echoed in numerous discussions of the 'new biography', in which, as we shall see, the relationship between the literary and the scientific and the importance of the study of 'character' are two of the dominant themes.

Cecil's claims also find a curious echo in the critical theorist Siegfried Kracauer's important critique of biography as 'an art form of the new bourgeoisie', published in 1930. The dissolution of character in the modern novel, Kracauer argues, has led to the elevation and increased popularity of biography: 'The moral of the biography is that, in the chaos of current artistic practices, it is the only seemingly necessary prose form.'[4] Yet, as I go on to explore, it would seem that critics and commentators in the early twentieth century were exploring fictional and biographical 'characters' in tandem, rather than perceiving biographical lives as offering a unity and plenitude no longer made available by the novelists.

A further dimension of early twentieth-century biography, which struck a number of commentators at the time, was the emergence of a new biographical theory and practice which crossed national boundaries and in which common biographical tenets were developed at the same historical moment in the work of writers between whom there was little, if any, actual contact. The central figures were Lytton Strachey, André Maurois, Emil Ludwig and the more marginal North American biographer – or, in his preferred term, 'psychographer' – Gamaliel Bradford; later in this essay I also discuss A.J.A. Symons and his 1934 'experiment in biography', *The Quest for Corvo*.

In an article titled 'The New Biography: Ludwig, Maurois and Strachey', published in *The Atlantic Monthly* of March 1929, George Alexander Johnston wrote:

> No feature of the literary history of Europe in the last few years is more remarkable than the simultaneous appearance in Germany, France, and England of a new conception of biography ... The amazing similarity both in philosophical conception and in literary style and structure of the work of these writers constitutes a problem of the highest interest.[5]

While Johnston was overstating the likenesses – as Mark Longaker wrote in his 1934 study of biography, 'There are marked similarities in the works of Strachey, Bradford, Maurois and Ludwig, but they obviously do not form a congenial group'[6] – we can work fruitfully with Johnston's perception of biographical 'newness' as a widespread cultural and literary phenomenon.

Commentators and critics both offered descriptions and definitions of the 'new biography' and attempted to account for the new or renewed popularity of the biographical genre. In addition to the numerous biographies published in the period, the 1920s and 1930s saw a spate of critical and theoretical works on biography, many of them written by biographers themselves, including William Thayer's *The Art of Biography* (1920),

James Johnston's *Biography: the Literature of Personality* (1927), Harold
Nicolson's *The Development of English Biography* (1927), André Maurois's
Aspects of Biography (1929), Mark Longaker's *Contemporary Biography* (1934)
and Emil Ludwig's *Die Kunst der Biographie* (1936), as well as a substantial
body of essays. Biographical works, in particular the collections of 'brief
lives' that appeared, were frequently prefaced by more theoretical reflections
on the biographer's art, signalling a marked self-consciousness about the
biographical form. Emil Ludwig (whose numerous biographies included
full-length studies of Goethe and Wilhelm II), André Maurois (whose first
biographies were highly romanticized studies of Shelley and Disraeli),
Gamaliel Bradford (author of such texts as *Bare Souls* and *A Naturalist of
Souls*), and Lytton Strachey (whose *Eminent Victorians* was the defining text
of the 'new biography') produced not only biographies but commentaries
on the genre. It is true, of course, that such commentaries tended to justify
rather than to critique the 'new biographical' methods, and thus it could be
argued that a strong and non-partisan biographical criticism did not emerge
at this time – a fact which may have contributed to the delayed development
of biographical theory, by contrast with, for example, theories of
autobiography.

What were the tenets and characteristics of the 'new biographers' and the
'new biography'? They included, or were held to include, a new equality
between biographer and subject, in contrast to the hero worship and
hagiography of Victorian eulogistic biography; brevity, selection and an
attention to form and unity traditionally associated with fiction rather than
history; the discovery of central motifs in a life and of a 'key' to personality,
so that single aspects of the self or details of the life and person came to stand
for or to explain the whole; and a focus on character rather than events.
While Maurois was committed to representations of a personality unfolding
through time, Ludwig and Bradford shared an anti-chronological aesthetic.
This reaction against chronology may seem paradoxical in the quintessen-
tially narrative genre of biography, but it is made explicable by the focus on
an essential self, transcending time, and, most markedly in Ludwig's work,
on the equivalences between biography and portraiture. The biographer is,
Ludwig asserts, a 'portraitist', whose problem is 'the discovery of a human
soul'. His portraitist is properly inductive and intuitive: he 'begins with the
concept of a character and searches the archives for what is at bottom the
corroboration of an intuition'.[7]

The tenets of modern biography are often defined in contrast to
'Victorian biography', although they were in part shared by a number of
later nineteenth-century critics and writers, including the editors of that

monumental enterprise, the *Dictionary of National Biography* (*DNB*), Leslie Stephen and Sidney Lee. The *DNB*'s instruction to its contributors was said to be 'No flowers by request', and good biographical practice was held to include concision, candour, and analysis and synthesis rather than the accumulation of facts. The representation of a total break between Victorian and modern biography may thus say as much – or more – about the moderns' need to demarcate themselves sharply from their immediate predecessors as about the differences themselves. As Richard Altick has argued, biography was seen as 'the literary emblem par excellence of Victorianism, a product faithful to the old era's habit of misapplied and exaggerated hero worship, with all its attendant hypocrisy and evasiveness'.[8] The 'new biography' comes to represent the radical ideological and cultural rupture between the Victorians and the moderns.

The break, in English literary contexts, is seen to start with the late nineteenth- and early twentieth-century auto/biographical texts of Samuel Butler and Edmund Gosse, who put paid, metaphorically and textually, to their Victorian fathers. Gosse, in *Father and Son* (1907), wields the Darwinian rhetoric which so agonized his father, the naturalist Philip Gosse, and represents his childhood self as engaged in a struggle for survival against his father's fundamentalism, while he depicts Gosse *père* as one of a dying species. For Desmond MacCarthy, Harold Nicolson and André Maurois, Edmund Gosse was Lytton Strachey's immediate precursor, enacting, as MacCarthy puts it, 'a tragic-comic clash between an age of belief and one of scepticism'.[9] The extraordinary impact of Strachey's *Eminent Victorians*, which was seen on its publication not only to have revolutionised biography but also to represent an absolute division between old and new, derived in the greatest part from its destruction through satire of Victorian heroes or 'fathers'. Furthermore, its critique of 'Victorian values' is so closely linked with its radical rewriting of biographical discourse that it came to mark the end not only of a way of writing lives, but of an age. Published in May 1918, five months before the Armistice, *Eminent Victorians* was perceived as the first text of post-war England, opening up to ridicule the workings of power and the blind submission to God and Country which had led to the mass slaughter of World War One.

The rhetoric of warfare emerges, in ironic form, in Strachey's 'Preface' to *Eminent Victorians*, a piece of writing so influential and so often echoed by subsequent biographers that it is worth quoting at some length. Arguing that the very weight of material emanating from the Victorians about their age had destroyed the possibility of its clear delineation, Strachey writes:

> It is not by the direct method of a scrupulous narration that the explorer of
> the past can hope to depict that singular epoch. If he is wise, he will adopt a
> subtler strategy. He will attack his subject in unexpected places; he will fall
> upon the flank, or the rear; he will row out over that great ocean of material,
> and lower down into it, here and there, a little bucket, which will bring up to
> the light of day some characteristic specimen, from those far depths, to be
> examined with a careful curiosity. Guided by these considerations, I have
> written the ensuing studies. I have attempted, through the medium of
> biography, to present some Victorian visions to the eye.[10]

Selection, impartiality and brevity are upheld as the guiding biographical
principles. Eschewing any pretence of, or aspiration to, completeness,
Strachey insists on the fragmentary quality of 'the truth which took my
fancy and lay to my hand', although he somewhat blurs the distinction
between the random or 'haphazard' and the particular in his choice of
biographical subjects. Cardinal Manning, Thomas Arnold, Florence
Nightingale and General Gordon may serve as representatives of
Church, Army, the Public Schools – 'the lives of an ecclesiastic, an
educational authority, a woman of action, and a man of adventure'[11] –
but Strachey's focus, in the body of the text, on his chosen subjects'
egotisms and idiosyncrasies puts the very notion of the representative
into crisis.

   The import of *Eminent Victorians*, Strachey suggests, is not only historical but biographical:

> Human beings are too important to be treated as mere symptoms of the
> past … The art of biography seems to have fallen on evil times in
> England … With us, the most delicate and humane of all the branches of
> the art of writing has been relegated to the journeymen of letters; we do not
> reflect that it is perhaps as difficult to write a good life as to live one.[12]

While biography is firmly claimed as an 'art', Strachey also plays with the
concept of the biographer as a biologist examining his specimens with a
curious but dispassionate eye.

   This aspect of Strachey's 'Preface' is echoed in Emil Ludwig's account of
the 'new biography' in his 1927 study *Genius and Character*.

> After a period which attempted to define man in terms of descent and
> breeding, we enter upon an era totally alien to the Darwinian mentality;
> once again we turn our attention to the personality *per se*, the personality
> almost devoid of temporal co-ordinates, considering the volume, intensity, and
> resistance of its vital forces, the restless fluid of its emotional configurations,
> and the balance between its impulse towards action and its repression through
> precept. Whereas our fathers asked, 'How did the individual harmonize with

his world?' our first question is, 'Does he harmonize with himself?' Questions of success and responsibility have been shifted from the environment back to the individual, so that the analysis which was formerly expended upon the milieu now seeks to penetrate within. Further, the renewed interest in memoirs is biological: and perhaps the portraitist of to-day, who is first of all a psychologist, is much nearer to the biologist than to the historian.[13]

The broader context here is that of the disciplinary and interdisciplinary configurations and disputes of the early twentieth century, to which biography is central. Positioned, like autobiography, on the fault-lines between literature, history and science, biography became perceived as a crucial tool for the scientific and ethnographic data-gatherers of the turn of the century. In 'An Open Letter to Biographers', the psychologist Havelock Ellis urged biographers to fulfil their proper role: 'In every man of genius a new strange force is brought into the world. The biographer is the biologist of this new life. I come to you to learn the origins of this tremendous energy.'[14] The obsession with 'genius' – also pursued in Ludwig's biographical projects – was in one sense continuous with the nineteenth-century preoccupation with 'Great Men', satirized so fully and frequently by Virginia Woolf, but it had also undergone a radical change with the development of interest in the psychology and even the pathology of genius.

In 1927, Leonard and Virginia Woolf's Hogarth Press published Harold Nicolson's *The Development of English Biography*. In the final chapter of his study, 'The Present Age', Nicolson argues that biography's lack of a distinct generic identity of its own and its consequent entanglement 'with other interests – with that, for instance, of history, fiction, and science', have made it uniquely sensitive to 'the spirit of the age': 'over no form of literary composition have the requirements of the reading public exercised so marked and immediate an influence. The development of biography is primarily the development of the taste for biography'.[15] When an age demands heroes, biography will supply them; when it asks for funeral monuments, this is the shape into which biography will transmute. In an age of scepticism, such as the one Nicolson inhabits, 'the reading public become dominantly interested in human behaviour, and biography, in order to meet this interest, becomes inductive, critical, detached and realistic .... The less people believe in theology the more do they believe in human experience. And it is to biography that they go for this experience.'[16] While the 'scientific' interest in biography demands an immensity of detail about the biographical subject, the desire for 'literary' biography requires that this material be organized with 'the perfection of literary form'.[17] The two approaches are, Nicolson argues, incompatible:

I would suggest, in the first place, that the scientific interest in biography is hostile to, and will in the end prove destructive of, the literary interest. The former will insist not only on the facts, but on all the facts; the latter demands a partial or artificial representation of facts. The scientific interest, as it develops, will become insatiable; no synthetic power, no genius for representation, will be able to keep the pace. I foresee, therefore, a divergence between the two interests. Scientific biography will become specialised and technical. There will be biographies in which psychological development will be traced in all its intricacy and in a manner comprehensible only to the experts; there will be biographies examining the influence of heredity – biographies founded on Galton, on Lombroso, on Havelock Ellis, on Freud; there will be medical biographies – studies of the influence on character of the endocrine glands, studies of internal secretions; there will be sociological biographies, economic biographies, aesthetic biographies, philosophical biographies. These will doubtless be interesting and instructive, but the emphasis which will be thrown on the analytical or scientific aspect will inevitably lessen the literary effort applied to their composition. The more that biography becomes a branch of science the less will it become a branch of literature . . . in general literary biography will, I suppose, wander off into the imaginative, leaving the strident streets of science for the open fields of fiction. The biographical form will be given to fiction, the fictional form will be given to biography. When this happens 'pure' biography, as a branch of literature, will have ceased to exist.[18]

Nicolson's account of the increasingly novelistic dimensions of biography in one of its aspects – opposed here to an equivalent growth in highly specialized 'scientific' biographies – is an aspect of, or anticipates, a range of twentieth-century intellectual and disciplinary debates, in which language is divided into its 'referential' and 'emotive' dimensions and functions, and in which 'science' and 'art' – 'the two cultures' – become increasingly polarized.

In 1928 André Maurois delivered the Clark Lectures at Cambridge University, published in English as *Aspects of Biography* in 1929, and named Nicolson's *Development of English Biography* as one of his central sources. He takes issue, however, with Nicolson's equation of the exact and the historical sciences, arguing that the writing of history and of biography should be brought into the literary domains of creativity and imagination: 'I hope to be able to show you,' Maurois writes,

> that art and science can be reconciled. A scientific book, perfectly constructed, is a work of art. A beautiful portrait is at once a portrait resembling his subject and an artistic transference of reality. It is perfectly accurate to say that truth has the solidity of stone and that personality has the lightness of a rainbow; but Rodin and the Greek sculptors before him have at times been

able to infuse into marble the elusive curves and the changing lights of human flesh.'[19]

In the chapter 'Biography Considered as a Work of Art', Maurois defends the biographical methods he adopted in his biographies of Shelley, *Ariel: a Shelley Romance* (1924), and of Disraeli, arguing that 'poetry' and 'rhythm' are as central to biography as to other forms of art, and are to be located in 'the recurrence, at more or less distant intervals, of the essential motifs of the work':

> A human life is always made up of a number of such motifs: when you study one of them, it will soon begin to impress itself upon you with a remarkable force. In Shelley's life the water motif dominates the whole symphony . . . In Disraeli's life there is a flower motif . . . there is an Eastern motif . . . and there is the antagonistic rain motif, that terrible English rain which sets out to extinguish the over-brilliant Eastern flame and succeeds.[20]

In 'Biography Considered as a Science,' Maurois argued against Nicolson's postulated future for biography and for 'that profounder truth which is poetic truth',[21] Maurois's belief, at least in the early stages of his long literary career, in the 'key to character', the attention he paid to the details of a life, his representations of inner thoughts and feelings, and his focus on the biographer's strong affective and empathetic identifications with his subject, were, as I have noted, some of the central tenets of the 'new biography'.

Maurois had entered into the Bloomsbury orbit when he came to London in the early 1920s to renew war-time acquaintances and to research his Shelley biography: he met the writer Maurice Baring, who introduced him to Harold Nicolson and Desmond MacCarthy. The centrality of biography to Bloomsbury culture and to its cult of the civilized individual is an important, and clearly highly class-inflected, dimension of the 'new biography' that I cannot explore fully here. *Aspects of Biography* is in many ways a 'Bloomsbury' text: the lectures were delivered a year after E.M. Forster's Clark Lectures, which subsequently became *Aspects of the Novel*, and which made the question of 'character' and 'personality' central to the analysis of fiction. *Aspects of Biography* also contains numerous laudatory references to Lytton Strachey, and closely debates with Harold Nicolson, as we have seen, and (though less overtly) with Virginia Woolf. When Maurois refers, in the passage quoted above, to the claim 'that truth has the solidity of stone and that personality has the lightness of a rainbow', he is alluding to Woolf's essay of 1927, 'The New Biography', one of the earliest namings of the genre. Woolf describes the divorce between the Victorians (represented by Sir Sidney Lee) and the moderns:

> 'The aim of biography,' said Sir Sidney Lee, who had perhaps read and written more lives than any man of his time, 'is the truthful transmission of personality,' and no single sentence could more neatly split up into two parts the whole problem of biography as it presents itself to us today. On the one hand there is truth; on the other there is personality. And if we think of truth as something of granite-like solidity and of personality as something of rainbow-like tangibility and reflect that the aim of biography is to weld these two into one seamless whole, we shall admit that the problem is a stiff one and that we need not wonder if biographers have for the most part failed to solve it.[22]

'The New Biography' was in part a review essay of Harold Nicolson's *Some People*. Like Woolf's *Orlando*, published in 1928, *Some People* is a hybrid work, a combination of autobiography, biography and fiction, whose guiding idea, as Nicolson explained, 'was to put real people in imaginary situations, and imaginary people in real situations'.[23] Such an admixture of fact and fiction was, for Woolf, the most striking feature of modern biography, as well as the most troubling, for although she applauded the creativity it afforded, she also expressed doubts about the combining of historical fact and artistic invention: 'Let it be fact, one feels, or let it be fiction; the imagination will not serve under two masters simultaneously.'[24] The balance between fact and fiction, she nonetheless suggests, has shifted in the modern age: 'it would seem that the life which is increasingly real to us is the fictitious life; it dwells in the personality rather than the act'.[25] Thus, by implication, biography is at one and the same time the modern genre *par excellence* and deeply in thrall to fiction and fiction-making.

The paradox that we 'know' characters in fiction far more fully than we do 'real life' figures, that they are imbued with far richer personalities and interiorities than we have access to in other contexts, increasingly became a rationale for the appropriation of novelistic strategies in biographical writing. Fictional characters, E.M. Forster wrote in *Aspects of the Novel*, 'are people whose secret lives are visible or might be visible; we are people whose secret lives are invisible'.[26] The 'perfect knowledge' we acquire of people in novels is 'a compensation for their dimness in life'.[27] While Forster sought to differentiate between fiction and history, novel and memoir, biographers were seeking, unsurprisingly, to represent that visibility of the secret life of the biographical subject that Forster reserved for fictional characters alone. Lytton Strachey's technique, for example, was to take phrases from letters and reported conversations and to turn them into representations of his subjects' thoughts and feelings; Maurois, in *Ariel* and *The Life of Disraeli*, simply laid claim, often without the felt necessity of written evidence, to knowledge of his subjects' inner lives. Calling upon E.M. Forster's distinction in *Aspects of the Novel* between the real man (*Homo sapiens*) and the character in a novel (*homo fictus*), the critic George Johnston claimed that the 'new biographer's' empathy with his subject amounted to a form of creation allied to that of the author of a novel:

> The new biography has so completely understood the principal actors in the history of the periods portrayed that it describes them as if it had created them. Thus we reach the paradox that the new biography produces the impression of reality because the principal actors create the illusion that they are the characters in a novel. If the reader of the new biography sometimes feels a sudden doubt whether these people ever lived at all, it is not because they seem improbable, but because they seem too probable to be real.
>
> Fiction does not seek to create mere illusion; it seeks to create the illusion of reality. And it is because the writer of fiction has been so successful in producing the sense of reality, and the traditional biographer, with his appeal to veracity, has been so unsuccessful, that the new biography has adopted the methods of fiction and has, by means of them, brilliantly succeeded in re-creating reality.[28]

The new biography, Johnston insists, employs the methods of fiction, but does not produce works of fiction. This nice distinction is treated with more caution by Woolf in 'The New Biography', in which she argues that the biographer treads the finest of lines when 'he carries the use of fiction too far', risking the loss of both 'the freedom of fiction' and 'the substance of fact'. Nonetheless, she recognizes that the focus on 'personality' and the created life has brought with it a desire for, in her words, 'the novelist's art of arrangement, suggestion, dramatic effect to expound the private life'.[29]

The importance of 'personality' and 'character' in literature and criticism of the early twentieth century may indeed be the central route into an understanding of the centrality and popularity of biography in the period. As the North American biographer Gamaliel Bradford wrote, in the introduction to his study *Wives*: 'The real object of the biographer, all that deeply and permanently interests him, is the analysis and synthesis of his subject's character.'[30] Bradford continues by pointing up the complexity of notions of 'character' and 'quality', and hence the difficulty or even impossibility of the biographer's task – that of giving some form of permanence and interpretative stability to 'this perpetual shift and change in the complexion of men's souls'.[31] James C. Johnston, in *Biography: the Literature of Personality*, a study whose stated aim is to elucidate the purpose and methods of biography, and thus to differentiate 'genuine biography' from the spate of meretricious journalistic biographical productions, writes:

> Herein lies the true province of biography in all its varied forms: indeed, centered upon temperament, individuality, character, personality – the frequently recurring terms in any discussion of genuine biography, particularly that which we are sometimes inclined to term 'the new biography' – the real objective of the biographer becomes that of writing not merely the story of a life, but rather of *life-writing*.[32]

Woolf's much-quoted assertion, in her essay 'Mr Bennett and Mrs Brown', that 'on or about December 1910 human character changed',[33] has been understood as her way of marking the birth of the modern, using the date of the first Post-Impressionist exhibition in London, which could be said to have changed modes of perception. Less attention, perhaps, has been paid to the fact that Woolf marks historical change in and through an alteration in 'character'. Modernism (though the term had not fully entered the critical and cultural lexicon) for Woolf, as for so many of her contemporaries, thus becomes strongly identified with questions of subjectivity, and with the problematic of representing 'character' or 'personality'. Her essay is a rejoinder to Arnold Bennett's claims that the moderns, or in Woolf's appellation, 'the Georgians', are incapable of representing 'character': Woolf plays with the complexities and multiple definitions of 'character', linking the term at one point to 'the character of one's cook', so that 'character' shades off into 'character-reference', the implication being that the Edwardians – Wells, Bennett, Galsworthy – depict their fictional characters in ways that look more like references or testimonials than they do depictions of complex modern subjectivities.

'Mr Bennett and Mrs Brown' is also a commentary on the 'new biography' in that it includes Lytton Strachey as one of the Georgians, alongside Forster, Eliot, Joyce and Lawrence, finding in his work a radicalism and an aesthetics of rupture that, by contrast with that of the poets and novelists, it has not, perhaps, fully retained. Woolf is by no means uncritical of the moderns (Strachey included), finding their destruction of tradition and convention a necessary way of breaking with outworn conventions, and yet damaging to the relationship and dialogue between writer and reader that is for her the point and purpose of the literary text:

> Again, in Mr Strachey's books, *Eminent Victorians* and *Queen Victoria*, the effort and strain of writing against the grain and current of the times is visible too. It is much less visible, of course, for not only is he dealing with facts, which are stubborn things, but he has fabricated, chiefly from eighteenth-century material, a very discreet code of manner of his own, which allows him to sit at table with the highest in the land and to say a great many things under cover of that exquisite apparel which, had they gone naked, would

have been chased by the men-servants from the room. Still, if you compare *Eminent Victorians* with some of Lord Macaulay's essays, though you will feel that Lord Macaulay is always wrong, and Mr Strachey is always right, you will also feel a body, a sweep, a richness in Lord Macaulay's essays which show that his age was behind him; all his strength went straight into his work; none was used for purposes of concealment or of conversion. But Mr Strachey has had to open our eyes before he made us see; he has had to search out and sew together a very artful manner of speech; and the effort, beautifully though it is concealed, has robbed his work of some of the force that should have gone into it, and limited his scope.[34]

For Woolf, the Georgians are transitional writers, and their production of 'the spasmodic, the obscure, the fragmentary, the failure' is to be tolerated because it heralds a new age – 'we are trembling on the verge of one of the great ages of English literature. But it can only be reached if we are determined never, never to desert Mrs Brown.'[35] 'Mrs Brown' becomes the figure of 'character' itself: female (as, Woolf hints, the future of fiction may well be) and at once elusive and deeply grounded in experience. The failure of writers adequately to represent 'character' resides, Woolf suggests, in a failure to measure up to the complex subjectivity to which we all have access. Thus, Woolf reminds her 'common reader':

> You have gone to bed at night bewildered by the complexities of your feelings. In one day thousands of ideas have coursed through your brains; thousands of emotions have met, collided, and disappeared in astonishing disorder. Nevertheless, you allow the writers to palm off on you a version of all this, an image of Mrs Brown, which has no likeness to that surprising apparition whatsoever.[36]

Whereas Forster was to claim that we know fictional characters more fully than we do individuals in the world, Woolf represents the self as the source of, and resource for, our knowledge of the inner life.

The growing impact of psychological and psychoanalytic theories on literary creation and criticism clearly played a central role in shaping the 'new biography' and its emphases on identity rather than event or action. The self-consciousness about form exhibited by biographers is accompanied by the perception, as in 'Mr Bennett and Mrs Brown', that the appropriate measure of psychological complexity in depicting the life of another is the psychological and experiential complexity of the biographer's own existence. 'Consider one's own life', 'Think of your own life', Virginia Woolf and André Maurois respectively enjoined, the one depicting the failure of Victorian biography to grasp and represent lived experience, the other arguing against the view that the self is reducible to a 'scientific' knowledge of its parts. Gamaliel Bradford referred to 'the immediate personal concern that accounts for our passionate interest in formal biography', while Emil Ludwig argued, in a slightly different vein, that the biographer 'must always perceive the rhapsody of his own life as though it were foreign to him ... If he is to make copies of men, he must see himself mirrored in mankind. It is not until his own life appears to him as symbolic that he is prepared to discern the symbolism behind the lives of others.'[37] Biography, it could be said, begins with self-analysis.

The distinction between biography and autobiography, which had become more marked in the course of the nineteenth century, thus becomes in some ways less absolute. A hundred years previously biography had been the parent genre, with 'self-biography' as a sub-genre in which biographical representation was turned, unusually, upon the self.[38] In the early twentieth century, either autobiographical consciousness, with its difficult self-exploration, has become a first reference point, or the two forms – biography and autobiography – are seen as equiprimordial.

The intense focus on 'character' in biography and in fiction also has an etymological dimension. The term 'character' stems from the Greek *kharratein*: to engrave. In Woolf's writing there is a recurrent play on 'character' as a printing term, and on the relationship between 'character' and 'type' – as deployed in one of her own 'biographical' experiments, *Jacob's Room* – to subvert received definitions of 'character' as psychological 'type' and to explore the concept of reading character as one would read a map or navigate a city. The novel also explores – as do *Mrs Dalloway, To the Lighthouse* and *The Years* – the question of what survives us, of how and on what we make our mark, inscribe our 'character'. In a different way, an implicit understanding of 'character' as mark or sign emerges in that aspect of the 'new biography' most prominent in North American contexts, in which an idealized model of essential selfhood replaces Stracheyan scepticism. 'Character' becomes inseparable from a concept of the permanency of 'impression' that was central to the Psychical Researchers of the late nineteenth and early twentieth centuries, whose claims for the afterlife were strongly predicated on the notion of 'a transcendental energy in living men' and 'an influence emanating from personalities which have overpassed the tomb'.[39] The widespread turn to Psychical Research and spiritualism more generally during and after the mass slaughter of World War One made its own mark on biography, although it could be said that biography has always been a 'haunted' form of writing, imparting a (textual) afterlife to the dead. Thus, James C. Johnston asserts: 'There can be only one legitimate purpose for biography of any kind: to keep alive the man's individuality', and he refers approvingly to Laura Spencer Portor's *Haunted Lives*:

> The key to a life, insists Laura Spencer Portor ... lies in the fact that all lives are 'haunted' by certain recurrent thoughts, influences, impressions, or realization, which, if the biographer will but seize and present to his readers, will leave a picture that no number of dates, or even events, can succeed in bringing to our minds ... the extent to which character is capable of crystallizing would obligate the biographer in any sort of method he might choose to see to it that his story possesses as much unity at least as the life itself holds.[40]

Bradford's 'psychography' (also the term applied by George Saintsbury to Sainte-Beuve's biographical writings) is equally predicated on the concept of a 'crystallizing' of character born out of 'recurrence':

> Out of the perpetual flux of actions and circumstances that constitutes a man's whole life, it seeks to extract what is essential, what is permanent and so vitally characteristic ... As we observe the actions of different men, we find that they follow certain comparatively definite lines, which we call habits ... The generalization of these habits of action, sometimes expressing itself very obscurely and imperfectly for the acute observer in features and manifestations of the body, constitutes what we call qualities. And the complex of qualities in turn forms the fleeting and uncertain total which we sum up in the word 'character' ... Character, then, is the sum of qualities or generalized habits of action. Psychography is the condensed, essential, artistic presentation of character.[41]

Underlying Bradford's aesthetics of biography – caught somewhat uneasily between concepts of the self as fixed or as fluid – we can glimpse the psychology of William James, with its double focus on the fixities of habitual action, in which semi-permanent traces are laid down in the mental mechanism through repetition and we become almost immutably what we are, and on the flux and flow of consciousness, in which there is no repetition: '*no state once gone can recur and be identical with what it was before ... What is got twice is the* same OBJECT ... our state of mind is never precisely the same.'[42] 'Habit has a physical basis', James insists, and the turn of biographers such as Bradford to habitual action as a key to character is frequently accompanied by an emphasis on habitual gesture, the authenticity of which is grounded in its non-volitional, automatic character. For Emil Ludwig, 'a man's daily habits ... were formerly inserted like curiosities, little bonbons for the reader's palate ... For us, today, the most trivial habit will often suggest the interpretation for some major trait of character.'[43] 'I long since learned', Bradford writes, 'that such material as the fifteen volumes of Sumner's collected works was of little or no value for my purposes. Again, a careless word, spoken with no intention whatever, a mere gesture, the lifting of the hand or the turning of the head, may fling open a wide window into a man's inmost heart.'[44] The perception of gesture as the mark of the uniqueness of the individual finds its more radical echo in the Freudian concept of the symptomatic gesture, and of bodies that speak the truths that minds disallow or disavow.

The intense focus on the gesture and the detail in the 'new biography' can work to 'crystallize' or essentialize 'character', as in the work of Ludwig (for whom, famously, the motive and meaning of Wilhelm II's life are concentrated in his withered arm and the 'inferiority complex' to which it led[45]) or, as in the far more radical and subversive writings of Strachey, to unravel identities. At the close of his *Queen Victoria*, Strachey undoes 'the life' by having the dying Queen remember her experiences in reverse chronology, turning back:

> To the Spring woods at Osborne, so full of primroses for Lord Beaconsfield – to Lord Palmerston's queer clothes and high demeanour, and Albert's face under the green lamp, and Albert's first stag at Balmoral, and Albert in his blue and silver uniform, and the Baron coming in through a doorway, and Lord M. dreaming at Windsor with the rooks cawing in the elm-trees, and the Archbishop of Canterbury on his knees in the dawn, and the old King's turkey-cock ejaculations, and Uncle Leopold's soft voice at Claremont, and Lehzen with the globes, and her mother's feathers sweeping down towards her, and a great old repeater-watch of her father's in its tortoise-shell case, and a yellow rug, and some friendly flounces of sprigged muslin, and the trees and the grass at Kensington.[46]

The passage is cinematic in its use of visual images and close-up techniques, and in its replaying in reverse time and motion of all that lived and biographical time have constructed. The images of childhood are at one and the same time enlarged and miniaturized, in accord with Susan Stewart's claim that 'we imagine childhood as if it were at the other end of a tunnel – distanced, diminutive, and clearly framed'.[47] Strachey also opens up an interior world conventionally reserved for the novelist, in which the subject is returned to her beginning, restoring, as Freud described the processes of the 'death drive', 'an earlier state of things'.

Strachey's use of detail also serves to make strange the familiar, and his biographical representations often take on a grotesque and even surreal aspect. The sketch of Lady Hester Stanhope, published in *Books and Characters* (1922), for example, opens thus:

The Pitt nose has a curious history. One can watch its transmigrations through three lives. The tremendous hook of old Lord Chatham, under whose curve Empires came to birth, was succeeded by the bleak upward-pointing nose of William Pitt the younger – the rigid symbol of an indomitable *hauteur*. With Lady Hester Stanhope came the final stage. The nose, still with an upward tilt in it, had lost its masculinity; the hard bones of the uncle and the grandfather had disappeared. Lady Hester's was a nose of wild ambitions, of pride grown fantastical, a nose that scorned the earth, shooting off, one fancies, towards some eternally eccentric heaven. It was a nose, in fact, altogether in the air.[48]

As Ruth Hoberman argues, Lady Hester's 'nose', although theoretically a synecdoche (the figure of speech in which part stands for whole) in fact operates metonymically, in 'a part-part, not part-whole relation to her self, suggesting her own alienated relationship to her society and her self'.[49] The biographical portrait closes with Lady Hester 'lying back in her bed – inexplicable, grand, preposterous, with her nose in the air'.[50] The part or detail – which, in the writings of Ludwig or Bradford, would ideally serve to represent the whole self – is here rendered 'inexplicable', excessive and absurd. In a related way, Strachey uses synecdoche in *Eminent Victorians* to undermine monumental ambition; the parts bring down (rather than represent or stand for) the whole. Hence Lytton Strachey's description of Cardinal Manning's 'remains':

> The Cardinal's memory is a dim thing today. And he who descends into the crypt of that cathedral which Manning never lived to see, will observe, in the quiet niche with the sepulchral monument, that the dust lies thick on the strange, the incongruous, the almost impossible object which, with its elaborations of dependent tassels, hangs down from the dim vault like some forlorn and forgotten trophy – the Hat.[51]

Synecdoche, the central device of Stracheyan biography, is also, in Domna Stanton's phrase, 'the idiolect of dandyism'.[52] 'Camp', Susan Sontag wrote, 'is the modern dandyism. Camp is the answer to the problem: how to be a dandy in an age of mass culture'.[53] Numerous biographies of the 1920s and 1930s, including those of Lytton Strachey and André Maurois, adopt the dandiacal or the 'camp' style, or take as their subjects figures such as Disraeli and Byron, whose 'dandyism' was combined with a fierce commitment to poetry and to politics. The status of the biographical subject – his factuality as well as his genius – secures the biography for literature and for history, while the style of many 'new biographies' allows them a share in the popularity of historical romances. One answer to the problem of 'how to be a dandy in an age of mass culture' was to become a 'new biographer'.

Against the high seriousness of Victorian biography, the 'new biography', of which Strachey's texts are the chief exemplars, is most typically defined by its uses of satire and irony. This essay has discussed some of the characteristic devices of early twentieth-century biography: shifts in size and scale, pointing up the relativity of the subject's status and value; a focus on the detail and the gesture. These related devices indicated, I have argued elsewhere, an uneasy relationship to the 'Great Man', his alternate elevation and diminution signalling an oscillation between hero worship and debunking.[54] To this I would add that the eccentricities of focus and of the imputation of value, and the homing in on the detail, are also defining details of camp style. As Andrew Ross writes in his essay 'Uses of Camp': 'Camp . . . involves a celebration, on the part of cognoscenti, of the alienation, distance and incongruity reflected in the very process by which hitherto unexpected value can be located in some obscure or exorbitant object.'[55] The Nose and the Hat, we could say, function as just such objects in Strachey's writings.

For a fuller exploration of the biographer as dandy we can now turn to the work of A.J.A. Symons. In a 1929 essay on 'Tradition in Biography', Symons argued against 'the timeworn chronological formula' of traditional biography in favour of a more 'telling order'[56]:

> The easiest, and one of many sound ways, is to lift the curtains on a hero fully developed and manifesting the idiosyncrasies which make him worth writing about, to follow his career until its end, illustrating meanwhile the changing of his character with the years; and then, at the finishing, to retrace the steps by which he had become what, in the first chapter, he was shown as being.[57]

The book for which A.J.A. Symons – dandy, bibliophile and self-styled 'speculator' – is best known is his 1932 biography of Frederick Rolfe, the turn-of-the-century writer and 'spoiled priest' who took as his alias 'Baron Corvo'. Symons called his text *The Quest for Corvo: An Experiment in Biography*: in the use of the term 'experiment' he was drawing attention, he wrote in a prefatory note, to his attempt 'to fulfil those standards which I endeavoured to set up in an essay on biographical tradition published by the Oxford University Press in 1929'. The nature of the 'experiment' lay to an extent in its ostensible indifference to chronology: Symons wrote that his interest 'in the early years of the eminent is far less than that which the tradition of biographical writing painfully imposes on its devotees' and that 'it is possible to reason backwards as well as forwards, to infer the child from the man; and I proposed to do so'.[58] This experimentation is more substantially based, however, in the foregrounding of the biographer's quest for his subject. This method (which, according to Symons's own biographer, his brother Julian Symons, writing in 1950, was 'emulated very little by later biographers'[59]) was in fact adopted by a number of late twentieth-century biographers, including Richard Holmes and Peter Ackroyd. The trope of detection enters in the image of one man tracking another across the territory, following (in) his footsteps. The elements which become more or less explicit are firstly, the biographer's identification with or desire for the subject whom he pursues, and, secondly, the nature of the 'evidence' and the means of its gathering.

For Symons, biographical desire is textually mediated through the friend (Christopher Millard, former secretary to Oscar Wilde's friend Robert Ross) by whom he is introduced to Rolfe's work. He opens his biography in this way:

> My quest for Corvo was started by accident one summer afternoon in 1925, in the company of Christopher Millard. We were sitting lazily in his little garden, talking of books that miss their just reward of praise and influence. I mentioned *Wylder's Hand*, by Le Fanu, a masterpiece of plot, and the *Fantastic Fables* of Ambrose Bierce. After a pause, without commenting on my examples, Millard asked: 'Have you read *Hadrian the Seventh*?' I confessed that I never had; and to my surprise he offered to lend me his copy – to my surprise, for my companion lent his books seldom and reluctantly. But, knowing the range of his knowledge of out-of-the-way literature, I accepted without hesitating; and by doing so took the first step on a trail that led into very strange places.[60]

The biography draws to a close with Symons's account of his meetings with one Maundy Gregory, a man fabulously but mysteriously wealthy, who is possessed, for a time at least, by a fascination with Rolfe's writings. Symons recounts his amazement when Gregory hands him one of Rolfe's missing novels: 'It had been found, I gathered, by one of his many 'agents' who, at considerable cost, had traced the original printer, and from the depths of a rat-haunted cellar salved five copies, the only survivors of the whole edition.' The biographical 'quest' Symons describes is a search for both 'the life' of Frederick Rolfe and for his lost manuscripts; the biography ends with Symons's discovery of the final missing novel 'in the depths of a literary agent's cupboard'.

> It was a deep satisfaction still to know that every one of the works which had been left and lost in obscurity when Frederick William Serafino Austin Lewis Mary Rolfe died suddenly and alone at Venice had been collected together by sympathetic hands, and that, alone, of living men, I had read every one. Nothing was left to be discovered; the Quest was ended. Hail, strange

tormented spirit, in whatever hell or heaven has been allotted for your
everlasting rest![61]

The biographical 'quest' is thus displaced onto the bibliographical search
and, with the discovery of the final missing manuscript, Rolfe can be laid
to rest.

Symons's own history in part explains the shift to bibliographical concerns. He was the largely self-taught son of a 'speculator' father and, as a
young man, 'spent hours in practising calligraphy, copying page after page
from the *Dictionary of National Biography* until he had achieved a tiny,
crabbed but beautiful Gothic script'.[62] (It is a nice irony that this 'new
biographer' invents his personal, decadent style by means of the *DNB*.) His
first entrepreneurial ventures included the creation of the First Edition Club
in the early 1920s, during which time he worked on a 'Nineties
Bibliography' and befriended the booksellers William and Gilbert Foyle,
who had opened a Rare Book Department in their bookshop and, in 1923,
became partners in the First Edition Club. Symons's first work on Rolfe
appeared in a paper delivered at a meeting of Ye Sette of Odd Volumes, 'a
select and distinguished dining Club', according to Julian Symons, and
subsequently published in Desmond MacCarthy's magazine *Life and
Letters*.

Symons died in 1941 at the age of 41, before completing a biography of
Oscar Wilde in which, Julian Symons writes, 'he planned to show the
distant world of the nineties in which Wilde achieved his successes of
conversation, drama and self-advertisement, and which he shocked by his
homosexuality'.[63] A.J.A. Symons was motivated to write a definitive life of
Wilde, his brother asserts, when he 'began to consider seriously the art of
biography and decided that English biography "has failed in beauty as in
truth"'. Although he gathered a vast amount of material, including the
'Wildeana' coming onto the collector's market, the writing of the life did
not come easily, and only five chapters had been written by the time of his
death. Wilde, or what he represented, was none the less central to Symons.
Wilde's son, Vyvyan Holland, remained a close friend after his encounter
with Symons at The First Edition Club in 1922, the meeting with which
Julian Symons opens the story of his brother's life. The reader's first image
of A.J.A. Symons – 'a very tall, thin young man, wearing a lavender-
coloured suit of an advanced cut', framed in the doorway – thus comes as
if through the eyes of Oscar Wilde's son.[64]

Rolfe and his biographer walk one of the more 'out of the way' paths of
literary history, as their *sui generis* status as writers might seem to preclude

them from functioning as representative texts. But the nexus of Rolfe and Symons, as well as Julian Symons's biography, opens up important aspects of early twentieth-century biography and its reception. Firstly, it emerged along with the new book clubs and literary venues of the 1920s, which were in many cases touched with the aesthetic and aristocratic hedonisms of the late nineteenth century, but were also part of a new commercial and literary culture. Secondly, for the collectors Symons mentions, the 1890s and its literary objects are the primary foci of bibliophilia, and the figure and image of Wilde are central. While Symons represents Rolfe's homosexuality as a fatal flaw and the source of his ruination, the milieu for and in which Symons writes is markedly homosocial. Books are the traffic between men, and biography in this period – which, despite the significant presence of women biographers, is almost always represented in the terms of one man writing the life of another – becomes a particularly charged genre.[65] The belief, imputed to Symons by his brother, that the problems of achieving beauty and truth in biography might be tested, if not resolved, through a biography of Wilde, is a telling one, suggesting a continuity between the *fin de siècle* and the 'new biography' of the 1920s and 1930s in ways which also bear on the periodizing of modernism more broadly.

This moment in literary and cultural history also relates to the ways in which norms of 'proper' masculinity (and femininity) and the moral imperatives of the established 'life course' so central to Victorian biography are radically disrupted in certain texts of the new biography. Symons's eschewal of chronology is not just a formal question; the more 'telling order' which he holds that the biographer should pursue disturbs conventional notions of formation and achievement. As William Epstein notes, Lytton Strachey showed, in his *Eminent Victorians*, how '"obscure recesses, hitherto undivined" divert the course of the miraculously lamplit pathway of the professional career'.[66]

Deviations from the conventional life-course are explored by Woolf in 'The New Biography' and in a later essay, 'The Art of Biography', in which she focuses on Lytton Strachey's writings. She argues that the biographer should not flout the law of factuality, but should exploit the 'proper creativeness' of 'fact', for facts, like fictions, are open to multiple interpretations. They are also subject to historical contingency and change and, as she writes in 'The Art of Biography', to 'changes of opinion: opinions change as the times change':

> What was thought a sin is now known, by the light of facts won for us by the psychologists, to be perhaps a misfortune; perhaps a curiosity, perhaps

neither one nor the other, but a trifling foible of no great importance one way
or the other. The accent on sex has changed within living memory. This
leads to the destruction of a great deal of dead matter still obscuring the true
features of the human face. Many of the old chapter headings – life at college,
marriage, career – are shown to be very arbitrary and artificial distinctions.
The real current of the hero's existence took, very likely, a different course.

    Thus the biographer must go ahead of the rest of us, like the miner's
canary, testing the atmosphere, detecting falsity, unreality, and the presence
of obsolete conventions. His sense of truth must be alive and on tiptoe.
Then again, since we live in an age when a thousand cameras are pointed, by
newspapers, letters, and diaries, at every character from every angle, he must
be prepared to admit contradictory versions of the same face. Biography will
enlarge its scope by hanging up looking glasses at odd corners. And yet from
all this diversity it will bring out, not a riot of confusion, but a richer
unity.[67]

The passage (and the essay from which it was drawn) raises a number of
crucial points, which I will use to address some remaining questions and
issues.

Woolf's allusion to the pointing cameras is a reminder that the 'new
biography' developed alongside the new media of the early twentieth
century. There are important connections to be made between biography
and the new arts of publicity and journalism that were also devoted to the
representations of lives, though in ways that often appeared to threaten
biography as a high-art form. The emergent art of film is a further crucial
context.[68] It may be that the 'new biography' is inflected by the cinematic
devices of detail, gesture and close-up and by cinematic subversions of linear
time and chronology (in, for example, parallel editing or flashback), but we
might also note the ways in which film borrowed from biography the
trajectory of a life as an appropriate cinematic theme and structuring
principle. Mark Longaker, writing in 1934, noted:

> In the past decade, the drama and the motion pictures have shown an
> unprecedented interest in the lives and personalities of historical figures . . .
> George Arliss's characterizations of Alexander Hamilton, Disraeli, and
> Voltaire; and Hartau's admirable interpretation of character in the French
> film *Napoleon* indicated that the motion pictures may in time afford an
> excellent medium not only for popularizing biography, but also for creating a
> vivid kind of portraiture.[69]

The second issue that concerns us here is Woolf's allusion to the changed
'accent on sex'. The example she gives of the changing nature of 'fact' is, we
can assume, the 'fact' of (homo)sexuality, while the passage serves to erode
the absolute nature of sexual difference: 'neither one nor another . . . of no

great importance one way or the other'. Woolf's own mock-biography *Orlando* which is, in Leon Edel's words, 'a fable for biographers',[70] stretches the boundaries of the individual beyond breaking-point: Orlando is alive during the three centuries of text-time, first as a man and then as a woman. Lytton Strachey's *Elizabeth and Essex*, published in the same year, suggests that the sexual identity of the Queen is ambiguous – 'was she a man?' – and turns to a Freudianism which tells a story in which the (male) child, when confronted with a naked Queen or a naked mother, will rapidly endow her with the 'manhood' she is observed to lack, made out of the materials of appearance: 'the huge hoop, the stiff ruff, the swollen sleeves, the powdered pearls, the spreading, gilded gauzes'.[71] Both *Orlando* and *Elizabeth and Essex* were strongly influenced by and contributed to contemporary debates about androgyny and sexual identity.

Woolf was, nonetheless, critical of *Elizabeth and Essex*, deeming it a failure. She does not refer to Strachey's use of psychoanalysis in the text, though his 'psychobiographical' portrait of Elizabeth met with Freud's full approval. As Freud wrote to Strachey:

> You are aware of what other historians so easily overlook – that it is impossible to understand the past with certainty, because we cannot divine men's motives and the essence of their minds and so cannot interpret their actions. With regard to the people of past times we are in the same position as with dreams to which we have been given no associations – and only a lay man could expect us to interpret such dreams as these. As a historian, then, you show that you are steeped in the spirit of psychoanalysis. And with reservations such as these, you have approached one of the most remarkable figures in your country's history, you have known how to trace back her character to the impressions of her childhood, you have touched upon her most hidden motives with equal boldness and discretion, and it is very possible that you have succeeded in making a correct reconstruction of what actually occurred.[72]

Freudian sexual theories provided Strachey with one answer to the question posed in *Elizabeth and Essex*: 'By what art are we to worm our way into those strange spirits, those even stranger projects?'[73] The 'correct reconstruction' of Elizabeth's motives and inner life is made through the 'universal story', the Oedipus legend. Yet Strachey also pursues a deviation from the life-course inscribed by the Oedipus narrative itself, a deviation generated by his explorations of women with power. As Perry Meisel notes, 'the book's psychoanalytic project is its beginning, not its end'.[74]

Strachey and Freud were, it could be argued, the two primary influences on biography in the 1920s, and their interrelation has a central bearing on the history of the British reception of psychoanalysis and of English-language Freud, with James Strachey, Lytton's brother, largely responsible for the work of translation. Biography was one of the major conduits by means of which psychoanalytic theory reached a general readership, and responses to Freud, positive and negative, emerged to a very large extent as responses to the new ways in which 'lives' were represented and interpreted. Freud was in fact notoriously ambivalent towards biography, warning his would-be biographer Arnold Zweig that 'biographical truth does not exist and if it did we could not use it',[75] but writing to Jung in 1909 that 'We [the psychoanalytic movement] must take hold of biography'.[76] Freud also produced the first 'psychobiography' in his *Leonardo da Vinci and a Memory of his Childhood* (1910), the text in which he also gives his most sustained account of biography as a genre, including the distortions caused by the biographer's identifications with and idealizations of his subject, using biographical speculation in, paradoxically, the service of 'correct reconstruction'. Freud, the founder of psychoanalysis, is also the founder of psychoanalytic biography as a genre.

The development of 'psychobiography', strongest in the United States, is a crucial aspect of the history of the 'new biography'. While a number of biographers in the 1920s retained a critical distance from Freudian theory, others, in John Garraty's words, 'began to see the possibilities – the insights into hidden motives, the escape from the limits of "factual" biography, the sensationalism inherent in an approach that emphasized sex, with its healthy effects on sales'.[77] Garraty, like many biographical critics, is clearly sceptical about the development of psychobiography. The sustained attacks on Freudian biography in the 1930s might well have contributed to its decline (though it remerged in the United States under the influence of ego-psychology): Bernard DeVoto's influential and highly positivist critique, for example, described psychobiography as an approximation to 'the art of the detective story, whose clues are also invented and whose deductions are also made to fit'.[78] The Freudian biography of the 1920s and 1930s may now seem both quaint and absurd, but there are surely interesting dimensions to the desire for and fascination with the new method by means of which lives could be told differently, and the texts of this period also made their contribution to the deeply imbricated histories of biography and of psychoanalysis.

In conclusion, I would suggest that the phenomenon of the 'new biography' and the significance of biography in the first decades of the century are not exhausted topics. Any attempt to reconstruct the priorities of early twentieth-century literary culture would need to give biography a much more central place than it has as yet received in literary and cultural histories. I have examined some of the preoccupations of biographers and their readers, including the focus on 'character' and 'personality' as a way of inscribing a 'modern' subjectivity. I have also suggested that the category of the 'new biography' often serves to hold together writers and texts with attitudes towards this subjectivity that are widely opposed. In looking at such questions, we begin to open up the complexity of the culture and the politics of biography, and the value of their further exploration.

Notes

1 The fullest recent account of early twentieth-century biography is Ruth Hoberman's *Modernizing Lives: Experiments in English Biography, 1918–1939* (Carbondale and Edwardsville: Southern Illinois University Press, 1987). Max Saunders' important study *Self-Impression: Life-Writing, Autobiografiction and the Forms of Modern Literature* (Oxford: Oxford University Press, 2010) is predominantly concerned with autobiography, but also contains extensive discussion of late nineteenth- and twentieth-century biographical writings. See also Richard D. Altick, *Lives and Letters: A History of Literary Biography in England and America* (New York: Greenwood Press, 1979); Ira Bruce Nadel, *Biography: Fiction, Fact and Form* (London: Macmillan, 1984); Perry Meisel, *The Myth of the Modern* (New Haven: Yale University Press, 1987); William H. Epstein, *Recognizing Biography* (Philadelphia: University of Pennsylvania Press, 1987); Leon Edel, *Writing Lives* (New York: Norton, 1984); John Garraty, *The Nature of Biography* (New York: Knopf, 1957).
2 Hesketh Pearson, *Ventilations: Being Biographical Asides*, quoted in Altick, *Lives and Letters*, p. 289.
3 David Cecil, 'Introduction' in *An Anthology of Modern Biography* (London: Nelson, 1936), p. ix.
4 Siegfried Kracauer, 'The Biography as an Art Form of the New Bourgeoisie' (1930), in *The Mass Ornament: Weimar Essays*, edited and translated by Thomas Y. Levin (Cambridge, MA: Harvard University Press, 1995), p. 103.
5 George Alexander Johnston, 'The New Biography: Ludwig, Maurois and Strachey', *The Atlantic Monthly* 143 (March 1929), p. 133.
6 Mark Longaker, *Contemporary Biography* (Philadelphia: University of Pennsylvania Press, 1934), p. 20.
7 Emil Ludwig, 'Introduction: On Historical Portraiture', *Genius and Character* (New York: Harcourt Brace and Co, 1927), pp. 13–17.
8 Altick, *Lives and Letters*, p. 289.
9 Desmond MacCarthy, 'Lytton Strachey and the Art of Biography', in *Memories* (London: MacGibbon and Kee, 1953), p. 37.
10 Lytton Strachey, *Eminent Victorians* (Oxford: Oxford University Press, 2003), p. 5.
11 Ibid., p. 5.
12 Ibid., p. 5–6.

13 Emil Ludwig, *Genius and Character* (London: Jonathan Cape, 1930), p. 14.

14 Havelock Ellis, 'An Open Letter to Biographers', in *Selected Essays* (London: Dent, 1936), p. III.

15 Harold Nicolson, *The Development of English Biography* (London: Hogarth Press, 1928), p. 135.

16 Ibid., p. 154.

17 Ibid., pp. 139–143.

18 Ibid., pp. 154–155.

19 André Maurois, *Aspects of Biography*, translated by S. C. Roberts (London: Appleton, 1929), p. 38.

20 Ibid., pp. 71–72.

21 Ibid., p. 103.

22 Virginia Woolf, 'The New Biography', in *The Essays of Virginia Woolf*, vol. 4, edited by Andrew McNeillie (London: The Hogarth Press, 1994), p. 473.

23 Nigel Nicolson, 'Introduction', in Harold Nicolson, *Some People* (Oxford: Oxford University Press, 1983), p. vii.

24 Woolf, 'The New Biography', p. 478.

25 Ibid., p. 478.

26 E. M. Forster, *Aspects of the Novel* (Harmondsworth: Penguin, 1990), p. 70.

27 Ibid., p. 69.

28 George Johnston, 'The New Biography', pp. 333–334.

29 Woolf, 'The New Biography', p. 478.

30 Gamaliel Bradford, *Wives* (New York: Harper, 1925), p. 12.

31 Ibid.

32 James C. Johnston, *Biography: the Literature of Personality* (New York: Century, 1927), pp. 18–19.

33 Virginia Woolf, 'Character in Fiction' (1924), in *The Essays of Virginia Woolf*, vol. 3, 1919–1924, pp. 420–438, 421.

34 Ibid., pp. 85–86.

35 Ibid., p. 87.

36 Ibid., p. 86.

37 Ludwig, *Genius and Character*, pp. 18–19.

38 See my discussion of the history of the autobiographical genre, and of autobiographical criticism, in Laura Marcus, *Auto/biographical Discourses: Theory, Criticism, Practice* (Manchester University Press, 1994), especially chapter I.

39 F. W. H. Myers, *Human Personality and its Survival of Bodily Death* (1903) (Norwich: Pilgrim Books, 1992), p. 173.

40 Johnston, *Biography: The Literature of Personality*, p. 242.

41 Gamaliel Bradford, *A Naturalist of Souls* (Boston: Houghton Mifflin, 1926), pp. 5–8.

42 William James, *Text Book of Psychology* (London: Macmillan, 1904), pp. 154–156. Italics in original.

43 Ludwig, *Genius and Character*, p. 16.

44 Bradford, *A Naturalist of Souls*, p. 13.

45 Emil Ludwig, *Kaiser Wilhelm II*, translated by Ethel Colburn Mayne (London: Putnam, 1926). Freud used Ludwig's biography of Wilhelm II to point up the inadequacy of the term 'inferiority complex', which 'haunts the pages of what are known as *belles letters*. An author who uses the term "inferiority complex" thinks that by so doing he has fulfilled all the demands of psycho-analysis and has raised his composition to a higher psychological plane. In fact, "inferiority complex" is a technical term that is scarcely used in psycho-analysis ... A historical personage of our own days, who is still alive though at the moment he has retired into the background, suffers from a defect in one of his limbs owing to an injury at the time of his birth. A very well-known contemporary writer who is particularly fond of compiling the biographies of celebrities has dealt, among others, with the life of the man I am speaking of [Ludwig's *Wilhelm II*]. Now in writing a biography it may well be difficult to suppress a need to plumb the psychological depths. For this reason our author has ventured on an attempt to erect the whole of the development of his hero's character on the sense of inferiority which must have been called up by his physical defect. In doing so, he has overlooked one small but not insignificant fact. It is usual for mothers whom Fate has presented with a child who is sickly or otherwise at a disadvantage to try to compensate him for his unfair handicap by a superabundance of love. In the instance before us, the proud mother behaved otherwise; she withdrew her love from the child on account of his infirmity. When he had grown up into a man of great power, he proved unambiguously by his actions that he had never forgiven his mother. When you consider the importance of a mother's love for the mental life of a child, you will no doubt make a tacit correction of the biographer's inferiority theory.' Freud, *New Introductory Lectures*, SE, pp. 65–66. Freud thus uses psychoanalytic theory to 'correct' Ludwig's inadequate psychoanalytic biography.
46 Lytton Strachey, *Queen Victoria* (1921) (Harmondsworth: Penguin, 1971), p. 246.
47 Susan Stewart, *On Longing* (Baltimore: Johns Hopkins University Press, 1984), p. 44.
48 Strachey, 'Lady Hester Stanhope', in *Books and Characters* (London: Chatto and Windus, 1922), p. 241.
49 Hoberman, *Modernizing Lives*, p. 45.
50 Strachey, *Books and Characters*, p. 249.
51 Strachey, *Eminent Victorians*, p. 108.
52 Domna Stanton, *The Aristocrat as Art* (Columbia: Columbia University Press, 1980), p. 160.
53 Susan Sontag, *Against Interpretation* (New York: Dell, 1966), p. 288.
54 See my essay '"Looking Glasses at Odd Corners": Biography and Psychoanalysis in the Early Twentieth Century', *New Comparison* 25, Spring 1998, 52–70.
55 Andrew Ross, *No Respect: Intellectuals and Popular Culture* (New York and London: Routledge, 1989), p. 146.

56 A. J. A. Symons, 'Tradition in Biography', in *Tradition and Experiment in Present-Day Literature* (Oxford University Press, 1929), p. 155.

57 Ibid., p. 156.

58 A. J. A. Symons, *The Quest for Corvo: An Experiment in Biography* (1934) (London: Quartet, 1993), p. 51.

59 Julian Symons, *A.J.A. Symons: His Life and Speculations* (Oxford University Press, 1986), p. 26.

60 A.J.A. Symons, *The Quest for Corvo*, p. 1.

61 Ibid., p. 283.

62 Julian Symons, *A.J.A. Symons*, p. 27.

63 Ibid., p. 246.

64 Ibid., p. 1.

65 I have not been able to do justice to biographies written by women in this period, which include substantial works by Edith Sitwell, Vita Sackville-West and Helen Waddell, as well as the experiments in life-writing of Gertrude Stein.

66 Epstein, *Recognizing Biography*, p. 148.

67 Woolf, 'The Art of Biography' (1939) *The Essays of Virginia Woolf*, edited by Stuart N. Clark (London: Hogarth Press, 2011), pp. 181–194, 186.

68 George Johnston, 'The New Biography', p. 340.

69 Longaker, *Contemporary Biography*, p. 5.

70 Edel, *Writing Lives*, p. 192.

71 Lytton Strachey, *Elizabeth and Essex* (1928) (Harmondsworth: Penguin, 1971), p. 13.

72 Freud, Letter to Lytton Strachey, 25 December 1928, in *Bloomsbury/Freud: The Letters of James and Alix Strachey 1924–25*, edited by Perry Meisel and Walter Kendrick (New York: Basic Books, 1985), pp. 332–333.

73 Strachey, *Elizabeth and Essex*, p. 12.

74 Meisel, *The Myth of the Modern*, p. 216.

75 Freud wrote to Arnold Zweig, 'Anyone who writes a biography is committed to lies, concealment, hypocrisy, flattery and even to hiding his own lack of understanding, for biographical truth does not exist, and if it did we could not use it.' Freud, Letter to Zweig, 31 May 1936, in *The Letters of Sigmund Freud and Arnold Zweig* edited by Ernst L. Freud (New York: Harcourt Brace Jovanovich, 1970), p. 127.

76 Freud, Letter to Jung, 17 October 1909, in *The Freud/Jung Letters* (abridged), edited by William McGuire (Harmondsworth: Penguin, 1991), p. 161.

77 Garraty, *The Nature of Biography*, p. 116.

78 Bernard DeVoto, 'The Sceptical Biographer', in James L. Clifford (ed.), *Biography as an Art: Selected Criticism 1560–1960* (Oxford University Press, 1962), p. 149.

CHAPTER 8

European Witness
Analysands Abroad in the 1920s and 1930s

The emigration, voluntary or enforced, of psychoanalysts from central Europe to Britain and the US from the 1930s onwards has been explored in depth and detail over the last decades, with important work on, among related topics, 'Freud in exile'.[1] Less fully documented and explored are the experiences, in the 1920s and 1930s, of those British analysands and trainee analysts who travelled to Vienna, Berlin or Budapest in order to be analysed by 'the masters', including Freud in Vienna, Sándor Ferenczi in Budapest, and Karl Abraham and Hanns Sachs in Berlin. While it is recognized that this was a familiar pattern in the training of early British analysts, the particularities of their experiences abroad (as well as those of analysands who were 'patients' rather than 'pupils', to use Freud's distinction) appear not to have been a significant focus of interest. This chapter is a preliminary exploration of this topic, and focuses on the activities of the Stracheys, particularly Alix Strachey, and of the writers Bryher and H.D., in the Berlin of the mid-1920s and the Berlin and Vienna of the late 1920s and early 1930s respectively.

Psychoanalysis developed as an international movement in the first two decades of the twentieth century, with the first International Psycho-Analytic Congress, held in Salzburg in 1908, attended by participants from America (A.A. Brill), Austria, England (Ernest Jones and Wilfred Trotter), Germany, Hungary and Switzerland. (Of the forty participants named by Ernest Jones, there is only one woman, Frieda Gross, wife of the analyst Otto Gross, from Austria.[2]) Jones also notes the occurrence of the first training analysis in 1907, that of Max Eitingon by Freud.[3] Jones himself was a frequent visitor to Vienna, in these early years and beyond; David Eder, with Jones, one of the first medical doctors to use psycho-analysis in his treatment, came to Vienna for a three-week analysis in early 1913, though Freud, too busy with other patients to take him on, referred him to Viktor Tausk.[4] In 1913, Eder also became the Secretary of the newly founded Branch Society in London of the International Association of Psychoanalysis, with Jones as President.

World War One was a period of retrenchment and restricted travel for psychoanalysts, but after the war, and with the extreme conditions of recession in Austria and Germany, it became a matter of necessity for Freud and other analysts to take on as many British and American patients and pupils, who could pay in hard currency, as possible. It was understood that these analysands would also facilitate the international dissemination of psychoanalytic thought and teaching. From the beginning of the 1920s, Freud took, in Jones's words, 'fewer patients, there being so many pupils, mainly from America and England, who wished to learn his technique'.[5] In 1922, Freud established the practice of inviting a number of analysts (in the first year, Karl Abraham, Sándor Ferenczi, Géza Róheim and Hanns Sachs) to come to Vienna to deliver lectures on theoretical topics, to supplement the work undertaken in individual training analyses.

Amongst the British who undertook analysis in Europe were James and Alix Strachey and Edward Glover, who went for training at the newly established Berlin Psychoanalytic Institute in 1921, and for analysis with Karl Abraham, who was also Alix Strachey's analyst in Berlin in the mid-1920s. The Institute, devoted to providing free analysis to patients who could not pay and making training analysis an essential part of its very substantial educational programme, received a large number of foreign visitors for shorter or longer periods and became, in the words of the Norwegian Ola Raknes, 'the central site for psychoanalytic education'.[6] Abraham initiated the lecture programme, to which Sachs made a substantial contribution, along with Horney, Ernst Simmel and others, and visitors including the Hungarian anthropologist and analyst Géza Róheim.

Edward Glover's brother James, who became James Strachey's analyst, was also analysed by Abraham in Berlin. James Glover had taken over the Medico-Psychological Clinic in Brunswick Square in 1918. The first British institution devoted to psychotherapy, including psychoanalytic methods, it was founded in 1913 by Jessie Murray, a doctor and Suffragist, along with her companion Julia Turner and with the financial and administrative involvement of the novelist May Sinclair. By 1917 it was substantially treating shell-shocked soldiers with various forms of physical and psycho-therapeutic treatments, but the need for more psychoanalysts became pressing. For a few years the Medico-Psychological Clinic co-existed alongside the London Psycho-Analytic Society, set up by Dr Ernest Jones in 1913, but it was this organization which finally replaced the Clinic after Jessie Murray's death in 1920.

As Suzanne Raitt notes in her biography of May Sinclair, the 'clinic was quietly repressed from psychoanalytic histories and from analysts' autobiographies'.[7] The Glovers – who became members of the British Psycho-Analytical Society – and Ernest Jones were soon engaged in fierce battles with the British medical establishment to defend the legitimacy of psychoanalysis. The eclectic nature of the institution where so many of their associates had been trained would not have helped their cause, nor would it have legitimized British psychoanalysis in the broader European and US psychoanalytic arenas. The controversy over lay analysis (that is, the legitimacy or otherwise of non-medically trained analysts), for example, was intense in the early 1920s. Raitt also suggests that their cause would not have been helped by the 'dominance in the movement of so many outspoken, intellectual – even, in the case of Murray and Turner, possibly lesbian – women'.[8]

The occlusion of the Clinic from psychoanalytic histories becomes striking when one observes that almost all the most familiar names in early British psychoanalysis were trained there and received their first analysis from Julia Turner. They included James Glover, Ella Freeman Sharpe, Mary Chadwick, Marjorie Brierley, Nina Searl, Sylvia Payne, and Susan Isaacs. A number of these analysts also went abroad for analysis and training. In addition to James and Edward Glover's analyses with Abraham in Berlin, Ella Freeman Sharpe, Sylvia Payne, Barbara Low and Mary Chadwick (the first child-analyst in Britain) were analysed in Berlin by Hanns Sachs. (Earlier, Sharpe and Low had been analysed by Ernest Jones.) Joan Riviere took a different route – she was analysed first by Jones and subsequently by Freud in Vienna.

Paul Roazen records that 'Edward Glover remembered Miss Sharpe in Germany walking along with lilies in her bosom, holding them as if they were a child.'[9] Sharpe, who had started her career as an English teacher and co-head of a Pupil Teacher's Training Centre, came to the Medico-Psychological Clinic in 1917, and went on to analysis with Sachs in Berlin in 1920. She went back as a student to Sachs and to Berlin at frequent intervals, and it was she who arranged for Sachs to visit London in 1924 in order to give the lecture series more famously given by Melanie Klein in Adrian and Karin Stephen's house in 1925 – the year before Klein moved permanently to England. (Sharpe became the analyst of Adrian Stephen, Virginia Woolf's brother, in 1926.)

Hanns Sachs, born in Vienna in 1881, initially trained as a lawyer. In 1904, he came to psychoanalysis through his reading of *The Interpretation of Dreams*. He abandoned his law career in its early stages and followed

Freud into psychoanalytic work, initially through writing and editing and, from 1920 onwards, through the training of analysts, when he was asked by the newly founded Berlin Psychoanalytic Institute to develop the new field of training analysis, including analysing psychoanalysts who were already practising. One of Freud's most trusted colleagues, Sachs became one of the group of seven – the Secret Committee – around Freud. Sachs remained in Berlin until 1932, when he was invited by the Harvard School of Medicine to become a training analyst in Boston, a function he continued until his death in 1947.

Sachs' publications were substantially contributions to applied psycho-analysis. Freud's 'dream book' remained a key text for him, as did the 1908 essay 'Creative Writers and Day-Dreaming'. Fascinated by the applications of psychoanalysis to the creative process and to the reception of works of art, and by the concept of the work of art as a 'collective day-dream', Sachs explored the idea of 'day-dreams in common'. In 1912 Freud entrusted to Sachs and Otto Rank the editing of the newly founded journal *Imago*, intended to develop the application of psychoanalytic knowledge to broader cultural and human-scientific spheres: Sachs continued this publication as *The American Imago* after his move to the U.S. Sachs was also involved in the film culture of Weimar Berlin: the director G.W. Pabst was a close friend. Sachs' cultural and aesthetic preoccupations fed his work with British training analysts such as Ella Sharpe, for whom language and literary representation were central to the understanding of psychic life, and for whom the role of 'sublimation' in creative activity was a life-long preoccupation. Sharpe's essays in the *International Journal of Psychoanalysis* included the 1930 essay 'Certain Aspects of Sublimation and Delusion', an exploration of the origins of, and magical thinking entailed in, the work of art. The essay closes with a discussion of 'the moving picture':

> The resources of science and art here converge in answer to man's deepest necessity and will consummate the most satisfying illusion the world has known. Future generations will be able to see the past as it really was. The great figures will move and live before them as they did even in life. They will speak with their authentic voices. There, in that darkened theatre, with all our knowledge and enlightenments we will not hesitate to reach out a hand through time to the first artist, painting his bison in the dim recesses of the cave.[10]

This relates in significant ways to the preoccupations of Hanns Sachs, as well as to those of the two women writers, Bryher (Winifred Ellerman) and her life-long companion, the American-born poet H.D. (Hilda Doolittle), to whom Sachs became particularly close and on whom the later part of this chapter is focused. Bryher's analysis with Sachs was undertaken as a form of training analysis, although this was not pursued to completion. H.D. was analysed first by Mary Chadwick in London, briefly by Sachs in Berlin and, finally, by Freud in Vienna in 1933–1934. H.D. and Bryher, like many of the British analysts and training analysts, were negotiating European cities in a period of cultural and political ferment, which intensified into the 1930s, and their experiences often brought into sharp relief the relationship between psychic and political life. This was also a time when psychoanalytic ideas about female sexuality, and, more particularly, female homosexuality, were being most fully formulated. The experiences of Bryher and H.D. – who identified as lesbian and as bisexual, respectively – in psychoanalysis, and, more particularly, in the so-called training analyses which might have allowed them to become analysts themselves, raises a number of issues in the history of an institution which has for much of its history excluded lesbians and gay men from its training programmes, and pathologized homosexuality itself. This then raises questions about an openness to difference possibly lost between the destruction of German and then Austrian psychoanalysis with the rise of fascism, and its recreation in Britain and the United States.

The extensive correspondence of H.D. and Bryher, and the other written records which they kept, provide exceptional insight into the period of their analyses. For H.D. in particular, the analytic hour was the central focus of her time in Vienna, but around this there were other hours to fill and routines to establish. The writing she produced during these periods – letters, journals, jottings – became not only a way of recording experience, but also of sustaining identity, as she organized her daily life around her 'hour' and the space of a room. She opened *Tribute to Freud* (1956), her retrospective account of her analysis with Freud, with these words:

> It was Vienna, 1933–1934. I had a room in the Hotel Regina, Freiheitsplatz. I had a small calendar on my table. I counted the days and marked them off, calculating the weeks. My sessions were limited, time went so quickly . . . I went down Berggasse, turned in the familiar entrance, Berggasse 19, Wien 19, it was. There were wide stone steps and a balustrade.[11]

H.D's letters from 1933 to 1934, to Bryher and to other close friends, reveal further dimensions of the relationship she developed with Freud, and of life in Vienna at the time in which National Socialism was rapidly taking hold. The early 1930s were also the years in which Bryher was most extensively committed to psychoanalysis, urging friends towards it (and frequently paying for their sessions), attending psychoanalytic lectures in Berlin and (in 1934) the Psychoanalytic Congress in Lucerne.

The correspondence between H.D. and Bryher in the early 1930s raises, as Susan Stanford Friedman notes, the question of leakage from the analytic encounter, against which Freud had warned in his 1913 essay 'On Beginning the Treatment'.[12] Deliberate preparation for the analytic session was, Freud suggested, a form of 'resistance . . . [which] will see to it that the most valuable material escapes communication'.[13] Such withholding might also be effected by other means. The patient 'may talk over the treatment every day with some intimate friend, and bring into this discussion all the thoughts which should come forward in the presence of the doctor. The treatment thus has a leak which lets through precisely what is most valuable.'[14]

The porosity of the border between the inside and the outside of 'the treatment' is striking in the case of H.D. and Bryher. It also raises broader questions about the communication of material arising in the analytic session to a third party, a topic explored by John Forrester in his work on psychoanalysis as gossip and as telepathy, in which he discusses the existence of a 'semi-permeable membrane' placed around the communication between analyst and analysand.[15] The analyst promises confidentiality to the patient; the patient makes no such explicit assurance, but, as we have seen, the understanding is that he or she will refrain from discussing the analysis with people outside. Gossip (which is explored in this context alongside telepathic communication, a thought-transmission through 'unofficial' channels) is the illicit mode of communication both attendant upon psychoanalysis and acting as threats to the attempt at discursive regulation: 'gossip is the underbelly of analysis, telepathy its shadow', while psychoanalysis is the 'science of gossip'.[16] Moreover, it allows for the possibility of 'gossiping about oneself' – something which, Forrester argues, is impossible in everyday life. The French Lacanian psychoanalyst Serge Leclaire has claimed that in highly psychoanalysed cultures, such as contemporary Paris, 'the question as to what is being said by friends and lovers on their respective couches can take on a greater analytic significance than the traditional Oedipus complex. The structure of gossip here replaces the family structure.'[17] I will return to these issues and to 'the logic of the ménage à trois' – with psychoanalysis as 'a theory of this third party' – in connection with Bryher and H.D.[18]

The Stracheys in Analysis

I want first to turn, more briefly, to one of the most fully documented experiences of the British analysand abroad: that of Alix Strachey (née

Sargeant-Florence), a number of whose letters to her husband James Strachey, written during the period of her analysis with Karl Abraham in 1924–1925, were published in the volume *Bloomsbury/Freud*.[19] The history of the Stracheys' encounter with psychoanalysis bears interestingly on the question of lay analysis in Britain. Ernest Jones, whose commitment to the medical training of analysts ran counter to Freud's own views on the topic, had strongly encouraged James Strachey to take up medical studies; Strachey gave up within a month. In May 1920, Jones wrote to Freud, at James's request, 'to ask if there is any hope of your taking him as for analysis . . . He is a man of 30, well educated and of a well-known literary family (I hope he may assist with translation of your works.')[20] Both James and Alix Strachey were analysed by Freud at this time, journeying to Vienna in 1920. Their translations of Freud's work (upon which James Strachey had in fact embarked before his first meeting with Freud) were to occupy the rest of their lives.

In July 1921 Freud wrote to Ernest Jones: 'Strachey and his wife might become very useful to you. They are exceptionally nice and cultured people though somewhat queer and after having gone through their analysis (what is not yet the case) they may become serious analysts.'[21] Alix's analysis with Freud was severely disrupted by illness – she spent several months in a sanatorium – and in 1924 she took up analysis again, this time with Abraham in Berlin, though this came to an abrupt end when he became seriously ill in 1925 – he died at the end of that year. James Strachey remained in London throughout most of the period of Alix's analysis. It was this separation which occasioned the letters describing Alix's life in Berlin, and James's work as an analyst and translator in London, as well as something of a territorial struggle between them. Alix resisted the idea that James might come for further analysis, either with Abraham in Berlin or with some other 'F-S' (father-surrogate), though he writes, rather pitifully, on 22 November 1924:

> Of course, the real point is that *I* want one *too*. I mean an analysis. For various reasons, also, besides the Lower one. Actually, I'm getting interested in the subject, & find I can't understand it. And also, but this is a secret of the deepest dye, I want to have a baby by you. – And it seems to me such a waste of time not to be being done while you're away, & while, incidentally, the motive's probably stronger.[22]

Life in Berlin itself – Alix was staying in a pension some distance from the centre – is represented by radio-cafés, ballet and theatre, and dances. She came to like and respect Hanns Sachs, but not to enjoy dancing with him:

'Yesterday I went to the *Union Palais de Danse* with Dr Sachs, & we, literally, hopped it together. Ah, well; I'd give a great deal to meet a tall, immaculate Briton in a "Smocking" & glide swiftly with straight knees over an empty, uncarpeted floor to the double rhythm of a saxophone Band.'[23] She wrote enthusiastically of the Russian ballet, of musical concerts and of visits to the Kino, but the balls and café-dances were her most frequent distraction, inadequate dancing partners notwithstanding, and one in which she was often accompanied by Melanie Klein, dressed, as Alix noted, in the style of Cleopatra. 'I had another all-night orgy', she wrote to James on 9 February 1925,

> at the 'Jury-freie' Dance. It was identical with the other Saturday (Frau Klein as Cleo; Simmel; a conversation about ψa [psychoanalysis] with a friend-of-the-sub editor of the *Vossische* [a conservative North German newspaper]; a dance or two in the rotating pack with one or two vague figures; a cup of coffee with a be-spectacled democrat; & a glass of beer (alas, not Sekt) with a paranoiac ex-officer nationalist whose speeches were simply incomprehensible to me from beginning to end & so home, in a tram, at 7.0 a.m.).[24]

The letters reveal the rising influence of Klein, in analysis with Abraham at the same time as Alix Strachey. Alix, indeed, says a good deal more about Klein's new theories than she does about her own analysis with Abraham, to the content of which, and perhaps following the psychoanalytic proscription on 'the leak', she barely refers (at least in the published letters). Her letters are, however, full of analytic gossip – 'fresh gossip', as she terms it[25] – as well as a psychoanalytically inflected commentary on the everyday world of Berlin: the 'radio pastry shop' she frequents 'is exactly like a Hitschmann diagram of the dream-mechanism, in which the loud-speaker = the gruesome, cavernous unc. & the Kontrolleur, the repressive Zensur'.[26]

Alix also wrote regularly to James about the lecture and discussion programme at the Berlin 'Poliklinik'. In the season running from October to December 1924, she chose three lecture series from the six on offer: Sachs on 'normal sexual development', Abraham on 'the history of character development', and Ernst Simmel on 'Die Angst'. (The other series were Sándor Rádo, 'Introduction to psychoanalysis', Franz Alexander, 'Neurosis and total personality' [*Gesamtpersönlichkeit*], and Max Eitington, Simmel and Rádo on 'Practical training in the introduction to psychoanalytic therapy'.) The following year she attended Rádo's lectures on 'Die Übertragung', finding them 'the most exhilarating': 'He covers the blackboard with diagrams showing the different processes which take place in the structure of the mind in (1) Hypnosis (2) Kathexis (3) Analysis . . . fiery zig-zags & concentric circles symbolizing analyst and analee . . . the result is purely Blakeian.'[27]

In London, James was also occupied with the psychoanalytic discussions taking place in London and Cambridge. He had been a member of the Apostles at the University, and he now returned to Cambridge not only to meet up with his fellow members in this dining and discussion club, but also to pursue developments in psychoanalysis with other adherents, including the mathematician Frank Ramsey, the scientist Lionel Penrose and the ecologist Arthur Tansley, many of whom had undertaken analysis with Freud in Vienna.[28] In London, the psychoanalytic discussion groups were frequently led by the women analysts (or, in James's parlance, 'the ladies'), including Ella Sharpe, Nina Searl, Mary Chadwick and M.G. Lewis. Child psychoanalysis was often the topic of the papers and discussion and, as James pointed out to a reluctant Alix, might be the province for her to enter as an analyst, given that it tended to be thought of as a suitable sphere for the non-medically trained (and for women). He was also extensively involved with meetings of the 'Glossary Committee' (convened to create a common lexicon of terms between the translators of psychoanalytic texts), as he worked on the Freud translations, which brought him into regular, and sometimes contentious, contact with analysts including John Rickman (who had been analysed by Freud in Vienna between 1920 and 1922), Ernest Jones and Joan Riviere. As he wrote to Alix (9 October 1924): 'They want to call "das Es" "the Id". I said I thought everyone would say "the Yidd". So Jones said there was no such word in English: "There's 'Yiddish,' you know. And in German 'Jude.' But there is no such word as 'Yidd.'" – "Pardon, me, doctor, Yidd is a current slang word for a Jew." – "Ah! A slang expression. It cannot be in very wide-spread use then." – Simply because that l.b. hasn't ever heard it.'[29]

James and Alix communicated on a very regular basis about the Freud translations, as they both worked on the texts for the Hogarth Press psycho-analytic publications, inaugurated in 1924. The process of translation from German into English becomes in some ways analogous to the process of cultural translation from one country to another. At times, Alix seems to have resisted such acculturation. On a number of occasions she compared Berlin social life unfavourably with Bloomsbury society, and English society more generally. It is perhaps unfair to single out one of the least appealing quotations from her letters, but the passage, describing a visit to a bicycle race at the 'Sport-Palast' does give a sense of her visceral, class-bound, response to aspects of Berlin life:

> What I really resented was being expected to look at those filthy, lower-class figures displaying their stupid, brutalized faces and bodies; instead of seeing lovely boys in dazzling skins & white shorts disporting themselves on green lawns in the open air – or at least well-bred horses cantering round, or something not quite so obnoxious to the senses. But it was interesting in its way – once.[30]

Food terms and analytic terms – different versions of the languages of appetite and desire – invariably appear in German in Alix's letters to James:

> So now I sit, stuffed with Sunday Braten in a stuffy, solitary room . . . I meant to tell you how exciting last night's Sitzung had been ... For Die Klein propounded her views and experiences on Kinderanalyse [and] demonstrated absolutely clearly that these children ... were already wrecked by the repression of their desires and the most appalling *Schuld bewusstein* (=too great, or incorrect oppression by the Ueberich).[31]

Alix's excitement about Klein's theories is palpable throughout the letters, and exists in strong contrast to James' comments about the material he was listening to in London (as he wrote on 18 March 1925, 'Tonight la Chadwick reads about some child analysis or other ...'[32]). Alix was particularly impressed by Klein's claim that transference in child analysis could only be effected if the analyst made clear the meaning of its symptoms and symbolic actions to the child, though she feared that Klein would encounter opposition when she presented the material in Vienna, not least from Anna Freud, 'that open or secret sentimentalist'.[33] The terms were being set for the controversy between Klein and Anna Freud that would dominate, and divide, the British psychoanalytic community in the years to come.

The Stracheys, and particularly Alix, played a significant role in arrangements for Klein's visit to London in 1925, which was in fact the first step towards her permanent move to England the following year. Alix helped Klein prepare the lectures she would give in London, translating two of the series of six lectures on child analysis, with James taking on three. With hindsight, aspects of Alix's admiration for Klein take on some irony, not least her approving assertion (in the light of subsequent revelations that the 'child patients' of a number of Klein's case studies were in fact Klein's own children) that she 'absolutely insists on keeping parental & educative influence apart from analysis & in reducing the former to its minimum'.[34] Alix was clearly deeply invested in the success of Klein's reception in London, and this would seem to bear some relation to her perception of her own roles as a mediator and as a translator, in the broadest sense, of psychoanalytic culture between Berlin/Vienna and London. Alix's Berlin years were, as Barbara Caine has noted, those of her most intense public engagement with psychoanalysis: on her return to London after Abraham's death she did not pursue an analytic career, though she would commit much of the rest of her life to the work of translating Freud.[35]

Bryher in Berlin, H.D. in Vienna

Two years after Alix Strachey's departure from the city, Bryher was in Berlin. The rest of this chapter explores the Berlin and Vienna years of Bryher and the poet H.D., Bryher's companion from their meeting in 1918 until H.D.'s death in 1961. H.D., born Hilda Doolittle in Pennsylvania in 1886, came to Europe in 1911, and settled in London, becoming part of the group surrounding Ezra Pound, and writing poetry as one of the group of 'Imagist' poets. She married the writer Richard Aldington, but the marriage broke down during World War One; a brief affair with the composer Cecil Gray resulted in pregnancy, and her daughter, Perdita, was born in 1919. Ill and isolated at the end of the war, she was supported by a young woman, who called herself 'Bryher', who had contacted her after reading H.D.'s first collection of poems, *Sea Garden*. In the 1920s, H.D. continued to write poetry and a series of semi-autobiographical novels, often using the background of Classical Greece, and frequently replaying in these narratives earlier episodes of sexual passion – lesbian and heterosexual – and the traumas of loss and betrayal. She entered into psychoanalysis in the early 1930s – this culminated in her analysis with Freud in Vienna in 1933 and 1934.

Bryher is a lesser-known figure. She was born in 1894 as Annie Winifred Ellerman, the daughter of Sir John Ellerman, the shipping magnate and financier who, on his death in 1933, was named as the richest man in Britain. She spent much of her early life travelling the world with her parents. She married twice – primarily to gain independence from her family – but was for the most part open about her lesbianism. She wrote throughout her life – beginning with fictionalized autobiographies and ending with historical novels. She was also extensively engaged with numerous publishing projects, including acting as co-editor of the film journal *Close Up*, which ran from 1927 to 1933 the years of the transition from silent to sound film. The editor of the journal was Kenneth Macpherson, a young Scottish artist with whom H.D. had fallen in love (he was some twenty years her junior), and whom Bryher married, ostensibly to provide a front for H.D.'s liaison, though more probably as a way of making sure she was not excluded from the ménage. Bryher and Macpherson legally adopted H.D.'s daughter at this time.

In the late 1920s and into the early 1930s, Bryher, H.D. and Macpherson were intensively involved in writing about film and in film-making itself. *Close Up* made a significant impact during the few years of its publication, drawing on a wide international group of writers, and publishing, for example, the first English-language versions of Eisenstein's film writings. There is a complete version of only one of the four films they made: *Borderline*, in which H.D. was the central actress. In the late 1930s Bryher bought the ailing journal *Life and Letters*, turning it into *Life and Letters To-Day* and supporting its transformation from Bloomsbury belletrism to internationalism and a far broader cultural remit. Before and during World War Two, she financially supported a number of the victims of the fascist regimes, including Walter Benjamin, and acted to help refugees escape from fascist Europe.

In the late 1910s, Bryher struck up a friendship with Havelock Ellis – he accompanied her and H.D. on a trip to Greece in 1920. She was also friendly with two of the women who were to play a central role in British psycho-analysis – Mary Chadwick and Barbara Low. She was much closer, however, to Hanns Sachs, whom she met in Berlin in the late 1920s, and who analysed her for a number of years. (She was living for a good part of the year in Switzerland at this time.) In the early 1930s she vicariously experienced H.D.'s analysis with Freud. From the thirties onwards there was close friendship with Melanie Klein's estranged daughter and son-in-law, Melitta and Walter Schmideberg ('the Bears'). She took care of Walter Schmideberg in Switzerland when he was ill and dependent – the nature of their relationship was obscure even to their closest friends.

In the early 1920s, Bryher wrote and published two autobiographical novels – *Development* (1920) and *Two Selves* (1923). These novels of for-mation delineate a growing divide between the norms of femininity and the boy that Nancy (Bryher's fictional alter ego) feels herself to be. Childhood represented the possible assumption of masculinity, while the trauma of the girls' school to which the female protagonist is sent as a teenager is that of a violent sexing against her own sense of gender identity. Bryher's narrative can thus be mapped on to Freud's account of gender identity as fundamen-tally undifferentiated until the girl reaches puberty and is channelled into feminine identifications.

'Oh to be a boy and have the world', Bryher writes in *Development*.[36] Boyhood becomes identified with adventure – in particular that of putting to sea (we recall Bryher's father's shipping lines): 'the door was locked; she could only wait at the window, desolate with lost adventure, desolate with a boyishness that might never put to sea'.[37] Solace comes only with literature – with *vers libre*, and with the Elizabethans, who give her images of girls who disguise themselves in boys' clothing, paramount among them Bellario. Bryher's first published article was on the girl page in Elizabethan literature.

Development was widely reviewed and for the most part well received. Bryher had sent a manuscript version to Havelock Ellis, whom she had approached for his views on cross-dressing and on the 'colour-hearing' (the attachment of particular colours to letters or phonemes) she had always experienced. As she wrote to H.D. in March 1919 of this visit:

> Then he [Ellis] brought out tea and we plunged into 'colour-hearing' and 'cross-dressing.' I should fill pages if I were to write all this down, so I shall have to wait and tell you all about it. Then we got on to the question of whether I was a boy sort of escaped into the wrong body and he says it is a disputed subject but quite possible and showed me a book about it. He said I should find it perhaps too difficult to read as it was very scientific. We agreed it was most unfair for it to happen but apparently I am quite justified in pleading I ought to be a boy, – I am just a girl by accident.[38]

At one level this model of the 'boy sort of escaped into the wrong body' represents turn-of-the-century sexological theories of homosexuality which psychoanalysis was largely to displace. At another level we can see how Bryher's gender perceptions map onto recent theorizations of early twentieth-century lesbianism as transsexualism, as in Jay Prosser's reading of Radclyffe Hall's *The Well of Loneliness*.[39] As Joanne Winning notes, from 1929 onwards Bryher collected articles and reports on sex-change operations and stories of individuals who crossed gender identities, material she did not supplement with articles on homosexuality until 1949.[40] In a letter of 1937, written to the analyst Walter Schmideberg, Bryher noted with disappointment that 'No research has been made in p.a. with regard to the girl who is really a boy. Freud made one study ["Psychogenesis of a Case of Homosexuality in a Woman"], and there are a few occasional references, that is all . . . Turtle [Hanns Sachs] knows much but never writes about it.'[41] Throughout her life, Bryher avidly collected books that spoke to the fantasy of gender transformation and/or to images of boyhood, including Elizabethan literature and Edwardian boys' adventure stories. In the early 1930s she met and subsequently pursued with a passion the German stage and screen actress Elizabeth Bergner, who had made her reputation playing Joan of Arc in the 1920s and continued to star in cross-dressed roles. When Bryher came to write historical novels after the war, the boy-player and the boy-adventurer were their heroes.

Turning now to Bryher's experiences of Berlin in the 1920s and early 1930s, we find only occasional references in letters to Berlin's notorious sexual freedoms, by contrast with, for example, the lesbian psychologist Charlotte Wolff's accounts (in her autobiography *Hindsight* (1980)) of visiting Berlin's numerous lesbian and cross-dressing clubs and her interest in Magnus Hirschfeld's *Institut für Sexualwissenschaften* [Institute for Sexual Sciences]. (Charlotte Wolff published a biography of Hirschfeld, *Magnus Hirschfeld: A Portrait of a Pioneer in Sexology* in 1986.) There was, nonetheless, a sexual charge to the responses of Bryher, H.D. and Macpherson to Berlin's modernity, which perhaps helped to sustain their ménage, for a time at least. Bryher's preoccupations and passions during Berlin's Weimar years also became a mirror-image of its cultural face, as she dashed between film, psychoanalysis and the Berlin Zoo, and appointed a Berlin architect – Henselmann – to build a Bauhaus dwelling in Switzerland, complete with a film studio that was never actually used. She called it 'Kenwin', a marriage of a kind between Kenneth (Macpherson) and herself (Winifred).

Bryher would later write of this period:

> I find myself unable to describe the atmosphere of that time. It was violent and strange and I felt more drawn into it than I had been into the literary world of Paris. Chance or destiny who knew, some people fitted into movies like a piece into a puzzle, they soared to the top for a few days or weeks, suddenly to make a fresh start, perhaps never to be heard of again. Work of any kind was hard to get, people in the early Thirties were literally starving. Yet because a camera caught not so much an expression as a thought beneath as if for the first time a lens could record an emotion or thought, we all seemed to be living in a world above ourselves, really something that was utterly new with no reflexions of other ages or thoughts about it.
>
> It was also linked for me with psycho-analysis. I felt that the analysis of that period had been invented just for my own pleasure, I loved it. I had asked 'why' ever since I could remember and now I was getting answers to my 'why' for the first time. It stirred my sense of history and eventually, I was allowed to attend the formal meetings, a carrot being tendered to me in the hope that I would forget the outside world and present myself as a candidate for training. I am sorry for the world today, now it has become a medical preserve and everything is standardized but in those days it was experimental ... I used to go to Dr Sachs, he lived in the Mommsenstrasse then, for my hour and in time was promoted to be allowed to go to the evening lectures, on theory and with examples.[42]

Bryher, in analysis with Sachs in Berlin, was taking seriously the idea of a training analysis, though she expressed her boredom at listening to lectures at the Berlin Institute: 'I was bored most of the time. Passive again – don't want to listen to other people on P.A. but want to get on the job myself!'[43] By 1931, meanwhile, both H.D. and Macpherson were in analysis with Mary Chadwick in London – H.D., apparently, to recover from the shock of Macpherson's turning away from her and into homosexual relationships; Macpherson as, it would appear, the price he had to pay for Bryher's continued financial support.

Psychoanalysis – Bryher's own, and that of the others for whom she was paying – became one way of orchestrating relationships at a new kind of level. Bryher wrote to H.D. on 25 April 1931:

> I am so sorry that you are having an unsettled time with the analysis. It must be analogous to having it happen all over again. I had a most friendly letter from Rvr. [Macpherson]. The most friendly since arrival! I hope he is being thoroughly vicious about me with Chaddie [Chadwick] because the things I dream about him – ! Even the Turtle [Sachs] chuckles.

Psychoanalysis – defined, we recall, by John Forrester through 'the logic of the ménage' – became a last-ditch attempt to preserve the logic of their ménage. In a letter to Bryher (2 June 1931), H.D. reported a furious argument with Macpherson: 'Just remember: all that I write in this confidential vein about K. is for you only, and the Herr Doctor. [I] told him what I thought was due him in the way of loyalty to our situation as THREE people, apart from ANY relationship between self and him, as lovers.'

Although Bryher warned against 'leaking' too much from psychoanalysis, she also wrote about her analytic sessions quite openly in her letters to H.D. Sexual identity was, unsurprisingly, the central question. On 8 June 1931, she wrote: 'The deeper I go the more male I get; it's queer. It seems to me funny one decides one's whole life by the time one is two. Or more or less so.'[44] 'My analysis sticks because almost as far back as memory I am "male" but there must have been one point Turtle [Sachs] says, where I decided to be "male". And till we find out we are stuck. It might come to-day and it might be months. And then afterwards only can I be prodded towards some definite attitude.' 'I have come to the bones as it were avec Turtle', she wrote in her next letter:

> There was apparently never question of compromise – there is with most – I said I wanted codpiece [penis] or nothing always in the unconscious and we have worked back this layer right to three. The thing that won't come up is what happened before three to make this so definite. Because compromise is apparently lacking all the way through. Turtle says it might come up tomorrow and it might not come up for years and until the situation is remembered remedial measures can't be applied. It all hinges on that one

thing. It is a nuisance though as I do want to get through and experiment on other people.[45]

(She later wrote to H.D. [16 March 1933], who was by then being analysed by Freud in Vienna: 'I am glad I am a "male" in your unconscious.'[46])

Bryher's considerable wealth certainly seems to have played a part in Sachs' ambitions for her to become a psychoanalyst. In the 1930s she started up a fund for training analysts in Vienna, gave money to the Verlag – Freud's publishing house for psychoanalytic works – and was gleeful about the dissension she caused between psychoanalytic groups in Vienna and London. Letters from 1934, after Sachs had left Berlin for Boston, show her at the Psychoanalytic Congress, which was held in Lucerne that year. In a letter to H.D. dated 28 August, she wrote: 'Jones has declared war on me. The Jones-Klein group are as mad as they can be that the dollars have gone to Sachs-Anna. I licked lips and giggled.'[47] 'I rather love it though', she added in a further letter, 'not because of scientific interests . . . but because of the dirt.'[48] 'Dirt' was Bryher's habitual term for 'gossip', and it sustained her analysis with Sachs: 'And the dirt! He dished it up so carefully in morsels, watching the effect on us . . . the choice bits I must keep till we see you but I can assure you it was Berlin at its most lurid.'[49]

Bryher's letters from this period, which frequently pit 'the moralists' in psychoanalytic circles against 'the strict Freudians', also suggest a division along the lines of sexual politics. In Berlin, it was the homosexual and analytical communities that were simultaneously put under threat and then destroyed. For Bryher, it was the 'English psychoanalysts' (many of them women), by contrast with those in Berlin, who represented moralism and a disapproval of homosexuality.

> I went to see Dorothy T. [Townsend] yesterday – she has been continuously ill since Christmas and asked me why I didn't have a little one as the aim of all analysis for women was to have a little one, and there was nothing so dreadful as lesbianism. Although the brother of Virginia Woolff [*sic*] is an analyst and has married – it is said – a Swede who likes girls. This is most discouraging from Dorothy but it seems part of the technique here for Stephen [Guest?] was always on about it.[50]

'I like Chaddie, love her', H.D. wrote to Bryher during her analysis with Mary Chadwick, 'but, rock-bottom she is ENGLISH . . . perhaps that is the worst and the best to say of anyone.'[51]

At the end of 1931, H.D. was in analysis with Sachs in Berlin, contrasting him favourably with Mary Chadwick: 'He is terribly kind and helpful, just the person for me, as he ties it all up into a dramatic whole, while with poor

Chaddie a lot of subterranean "morality" somehow had to creep in.'[52] And, on Christmas Day, 1931, in Vienna with Sachs: 'I have done with Tee what I did not do with Chaddie. I have evidently shunted over the repressed father-complex to him.'[53] In 1932, she was reading intensively from psycho-analytic journals and books and mentioning 'talk of my possibly going to Freud himself in Vienna'.[54]

In the spring of 1933, as *Close Up* entered its final year, H.D. travelled to Vienna for psychoanalysis with Freud, bearing Sachs's recommendation.[55] There were in fact two separate periods of analysis with Freud – from March to June 1933 and from October to December 1934. What had led her there, H.D. wrote, was the feeling that her creativity was blocked and that 'I wanted to free myself of repetitive thoughts and experiences' – always linked for her with World War One and with her 'war-phobia.'[56] She referred to herself as a 'student' of Freud and not a patient, though the question of the analysis as a training analysis seems not to have been pursued.

Tribute to Freud encompasses two separate works. The first of these, 'Writing on the Wall', was written in London in the autumn of 1944, without recourse, H.D. alleged, to the notebooks which she had kept in Vienna in the spring of 1933. It was written as a construction or reconstruc-tion, echoing the terms of Freud's 1937 essay 'Constructions in Analysis', in which (in ways which have a particular bearing on the analysis with H.D.) he drew an extended analogy between the work of the archaeologist and the analyst. 'Writing on the Wall' appeared in the journal *Life and Letters To-Day* in 1945–1946. The second piece, 'Advent' (which H.D. referred to in a note as a continuation of 'Writing on the Wall' or as its prelude) was taken directly, H.D. wrote, from the notebooks of 1933 (which were sub-sequently lost or destroyed), but not assembled until December 1948. The issue of the Vienna notebooks was a loaded one, because Freud seems to have asked her neither to prepare for nor to take notes on the analytic sessions: 'He does not, apparently, want me to take notes, but I must do that.'[57] She did in fact abandon the notebook during the first period of analysis, but continued to write in some detail to Bryher about her sessions with Freud. For Bryher, in particular, the question of historical record was always central, and she kept and filed correspondence and other personal documents with immense care and with regard to their significance as historical and auto/biographical source materials.

H.D.'s letters of this period reveal dimensions of the analysis not explored in the two memoirs, including a set of highly complicated nego-tiations at the time of the birth of Freud's beloved chow Yofi's puppies, one or both of which Freud wished to give to the Bryher household, and which also became caught up in the analytic transference: 'I had horrible dreams last night, I suppose the puppy equates death, impregnation and so on.'[58] At this time, H.D. was also sending Bryher detailed reports of her dreams, and in particular one which Freud had told her 'represents the whole of my life in a sequence of detached yet continuous incidents'.[59] For H.D., the dream's value lay its 'new combinations, all founded on the most trivial incident yet with a universal or astrological symbolism'. Her astrology, she suggested, redeemed the 'star-values' of her father, an astronomer who measured the stars with, as she puts it, 'a cold hermit logic and detachment', and the association of whom with Freud ('the Professor') was central to the analysis.

The crisis engendered by Freud's proposed gift of the puppy, or puppies, also became imbricated with H.D.'s curious account of his 'new' theory of female sexuality, and her perception that she and Bryher must not disrupt the working out of his ideas, to which they were instrumental:

> Papa [Freud] has a complete new theory but he says he dare not write it because he does not want to make enemies of women. Apparently, we have all stirred him up frightfully. His idea is that all women are deeply rooted in penis-envy, not only the bi-sexual or homo-sexual woman. The advanced or intellectual woman is [more] frank about it. That is all. But the whole cult and development of normal-womanhood is based on the same fact; the envy of the woman for the penis. Now this strikes me as being a clue to everything. The reason women are FAITHFUL, when men are not, the reason a Dorothy R. [Richardson] or a Cole will stick like grim-death to some freak like Alan or Gerald, the reason mama or my mother went insane at the oddest things, the reason for this, the reason for that. I was awake all last night and up this morning just after 7 ... as this seemed to convince me more than anything. What got me, was his saying that the homo woman is simply frank and truthful but that the whole of domestic womanhood is exactly the same, but has built up its cult on deception. Well, he did not say deception. He just flung out the idea. I screamed at him, 'but the supreme compliment to WOMAN would be to trust women with this great secret.' I said Br, the princess [Marie Bonaparte] and myself would appreciate it, and keep it going. Or something like that. Anyhow, do you see what I mean??? We have evidently done some fish-tail stirring, and if papa bursts out like the Phoenix with his greatest contribution NOW, I feel you and I will be in some way, responsible. This is a thing, for instance, that Chaddie [Mary Chadwick] fought against, and tried to make out that the monthly is interesting and that men envy women. Well, men do. But the whole thing must be 'built on a rock' anyhow, and I feel that S.F. is that rock, and that perhaps you and I (as I did say half in joke) ARE to be instrumental in some way in feeding the light.[60]

It is of course surprising to find H.D. proclaiming 'penis-envy' as a new discovery in the 1930s, when Freud had in fact first discussed it in the 1908 essay 'On the Sexual Theories of Children' and allied it to his theory of the little girl's 'castration complex' in 'On Narcissism' (1914). The context for her letter was almost certainly the reformulation of theories of female sexuality, and of female homosexuality, by analysts such as Karen Horney, Helene Deutsch and Ernest Jones in the late 1920s, to which Freud was responding in his writings on female sexuality in the early 1930s, including the 1932/33 essay 'On Femininity.' Here Freud asserted that 'One cannot very well doubt the importance of envy for the penis':

> The wish to get the longed-for penis eventually in spite of everything may contribute to the motives that drive a mature woman to analysis, and what she may reasonably expect from analysis – a capacity, for instance, to carry on an intellectual profession – may often be recognized as a sublimated modification of this repressed wish.[61]

In his 1927 essay on 'The Early Development of Female Sexuality', Jones had argued against the notion of 'penis-envy' as a stage in the development of heterosexual women (and for a concept of 'aphanisis', a fear of the extinction of the capacity for sexual enjoyment) common to boys and girls. He thus reserved 'penis-envy', which he had discredited as an explanation of feminine development, as an explanation of the etiology of homosexual women.[62] H.D.'s proclamation might in part be seen as an attempt, from within the terms offered to her by Freudian theory, to refuse Jones's way of differentiating between heterosexual and homosexual women. She suggests, indeed, that homosexual women are the measure of women *tout court*, acknowledging what the others deny. At the same time, she seems to have resisted the concept of womb-envy developed by Helene Deutsch and others, linked as it was to representations of motherhood as definitional of femininity. Her eccentric, or anachronistic, 'discovery' might thus be understood as an attempt to fight back against 'the moralists'. It is striking that, of the British women analysts working at this time, it was Ella Freeman Sharpe (with her absorption in questions of art and aesthetics) to whose work H.D. was most drawn.

The debates and differences within psychoanalytic theories and techniques to which H.D. alluded in her letters to Bryher do not appear in any very direct way in 'Writing on the Wall' or 'Advent' (both works subsequently published as *Tribute to Freud*), although there are points at which she hints at discomfort with his views on femininity and female sexuality, an 'argument' between them made more explicit in her poem 'The Master'.[63]

In 'Advent', she writes (following a description of a dream in which she had used 'my little bottle of smelling-salts' to *salt* her typewriter, her interpretation of which is that she would come to 'salt my savorless writing with the salt of the earth, Sigmund Freud's least utterance') of the annoyance she had experienced with 'the Professor in one of his volumes':

> He said, as I remember, that women did not creatively amount to anything or amount to much, unless they had a male counterpart or a male companion from which they drew their inspiration. Perhaps he is right and my dream of 'salting' my typewriter with the tell-tale transference symbol is further proof of his infallibility.[64]

The dream thus confirmed for her, in the terms of her letter to Bryher, 'SF' as the 'rock': disagreement, 'annoyance', become merely superficial.

'Writing on the Wall' moves backwards and forwards in actual time, recounting, for example, H.D.'s last meeting with Freud in London, soon before his death in 1939, as well as in the time of memories and dreams. 'Length, breadth, thickness, the shape, the scent, the feel of things', H.D. wrote. 'The actuality of the present, its bearing on the past, their bearing on the future [. . .] Past, present, future, these three – but there is another time-element, popularly called the fourth dimensional.'[65] I have already mentioned the significance of time (the hour) and space (the space of the room) for the analysand; The 'Writing on the Wall' returns again and again to the space of Freud's consulting rooms. His collection of Classical, Egyptian and Indian antiquities was of the greatest significance to H.D., and indeed the statuettes, rings and coins were the coinage, the common currency of the analysis. Freud, she wrote to Kenneth Macpherson, 'dashes in and out of his rooms to find me some little god or other that has happened in to the conversation'.[66] 'Some words "to greet the return of the Gods" (other people read: Goods)', Freud wrote to H.D. after she had sent him gardenias and an unsigned card – 'to greet the return of the Gods' – to welcome him and his collection to London in the Autumn of 1938.[67] Gods or goods – Freud's response appears to refer to her argument, perhaps never fully voiced, with what she saw as his materialism and rationalism. Religion, myth and psychoanalysis were inextricably intertwined for her:

> The doll is the dream or the symbol of this particular child, as these various Ra, Nut, Hathor, Isis, and Ka figures that are dimly apprehended on their shelves or on the Professor's table in the other room are the dream or the symbol of the dream of other aspiring and adoring souls. The childhood of the individual is the childhood of the race, we have noted, the Professor [Freud] has written somewhere.[68]

'We touched lightly on some of the more abstruse transcendental problems, it is true', H.D. writes,

> but we related them to the familiar family-complex. Tendencies of thought and imagination, however, were not cut away, were not pruned even. My imagination wandered at will; my dreams were revealing, and many of them drew on classical and Biblical symbolism. Thoughts were things, to be collected, collated, analyzed, shelved, or resolved. Fragmentary ideas, apparently unrelated, were often found to be part of a special layer or stratum of thought and memory, therefore to belong together; these were sometimes skilfully pieced together like the exquisite Greek tear-jars and iridescent glass bowls and vases that gleamed in the dusk from the shelves of the cabinet that faced me where I stretched, propped up on the couch in the room in Berggasse 19, Wien XIX. The dead were living in so far as they lived in memory or were recalled in dream.[69]

The image of analytic discourse – free association and dream interpretation – as the piecing together of the precious fragments of a bowl or vase – of something that holds or contains – runs throughout the text, and again recalls the terms of Freud's essay 'Constructions in Analysis'. At other times it transmutes into the image of the mind as a vessel seemingly whole, but precariously close to shattering:

> There are dreams or sequences of dreams that follow a line like a graph on a map or show a jagged triangular pattern, like a crack on a bowl that shows the bowl or vase may at any moment fall in pieces; we all know that almost invisible thread-line on the cherished glass butter-dish that predicts it will 'come apart in me 'ands' sooner or later – sooner, more likely.[70]

Here the image of the bowl (of the unconscious) has become homely, domestic – an aspect of the mystery that resides in the everyday. 'I was here because I must not be broken', H.D. wrote, after describing the shock she experienced when Freud suddenly burst out, beating with his fist on the analytic couch – 'The trouble is – I am an old man – *you do not think it worth your while to love me*'[71] – concerned that Freud might feel that she needed to be broken in order to be remade. 'Did he think', she asks, 'it was easy to leave friendly, comfortable surroundings and come to a strange city, to beard him, himself, the dragon, in his very den?' She refers, too, to 'women broken by wars', as she felt herself to have been broken by World War One, and as she would be broken by World War Two. There was thus no obvious question of a 'cure' by the analysis, though she was able to write again.

In her 2009 study of archaeology and modernism, *Knossos and the Prophets of Modernism*, Cathy Gere gives a compelling account of the significance for modernist writers and thinkers of the archaeologist Arthur

Evans's discoveries (and reconstructions) of the world of ancient Crete, which he (and a number of his contemporaries and followers) identified as a matriarchal society.[72] Gere discusses this as the context for Freud's account, in the 1931 essay on 'Female Sexuality', of the 'early, pre-Oedipus phase in girls', which, in Freud's words, 'comes to us as a surprise, like the discovery, in another field, of the Minoan-Mycenean civilization of Greece'.[73] In the essay Freud writes, in terms close to the archaeological analogies of 'Constructions in Analysis', of the difficulty of grasping in analysis 'the sphere of this first attachment to the mother ... so grey with age and shadowy and almost impossible to revivify – that it was as if it had succumbed to an especially inexorable repression'.[74] However, he suggests that it may be that women analysts (he instances Jeanne Lampl-de Groot and Helene Deutsch) 'have been able to perceive these facts more easily and clearly because they were helped in dealing with those under their treatment by the transference to a suitable mother-substitute'.[75] The analysis with H. D., coming two years after this essay and in the same year as Freud's essay 'On Femininity', appears to have been imbricated in the terms both of Freud's 'discovery' and of the archaeological topoi through which he conceptualized it. H.D. refers directly, in 'Advent', to discussion with Freud of Sir Arthur Evans and his work, of 'the Crete mother-goddess', and of her mother-fixation, which the analysis revealed.

As Gere writes: 'Psychoanalysis and archaeology shared the same backward chronology.'[76] She finds this same structure in H.D.'s accounts of her analysis, suggesting that 'Advent' in particular should be understood not merely as a construction or reconstruction, but as a fake or forgery, akin to those which dominated archaeological 'finds' and the narratives (in which 'myth' masquerades as 'history') which they generated. She argues that H.D. deliberately destroyed the 1933 notebook on which 'Advent' is said to draw in order to conceal the fact that it showed so little engagement with the increasingly desperate political and historical situation in the Vienna of these years. 'Advent', Gere suggests, writes into its retrospective account (which masquerades as a document of the times) a 'constant pre-vision of disaster', in H.D.'s words.[77] Through this strategy H.D. constructs herself in retrospect, Gere argues, as a prophetess of the catastrophe to come.

'Already in Vienna', H.D. wrote in 'Writing on the Wall', 'the shadows were lengthening or the tide was rising'.[78] She wrote of picking up confetti-like tokens outside her hotel, on which were written 'mottoes' ('Hitler gives bread', 'Hitler gives work'), of swastikas chalked on the Berggasse pavement, and of rifles stacked at street corners. In 'Advent' she wrote directly about the ways in which she felt silenced in her analytic sessions in this context. She recalls a disturbing childhood memory, of her brothers putting salt on a caterpillar, which 'writhes, huge like an object seen under a microscope, or looming up it is a later film-abstraction':[79] 'No, how can I talk about the crucified Worm? I have been leafing over papers in the café, there are fresh atrocity stories. I cannot talk about the thing that actually concerns me, I cannot talk to Sigmund Freud in Vienna, 1933, about Jewish atrocities in Berlin.'[80] For Gere, it is claims such as these through which, more than a decade later, H.D. composed her retrospective account of analysis with Freud in the early 1930s, layering them over an original absence.

Gere's level-headed account of H.D.'s mysticism provides, in many ways, a refreshing contrast to the over-wrought prose which characterizes a good deal of the critical work on this writer. The connections she draws between modern archaeology and modernist culture are expert and convincing. Yet I am not fully persuaded by her own constructions in the case of H.D.'s memoirs of this time. H.D. habitually destroyed drafts and manuscripts once a fair or published version came into being: there is no reason to suppose that the destruction (if that is was it was) of the Vienna notebooks was a particularly charged act of suppression. The extensive letters written and received by H.D. at this time are strongly engaged with the political realities on the streets, and she explicitly comments in her letters on her unusual absorption in the daily newspapers: the *New York Times*, one of the papers she read regularly, presented particularly extensive coverage of the situation in Germany and Austria at this time. It is certainly true that she wrote to Bryher at the time of her analysis that she hated wasting her psychoanalytic hour on politics, but this was a view with which Freud would almost certainly have concurred. Indeed, in April 1933, Freud wrote to Ernest Jones that:

> Despite all the newspaper reports of mobs, demonstrations, etc., Vienna is calm, life undisturbed. We can expect with certainty that the Hitler movement will spread to Austria, is indeed already here, but it is very unlikely that it will present a similar danger as in Germany ... In such a way we lull ourselves into – relative – security.[81]

More interesting then, than any imputation of 'faking' or 'forgery', might be a fuller consideration of the ways in which relationships between 'inner' and 'outer' realities, psychoanalysis and politics, were playing themselves out in the Europe of the 1930s. Freud was writing extensively, in this period, on war, aggression, and anti-Semitism: anxiety, ambivalence and the origins of love and hate were at the heart of psychoanalytic theories more generally in the first part of a century which was devastated by two world wars. The experiences of analysands abroad at this charged time make their own, very particular, contribution to an understanding of the ways in which psyche and polis intersect, as well as to the ways in which we conceptualize this very divide. Our understanding of psychoanalysis as an international movement would be illuminated and enlarged by further exploration of the encounters and experiences of those many analysands and analysts who undertook foreign travel in a volatile Europe, in the service of the journey into the interior.

Notes

1 See, for example, essays in the volume *Freud in Exile: Psychoanalysis and Its Vicissitudes*, edited by Edward Timms and Naomi Segal (New Haven and London: Yale University Press, 1988).

2 Ernest Jones, *The Life and Work of Sigmund Freud*, vol. 2 (New York: Basic Books, 1955), pp. 40–41.

3 Jones, *The Life and Work of Sigmund Freud*, vol. 2, pp. 31–32. Eitingon, Jones writes, then a medical student in Zürich, came to Vienna in January 1907 to consult Freud over a severe case he was interested in: 'He passed three or four evenings with Freud and they were spent on personal analytic work during long walks in the city. Such was the first training analysis!'

4 Jones, *The Life and Work of Sigmund Freud*, vol. 2, p. 98.

5 Jones, *The Life and Work of Sigmund Freud*, vol. 3 (New York: Basic Books, 1957), p. 78.

6 See the anniversary volume, *Zehn Jahre Berliner Psychanalytisches Institut (Poliklinik und Lehranstalt) 1920–1930* (Vienna: Internationaler Psychoanalytischer Verlag 1930; reprinted by Anton Hain KG, Meisenheim, 1970).

7 Suzanne Raitt, *May Sinclair: a Modern Victorian* (Oxford: Oxford University Press, 2000), p. 139. For discussion of the Clinic, see also Sally Alexander, 'Psychoanalysis in Britain in the early twentieth century: an introductory note', in *History Workshop Journal* 45 (1998): 135–143.

8 Raitt, *May Sinclair*, p. 139.

9 Paul Roazen, *Oedipus in Britain: Edward Glover and the Struggle Over Klein* (New York: Other Press, 2000), p. 33.

10 Ella Freeman Sharpe, *Collected Papers on Psychoanalysis* (London: Hogarth Press and The Institute of Psycho-Analysis, 1950), p. 136.

11 H. D., *Tribute to Freud* (Manchester: Carcanet Press, 1985), p. 3.

12 Susan Stanford Friedman, *Analyzing Freud: Letters of H.D., Bryher and Their Circle* (New York: New Directions Publishing, 2002), p. xxii

13 Freud, 'On Beginning the Treatment', *SE* vol. 12, p. 136.

14 Ibid.

15 John Forrester, 'Psychoanalysis: gossip, telepathy and/or science?', in *The Seductions of Psychoanalysis: Freud, Lacan and Derrida* (Cambridge: Cambridge University Press, 1990), pp. 243–259.

16 Ibid., p. 253.

17 Ibid., p. 258.

18 Ibid., p. 224.

19 *Bloomsbury/Freud: The Letters of James and Alix Strachey 1924–1925*, edited by Perry Meisel and Walter Kendrick (New York: Basic Books, 1985).

20 Jones, Letter to Freud, 7 May 1920 in *The Complete Correspondence of Sigmund Freud and Ernest Jones 1908–1939*, edited by R. Andrew Paskauskas (Cambridge, Mass: Harvard University Press, 1993) p. 378.

21 Freud, Letter to Jones, 14 July 1921, in Paskauskas, p. 431.

22 James Strachey, Letter to Alix, 22 November 1924, in *Bloomsbury/Freud*, p. 125.

23 Alix Strachey, Letter to James, 5 December 1924, in *Bloomsbury/Freud*, p. 137. Italics in original.

24 Alix Strachey, Letter to James, 9 February 1925, in *Bloomsbury/Freud*, p. 199.

25 Alix Strachey, Letter to James, 11 November 1924, in *Bloomsbury/Freud*, p. 114.

26 Alix Strachey, Letter to James, 5 December 1924, in *Bloomsbury/Freud*, p. 137.

27 Alix Strachey, Letter to James, 21 May 1925, in *Bloomsbury/Freud*, p. 271–272.

28 For detailed histories of the Cambridge psychoanalytic networks, see the work by Laura Cameron and John Forrester: '"A nice type of the English scientist": Tansley and Freud', *History Workshop Journal* 48 (1999): 65–100; 'Tansley's Psychoanalytic Network: An Episode out of the Early History of Psychoanalysis in England', *Psychoanalysis and History* 2, no. 2 (2000): 189–256. See also John Forrester, 'Freud in Cambridge', *Critical Quarterly* 46, no. 2 (2004): 1–26; '1919: Psychology and Psychoanalysis, Cambridge and London – Myers, Jones and MacCurdy', *Psychoanalysis and History* 10, no. 1 (2008): 37–94.

29 James Strachey, Letter to Alix, 9 October 1924, in *Bloomsbury/Freud*, p. 83.

30 Alix Strachey, Letter to James, 10 March 1925, in *Bloomsbury/Freud*, p. 231.

31 Alix Strachey, Letter to James, 14 December 1924, in *Bloomsbury/Freud*, p. 145.

32 James Strachey, Letter to Alix, 18 March 1925, in *Bloomsbury/Freud*, p. 237.

33 Alix Strachey, Letter to James, 14 December 1924, in *Bloomsbury/Freud*, p. 146.

34 Alix Strachey, Letter to James, 11 February 1925, in *Bloomsbury/Freud*, p. 201.

35 See Barbara Caine, 'The Stracheys and Psychoanalysis', *History Workshop Journal* 45 (1998): 145–169.

36 Bryher, *Development*, in *Bryher: Two Novels*, edited by Joanne Winning (Madison: Wisconsin University Press, 2000), p. 136.

37 Ibid., p. 154.

38 Bryher, Letter to H.D., 20 March 1919. The letters of Bryher and H.D. are held in the Beinecke Rare Book and Manuscript Library, Yale University. Many of the letters from the period I am considering have also been published in Stanford Friedman, *Analyzing Freud*.

39 Jay Prosser, '"Some Primitive Thing Conceived in a Turbulent Age of Transition": The Transsexual Emerging from *The Well*', in *Palatable Poison:*

Critical Perspectives on The Well of Loneliness, edited by Laura Doan and Jay Prosser (New York: Columbia University Press, 2001), pp. 129–144.

40 Introduction to *Bryher: Two Novels*, xxx.

41 Quoted in Maggie Magee and Diane C. Miller, *Lesbian Lives: Psychoanalytic Narratives Old and New* (New York: Analytic Press, 1996), p. 26.

42 Bryher, 'Berlin' (2 page typescript). Beinecke Library, Bryher papers, Box 72, Folder 2855.

43 Bryher, Letter

44 Bryher, Letter to H.D., 8 June 1931.

45 Bryher, Letter

46 Stanford Friedman, *Analyzing Freud*, p. 105.

47 Stanford Friedman, *Analyzing Freud*, p. 408.

48 Bryher, Letter to H.D., 28 August 1934.

49 Bryher, Letter

50 Bryher, Letter

51 H.D., Letter to Bryher, 2 June 1931.

52 H.D., Letter to Bryher, 3 December 1931.

53 H.D., Letter to Bryher, 25 December 1931.

54 H.D., Letter

55 See *Close Up: Cinema and Modernism*, edited by James Donald, Anne Friedberg and Laura Marcus (London: Continuum, 1998) and Laura Marcus, *The Tenth Muse: Writing about Cinema in the Modernist Period* (Oxford: Oxford University Press, 2007).

56 H.D., *Tribute to Freud*, p. 13.

57 Ibid., p. 165.

58 H.D., Letter to Bryher, 27 April 1933.

59 H.D., Letter to Bryher, 28 April 1933.

60 H.D., Letter to Bryher, 3 May 1933.

61 Freud, 'On Femininity', *SE* vol. 22, p. 125.

62 Ernest Jones, 'The Early Development of Female Sexuality', *International Journal of Psycho-Analysis* 8 (1927): 459–472.

63 See Stanford Friedman, *Analyzing Freud*, pp. 227–228.

64 H.D., *Tribute to Freud*, p. 149.

65 Ibid., p. 23.

66 H.D., Letter to Kenneth Macpherson, 15 March 1933.

67 H.D., *Tribute to Freud*, p. 11.

68 Ibid., p. 38.

69 Ibid., pp. 13–14.

70 Ibid., p. 93.

71 H.D., *Tribute to Freud*, italics in original, p. 16.

72 Cathy Gere, *Knossos and the Prophets of Modernism* (Chicago: Chicago University Press, 2009).

73 Freud, 'Female Sexuality', in *SE* vol. 21, p. 226.

74 Ibid., p. 226.

75 Ibid., p. 227.

76 Gere, *Knossos and the Prophets of Modernism*, p. 155.
77 H.D., *Tribute to Freud*, p. 139; Gere, *Knossos and the Prophets of Modernism*, p. 192.
78 H.D., *Tribute to Freud*, p. 58.
79 Ibid., p. 134.
80 Ibid., p. 135.
81 Paskauskas, *Complete Correspondence of Sigmund Freud and Ernest Jones*, p. 716.

CHAPTER 9

Dreaming and Cinematographic Consciousness

The year 1895 was a key year in the histories of both psychoanalysis and cinema. On 24 July 1895, Freud dreamed the 'Dream of Irma's Injection', the Specimen Dream of *The Interpretation of Dreams*. 'Do you suppose', Freud wrote to Wilhelm Fliess in a letter describing a later visit to Bellevue, the house where he had had the dream, 'that someday one will read on a marble tablet on this house':

> Here, on July 24th, 1895
> the secret of dreams
> revealed itself to Dr. Sigm Freud.[1]

During September and October 1895, Freud wrote the uncompleted *Project for a Scientific Psychology*, which, as James Strachey noted in his editorial introduction to *The Interpretation of Dreams*, contains sections constituting a first approach to a coherent theory of dreams.[2] *The Interpretation of Dreams* was, Freud himself claimed, 'finished in all essentials at the beginning of 1896'.[3]

The Lumière brothers' Cinématographe gave its first public presentation (to the Société d'Encouragement de l'Industrie Nationale in Paris) on 22 March 1895, exhibiting their film *Workers Leaving the Lumière Factory* as an example of the progress being made in photography. Its immediate success was unexpected. The film is both the most unmediated of early *actualité* films, and a complex act of historical reflexivity: the workers at Lumière *père*'s photographic plate factory look into the camera, which would transform the very act of looking and turn still into moving images. George Méliès's trick-films, which directly exploited the relationship between dream and film, followed soon after.

Psychoanalysis and cinema thus emerged in tandem at the close of the nineteenth century: twin sciences or technologies of fantasy, dream, virtual reality and 'screen memory'. In the following century, a vast body of literature has explored the complex historical and conceptual relationship between the two fields. Psychoanalytic film theory has turned to a wide range of Freud's writings – on fetishism, on femininity, on fantasy, on 'scopophilia' – as part of this exploration, and with a focus on cinematic spectatorship. Dreams and dream-theory have nonetheless retained a privileged role in the 'parallel histories' of psychoanalysis and cinema, just as dreams have a privileged role in psychoanalysis itself.

Practitioners and theorists of psychoanalysis have found the film–dream relationship a compelling one for their understanding of unconscious processes, while philosophers have turned to this relationship in their explorations of the workings of consciousness, and of the relations of space and time particular to dreams and to cinema. From the first decades of the twentieth century, cultural commentators have explored the primacy of 'wish fulfilment' in the narrative structures of films, and as equivalent to its function in dreams and daydreams. The cinema as a 'dream factory' is an early designation. For film-makers themselves, dreams and dream-states seemed from the outset to be an essential part of film's ontology: while 'dream sequences' within films may seem to be bounded, they are never fully sealed off from the film-space which contains them. It has been said, moreover, that we can watch films precisely because we are dreamers: for Hugo von Hofmannsthal, 'a secret instinct is appeased' in film spectatorship, 'an instinct familiar to the dreamers of dreams'.[4] Elsewhere we find the implication that the film has in some sense replaced the dream in and for the twentieth century: the argument might then run that we know how to watch films because we have in the past been dreamers.

Such ideas suggest a 'total world' equivalence in their accounts of filmic and oneiric universes. Yet the fascination with film and dream often seems to situate their interrelationship on borderlines and thresholds: between sleeping and waking; inner and outer; visual and verbal; stasis and motion; reality and simulacra. It is such borderlines and thresholds that this chapter in part explores.

'Cinema' [Kino] and 'film' are absent from Freud's theoretical work, appearing neither as topics nor as analogies in the *Standard Edition*, though we can find references to photography and to other optical technologies and instruments of vision, including the microscope and the telescope, deployed as analogues for the workings of consciousness and the unconscious. By contrast, Freud's contemporary Henri Bergson made the 'cinematograph' and the 'cinematographical' central to his theorizations of mind and reality, even as he expressed doubts about film (whose 'movement' is in one way illusory, and which mechanistically segments and spatializes time into discrete and identical units rather than producing it as continuous flow) as an appropriate analogue for time and motion: 'rests placed beside rests will never be equivalent to a movement'.[5] A number of film theorists – both early and late twentieth century – have wanted to argue that Bergson's understandings of time and consciousness are ultimately cinematic, despite his expressions of ambivalence and even hostility towards film, and that his writings – whether overtly debating the question of the cinematographic or not – are the founding texts of philosophy and film.[6] It is also worth noting that Bergson's models of the cinematographic would have been drawn largely from late nineteenth- and early twentieth-century (pre)cinematic experiments (beginning with Étienne-Jules Marey's 'chronophotography', which experimented with the representation and analysis of movement) rather than with the later narrative cinema.[7]

Underlying Freud's silence on the question of cinema might well have been a resistance to the 'modernization' or mechanization of thought and consciousness; as I discuss below, Freud, in the essay on 'The Uncanny' in particular, is resistant to the connection of 'the uncanny' and its manifestations with the 'novel and unfamiliar'[8] (which could include the new technologies of vision and animation), firmly linking it instead with the archaic and the always-known. For Freud to embrace photography as an analogue for unconscious life, as in his use of Francis Galton's 'composite photography' to analogize 'condensation' in the dream-work, but to remain silent on the question of cinema might suggest a habit of nineteenth-century thought resistant to some of the innovations of the twentieth century. There might also have been an ambivalence towards the primacy of the visual which, in *The Interpretation of Dreams*, is represented as a regression, redeemed for meaning and for culture by the highly verbal and textual work of secondary revision, narration and interpretation. We could usefully compare Freud's approach with that of Bergson in his essay on dreams (published in France in 1901, and in an English version in 1913).[9] There are similarities, including foci on inscriptions and on the unfathomable mysteries of dream-life, the latter taking both thinkers into the realms of psychical research and telepathy. Bergson's account, however, is more overtly concerned than Freud's with the hallucinatory and visual aspects of dreams, including the phenomena of hypnagogia and the phantasmagoric, a concern linked to Bergson's understanding of human subjectivity as both mingled with and emerging out of a universe of images.

The approach of Havelock Ellis's *The World of Dreams* to the visual arena also provides a significant contrast with Freud's approach. Ellis wrote that 'The commonest kind of dream is mainly a picture, but it is always a living and moving picture, however inanimate the objects which appear in vision before us would be in real life.' Fascinated by the hypnagogic state – 'the porch to sleep and dreams'[10] – he discussed the ways in which hypnagogic imagery crosses the threshold from waking to sleeping. Imagery in motion is at times analogized through the kaleidoscope, as a way of representing the renewal of the stream of sleeping consciousness. Echoing Baudelaire's image, in 'The Painter of Modern Life', of the flâneur as 'a kaleidoscope gifted with consciousness', Ellis writes: 'if the kaleidoscope were conscious we should say that each picture had been suggested by the preceding pattern – but yet definitely novel'.[11] Elsewhere Ellis makes the magic lantern the more appropriate analogue: 'The movement of the cinematograph, indeed, scarcely corresponds to that fusion of heterogeneous images which marks dream visions. Our dreams are like dissolving views in which the dissolving process is carried on swiftly or slowly, but always uninterruptedly.'[12] This is one of only two references in *The World of Dreams* to the cinematograph – later in the text Ellis refers to the dream as 'a kind of cinematographic drama which has been condensed and run together in very much the way practiced by the cinematographic artist'[13] – and it is striking that Ellis includes it as one among a number of optical instruments or shows, not only undifferentiated from its precursors, but less absorbing in its assumed inability to fuse and dissolve images.

Freud may not (or not only) have neglected the cinema on the grounds of its modernity, its seeming lack of attachment to the already-known, but because of its association with optical toys (or optical instruments become toys) such as the kaleidoscope, which, for so many of the nineteenth-century commentators he critiques in the first chapter of *The Interpretation of Dreams*, implied not a pattern of difference (as it does for Ellis) but a disordered and chaotic visual regime – precisely the charge from which Freud wishes to redeem dreams and dreaming. For James Sully – whose writings on dreams, in particular his essay 'The Dream as a Revelation' (1893) along with other aspects of his psychology, were acknowledged influences on Freud – 'Nothing is more striking in our dreams than the kaleidoscopic transformations, the new scene having no discoverable relation to its predecessor, yet being confusedly identified with it in the jumble of the nocturnal phantasmagoria'.[14]

The absence of 'film' in Freud's work does not, however, diminish the perception that there is a profound relationship between psychoanalysis and cinema, and the few 'glancing' references to film in Freud's writings and in the biographical literature on Freud become highly charged. In the second volume of *Sigmund Freud: Life and Works*, Ernest Jones writes of a visit to the cinema in New York in 1909: 'We all dined together in Hammerstein's roof garden, afterwards going on to a cinema to see one of the primitive films of those days with plenty of wild chasing. Ferenczi in his boyish way was very excited at it, but Freud was only quietly amused; it was the first film they had seen.'[15] Stephen Heath argues that if Jones is right in claiming that this was Freud's first encounter with cinema, his disinterest becomes even more marked: there were some eighty cinemas in Vienna at this time.[16] In fact, a letter written by Freud to his family from Rome in September 1907 (published in Ernst Freud's edition of Freud's letters and in a different English translation in Jones's biography of Freud, though Jones himself notes no contradiction[17]) provides an earlier, and much fuller and more appreciative, account of cinematic viewing, as Freud describes watching open-air projections of lantern slides on the Piazza Colonna:

> They are actually advertisements, but to beguile the public these are inter-spersed with pictures of landscapes, Negroes of the Congo, glacier ascents and so on. But since these wouldn't be enough, the boredom is interrupted by short cinematographic performances for the sake of which the old children (your father included) suffer quietly the advertisements and monot-onous photographs. They are stingy with these tidbits, however, so I have had to look at the same thing over and over again. When I turn to go I detect a certain tension in the attentive crowd which makes me look again, and sure enough a new performance has begun, and so I stay on. Until 9 P.M. I usually remain spellbound; then I begin to feel too lonely in the crowd, so I return to my room to write to you all.[18]

As Jonathan Crary notes at the close of his study *Suspensions of Perception: Attention, Spectacle and Modern Culture*, Freud says nothing of the content of the cinematographic performances.[19] The spell-binding nature of the spectacle is precisely the display of its own visibility, and this is to be situated as an historical moment in the early history of cinematic reception. I would add that Freud's account is interestingly structured around the phrase and the concept of 'look[ing] again', which is itself multiplied as repetition (seeing the same thing over and over again), return (being called back to look again) and renewal (looking again as seeing anew). For Crary, Freud's account offers a specifically modernized, urban vision, as the advertisements and the images of foreign lands as touristic spectacle play over the surfaces of the ancient city and its buildings.

Freud's vivid description provides a counterpoint to the view that he was hostile to cinema where he was not indifferent to it. There is no overt suggestion, however, that he saw in the cinematic spectacle an analogue for psychic life, nor that he wished to transmute the Roman holiday experience into the work of theoretical reflection. By contrast, Lou Andreas-Salomé's journal entry on 15 February 1913 recounts both her pleasure in the movies and her thoughts on film and psychic life:

> A few purely psychological considerations deserve to be added to the many things that might be said in vindication of this Cinderella of aesthetic criticism. One has to do with the fact that only the technique of the film permits the rapid sequence which approximates our own imaginative faculty; it might even be said to imitate its erratic ways . . . The second consideration has to do with the fact that even though the most superficial pleasure is involved, we are presented with an extraordinarily abundant variety of forms, pictures, and impressions . . . Here in Vienna it was Tausk who took me to the movies despite work, weariness, and lack of time.[20]

Andreas-Salomé makes the crucial link between cinema and consciousness. This connection was explored at length by the psychologist Hugo Münsterberg, whose work I discussed in Chapter 4. In *The Film: A Psychological Study* (1916), one of the earliest works of film aesthetics, he wrote that film 'unfold[s] our inner life, our mental play [in] tones which are fluttering and fleeting like our own mental states'.[21] 'The massive outer world has lost its weight, it has been freed from space, time, and causality, and it has been clothed in the forms of our own consciousness', Münsterberg argued.[22] His post-Kantian aesthetic not only connected cinema and consciousness, but made cinema (as did Andreas-Salomé) the reflector of a particularly modernized consciousness, imaged in the terms of a Baudelairean metropolitan modernity, in which 'the fleeting, passing surface suggestion' is imbued with depth and fullness only through 'our mental mechanism', as the gift of consciousness to the phenomenal world. Linking 'cut-back' or flash-back to 'the mental act of remembering' and close-up to 'the mental act of attending', Münsterberg wrote: 'It is as if the outer world itself became molded in accordance with our fleeting turns of attention or with our passing memory ideas.'[23]

Freud was silent on the topic of film's capacity to 'unfold our inner life'. He did speak out, however, on the issue of using film as a way of representing psychoanalytic theory. The most charged moment came in 1925, when Karl Abraham wrote to Freud, telling him that he had been approached by a director (Eric Neumann) of Ufa (Universum Film Aktiengesellschaft), about the possibility of a film exploring psychoanalytic concepts. Letters between Abraham and Freud chart Abraham's growing enthusiasm for the project and Freud's continuing resistance:

> My chief objection is still that I do not believe that satisfactory plastic representation of our abstractions is at all possible. We do not want to give

our consent to anything insipid. Mr. Goldwyn was at any rate clever enough
to stick to the aspect of our subject that can be plastically represented very
well, that is to say, love. The small example that you mentioned, the
representation of repression by means of my Worcester simile [a reference
to the analogy of the invader to illustrate repression and resistance], would
make an absurd rather than instructive impact.[24]

Freud may well have felt that his *Introductory Lectures* had already analogized and dramatized psychoanalytic abstractions to a sufficient degree: to
represent analogies in cinematic form would thus be to further substantiate
the dramatized example rather than the concept of which it was an illustration. The film was made, however, as *Secrets of a Soul*, directed by
G.W. Pabst. Abraham and Hanns Sachs acted as advisors, and Sachs
wrote the pamphlet which accompanied the film and explained some of
the psychoanalytic concepts it explored.

Sachs's introduction to psychoanalysis had come with his reading of *The
Interpretation of Dreams* in 1904. He abandoned his law career in its early
stages, and followed Freud into psychoanalytic work, initially through
writing and editing, and, in 1920, through the training of analysts.
Freud's dream book remained a key text for him, as did Freud's 1908
essay 'The Creative Writer and Day-dreaming'. Fascinated by the application of psychoanalysis to the creative process and to the reception of works
of art, and by the concept of the work of art as a 'collective day-dream',
Sachs explored the idea of 'day-dreams in common', a concept which
became central to the articles he wrote on film in the late 1920s and early
1930s for the film journal *Close Up*.[25] In an article on 'Film Psychology',
Sachs also opened up the relationship between conscious and unconscious
knowledge in relation to dream and film, suggesting that the film-work
functions not only by analogy, but also by contrast with the dream-work:[26]
while the dream disguises unconscious wishes and desires as a way of
eluding the censor, the film reveals them. In this sense, the film could be
said to be closer to dream interpretation, with its emancipatory potential,
than to the dream itself.

The *Secrets of a Soul* pamphlet describes at length and in detail the action
of the film as an illustration of central Freudian concepts: repression,
sublimation, displacement, condensation.[27] There is, however, virtually
no analysis of the ways in which the filmic medium might itself be operating
in ways analogous to the psychic apparatus; the film seems to function at
this stage for Sachs as pure illustration, though the dream sequences in
the film use devices, such as superimpositions and fade-outs, which other
of his contemporaries were readily mapping onto the processes of the

dream-work. In some senses, then, the pamphlet serves to neutralize or, at least, to instrumentalize the cinema.

Sachs's partial occlusion of the cinematographic in the *Secrets of a Soul* pamphlet is found in a different guise and in a far more extreme form a few years earlier, in Freud's comments on Otto Rank's study *The Double* in his essay on 'The Uncanny'.[28] Freud discusses Rank's exploration of the connections 'which the "double" has with reflections in mirrors, with shadows, with guardian spirits, with the belief in the soul and with the fear of death', as well as his theory that the evolution of the idea of the double functioned as a form of preservation against extinction. In a footnote he adds: 'In Ewer's *Der Student von Prag*, which serves as the starting point of Rank's study on the "double," the hero has promised his beloved not to kill his antagonist in a duel. But on his way to the duelling-ground he meets his "double," who has already killed his rival.'[29] Ewers indeed wrote the script for *The Student of Prague* (1913), but it is striking that Freud makes no reference to the film itself, referring to the narrative in entirely literary terms.

If we turn to Rank's *The Double* (1914), however, we find in his first paragraph the following lines: 'Psychoanalysis need not shy away even from some random and banal subject, if the matter at hand exhibits psychological problems whose sources and implications are not obvious. There should be no objection, then, if we take as a point of departure a "romantic drama," which not long ago made the rounds of our cinemas.'[30] While Rank does add that 'Those whose concern is with literature may be reassured by the fact that the scenarist of this film, *The Student of Prague*, is an author currently in vogue and that he has adhered to prominent patterns, the effectiveness of which has been tested by time', he goes on to make a direct connection between cinematic and psychic processes.[31] As he writes:

> Any apprehension about the real value of a photoplay which aims so largely at achieving external effects may be postponed until we have seen in what sense a subject based upon an ancient folk-tradition, and the content of which is so eminently psychological, is altered by the demands of modern techniques of expression. It may perhaps turn out that cinematography, which in numerous ways reminds us of the dream-work, can also express certain psychological facts and relationships – which the writer often is unable to describe with verbal clarity – in such clear and conspicuous imagery that it facilitates our understanding of them. The film attracts our attention all the more readily since we have learned from similar studies that a modern treatment is often successful in reapproaching, intuitively, the real meaning of an ancient theme which has become either unintelligible or misunderstood in its course through tradition.[32]

The broader context for Rank's discussion is the uncanniness of cinema itself, described so often by early commentators as a world of shadows. 'This is not life but the shadow of life and this is not movement but the soundless shadow of movement', Maxim Gorki wrote in July 1896, describing a showing of the Lumière brothers' first films: 'It is terrifying to watch but it is the movement of shadows, mere shadows. Curses and ghosts, evil spirits that have cast whole spirits into eternal sleep come to mind and you feel as though Merlin's vicious trick is being played out before you.'[33] For cinema's first spectators, the realism of early films, combined with their unlifelike absence of sound and colour, seems to have provoked, in Yuri Tsivian's words, 'the uncanny feeling that films somehow belong the world of the dead' and that 'cinema is a convenient metaphor for death'.[34]

A phenomenological fear is present at the origins of cinema, and is strikingly reinvoked in German expressionist cinema of the 1910s and 1920s: films such as *The Student of Prague*, *The Cabinet of Dr. Caligari*, and *Nosferatu* do not merely constitute an episode in the history of cinema, but act as figurations of the materiality and the phenomenology of film *and* of fear. Such films, with their shadows, their mirrors and their doubles, inform – in however oblique and occluded a way – many of the terms and the images of Freud's writings of the period, in particular the essay on 'The Uncanny'. This, like Rank's *The Double*, attempts to negotiate the relationship between the archaic and the modern: the animations and automations – anthropologically conceived – of primitive mentation and belief, and of the new technologies, with their power to bring still things to life and to represent (though Freud does not of course make the connection to filmic representations) 'dismembered limbs, a severed head, a hand cut off at the wrist ... feet which dance by themselves'.[35] Moreover, and as Friedrich Kittler suggests, psychoanalysis and film – science and technology – together extend *and* implode the life of the Romantic double.[36] The fundamental link between the two fields overrides Freud's silence on the question of the cinematic in his thoughts on 'the double' and 'the uncanny'.

In the quotation from Rank, cited above, a specific equation is made between cinematography and the dream-work. The plethora of psychoanalytic and psychological studies of dream-life in the 1920s and 1930s was, I would argue, linked to the development of film aesthetics, while writings on dreams and dream-life in the early twentieth century found new forms of association and analogy in film. The intense debates over visual/verbal representations in the transition from silent to sound film in the 1920s had highly significant counterparts in the discussions over the visual or verbal dimensions, and the alphabetical or pictorial scripts, of dream-language.

Time and again in early film theory we find the paradox that this art or science of modernity is being framed in the terms of a primitive or archaic consciousness, mapping onto Freud's exploration of the 'regressive' transmutation of ideas into visual pictures in his dream, and his account of visual thinking as 'primitive' mentation.

Freud's account of the 'apparatus' of the mind had a crucial influence on later filmic 'apparatus theories', most notably the work of film theorists such as Jean Louis Baudry and Christian Metz who, in the 1970s, made a theoretical return to the machinery and apparatus of the cinema, constructing, as Stephen Heath notes, a conceptual synthesis of the technological and the metapsychological.[37] Film theory's fascination with psychoanalysis also has its counterpart in psychoanalytic literature's deployment of film. Analysts and theorists have taken up the cinematic dimensions of such concepts as 'projection', 'scene' and 'screening'. I have discussed elsewhere the centrality of such terms for Ella Freeman Sharpe in her book *Dream Analysis*, for Bertram Lewin in his work on the 'dream screen', and, most recently, for Didier Anzieu in his formulations of 'the skin ego'.[38] For these psychoanalytic theorists, projections, such as we have in dream-images, require a screen. As Ella Freeman Sharpe stated, in her account of the dream-mechanisms of 'dramatization' and 'secondary elaboration': 'A film of moving pictures is projected on the screen of our private inner cinema'.[39] One of the dreams Sharpe analyses is an anxiety dream in which:

> A man is acting for the screen. He is to recite certain lines of the play. The photographers and voice recorders are there. At the critical moment the actor forgets his lines. Time and again he makes the attempt with no result. Rolls of film must have been spoilt.[40]

In Sharpe's analysis of the dream, the associations reveal an infantile situation in which 'the dreamer was once the onlooker when his parents were "operating" together. The baby was the original photographer and recorder and he stopped the parents in the "act" by noise. The baby did not forget his lines!':

> The 'return of the repressed' is given in the dream by the element 'rolls of film must have been wasted' telling us by the device of metonymy, of a huge amount of faecal matter the baby was able to pass at that moment.
>
> Illustrated in this dream are some of the profoundest activities of the psyche. We have the recording of sight and sound by the infant and the incorporation by the senses of sight and hearing of the primal scene. We have evidence of this incorporated scene by its projection into the dream dramatization. The modern invention of the screen of the cinema is pressed into

service as the appropriate symbol, the screen being the modern external device corresponding to the internal dream picture mechanism.[41]

Sharpe's analysis echoes (while also making explicit the film/dream analogy) Freud's account of one of the most famous dreams of psychoanalysis, his patient 'the Wolf-Man's' childhood dream of observing, through a window, a number of white wolves sitting on a tree and looking at him. 'He had woken up and seen something', Freud comments. 'The attentive looking, which in the dream was ascribed to the wolves, should rather be shifted on to him. At a decisive point, therefore, a transposition has taken place.'[42] Behind the content of the dream, Freud suggests, lies the 'primal scene', the '*Urszene*', in which the very young child observed the parents' sexual intercourse.

In Sharpe's analysis, the transposition from observer to observed noted by Freud revolves around the image of the 'screen' as both interior (the 'inner private cinema') and 'exterior' ('the modern external device'). The perception both extends and renders cinematographic Freud's claim in 'A Metapsychological Supplement to the Theory of Dreams' that 'A dream is … among other things, a *projection*: an externalization of an internal process' and, in 'The Ego and the Id', that 'The ego is first and foremost a bodily ego: it is not merely a surface entity, but is itself the projection of a surface'.[43] Freud's emphases in this essay on the ego as a bodily 'projection', and on the body and its surface as a 'place from which both external and internal perceptions may spring', allow us to bring together the concepts of 'projection' as 'prosthesis' (the body extended or projected into the world) and as a 'screening', whereby not only the subject's body but his/her relationship to the 'skin' – the screen/surface of the other (the mother) – is projected or imaged.[44]

In Bertram Lewin's important work of the 1940s, the 'dream screen' becomes the hallucinatory representation of the mother's breast, which once acted as a prelude to sleep, while the forgetting of dreams is often imaged as a rolling up or away of the dream screen, repeating the experience of the withdrawal of the breast.[45] In a more recent study, and returning to the Wolf-Man, Lewin explores the ways in which events in motion (para-digmatically the parents 'operating' together in the 'primal scene') are remembered as 'stills': 'They are as if immobilized for better viewing'.[46] 'Screen memories', it could be said, 'freeze-frame' the moving picture. By extension, Freud's photographic analogies could be taken not merely as pre-cinematic concepts, but as ways of understanding the stillness of which the moving (cinematic) image is truly composed.

Lewin, in making a distinction between the screen and the dream-images projected onto it, allows for a distinction to be drawn between sleep (the blank screen) and dream (the play and projection of visual images). The distinction between sleep and dream is relatively untheorized in *The Interpretation of Dreams*, as are threshold states between sleeping and waking. It is such states to which I now turn, in relation to cinema and film spectatorship, and in part as a way of pursuing the question of the archaic, the modern, and their interrelationship.

My starting point comes in the opening section of chapter 2 of *The Interpretation of Dreams*, the preamble to the analysis of the specimen dream, the dream of Irma's injection. Freud is describing his development of the techniques of free association and their relationship to dream interpretation. This method of interpretation, he writes, 'involves some psychological preparation of the patient. We must aim at bringing about two changes in him: an increase in the attention he pays to his own psychical perceptions and the elimination of the criticism by which he normally sifts the thoughts that occur to him.'[47] The distinction Freud draws – as Strachey translates it – is between the 'frame of mind of a man who is reflecting' and 'that of a man who is observing his own psychical processes'. While attention is concentrated in both cases, the man who is reflecting is exercising his *critical* faculty, and censoring his thoughts. The self-observer, by contrast, need only suppress his critical faculty to enable 'innumerable ideas [to] come into his consciousness of which he could otherwise never have got hold'. Freud continues:

> What is in question, evidently, is the establishment of a psychical state which, in its distribution of psychical energy (that is, of mobile attention), bears some analogy to the state before falling asleep – and no doubt also to hypnosis. As we fall asleep, 'involuntary ideas' emerge . . . . [and] change into visual and acoustic images.[48]

The abandonment of the critical function is also to be found, Freud argues, in poetic creation.

The significant phrase in this section of *The Interpretation of Dreams* is 'mobile attention', and I want now to link the concept to those modes of (in)attention and reduced wakefulness that so preoccupied critical theorists such as Siegfried Kracauer and Walter Benjamin, and which the film theorist Christian Metz explored, in a different conceptual and historical context, and more directly in relation to film and dream, in *The Imaginary Signifier*.[49] The film–dream analogy functions not only as a correlation between dream-work and film-work, but through the concept of states – film-states and dream-states – which converge in the transitional space between sleeping and waking. As Kracauer stated in his *Theory of Film*: 'Lowered consciousness invites dreaming.'[50]

The work of Benjamin is of significant interest here. Axel Honneth has argued that Benjamin took from American pragmatism and French versions of *Lebensphilosophie* (especially the work of Bergson) a fascination with religious and aesthetic experiences as 'borderline experiences in which reality as a whole is experienced as a field of subjective forces'.[51] Hence Benjamin's preoccupation with situations of reduced attention or half-wakefulness – flânerie, reading, listening to music, intoxication, artistic creation – and above all, moments of awakening, 'when the environment's perceptual stimuli cannot yet be instrumentally classified in accordance with everyday routine'.[52] In ways at least analogous to Freud's distinction between reflection and self-observation – the latter allied to free association – Benjamin suggests, in Honneth's words, that 'when our purposively directed concentration is low, we tend to experience reality as a field of surprising correspondences and analogies'.[53] Modernity, for Benjamin, with its demands for instrumental, purposive, rational attention, threatens the 'anthropologically based potential for intensifying experience by reducing attention'.[54]

Film plays a most complex and ambiguous role in this model. The loss of aura, which the cinema – among other modern technologies – embodies, could be seen (as Honneth sees it) as a deprivation of those experiences of the shattering of the self and of reduced attention. Yet Benjamin's film viewer is also a centreless subject, responding to the 'shock' of cinematic experience – its radical disruptions and 'changes of scene and focus which have a percussive effect on the spectator'[55] – 'in a state of distraction'. The cinema trains the spectator, Benjamin seems to suggest, in the transformed mode of perception demanded by modern life. For Siegfried Kracauer, writing a decade earlier, 'distraction' – originally a negative attribute, opposed to contemplative concentration – takes on a positive aspect as it becomes anchored in a non-bourgeois mode of visual and sensorial experience, a form of attention or inattention appropriate to the fragmentary, discontinuous nature of the modern visual media.

Kracauer's *Theory of Film* (published in 1960, but including earlier material) explores the relationship between dreaming and cinema through 'the two directions of dreaming': towards and into the object and 'away from the given image into subjective reveries'.[56] These two apparently opposed movements of dreaming are, in fact, intertwined:

> Trance-like immersion in a shot or a succession of shots may at any moment yield to daydreaming which increasingly disengages itself from the imagery occasioning it ... Together the two intertwined dream processes constitute a veritable stream of consciousness whose contents – cataracts of indistinct fantasies and inchoate thoughts – still bear the imprint of the bodily sensations from which they issue.[57]

The relations of 'inside' and 'outside' here strongly recall Freud's emphases, noted above, on the ego as a bodily 'projection', and remind us of the extent to which mind/body and inner perception/outer world dichotomies are dissolved in Freudian dream theories.

The work of Christian Metz leads us back to the question of cinema spectatorship as a mode of reduced attention on the borderlines of sleep and wakefulness:

> [T]he filmic flux resembles the dream flux more than other products of the waking state do. It is received, as we have said, in a state of lessened wakefulness. Its signifier (images accompanied by sound and movement) inherently confers on it a certain affinity with the dream, for it coincides directly with one of the major features of the dream signifier, 'imaged' expression, the considerations of representability, to use Freud's term.[58]

Throughout Part III of *The Imaginary Signifier* – 'The Fiction Film and its Spectator' – Metz sets dream, daydream and film alongside and against each other through the question of degrees of sleep and wakefulness. Film and dream 'are interwoven ... by differences'. The filmic state 'is marked by a general tendency to lower wakefulness'; 'The filmic and dream states tend to converge when the spectator begins to doze off [s'endormir] ... or when the dreamer begins to wake up. But the dominant situation is that in which film and dream are not confounded: this is because the film spectator is a man awake, whereas the dreamer is a man asleep.'[59] Nonetheless, 'the filmic situation brings with it certain elements of motor inhibition, and it is in this respect a kind of sleep in miniature, a kind of waking sleep ... To leave the cinema is a little like getting up: not always easy (except if the film was really indifferent).'[60] 'The spectator puts himself into a state of lessened alertness ... Among the different regimes of waking, the filmic state is one of those least unlike sleep and dreaming, dreamful sleep'. Metz's procedure, however, is not to rest with such formulations, but to introduce new terms for comparison – in this case, the daydream – so that he concludes with the image of the film as a force field in which distinct regimes of consciousness – reality, dream and daydream – are momentarily – but only momentarily – reconciled.

In the final part of this chapter I turn to the significance of the border-line for film, dream and modernism. The transitional states between sleeping and waking, and the experiences of going to sleep and of waking up, are central to modernist literature: Proust is the crucial example here. The works of modernist literature most intensely engaged, implicitly or explicitly, with film are also those most preoccupied with the representa-tion of states of going to sleep, sleeping and awakening; for example, Virginia Woolf's *To the Lighthouse* (1928), which is bound up with the representation of reduced attentiveness and lowered wakefulness, as in Mrs Ramsay's evening reverie: 'All the being and the doing, expansive, glittering, vocal, evaporated; and one shrunk, with a sense of solemnity, to being oneself, a wedge-shaped core of darkness, something invisible to others.'[61] The central section of the novel, 'Time Passes', is film-minded in its representations of sound 'folded in silence'[62] and of the animation of the object world. It begins and ends with the processes of going to sleep and awakening – the last word of the section is indeed 'Awake'[63] – while its centre is a correlation between dream and the play of projected images on a surface which suggests a cinematic consciousness. The last part of the novel – 'The Lighthouse' – returns to the realms of daydream, reverie, memory and hauntings.

The importance of 'the borderline' and of transitional states emerges, in a rather different way, in the film writings of H.D., a central figure, as I touched on in the previous chapter, for the interrelations of psychoanalysis and cinema, both historically and conceptually. In her articles for the film journal *Close Up* in the late 1920s – also the forum for Hanns Sachs's writings on cinema – H.D. describes the processes of an initial resistance to film which we could link to the resistance to sleep, understood as a fear of the loss of identity and even of death. As Freud writes in 'A Metapsychological Supplement to the Theory of Dreams', the ego, in extreme cases, 'renounces sleep because of its fear of its dreams'.[64]

In her article on the Russian film *Expiation* (*Before the Law*, or *Sühne*), Lev Kuleshov's 1926 adaptation a Jack London story, with a screenplay by the Russian formalist critic Viktor Shklovsky, H.D. writes of the ways in which, about to enter the cinema to watch the film, she finds herself impelled to create a form of pre-filmic experience from the vision of the street: 'I so poignantly wanted to re-visualize those squares of doors and shutters and another and another bit of detail that of necessity was lost at first that I did illogically (I was already late) climb back.'[65] She enters the cinema when the film is a third over:

Rain poured over a slab of earth and I felt all my preparation of the extravagantly contrasting out of doors gay little street, was almost an ironical intention, someone, something 'intended' that I should grasp this, that some mind should receive this series of uncanny and almost psychic sensations in order to transmute them elsewhere; in order to translate them.[66]

Film and pre-film (the 'dimensional dream-tunnel' of the street) are brought into an 'uncanny' relationship, allowing H.D. as spectator to 'translate' the 'remote and symbolical' dimensions of the film. *Expiation* is something beyond the limit, 'the word after the last word is spoken', 'taking the human mind and *spirit* further than it can go'.[67] H.D.'s film aesthetics and her model of vision are predicated on symbol, gesture, 'hieroglyph',[68] and her film writing tends to provide not retrospective judgement on a film, but a performative running commentary on the processes of spectating which becomes a form of 'inner speech', acting as a screen onto which the film images can be projected.

Her article on *The Student of Prague* (Hendrik Galeen's 1926 version, with Conrad Veidt in the title role) describes or enacts a spectatorial procedure similar to that in *Expiation*, an initial resistance to film, an irritated awareness of her surroundings, a disorder: 'Something has been touched before I realise it, some hidden spring; there is something wrong with this film, with me, with the weather, with something', and then a moment of understanding and an increasing absorption in the film, until its close, when she 'awakens' to the discordant voices of her fellow spectators: 'A small voice . . . will whisper there within me, "You see I was right, you see it will come. In spite of 'Gee' and 'Doug Fairbanks' and 'we must have something cheerful', it must come soon: a universal language, a universal art open alike to the pleb and the initiate."'[69] The promise of the film as 'universal language' – which did not survive the transition to sound film for H.D. – becomes increasingly inseparable from a model of the 'universal language' of the dream. In her account of viewing *The Student of Prague*, she emphasized the 'hieroglyphic' dimensions of the film's landscapes and the 'hieratic' movement of the actors' bodies: 'The little tree twists and bends and makes all the frantic gestures of the little tree at the cross-roads under which Faust conjured devils . . . . That little man [Punchinello] . . . is a symbol, an asterisk, an enigma'.[70]

The intertwining of (silent) cinema and psychoanalysis was cemented for H.D. by the cinema of Pabst, whose *Secrets of a Soul* was, as I have noted, supervised by Hanns Sachs, H.D.'s analyst for a brief period. H.D. not only wrote for *Close Up*, she also acted in the films directed by one of the journal's editors, Kenneth Macpherson.[71] The most ambitious film, *Borderline*, in which she acted alongside Paul Robeson, took *Secrets of a Soul* as a central model, including the publication of a pamphlet, written by H.D. (though published anonymously) to explain the film. '*Borderline*', she wrote in the pamphlet, 'is a dream and perhaps when we say that we have said every-thing. The film is the art of dream portrayal and perhaps when we say we have achieved the definition, the synthesis toward which we have all been striving'.[72]

Borderline also shows the strong influence of *Expiation*, particularly on H.D.'s film performance. In her article on Kuleshov's film, H.D. focused on the acting style, and in particular the gestures, of the one woman in the film, the character Edith, played by the actress Aleksandra Khokhlova (Kuleshov's life-partner), writing:

> She has a way of standing against a sky line that makes a hieroglyphic, that spells out almost visibly some message of cryptic symbolism. Her gestures are magnificent. If this is Russian, then I am Russian . . . . Edith stalks out to fulfil the bidding of justice . . . Joan of Arc, all the women from Pallas Athene to Charlotte Corday that have personified some grave principle is in her fanatic gesture, in her set gargoyle posture, in her lean attenuated determination . . . This sort of raw picked beauty must of necessity destroy the wax and candy-box 'realism' of the so much so-called film art. It must destroy in fact so much that perhaps it does 'go' as one of our party said 'too far' . . . Edith is a great locust, a sort of Flemish saint, a worn-down, sea-wind battered statue that has been rubbed raw by weather, hardly any personal significance in the figure; it certainly has gone too far.[73]

'If this is Russian, then I am Russian': H.D.'s identification with the figure of Edith would be enacted in *Borderline*, in her use of gesture and her performance of neurosis and madness in that film, and in the film's imagery, with its stuffed sea-gull against the blowing curtains of an open window becoming a metonymy for the 'worn-down, sea-wind battered statue that has been rubbed raw by weather'. H.D. used similar terms to describe her fictional alter ego, Raymond Ransome, in the autobiographical short story *Two Americans*, which describes a meeting with Paul Robeson (Saul Howard in the story): 'Weather-worn marble, Raymonde Ransome, faced Saul Howard, seared bronze'.[74] The images are also indicative of H.D.'s fascination with the relationship between statuary and the moving body/image, a central aspect of her modernist Classicism: 'Is it true that move-ment of the human body throws out, as it were, a sort of charted series of tabulated vibrations, so that just that circular turn, Greek bronze on rotating pedestal, did this thing?', asks her narrator in *Two Americans*.[75] The redefinition of 'beauty' brought about by Khoklova as Edith, at the heart of H.D.'s appreciation, and contrasted with Hollywood's despoliation of screen beauty (imaged in other of her cinema articles by Greta Garbo) in the figure of the 'vamp', was also central to Bryher's briefer description of *Expiation*, in *Film Problems of Soviet Russia*. There Bryher wrote of the film: 'It must have been the first time, considering the date, that mind was shown on the screen, instead of mere body.'[76]

In the spring of 1933, as *Close Up* entered its final year, H.D. travelled, as I discussed in the previous chapter, to Vienna for psychoanalysis with Freud, bearing Sachs's recommendation. She did not refer to her work in and on film in her accounts of the analysis – 'Writing on the Wall' (1945/46) and 'Advent' (1933/48), published together as *Tribute to Freud* in 1985 – but it seems likely that she saw her sessions with Freud as a way of continuing, or perhaps replacing, the work of film, finding in dream and symbolic interpretation an equivalent to, and extension of, the 'language' of the silent cinema, which she invested with both individual and 'universal' meaning.

The 'shapes, lines, graphs' of dreams are, H.D. writes, 'the *hieroglyph of the unconscious*'.[77] In an echo of Freud's repeated references in *The Interpretation of Dreams* to the popular newspaper *Fliegende Blätter* – in one of which he compares the work of 'secondary revision' with 'the enigmatic inscriptions with which *Fliegende Blätter* has for so long entertained its readers'[78] – H.D. discusses 'the newspaper class' of dreams, implicitly suggesting the ways in which the diurnal newspaper itself provides the materials for the 'day's residues':

> The printed page varies, cheap-news-print, good print, bad print, smudged and uneven print – there are the great letter words of an advertisement or the almost invisible pin-print; there are the huge capitals of a child's alphabet chart or building blocks; letters or ideas may run askew on the page, as it were; they may be purposeless; they may be stereotyped and not meant for 'reading' but as a test.[79]

The passage recalls the debates about film captions and intertitles in the 1920s, and their indeterminate nature as speech or writing, as in the Hungarian film theorist Béla Balázs's account of the ways in which emotions in the silent film were 'made visible in the form of lettering . . . It was an accepted convention, for instance, that alerting alarm-signals rushed at us from the screen with tousled letters rapidly increasing in space . . . At other times a slowly darkening title signified a pause full of meaning or a melancholy musing.'[80] The 'enigmatic inscriptions' to which Freud refers are also the alphabets or hieroglyphs of film and dream.

In *Tribute to Freud*, as in other of her autobiographical writings, H.D. represents her childhood memories and dreams as moments of vision which are also moments in a history of pre-cinema and cinema, and autobiography becomes intertwined with a history of optics (lenses, daguerreotypes, transparencies.) Most strikingly, there is the 'writing on the wall', her 'visionary' experience in Corfu in the early 1920s, which Freud saw as a 'dangerous symptom'[81] and H.D. viewed as her most significant life experience. She recounts, frame by frame, the inscription of hieroglyphs, images projected on a wall in light not shadow. The first are like magic-lantern slides, the later images resemble the earliest films. 'For myself', she writes, differentiating her position from that of Freud, 'I consider this sort of dream or projected picture of vision as a sort of halfway state between ordinary dream and the vision of those who, for lack of a more definite term, we must call psychics or clairvoyants.'[82] Later in the text, she recalls an earlier dream or 'flash of vision' of a carved block of stone, a solid shape that appeared before her eyes 'before sleeping or just on wakening'.[83] 'Crossing the line', 'crossing the threshold' are H.D.'s signature phrases: they refer both to the blurred borderline between ordinary experience and 'psychic' life, and to the threshold between the states of sleeping and waking. In this indeterminate zone, films and dreams share a reality.

For H.D., remembered scenes, recalled in the analytic session, 'are like transparencies, set before candles in a dark room', and the network of memories builds up to become a surface, onto which 'there fell inevitably a shadow, a writing-on-the-wall, a curve like a reversed, unfinished S and a dot beneath it, a question mark, the shadow of a question – *is this it?*'[84] Throughout *Tribute to Freud* (and its companion text, *Advent*) we are led around (as in a cinematic panning-shot) the space of Freud's consulting room in Vienna, following the line of its walls, the fourth of which is a wall which is not a wall, its folding-doors opening onto a connecting room, the 'room beyond' which 'may appear very dark or there may be broken light and shadow'.[85] She links this 'fourth wall', and the room beyond, which contains Freud's books and antiquities, to the 'fourth dimension', the dimension explored by numerous modernist artists and writers in their explorations of mysticism and the occult and which was, for Sergei Eisenstein, writing in *Close Up*, the dimension of the Kino. It is the 'fourth wall' and the 'room beyond' which both H.D. and Freud face or look towards, as she lies on the couch with Freud seated in the corner behind her, his cigar smoke rising in the air.

In *Advent*, the account of her analysis with Freud based most closely on the notes she made at the time, H.D. represents Freud as absorbed by particular aspects of her Corfu experience, the Writing on the Wall of her hotel room, including:

> the lighting of the room, or possible reflections or shadows. I described the room again, the communicating door, the door out to the hall and the one window. He asked if it was a French window. I said, 'No – one like that,' indicating the one window in his room.[86]

In *Advent*, the space of the hotel room, the scene of the Writing on the Wall, becomes increasingly identified with the space of Freud's consulting room, an identity to which his own insistent questioning would seem to point. If both spaces are the sites of projection, of picture-writing, of a Writing on the Wall, then psychoanalysis too becomes a cinematographic arena, with both analyst and analysand facing towards a surface – wall or screen – onto which memories and imaginings are projected. That the wall or screen is also an open, or 'communicating', doorway into the 'room beyond' creates a further connection between psychoanalysis and film, in the conception of a fourth dimensionality and, in Walter Benjamin's phrase, an 'optical unconscious'.[87]

As H.D.'s *Tribute to Freud* helps us to understand, Freud's near-silence on the question of cinema (a silence with which H.D., despite all her recent and intense engagement with film, appears to have colluded) conceals the profundity of the relationship between psychoanalysis and film. Psychoanalysis is itself a form of cinema, the projection and play of sign, image and scene upon a screen which, like H.D.'s representations of Freud's 'fourth wall', is at once past, present and future and simultaneously absent and present, wall and notwall. In this reading, the absence of filmic analogies in Freud's writings need not signal an indifference towards cinema. In the absence of analogy, a connection more intricate and intimate begins to emerge.

Notes

1 *The Complete Letters of Sigmund Freud to Wilhelm Fliess 1887–1904*, edited by Jeffrey Moussaieff Masson (Cambridge, Mass: Harvard University Press: 1985), p. 417.

2 Freud, *The Interpretation of Dreams*, *SE* vol. 4, p. xv.

3 Ibid., p. 22.

4 Hugo von Hoffmansthal. 'A Substitute for Dreams' (Translation of *'Der Ersatz für die Träume'* (1921)) in *The London Mercury* IX (1923–1924): 177–1799, 179.

5 *Creative Evolution* (*L'Evolution créatrice* (1907)), translated by Arthur Mitchell. (London: Macmillan, 1911), p. 329.

6 See in particular the work of Gilles Deleuze, especially *Cinéma 1: L'imagemouvement* (Paris: Editions de Minuit, 1983), translated by Hugh Tomlinson and Barbara Habberjam (Minneapolis: University of Minnesota Press, 1986) and

Cinema 2: L'image-temps (Paris: Editions de Minuit, 1985), translated by Hugh Tomlinson and Robert Galeta (Minneapolis: University of Minnesota Press, 1989).

7 Mary Ann Doane has argued for a conceptual and historical link between Freud and Marey, in that both psychoanalysis and chronophotography were attempts to correlate storage and time. See Mary Ann Doane, 'Freud, Marey and the Cinema', in *Endless Night: Cinema and Psychoanalysis, Parallel Histories*, ed. Janet Bergstrom (Berkeley and Los Angeles: University of California Press, 1999), pp. 57–87.

8 Freud, 'The Uncanny', *SE* vol. 17, p. 221.

9 Henri Bergson, *Dreams*, trans. translated by Edwin E. Slosson (London: Unwin, 1914).

10 Havelock Ellis, *The World of Dreams* (London: Constable, 1911), p. 32.

11 Ibid., p. 21.

12 Ibid., p. 36.

13 Ibid., p. 214.

14 James Sully, 'The Dream as a Revelation', *Fortnightly Review*, 59 (March 1903), 354–365. It should be noted that Sully is not dismissing the value of dreams, but rather representing 'the nocturnal phantasmagoria as a source of preternatural delight, as an outlet from the narrow and somewhat gloomy enclosure of the matter-of-fact world, giving swift transition into the large and luminous spaces of the imagination'.

15 Ernest Jones, *Sigmund Freud: Life and Work*, vol. 2 (London, Hogarth: 1955), p. 62.

16 Stephen Heath, 'Cinema and Psychoanalysis: Parallel Histories', in *Endless Night: Cinema and Psychoanalysis, Parallel Histories*, edited by J. Bergstrom (Berkeley: University of California Press, 1999), p. 25.

17 Jones, *Sigmund Freud*, pp. 40–41.

18 Sigmund Freud, *The Letters of Sigmund Freud*, edited by Ernst L. Freud, translated by Tania and James Stern. (New York: Basic Books, 1975). p. 261–262. Date of letter: 22 September 1907.

19 Jonathan Crary, *Suspensions of Perception: Attention, Spectacle and Modern Culture* (Cambridge, Mass: MIT Press, 1999), p. 366.

20 Lou Andreas-Salomé, *The Freud Journal*, translated by S. A. Leavy (London: Quartet, 1987), p. 101.

21 Hugo Munsterberg *The Film: A Psychological Study* (New York: Dover, 1970), p. 72.

22 Ibid., p. 95.

23 Ibid., p. 41.

24 *The Complete Correspondence of Sigmund Freud and Karl Abraham*, ed. Ernst Falzeder (London and New York: Karnac, 2002), p. 547..

25 The *Close Up* essays discussed in this essay have been anthologized in *Close Up 1927–1933: Cinema and Modernism*, edited by James Donald, Anne Friedberg and Laura Marcus (London: Cassell, 1998).

26 Hanns Sachs, 'Film Psychology', *Close Up* 3, no. 5 (1928).

27 Hanns Sachs, *Psycho-Analyse: Rätsel des Unbewussten* (Berlin: Lichtbild-Bühne, 1926).

28 Sigmund Freud, 'The Uncanny', *SE* vol. 17, pp. 234–235.

29 Ibid., p. 236.

30 Otto Rank, *The Double: A Psychoanalytical Study*, translated by Harry Tucker (London: Maresfield, 1989), p. 3.

31 Ibid., pp. 3–4.

32 Ibid., p. 4.

33 Richard Taylor and Ian Christie (eds.), *The Film Factory: Russian and Soviet Cinema in Documents 1896–1939* (London: Routledge, 1988), p. 25.

34 Yuri Tsivian, *Early Cinema in Russia and Its Cultural Reception*, translated by Alan Bodger (Chicago: Chicago University Press, 1994), p. 6.

35 Freud, 'The Uncanny', *SE* vol. 17, p. 244.

36 Friedrich Kittler, *Literature, Media, Information Systems* (Amsterdam: Overseas Publishers Association, 1997).

37 Stephen Heath, *Questions of Cinema* (Bloomington: Indiana University Press, 1981), p. 223.

38 Laura Marcus, *Sigmund Freud's* The Interpretation of Dreams: *New Interdisciplinary Essays* (Manchester: Manchester University Press, 1999), pp. 33–43.

39 Ella Freeman Sharpe, *Dream Analysis* (London: Hogarth, 1937), p. 58.

40 Sharpe, *Dream Analysis*, pp. 76–77.

41 Ibid.

42 Freud, 'From the History of an Infantile Neurosis', *SE* vol. 17, pp. 7–122, 34–35.

43 Freud, 'A Metapsychological Supplement to the Theory of Dreams', *SE* vol. 14, p. 223; Freud, 'The Ego and the Id', *SE* vol. 19, p. 26.

44 Freud, 'The Ego and the Id,' *SE* vol. 19, p. 25.

45 Bertram Lewin, 'Sleep, the mouth and the dream screen', *Psychoanalytic Quarterly* 15 (1946): pp. 419–434.

46 Bertram Lewin, *The Image and the Past* (New York: International Universities Press, 1968), 16–17.

47 Freud, *The Interpretation of Dreams*, *SE* vol. 4, p. 101.

48 Ibid., p. 102.

49 Christian Metz, *The Imaginary Signifier: Psychoanalysis and the Cinema*, translated by C. Britton, A. Williams, B. Brewster and A. Guzzetti (Bloomington: Indiana University Press, 1982).

50 Siegfried Kracauer, *Theory of Film: The Redemption of Physical Reality* (New York: Oxford University Press, 1965), p. 163.

51 Axel Honneth, 'A communicative disclosure of the past: on the relation between anthropology and philosophy of history in Walter Benjamin', in *The Actuality of Walter Benjamin*, edited by L. Marcus and L. Nead (London: Lawrence and Wishart, 1998), p. 120.

52 Ibid., p. 122.

53 Ibid.

54 Ibid., p. 123.

55 Walter Benjamin, 'The Work of Art in the Age of Its Technological Reproducibility', in *Walter Benjamin. Selected Writings* vol. 3, translated by Edmund Jephcott et al. (Cambridge, MA: Harvard University Press, 2002), p. 119.

56 Kracauer, *Theory of Film*, p. 165.

57 Kracauer, *Theory of Film*, p. 166.

58 Metz, *The Imaginary Signifier*, p. 124.

59 Ibid., p. 198.

60 Ibid., p. 117.

61 Virginia Woolf, *To the Lighthouse* (Harmondsworth: Penguin, 1992), p. 69.

62 Ibid., p. 142.

63 Ibid., p. 155.

64 Freud, 'A Metapsychological Supplement to the Theory of Dreams', *SE* vol. 14, p. 225.

65 H. D., 'Expiation', *Close Up* 2, no. 5 (1928): 5–49.

66 Ibid., 39–40.

67 Ibid., 44.

68 Ibid., 42.

69 H. D., 'Conrad Veidt: The Student of Prague,' *Close Up* 1, no. 3 (1927): 34–44, 44.

70 Ibid., p. 35.

71 *Close Up* was edited by Kenneth Macpherson and by Bryher (Winifred Ellerman). Bryher was also analysed by Hanns Sachs, and writes about him in her memoir *The Heart to Artemis: A Writer's Memoirs* (London: Collins, 1963).

72 *Borderline: A POOL film with Paul Robeson* (1930), reprinted in *Close Up: Cinema and Modernism*, edited by James Donald, Anne Friedberg and Laura Marcus (London: Cassell, 1998), pp. 221–236

73 H.D., *'Expiation'*, pp. 42–3, 48.

74 H. D., *Two Americans* (Dijon, Darantiere, 1934), p. 96.

75 Ibid., p. 110.

76 Bryher, *Film Problems of Soviet Russia* (Territet: POOL, 1929), p. 24.

77 H. D., *Tribute to Freud* (Manchester: Carcanet, 1985), p. 93 (emphasis in the original).

78 Freud, *The Interpretation of Dreams*, *SE* vol. 5, p. 500.

79 H.D., *Tribute to Freud*, p. 92.

80 Béla Balázs, *Theory of Film*, translated by Edith Bone (London: Dobson, 1952), p. 183.

81 H.D., *Tribute to Freud*, p. 41.

82 H.D., *Tribute to Freud*, p. 41.

83 Ibid., p. 64.

84 Ibid., p. 30.

85 Ibid., p. 23.

86 Ibid., p. 170.

87 Benjamin, 'Work of Art', p. 117.

CHAPTER 10

Directed Dreaming
Dorothy Richardson's Pilgrimage and the Space of Dreams

Dorothy Richardson's 'A Sculptor of Dreams', published in *The Adelphi* in October 1924, was a review essay of Mary Arnold-Forster's (Mrs H.O. Arnold-Forster's) *Studies in Dreams*, which had appeared in 1921.[1] Richardson's discussion of the book fell into two parts: the first a consideration of Arnold-Forster's accounts of dreams and dreaming, and the second an account of Richardson's own model of good dreaming or, more precisely, good dreamlessness. My focus is also two-fold, looking both at Richardson's responses to *Studies in Dreams* and at the place or space of dreams in her multi-volume novel *Pilgrimage*, the first book of which, *Pointed Roofs*, was published in 1915.

For Richardson, Arnold-Forster's text posed the question, 'To dream, or not to dream', though, Richardson noted, this was a query that the author, 'herself a born dreamer', neglected, assuming in her readers the same full dream-life that she herself enjoyed.[2] Situating herself among those who do not dream, or whose dreams are so infrequent that they may be called those who do not dream, Richardson turned her attention to the 'man of many dreams',[3] for whom *Studies in Dreams* would create a particular dilemma. Arnold-Forster's study, which explored the possibilities of 'dream control' and the cultivation of 'the art of happy dreaming', had, Richardson argued 'achieved nothing less than the destruction of the dream as a free booter and its reconstruction as a controllable human faculty'.[4] The dreamer was thus left, Richardson suggested, with an 'uncomfortable choice': 'once aware not only that he may influence the material of which his dreams are built, [he] must either accept a discipline or turn away to sorrowful possession of his disorderly wealth'.[5] What he could no longer do is 'regard dreams as the uncontrollable antics of his unknown self'.[6] Arnold-Forster was, in Richardson's words, 'of those who are, so to say, permanently conscious, thinking as they go, all the time in words', and this 'permanently conscious thought' was revealed nowhere more clearly than in her attitude towards 'wandering thought, a state of mind she regards as possible only quite rarely, and then only as spree or experiment'.[7] We can begin to see how radically opposed Richardson would be to Arnold-Forster's conceptions of thought and consciousness, though her review was not a strongly critical one. It expressed less intellectual disagreement than the gulf that exists between, as she framed it, the dreamer and the one who does not dream.

Richardson alluded to, but did not directly address, the deep hostility to Freudian dream-theory and its sexual and symbolic underpinnings that motivated *Studies in Dreams*. As Arnold-Forster argued:

> Nightmares and dreams of fear exist, other ugly and evil imaginings may also be hidden away out of sight, and all these conceptions, side by side with our uncounted half-forgotten memories of fair and happy things, are set free when the will that controls them is wholly or partially suspended at night. But I believe that not only are these sinister visions and interpretations exaggerated, but I shall also hope to show that, in sleep, we are not, or need never be, left at their mercy, because we can if we choose exercise a real and effective control over the nature of our dreams.[8]

The question of 'dream control' did not, Arnold-Forster argued, 'come within the scope of other books', and Richardson followed her in this claim when she argued that *Studies in Dreams* had, albeit unwittingly, created havoc in the fabric of up-to-date ideas on the subject of dreams.

However, Arnold-Forster's text is in fact part of an established tradition of writing on the concept and practice of 'directed dreaming', the most recent manifestation of which is 'lucid dreaming', sometimes defined as 'dreaming with awareness'. Some contemporary writers on the topic suggest that 'lucid dreams' might be used to practise or perfect our imperfect skills – a spot of oneiric car-mechanics, perhaps – giving a whole new meaning to the term 'night school'. All writings on 'lucid dreaming' spend considerable time on lucid dreaming techniques and the promotion of awareness of the dream state and dream control, which apparently comes only with considerable practice. Techniques include waking oneself at regular intervals in order to recall dreams and write them down, and prolonging or stabilizing lucid dreams, usually through forms of spatial orientation. The current *doyen* of lucid dreaming, the sleep researcher Stephen LaBerge, proposed the now favoured technique of *Dream Spinning*:

> As soon as the visual imagery of your lucid dream begins to fade, quickly, before the feel of your dream body evaporates, stretch out your arms and spin like a top (with your dream body, of course). It doesn't matter whether you

pirouette, or spin like a top, dervish, child or bottle, as long as you vividly feel your dream body in motion. This is not the same as imagining you are spinning: for the technique to work, you must feel the vivid sensation of spinning.[9]

The longer history of 'directed dreaming' includes such texts and movements as the dream experiments of Alfred Maury, described in his *Sleep and Dreams* of 1861.[10] This was closely followed by the anonymously published study by the Marquis d'Hervey de Saint-Denys, *Les rêves et les moyens de les diriger* ('Dreams and How to Guide Them') of 1867.[11] Freud's dream diaries, kept from the 1880s, were the foundation for *The Interpretation of Dreams*, itself a text in which autobiography becomes a method. Late nineteenth-century novelists also had a particular fascination with dream-states, particularly in their relation to concepts of double or dual consciousness. In the 1910s and 1920s, and in part as a direct outcome of the First World War, there was an increased interest not only in dreams, but more particularly in pre-cognitive and directed dreaming, as in J.W. Dunne's extremely influential *An Experiment in Time* (1927). The history of dream-recording should also, of course, include Surrealist auto-experiments in dreaming, in particular those of André Breton, Robert Desnos and René Crevel. Mass-Observation, the 'anthropology of ourselves' founded in England in the 1930s, was in its first stages influenced by Surrealism, and one of its central activities, emerging out of war-consciousness and the kind of dreams brought about by war-time existence, was the study of dreams. Mass-Observers were asked to keep records of their own dreams and nightmares, and of 'dominant images' in dreams. In all of these instances, dreaming became a 'project'.

Directed Dreaming

Hervey de Saint-Denys (b. 1822), an aristocrat who became a Professor of Chinese at the Collège de France, described his childhood passions as those of dreaming and drawing, passions he combined by starting to keep, when he was 13, a regular diary of his dreams, which ran to twenty-two notebooks filled with coloured illustrations covering a period of more than five years of dreams. His project was to develop his skills as a dreamer. *Les rêves et les moyens de les diriger* was both an exploration of what Freud would later call the dream-work and a guide to directed dreaming. Again anticipating Freud, Hervey gave accounts of dream-images and dream-mechanisms in terms recognizable as those of condensation, displacement and secondary revision, and there is a similar sense of the incorporation into the dream of the 'day's residues', though he explicitly linked this to the fact that his attentiveness to his dreams, his practice of 'analyzing and describing them during the day, meant that they, as elements of my ordinary intellectual life, came to form part of the body of reminiscences my mind could draw upon while I was asleep'.[12] The next step was to fix his attention in his dreams 'on particular details which interested me, so that on waking I might have a more clearly defined memory of them'.[13]

The emphasis on 'attention' in Hervey's text brings it into the frame of the late nineteenth-century psychology of attention. It was not until the later nineteenth century that 'lucid' or 'directed' dreaming was firmly tied in to the 'disciplinary' aspects of attentiveness: in Jonathan Crary's words, 'a repressive ... defense against all potentially disruptive forms of free association'.[14] There may be a hint of this, however, in Hervey's contrast between the lucidity of deep dream-sleep and a 'transitory period between waking and sleeping in which anarchy reigns among our ideas and confusion among the images representing them'.[15]

Hervey practiced elaborate and idiosyncratic experiments in controlling his dreams by introducing sensations. He frequently drew comparisons between dream-consciousness and dreaming and the new optical instruments and technologies of his time – particularly the camera, the photograph and the magic lantern. His dreams also represented, and often had the qualities of, prints or engravings, and dream-awareness consisted substantially in the close observation of visual and architectural detail within the dream. Hervey most often explored dream-attention as a question of focus. If a dream-landscape began to fade, signalling that sleep was becoming less deep, the dream could be continued and the intensity of sleep regained by the concentration of attention 'on one of the small objects whose image still remains – the leaf of a tree for instance. This image will gradually regain the clarity it has lost, and you will see the vividness and colour of the shapes gradually re-established, just as if you were focusing the image from a lantern slide in a darkened room.'[16] If the dreamer wished to change the dream-scene, it was suggested that he put his hand over his eyes in the dream to cut off vision.

There is a complex relationship between what Hervey called 'the moving panorama of our visions' and the stasis of the photographic image which operated for him as an analogy for memory and dream-consciousness. Recurrent images of train travel, associated with reverie, and city perambulations were a further aspect of his desire to put (still) visual images into motion. It was imagination, he suggested, that gave to memory the ability to turn a 'two-dimensional stationary picture' into 'a moving, living figure'.[17]

At two different points in the text, he offered accounts of the ways in which the 'capricious mutations' within dreams were captured by a caricaturist, Grandville, who 'drew a series of outlines in which a pirouetting dancer turned into a frantically whirling bobbin. This phenomenon occurred particularly in moments of greatest passivity, in which the mind rested, as if seated in a theatre, watching distractedly, as a series of images of greater or lesser clarity passes before its eye.'[18] At a later point in the text Hervey referred to the occurrence in a dream of 'the spectacle of two superimposed images, the one appearing fixed and solid, the other moving and transparent'.[19] There are proleptic hints here of Freud's preoccupation with the co-existence of the permanent and the mutable, of the retentive and receptive surfaces of the mental apparatus, but my primary interest here is in the interplay of, and the border or boundary-crossing between, stasis and motion, as well as that between waking and dreaming in the discourses of controlled or directed dreaming.

In a chapter on 'Transformations and Transitions in Dreams', Hervey described a dream experiment involving the reading of passages from Ovid's *Metamorphoses* in which Proteus's daughters are changed by Venus into stone, as a punishment for their denial of her divinity and for their prostituting themselves, and Pygmalion's creation of the statue of a woman which Venus brings to life. Hervey painted the scene of enlivenment or vivification while keeping a piece of orris root in his mouth. He then arranged for this substance to be passed between his lips as he slept, and dreamed of being in a theatre with an actress from the Comédie Française, and of Miss X, scantily attired: '"How do you like me like this?" she asked, coming towards me . . . "[20] The route of associations Hervey traced were formulations of a dream-work, with an interplay of primary and secondary ideas.

In the Ovidian structure of Hervey's dream experiments that which is animate, mobile – the daughters of Proteus – is turned to stone, while Pygmalion's stone statue is animated into life and motion. This interplay or exchange between the animate and the inanimate was repeated in a further experiment involving a Chinese album which Hervey possessed, showing a series 'of palaces, countrysides and more or less fantastic scenes' and numerous human figures. He studied the paintings closely while sniffing some powdered flowers – 'an oriental product with a particularly distinctive scent'. The scent was then administered while he slept. His dreams on these occasions took one of two forms. On three occasions, he saw some of the subjects of the Chinese album in movement. On two occasions, 'by a somewhat remarkable process of reversal' he saw 'real scenes, friends or acquaintances' appearing not in the guise of real objects, 'but in the form of a collection of engravings and watercolours, lifeless and two-dimensional'.[21]

By taking their own dreams as examples and paradigms, Maury and Hervey inaugurated a tradition of dreaming as auto-experimentation, which became central to Freud's work on dreams. Freud's dream diaries, kept from the 1880s, were a foundation for *The Interpretation of Dreams*. While at one level the concept of lucid, controlled or directed dreaming would seem to be antithetical to Freudian dream-theory, with its emphasis on dreams as a highly encoded message from psychic regions inaccessible to consciousness, Freud's letters to Wilhelm Fliess recount the progress of his self-analysis as a process which transgresses the boundaries between waking and sleeping:

> For the last four days my self-analysis . . . has continued in my dreams and has presented me with the most valuable elucidations and clues. At certain points I have the feeling of being at the end, and so far I have always known where the next dream-night would continue.[22]

As J. B. Pontalis writes: 'for a certain time [Freud] literally made appointments with his dreams and, even more astonishingly, his dreams kept the appointments'.[23] When Fliess suggested that Freud leave out the account of one of his dreams from the dream book, Freud complied with regret, asking Fliess to 'Let me know at least which topic it was to which you took exception . . . So that I can omit what you designate in a substitute dream, because I can have dreams like that to order.'[24]

The structure and the narrative drive of *The Interpretation of Dreams* makes the text itself into a kind of directed dream. Hervey sought to show that will and attention are to be found in dreams, and thus that dreams could be directed, by an account of a dream in which he saw himself riding on horseback to a fork in the road which appears before him: 'The right-hand path disappears into a thick wood, the left-hand path leads to some sort of ruined manor house. I feel at liberty to turn either right or left, and therefore to decide for myself whether I shall evoke ideas and images relating to the ruins or to the wood.'[25] Freud wrote to Fliess that *The Interpretation of Dreams* 'is planned on the model of an imaginary walk. First comes the dark wood . . . then there is the cavernous defile . . . and then, all at once, the high ground and the open prospect and the question: "Which way do you want to go?"'[26] The reader is guided through the text as a dreamer.

More generally, the wish-fulfilment theory of dreams turns all dreaming into a kind of directed dreaming, an aspect of Freudian theory picked up by Sandor Ferenczi in a note on 'Dirigible Dreams' published in 1912. He commented on the dreams of a patient in which the transition between different scenes within a dream occurs in a motivated rather than unmotivated way, the dreamer reporting the transition between scenes in these terms: 'at this moment I thought to myself this is a bad dream; the dream must be solved in a different way'. In this way a change of scene could be effected in the dream, and the material, and its outcome, worked through to a satisfactory conclusion. In Ferenczi's words:

> The insight into the motives of the scene-changes in these dreams may be used in general for explaining the connexion between several dreams dreamt in the same night. The dream elaborates from all sides the particular dream thought which occupies the mind, drops one dream-scene when there is a danger that the wish-fulfilment will fail, tries a new kind of solution, and so on, until finally it succeeds in bringing about a wish-fulfilment which satisfies, with a compromise, both instances of the mind.[27]

Other turn-of-the-century models of lucid or directed dreaming abounded. An imitation of Hervey's technique of dream-direction was practiced by the Dutch psychiatrist Frederik Van Eeden, who began to use similar methods to Hervey's to study and then to guide his dreams in 1896. He first presented his observations in the form of a novel, *The Bride of Dreams*, but a paper delivered at a meeting of the Society for Psychical Research described in direct terms his experiences with demon-dreams and with lucid dreams, in which he directed himself to meet dead people whom he had known in life. Hervey's experiments may also have influenced George du Maurier's 1891 novel *Peter Ibbetson*, in which two separated lovers meet every night in their dreams and together explore their childhoods and the historical past, moving, as apparitions, alongside their former selves and their ancestors. This anticipates responses to early cinema (as *La Poste* wrote of the Lumière's first screenings at the end of 1895: 'When everyone can photograph their dear ones, no longer in a motionless form, but in their movements, their activity, their familiar gestures, with words on their lips, death will have ceased to be absolute.'[28]), while at the same time exploring the concept of dreaming as time travel. This would be taken up by J.W. Dunne in *An Experiment in Time*, which used relativity theory to argue for the possibility of dreaming of future events. The method of lucid or directed dreaming was called 'dreaming true' in *Peter Ibbetson*, and was intertwined with du Maurier's (or his narrator's) polemics on the potential for the expansion of human consciousness through 'dreaming true', and for the perfectibility of the human race, usually framed in eugenicist terms. Prior to learning 'true dreaming', the narrator's sleep was 'full of dreams':

Terrible nightmares, exquisite visions, strange scenes full of inexplicable reminiscence; all vague and incoherent, like all men's dreams that have hitherto been; *for I had not yet learned how to dream.*

A vast world, a dread and beautiful chaos, an ever-changing kaleidoscope of life, too shadowy and dim to leave an lasting impression on the busy waking mind; with here and there more vivid images of terror or delight, that one remembered for a few hours with a strange wonder and questioning, as Coleridge remembered his Abyssinian maid who played upon the dulcimer . . .

But there is one thing which, as a schoolboy, I never dreamed – namely, that I, and one other holding a torch, should one day, by common consent, find our happiness in exploring these mysterious caverns of the brain; and should lay the foundations of order where only misrule had been before; and out of all those unreal, waste, and transitory realms of illusion, evolve a real, stable, and habitable world, which all who run may reach.[29]

The passage is indicative of the ways in which the late nineteenth-century utopia of 'lucid' or 'directed' dreaming became a way of channelling Romantic vision, turning misrule into order. The kaleidoscope image is also significant, for it occurred, as I discussed in the previous chapter, with marked frequency in the writings of nineteenth-century writers on dream psychology, where, as for du Maurier, it represented a chaotic image-show. 'Dreaming true', 'lucid dreaming', in *Peter Ibbetson*, was analogized by the *camera obscura* on Ramsgate pier: 'one goes in and finds one's self in total darkness; the eye is prepared; one is thoroughly expectant and wide-awake. Suddenly there flashes on the sight the moving picture of the port and all the life therein, and the houses and cliffs beyond; and farther still the green hills, the white clouds, and blue sky' – and by an image of the unconscious memory as the product of a brain which contains 'something akin both to a photographic plate and a phonographic cylinder, and many other things of the same kind not yet discovered; not a sight or a sound or a smell is lost; not a taste or a feeling or an emotion'.[30] Mind and memory, as well as the new technologies, were thus imaged as storage systems.

Robert Louis Stevenson's dream-life, which he described in an article entitled 'A Chapter on Dreams', published in *Scribner's Magazine* in January 1888, is a variant on directed dreaming, with Stevenson's claim to use the help of his 'little people' or 'brownies' as collaborators in the writing of his novels. Opening his account by describing his own experiences in the third person before he claims them as his own – a strategy of doubling central to Stevenson's fictions, to his authorial collaborations (as with his stepson Lloyd Osbourne), and to the structures of dreaming itself – Stevenson wrote:

When he lay down to prepare himself for sleep, he no longer sought amusement, but printable and profitable tales; and after he had dozed off in his
box-seat, his little people [the 'brownies'] continued their evolutions with
the same mercantile designs. All other forms of dream deserted him but two:
he still occasionally reads the most delightful books, he still visits at times the
most delightful places; and it is perhaps worthy of note that in these same
places, and to one in particular, he returns at intervals of months and years,
finding new field-paths, visiting new neighbours, beholding that happy
valley under new effects of noon and dawn and sunset. But all the rest of
the family of visions is quite lost to him: the common, mangled version of
yesterday's affairs, the raw-head-and-bloody-bones nightmare, rumoured to
be the child of toasted cheese – these and their like are gone; and, for the
most part, whether awake or asleep, he is simply occupied – he or his little
people – in consciously making stories for the market.[31]

As in *Peter Ibbetson*, this passage from Stevenson implied the vanquishing of
the fierce dreams of Romanticism. 'The raw-head-and-bloody-bones nightmare', in Stevenson's phrase, was to be mastered by the strategies of
controlled or directed dreaming, even as Stevenson created his own fictional
nightmares. Here we see the use of the concept of the dream to define a shift
from the notion of literature as inspiration, possession, to the practice,
proscribed by Coleridge, in *Biographia Literaria*, of pursuing literature as
a trade. More precisely, Stevenson was suggesting that the possessing
agents – his 'brownies' – could be profitably harnessed to the means of
production. This would become the basis for the argument Arnold-Forster
had with the writings of Henri Bergson in *Studies in Dreams*: Bergson
claimed that Stevenson was not truly dreaming, because he had not with-
drawn interest from the world, whereas for Arnold-Forster Stevenson's was
in fact the truest form of dreaming.[32]

The narratives of 'directed dreaming' at the turn of the century were
rarely far removed from those of mediumship and, indeed, spiritualism, as
in the dream experiments of Frederick Myers. In Andrew Lang's study of
1897, 'dreams' and 'ghosts' were readily conjoined, in both his title and his
thought. 'The alleged events of ghostdom – apparitions of all sorts – are
precisely identical with the every-night phenomena of dreaming, except for
the avowed element of sleep in dreams', Lang wrote. He added: 'In dreams,
time and space may be annihilated, and two severed lovers may be made
happy . . . the comparatively rare cases in which two or more waking people
are alleged to have seen the same "ghost," simultaneously or in succession,
have *their* parallel in sleep, where two or more persons simultaneously
dream the same dream.'[33] *Peter Ibbetson* would seem to underlie much of
this discussion. The phrase 'time and space may be annihilated' is also

striking: we find it and its variants time and again in discussions of the
phenomena of late nineteenth- and twentieth-century modernity – in
particular new forms of communication, such as wireless telegraphy,
train travel and the emergent art of the cinema – suggesting that the
dream-apparatus might also be perceived as one of the technologies of
modernity.

In the 1910s and 1920s, and in part as a direct response to the First World
War, there was an increased interest not only in dreams but more particularly in pre-cognitive and directed dreaming. Dunne, in his *An Experiment
in Time*, was interested in the crossing of boundaries between past and
future in the dream, and he set out to prove 'that dreams – dreams in
general, all dreams, everybody's dreams – were composed of images of past
experience and images of future experience blended together in approxi-
mately equal proportions'. The effect, he argued, 'was one which was
apparent only to definitely directed observation, and its failure to attract
general attention was, thus, sufficiently explained'.[34] Arnold-Forster's
Studies in Dreams explored in particular war-dreams in which the author
as dreamer redirected the course of events, and argued, as we have seen, that
will, morality, and judgement are all fully operative in dream-consciousness.
The question of the desire for controlled or directed dreaming as a response
to war trauma was a particularly significant aspect of *Studies in Dreams* and
raised for Arnold-Forster the central question of whether the mind, waking
or sleeping, could ever be fully disengaged – or 'disinterested' in the terms
Henri Bergson used to describe the dream state – during states of emergency
such as war-time, an issue also at the heart of the Mass-Observation dream
diaries.

'A Sculptor of Dreams'

There are aspects of Arnold-Forster's *Studies in Dreams*, above and
beyond the question of controlled dreaming, which might have been
expected to interest or engage Richardson more fully than they appear
to have done. For example, Arnold-Forster was particularly caught up
with the question of flying or gliding in dreams, an aspect of dreaming
also central to James Sully's accounts of the phenomenon in 'The Dream
as a Revelation', and highly enthusiastic about the flying-costume
that she often wore in her dreams. This she described as a 'flying dress'
of 'straight close folds which fall three or four inches below my feet' so
that they could not be seen as she glided just above the surface of the
streets: 'no one can see now that I am not walking just as they are'.[35]

Dream-costumes aside, such forms of 'hovering' find their echo in *Pilgrimage*, as do Arnold-Forster's preoccupations – shared by James Sully, Havelock Ellis and Henri Bergson in their studies of dreams – with transitional states between sleeping and waking, with the intensely visual, cinematographic aspects of the dream state, and, perhaps above all, with the question of time and narrative in dreaming and in the recollection of dreams. 'I suspect', Sully wrote in 1893, 'that we are much less creators in our dreams than we are apt to suppose, and that the rush of apparently new imagery which sometimes threatens to whelm the spirit, is but a sudden tidal return of the swiftly receding past'.[36] For Arnold-Forster: 'The dream should first be allowed to unroll itself very quietly *backwards* in a series of slowly moving pictures, starting from the end and going back slowly through scene after scene to its beginning, until the whole dream has been seen.'[37]

In 'A Sculptor of Dreams' Richardson expressed a strong resistance to the willed recall of dreams, as to dreaming in general: 'There is, for me, not only no attraction in the art of dreaming, but an aversion so strong that I am aware, while a dream is in progress, of an annoyed sense of being derailed, of wasting time. Most certainly I do not wish to learn to dream.'[38] She particularly resisted the idea of the 'necessity of spending the wakening moments'[39] of each morning in recalling and noting down the features of the night's dream. This would be, in her phrase, a 'morning sacrifice',[40] and it is not too difficult, if one has a knowledge of *Pilgrimage*, and its relationship to the space–time of the day, to comprehend why Richardson would express a resentment of the use of the day in the service of the night (as opposed to sleep serving to renew the self for the day). Yet Arnold-Forster's account of dream-recollection as the unrolling of the dream into the past, and the focus throughout her text on what she calls 'borderland states' would not seem, on the surface, to be radically opposed to the experience which Richardson proffers as her model of ideal dreaming (or non-dreaming). She recounted, in 'A Sculptor of Dreams', an experience of waking from deep sleep, 'profound slumber',

> to find myself, there is no other way, to put it, busily alive in the past, and at the same time onlooker at myself living . . . As actor, my known self . . . was living through whole strands of life, not in succession, but as it were all in one piece . . . and was at the same time aware of the inquisitor presenting them, sharing the life and making judgements . . . with a gaiety bordering on amusement and enchanting altogether.[41]

The nightly task of perfect sleep, she suggested (in ways that echo early twentieth-century time-philosophies, and in particular concepts of 'tensed' and 'untensed' time in the writings of the British Idealist philosopher John McTaggart) might be 'a direct consideration of things as they are, undisturbed by the sense of time and place, and sometimes of an undisturbed consideration of all that we are. Not a review, as one reviews life in memory, but a current possession, from a single point of consciousness, of our whole experience intact, and a consequent arrangement of the immediate future'.[42] This account of 'perfect sleep', it should be said, might also define her project in the thirteen volumes of *Pilgrimage*, both in relation to time and experience and to the doubled self.

Richardson's biographer Gloria Fromm, in her discussion of 'A Sculptor of Dreams', argued that 'what Dorothy Richardson was describing was an experience of profound *consciousness* – such as might come to a psychoanalyst turned upon himself and purified of all resistance – a sense of staggering self-sufficiency'.[43] Joanne Winning extends this reading, arguing that the two selves represented in the dream, the one existing in the past and the other in the present, echo the split between the writing self and the recreated self, Miriam Henderson. The pleasure of the experience Richardson described in the essay derived from the sense that neither the past self, nor the past, was lost. The journey in the dream seems, in Winning's words, 'to be the analytic one that she refuses to make "in waking life" because of the pain and the terror of it. This dream is memorable for the emotional resolution it provides – the union of her two selves; and the realization that her past self remains alive in the past brings about "healing blows."'[44]

This analysis convinces, both as an account of the dream-experience and of the project of *Pilgrimage* more broadly. We might also, however, situate the dream-experience less as a form of, or substitute for, psychoanalysis, than in the general context of early twentieth-century dream-theories, and in particular those of Bergson. Richardson's experience is differentiated most fully from Arnold-Forster's 'directed dreaming' not by its divorce from a form of 'work' – Richardson referred to the 'nightly task' of sleep – but through its lack of susceptibility to will and control. It is revealed in progress only by an accident, by a wakening that must not be the product of 'noise or any other warning disturbance'.[45] It arose, Richardson wrote, out of a state of 'profound slumber'. This last phrase was that used in the English translation (published in 1913/14) of Bergson's essay *Dreams*, in which he differentiated between the kind of dreams that might work through or over what Freud had called the day's residues, arising from the events about 'which we have thought most distractedly', in Bergson's words, and those that emerge 'in very profound slumber' in which 'the law that regulates the reappearance of memories may be very different':

We know almost nothing of this slumber. The dreams which fill it are, as a general rule, the dreams which we forget. Sometimes, nevertheless, we recover something of them. And then it is a very peculiar feeling, strange, indescribable, that we experience. It seems to us that we have returned from afar in space and afar in time. These are doubtless very old scenes, scenes of youth and infancy that we live over then in all their details, with a mood which colours them with that fresh sensation of infancy and youth that we seek vainly to revive when awake.[46]

Whereas Freud found something new and something old in all dreams, Bergson divided dreams into two classes – ordinary dreams, arising from distracted thoughts, 'which do not bear the mark of effort', and the dreams arising from 'profound slumber' which suggest to him not only the mechanisms of unconscious memory, but 'the more mysterious phenomena which are raised by 'psychical research', more particularly telepathy. As with Freud's invocation of the 'navel' of that dream, that point beyond which interpretation cannot go, Bergson stops 'upon the threshold of the mystery'.[47]

Richardson, I would suggest, was uninterested in dreaming as the processing of the day's residues: that material which has barely caught waking attention but that has attached itself, as it were, round the edges. For Freud, Ellis and Bergson, these residues are often represented as the by-products of the life of the street and the fleeting aspects of urban modernity. The completeness of Miriam's day in *Pilgrimage* and the quality of her attention to it – which does not preclude 'wandering consciousness' – seems to leave no such 'residues'. Richardson was instead drawn, it would seem, to Bergson's second category of dreams: not the 'ordinary' dream but that brought about in and by 'profound slumber'.

These speculations can be tested by a turn to the representation of sleep and dreams in *Pilgrimage* itself. There are only two narrative or narrated dreams in the whole of *Pilgrimage*, the first occurring on the opening pages of *Pointed Roofs*, when Miriam, waking on the morning of her departure for Germany, recalls that she has been dreaming about the unwelcome reception she would receive from the women there: 'She had dreamed that she had been standing in a room in the German school and the staff had crowded round her, looking at her. They had dreadful eyes.'[48] The second dream occurs at the close of *Honeycomb*, when Miriam is with her mother at the seaside, just before her mother's suicide. Her mother's sleeplessness is at one with the weight of the night which produces the dream rather than healing sleep: Miriam 'dreamed she was in the small music-room in the old Putney school, hovering invisible'.[49] Her friend Lilla plays the piano, first 'steadily and vigorously', and then in 'a blur of wrong notes'. 'Miriam rejoiced in her heart. What a fiend I am'. She is woken from the dream, into the darkness and 'the unbroken sleeplessness of the room', by the sound of her mother 'sighing harshly'.[50]

Is Miriam, then, like her creator, so infrequent a dreamer as to count as one who does not dream? In fact, we are told (or Miriam tells others) of her recurrent dreams, though the text rarely narrates them, most of them being linked to memories of the childhood garden – where they become merged with the 'bee-memory' – and/or to exile from the garden: 'I often dream I am there [in the garden at Abingdon] and wake there, and for a few minutes I could draw the house . . . and I feel then as if going away were still to come, an awful thing that had never happened', Miriam tells Michael Shatov.[51] In *Revolving Lights*, Miriam remembers the last summer of her school-days, 'a sunlit flower-filled world opening before her . . . To that other world she was still going forward. One day she would suddenly come upon it, as she did in her dreams'.[52] McTaggart's philosophy is invoked in this part of the novel sequence: the blending of past experience and images of future experience further anticipates Dunne's *An Experiment in Time*, in which he sought a way to break down, in thought and dream, the barrier which divides our knowledge of the past from our knowledge of the future.

In *Pointed Roofs*, Miriam awakens into stillness after a terrible storm, becoming aware of 'the faint scent of her soap-tablet' – linked at other times to the fragrance of the remembered garden: 'She felt that her short sleep must have been perfect . . . She remembered that she had dreamed her favourite dream – floating through clouds and above tree-tops and villages . . . She had almost brushed the tree-tops, that had been the happiest moment . . . She stirred . . . "It's me," she said, and smiled.'[53] Self-possession is thus closely linked to 'perfect' sleep and the 'favourite dream'.

The other class of sleep- or dream-states in *Pilgrimage* come closest to the experience Richardson recounted in 'A Sculptor of Dreams', and they are linked to sleeping 'out of place' or 'out of time': that is, to sleeping outside and/or to sleeping during the day. In *The Tunnel*, Miriam spends a day by the sea with her 'new woman' friends Jan and Mag, during which they fall asleep at the foot of the cliffs. Miriam is awoken by the shouting of a group of boys:

> Waking in the daytime is *perfect* happiness. To wake suddenly and fully, nowhere; in Paradise; and then to see sharply with large clear strong eyes the things you were looking at when you fell asleep . . . She closed her eyes and drifted drowsily back to the moment of being awakened by the sudden cry . . . In the instant before her mind had slid back . . . she had been perfectly alive, seeing; perfect things all round her, no beginning or ending . . . the

moment she had just lived was the same, it was exactly the *same* as the first
one she could remember, the moment of standing, alone, in bright sunlight
on a narrow gravel path in the garden at Babington between two banks of
flowers, the flowers level with her face, and large bees swinging slowly to and
fro . . . It was the same moment.[54]

Here the experience recounted in 'A Sculptor of Dreams' is identified with
the first memory.

In *Dawn's Left Hand*, Miriam's attempt to describe her friend and soul-
mate Amabel to Hypo Wilson (the H.G. Wells character in *Pilgrimage*) is
interrupted, in the narrative, by a passage in which she recalls a Sunday
morning spent together with Amabel, after an evening at Mrs Bellamy's
gathering, where she and Amabel 'suddenly met and were both filled with
the same longing, to get away and lie side by side in the darkness describing
and talking it all over until sleep should come without any interval of going
off into the seclusion of our separate minds'. In the morning,

> I leaned my head back and for a few seconds was asleep for the first time in
> broad daylight, and woke so thoroughly refreshed that I said without think-
> ing: 'This is the birthday of the world,' and, while she flew to fling herself
> down at my knees, I was back in the moment of seeing for the first time those
> flower-beds and banks of flowers blazing in the morning sunlight . . . And I
> told her of it and that it must have been somewhere near my third birthday,
> and her falling tears of joy and sympathy promised that never again should
> there be in my blood an unconquerable fever.[55]

These two episodes of sleeping in the daylight, in the company of another
woman or women, have their counterpoint and contrast in *Revolving Lights*,
in which Miriam, staying at the Wilsons', sleeps out at night in the garden
with Alma and Hypo. As Hypo 'sleepily' tries to discourage Miriam from
talking, she thinks: 'There was to be no time of being out in the night with
him. He was too far off . . . They were all more separated than in their
separate rooms indoors . . . She lay waiting for the night to turn to night.'
But, she discovers,

> there is no night . . . Day, not night, is forgetfulness of time. Its movement is
> a dream. Only in its noise is real silence and peace. This awful stillness is
> made of sound; the sound of time, pouring itself out; ceaselessly winding off
> short strips of life, each life a strip of ceaseless light, so much, no more,
> lessening all the time.

This, then, is time passing – and the model is one of subtraction rather
than accumulation. 'Night is torment', Miriam thinks. 'That is why people
go to sleep.'[56]

The significance of these three scenes of 'extraordinary' sleep – sleep during the daytime, sleep (or sleeplessness) in the outdoors at night – is two-fold: they are ways of realizing sleep, and, because they are about sleeping in the company of others, 'shared' sleep, the 'absence of division' between night and day, in the terms posed at the close of 'March Moonlight', is, potentially, an absence of division between self and other.[57] 'Perfect sleep' thus embodies both 'the utopia of individualism' (which Stephen Heath sees as the heart of *Pilgrimage*) and the possibility of absolute relationship, and it is inextricably intertwined, in *The Tunnel* and in *Dawn's Left Hand*, with the relationship between women. The episode in *Revolving Lights* points in a different direction – the presence of Hypo (and Alma) Wilson renders Miriam more isolated, not less, and she realizes not healing sleep but the night and the entropic dimensions of time and the universe. The sound of time is 'a harsh hissing sigh, far away; gone', which is at one level the sound of 'the unconscious sea' but also seems to recall the 'sighing harshly' of Miriam's sleepless mother on the night before her suicide and her conviction of her 'desertion'. When sleep comes to Miriam, lying on the Wilsons' lawn, it is 'angry sleep leading direct to this open of morning': 'Alma, folded in her dressing-gown, disappearing into the house. The tumbled empty bed on the lawn, white in the open stare of the morning. Everything that happened seemed to be a conspiracy to display empti-ness.'[58] This is a form of desolation, a pitilessness, and an absence of reciprocity in which the 'open stare' countenances no returning look, with echoes of *To the Lighthouse*, and of Lily Briscoe's empty canvas, 'with its uncompromising white stare'.[59] The scenes of sleep and dream in *Pilgrimage* thus lead to the extremes of experience: to both the ecstasy of being and back to 'the horror that had wrenched her life in twain'.[60]

So far I have discussed the ways in which sleep and dreams are thematized in *Pilgrimage*. But the question of the 'space' of dreams in Richardson's text is also one of narrative structure and of the representation of narrative time. At times the text depicts the space between the end of one day and the beginning of the next as a break rather than a transition; at other times Richardson represents the extension of the day through the broken flow of consciousness before sleep. On occasion, there is a resistance to sleep, not, as Freud suggested, because of the ego's fear of its dreams, but because 'She loved the day that had gone; and the one that was coming.'[61] Between the end of chapter 4 and the beginning of chapter 5 of *Deadlock*, the white space of the page is the space of the night. Miriam has discovered writing and on the little table in the window-space of her room the 'paper-scattered lamplit circle was established as the centre of life'.[62] The chapter closes with the table 'free and untouched'. The next chapter opens: 'The spell of the ink-stained table had survived the night.'[63] Here the space of the night is not occluded, but the focus is on the continued existence of the desire for writing, embodied and embedded in the little table, through the night, as if there had indeed been a danger that it would not survive the night but would have been dispelled and dispersed in the space between the days.

In *Oberland*, there is a more radical representation of continuity between the end of one day and the beginning of the next. Chapter 2 ends with Miriam borne down 'into the uttermost depths of sleep'[64]: 'From which', chapter 3 begins, 'she awoke in light that seemed for a moment to be beyond the confines of the earth. It was as if all her life she had travelled towards this radiance, and was now within it, clear of the past, at an ultimate destination.'[65] The sentence carries on over the space of the night, in an interlude in *Pilgrimage* in which the world is so given over to light that night has lost even the power of interruption.

Where, in conclusion, is the space of dreams in *Pilgrimage*? Richardson's work could clearly be situated alongside those other modernist texts to which sleep and dreams are central: Woolf's *To the Lighthouse*, Joyce's *Ulysses* and *Finnegans Wake*, and Proust's *A la recherche*. These writers, as I discussed in Chapter 9, were caught up with the borders or boundaries between sleeping and waking, as in Walter Benjamin's focus on the threshold arenas of awakening and his preoccupation with situations of reduced attention or half-wakefulness. Whereas, however, the self for Proust is radically dispersed in and by sleep, having to be reconstituted every day, for Richardson it is renewed, as sleep renews the day.

The question of the space of dreams is, of course, also linked to the representation of the night in *Pilgrimage*, at its fullest in *The Trap*, which contains much of the night, and in which Miriam's dislike of her roommate Selina Holland comes to centre on her obliviousness to the world of the night in Flaxman's Court (the novel's name for Woburn Walk in Bloomsbury). It is not so much that Miss Holland sleeps through its disturbances as that she is oblivious both to her own unconsciousness of them and to the world of the night through which she sleeps.

The philosopher Maurice Blanchot's short essay 'Sleep, Night' (included in his *The Space of Literature*) takes us a little further into these issues and representations. Blanchot differentiates between sleep and dream, which is 'closer than sleep to the nocturnal region. In the night one cannot sleep . . . this interminable "day" is the approach of time's absence, the threat of the outside where the world lacks'. In contrast, Blanchot writes: 'By means of sleep, day uses night to blot out the night. Sleep belongs to the world; it is a task.'[66] We recall here Richardson's invocation, in 'The Sculptor of Dreams', of the 'nightly task' of 'perfect sleep'. 'You must sleep', Blanchot writes: 'this is the watchword which consciousness assigns itself, and this commandment to renounce the day is one of day's first rules.' Whereas 'Bergson saw behind sleep the totality of conscious life minus the effort of concentration', Blanchot argues that

> on the contrary, sleep is intimacy with the center. I am, not dispersed, but entirely gathered together where I am ... Sleep signifies that at a certain moment ... I must stop and manfully transform the instability of myriad possibilities into a single stopping point up which I establish and re-establish myself ... The meaning of sleep lies precisely in its being vigilant existence concentrating upon certitude ... so that the morning's newness can welcome it and a new day can begin.'[67]

It is in very similar terms that I see the representation of, and relationship between, sleep, dream, night and day in *Pilgrimage*. The question might also be raised, however, of whether some of the qualities of dream-life explored in this chapter – the role of urban phantasmagoria, the interplay of stasis and movement, the annihilation of time and space – might not also connect more closely to waking consciousness in *Pilgrimage* and the space of the day. The yet broader issue is whether *Pilgrimage*, with its interplay between first and third person, understood in psychoanalytic terms as the very structure of fantasy and dream, its 'penetration' of space and its mode of narration interminable, should in fact be understood as a dream text *tout court*.

Notes

1 Dorothy Richardson, 'A Sculptor of Dreams', *Adelphi* 2 (October 1924): 422–427.
2 Ibid., 422.
3 Ibid., 423.
4 Ibid., 422.
5 Ibid., 423.
6 Ibid., 423.
7 Ibid., 423.
8 Mary Arnold-Forster, *Studies in Dreams* (London: George Allen and Unwin, 1921), p. 39.
9 Stephen LaBerge, *Exploring the World of Lucid Dreaming* (New York: Ballantine Books, 1997), p. 118.
10 Alfred Maury, *Le sommeil et les rêves* (Paris: Didier, 1865).
11 Hervey de Saint-Denys, *Les Rêves et les moyens de les diriger* (1867) (Paris: Tchou, 1964). A shortened version of the text was published in translation as *Dreams*

and How to Guide Them (London: Duckworth, 1982). The quotation is from the translation.

12 Ibid., p. 25.

13 Ibid.

14 Jonathan Crary, *Suspensions of Perception: Attention, Spectacle and Modern Culture* (Cambridge, Mass: MIT Press, 1999), p. 17.

15 Hervey de Saint-Denys, *Dreams and How to Guide Them*, p. 63.

16 Ibid., p. 49.

17 Ibid., p. 71.

18 Ibid., p. 38–39.

19 Ibid., p. 137.

20 Ibid., p. 125.

21 Ibid., p. 155.

22 Sigmund Freud, letter to Wilhelm Fliess, 3 October 1897, in *The Complete Letters of Sigmund Freud to Wilhelm Fliess 1887–1904*, edited and translated by Jeffrey Moussaieff Masson (Cambridge, Mass: Harvard University Press, 1985), p. 268.

23 J.-B. Pontalis, 'Dream as an object', in *The Dream Discourse Today*, edited by Sara Flanders (London: Routledge, 1993), p. 111.

24 Freud, letter to Wilhelm Fliess, 9 June 1898, *Complete Letters of Sigmund Freud to Wilhelm Fliess*, p. 315.

25 Hervey de Saint-Denys, *Dreams and How to Guide Them*, p. 53.

26 Freud, letter to Wilhelm Fliess, 6 August 1899, *Complete Letters of Sigmund Freud to Wilhelm Fliess*, p. 365.

27 Sandor Ferenczi, *Final Contributions to the Problems and Method of Psychoanalysis*, edited by Michael Balint (London: Hogarth Press and the Institute of Pychoanalysis, 1955), p. 314.

28 *La Poste*, 30 December 1895 ; quoted in Noel Burch, *Life to Those Shadows*, translated by Ben Brewster (London: British Film Institute, 1990), p. 21.

29 George de Maurier, *Peter Ibbetson* (London: Osgood, McIlvaine and Co., 1896), pp. 72–74.

30 Ibid., pp. 198, 208.

31 Robert Louis Stevenson, *The Strange Case of Dr. Jekyll and Mr Hyde and Other Tales of Terror* (London: Penguin, 2002), pp. 138–139.

32 Henri Bergson, *Dreams*, translated by Edwin E. Slosson (London: T. Fisher Unwin, 1914), pp. 30–31.

33 Andrew Lang, *The Book of Dreams and Ghosts* (London: Longmans, Green, and Co., 1897), pp. 2–3.

34 J. W. Dunne, *An Experiment in Time* (1927) (London: Faber, 1934), pp. 59, 90.

35 Arnold Forster, *Studies in Dreams*, pp. 74–75.

36 James Sully, 'The Dream as a Revelation', *Fortnightly Review* 59 (March 1893), 354–365.

37 Ibid., p. 79.

38 Richardson, 'A Sculptor of Dreams', p. 425.

39 Ibid., p. 425.

40 Ibid.
41 *The Adelphi*, 2.5 (October 1924), p. 426.
42 Ibid., pp. 426–427.
43 Gloria Fromm, *Dorothy Richardson: A Biography* (Athens, GA and London: University of Georgia Press, 1994), p. 173.
44 Joanne Winning, *The Pilgrimage of Dorothy Richardson* (Madison: University of Wisconsin Press, 2000), p. 76.
45 Richardson, 'A Sculptor of Dreams', p. 425.
46 Bergson, *Dreams*, pp. 60–61.
47 Ibid., p. 62.
48 Dorothy Richardson [volume and page numbers refer to the Virago edition], *Pilgrimage*, 4 vols. (London: Virago Press, 1979), vol. 1, p. 21.
49 Ibid., vol. 1, p. 184.
50 Ibid., vol. 1, p. 185. The dream is rendered open to analysis through the terms that the text has already offered. Lilla has been differentiated by Miriam from those dreadful, smiling women she encounters elsewhere, and an identification with her has been made explicit. The text has also described Miriam's 'masculine' style of piano-playing and her large hands. Just before the dream, she has found a new way of playing the piano to soothe her mother, 'carefully avoiding pressure and emphasis . . . She had a clear sense of manhood', vol. 1, p. 471.
51 Ibid., vol. 3, p. 124.
52 Ibid., vol. 3, pp. 334–345.
53 Ibid., vol. 1, pp. 149–50.
54 Ibid., vol. 2, pp. 212–213.
55 Ibid., vol. 3, p. 243.
56 Ibid., vol. 3, pp. 357–358.
57 Ibid., vol. 4, p. 648.
58 Ibid., vol. 3, p. 359.
59 Virginia Woolf, *To the Lighthouse* (London: Penguin, 1992), p. 171.
60 Richardson, *Pilgrimage* (London: Virago, 1979), 1. 250.
61 Richardson, *Pointed Roofs,* vol. 1 of *Pilgrimage* (London: Virago, 1979), p. 111.
62 Ibid., vol. 3, p. 134.
63 Ibid., vol. 3, p. 135.
64 Ibid., p. 48.
65 Ibid., vol. 4, p. 49.
66 Maurice Blanchot, 'Sleep, Night', in *The Space of Literature*, translated by Ann Smock (Lincoln: University of Nebraska Press, 1982), p. 264.
67 Ibid., p. 266.

CHAPTER II

'In the Circle of the Lens'
Woolf's 'Telescope' Story, Scene-Making and Memory

On 31 January 1939, Virginia Woolf noted in her diary: 'I wrote the old Henry Taylor telescope story that has been humming in my head these 10 years.'[1] The short story to which she was referring was published as 'The Searchlight' in the posthumous *A Haunted House and Other Stories*. The 'humming' had, however, already been transferred to the page ten years previously, when Woolf wrote a story which she entitled 'What the Telescope Discovered', followed a year later by the incomplete 'Incongruous/Inaccurate Memories'. In all, Woolf produced some fourteen different drafts of 'the telescope story', with fragments of other drafts. A number of the later draft versions set the scene at Freshwater on the Isle of Wight, where Woolf's great-aunt Julia Margaret Cameron, a pioneer photographer, and her close neighbour and friend the Poet Laureate Alfred Tennyson were living in the mid-nineteenth century.

While some of the drafts of Woolf's 'telescope story' are dated, others are not, leading to uncertainties about the chronology of the story's composition. J.W. Graham, in an article published in 1976 that was the first to look in detail at the variant drafts, took the published version, 'The Searchlight', as the culminating narrative for Woolf. He noted the date of the first of the 'Searchlight drafts' as 31 January 1939 (the date Woolf gives in her diary), but records three subsequent, though undated, typescripts. The last of these was, he argued, clearly the work of a professional typist and hence a 'final' version. His argument was that

> [Woolf] began to draft the story in what was to prove its final form, then abandoned it for the very different Freshwater version, and then decided to return to the version drafted some two years earlier. Whatever her reasons for inventing the Freshwater version, the fact that she abandoned it is more pertinent to the present discussion, because it suggests that finally, after at least six drafts, she found this form of the story fundamentally inadequate.[2]

In a more recent article, Jane de Gay has queried Graham's chronology, noting that the version of 'The Searchlight' published by Susan Dick in

Virginia Woolf: The Complete Short Fiction came to light after Graham had published his article, and its professional typing can be dated as no later than September 1940. The Freshwater story was begun in 1941, after Woolf had (bar some very minor revisions) completed the draft subsequently published as 'The Searchlight'. De Gay suggests that 'the Freshwater story of 1941 had its own momentum, and that with its different framing narrative and title, it was developing away from the Ivimey version and the searchlight motif'.[3] For de Gay, the composition of the Freshwater story was driven by Woolf's interests in Julia Margaret Cameron, Victorian photography and the writing of a non-patriarchal history. In this reading, the photograph replaces the searchlight and the telescope to become the story's central motif.

Whereas J.W. Graham sought to establish a definitive version of the text, which he locates in the 'final' typescript of 'The Searchlight', Jane de Gay perceives the Freshwater drafts as texts subsequent to, and independent of, the published version of the story and not as 'inadequate' earlier variants of it. The differences between these two positions have a broader critical significance, which bears some relation to the shift in recent decades from 'textual criticism', the purpose of which is to produce an authoritative text, to 'genetic criticism', which, in the words of one critic, 'uses preparatory material, variant textual states or any other evidence of the compositional process for purposes of interpretation and evaluation'.[4] Yet while Jane de Gay queries Graham's location of the authoritative text, she still seeks to establish an autonomous Freshwater version of 'the telescope story.'

My interest, like that of de Gay, lies substantially in the 'Freshwater' versions of the narrative, but these seem to me not altogether distinct from the version published as 'The Searchlight'. The interplay of all the textual variants, from 1929 through to 1941, opens up significant issues of creation and composition, and of the 'scene-making' at the heart of Woolf's writing. Questions of autobiography and life-writing are raised in and by construction of 'the telescope story' which relate to genesis and literary genetics in a number of senses and in a number of ways, including structure and theme. They turn on what has brought not only writing, but also the very self into being. They also bring to the fore the question of 'framing' in Woolf's short fiction, and the question of the 'frame' becomes inseparable from issues and problems of narrative motivation – that is, the issue of how to construct a narrative rationale as well as a casing for a 'scene'.

At the heart of all of Woolf's versions of her telescope story is a passage from the autobiography of the nineteenth-century writer and Colonial Office official

Sir Henry Taylor, published in two volumes in 1877 (privately printed) and then in 1885. In the autobiography, Taylor described his early years, recalling how he had lived for a time in 'an old square ivy-covered border tower' in the North of England, always isolated from other people, but particularly so one summer when his father and stepmother were away. He wrote:

> All the day long I saw no one but the servants, except that I sometimes looked through a telescope ... at the goings on of a farmstead on a road which skirted our grounds at the farther end. Through this telescope I once saw a young daughter of the farmer rush into the arms of her brother, on his return after an absence, radiant with joy. I think this was the only phenomenon of human emotion which I had witnessed for three years.[5]

He then returns, in Graham's words, to 'the leisurely chronicle of his Victorian life'.[6]

In Woolf's retellings of this episode, the embrace seen through the telescope is not that between siblings but between lovers, and the young man (not always identified in the various drafts as Henry Taylor) is impelled, when he sees the embrace, the kiss, in his lens, to run out of his tower and towards, or into, his life. She also revises the scene so that the telescope is focused on the sky before it is turned to the earth. The young man thus becomes an amateur astronomer, opening up a link between her story and Thomas Hardy's novel of 1882, *Two on a Tower*, in which the youthful hero, all of whose passions are for the stars and the sky, enters into a relationship, and subsequently a clandestine marriage, with the woman on whose estate the tower with its telescope sits. In his 1895 Preface to the novel Hardy wrote: 'This slightly built romance was the outcome of a wish to set the emotional history of two infinitesimal lives against the stupendous background of the stellar universe, and to impart to readers the sentiment that of these contrasting magnitudes the smaller might be the greater to them as men.'[7] A recent critic has argued of *Two on a Tower*: 'Although new configurations of time and space had the potential to dwarf psychologically the human imagination, Hardy's cosmological narratives effectively divulge ... ways in which readers may productively scrutinise their own life stories as well as the cultural evolution of the species.'[8]

The echoes of Hardy's novel in Woolf's 'telescope story' are connected to her own fascination with relations of distance and proximity and between human experience and the dimensions of time and space. The centrality of Victorian science and scientific knowledge to Hardy's novel, one strand of which is the crucial link between astronomy and photography, is also one of the numerous sub-texts and inter-texts of Woolf's story.

The published version of the story, 'The Searchlight', is not connected to Freshwater, and Sir Henry Taylor is absent from the scene. A Mrs Ivimey, a society-lady, stands on the balcony of a London club before going with her party to the theatre. The searchlights of the war-years illuminate the scene, the story thus opening up the concepts, also at the heart of *Between the Acts*, of the theatre of war and of the 'interval' between acts and events. The beam of light the searchlights cast motivates Mrs Ivimey to tell the story of her great-grandfather, who as a boy lived in an isolated tower, and one day turned his telescope from the skies to the earth. She enacts, with her fingers, the focusing of the telescope – 'She made another quick little movement as if she were twirling something': '"He focussed it," she said, "He focussed it upon the earth. He focussed it upon a dark mass of wood upon the horizon. He focussed it so that he could see . . . each tree . . . each tree separate . . . and the birds . . . rising and falling . . ."'9 As Holly Henry notes in her recent study *Virginia Woolf and the Discourse of Science: The Aesthetics of Astronomy*, the elliptical interruptions mean that the reader 'must physically pause as the sentence is focused through the mechanisms of the ellipses and repetition of the words "focussed," "each" and "lower",' while Mrs Ivimey, 'who narrates her tale while miming the act of peering through an imaginary telescope, looks back in time to glimpse a crucial moment which marks the beginning of her life', her great-grandfather having married the young woman spied through the telescope.10 The telescope is thus understood as a device that allows for a simultaneous co-existence of the past and present. The young woman is Mrs Ivimey's great-grandmother, and it is thus her own origin or genesis – 'metaphorically, a primal scene', as Julia Briggs notes – that Mrs Ivimey 'sees'.11

Holly Henry has made the published version of the story a central plank in her study, connecting it to Woolf's fascination with telescopic vision, astronomy and the popularization of science in the early twentieth century, and to the links between 'telescopes, searchlights and war'.12 For Henry, the interest of 'The Searchlight' is the question of telescopic vision, which, she argues, shaped Woolf's 'narrative scoping strategies'.13 I want to extend this focus in order to explore both what Woolf may have wanted from 'the scene' and the issue of memory. The story, in its various manifestations, was bound into the two periods in Woolf's life – the mid–late 1920s and the mid–late 1930s – when, in her writing, she was considering the question of memory, her childhood and her mother's life most intensely.14

The earliest draft of the 'telescope story', titled 'What the Telescope Discovered', was written in 1929.15 It has no framing narrative and does not name the young man in his tower as Henry Taylor. It describes a boy in his tower on a lovely evening in which there is complete stillness in the air, but a 'mysterious throbbing outside'. He turns his telescope from moon to earth and gradually brings a nearby farm 'more and more clearly into view . . . He gazed and gazed as if he were exploring a new world.' He sees a servant girl coming out of a door, and a farm boy seizing her 'in his arms'. 'He could see every movement – he could see the boys face flush and the girl half struggle from him and then give herself up to his embrace. He kept his telescope turned on them through the telescope. He kept it motionless fixed motionless upon them.' Then he rushes out of the tower 'not knowing where he went or where he looked to find. Through the telescope he had discovered a new world.'

A 1930 version – 'Incongruous/Inaccurate Memories' – identifies the story as that of Sir Henry Taylor.[16] The opening frame here (as in the draft called 'Ghosts') suggests that 'scenes' in narrative can transcend their immediate contexts: 'these expansions and transformations are not travesties, but that the changes and rearrangements are only the . . . unfurling of a scene which when dropped into sympathetic waters. It is the natural effect of words when they are for some reason highly charged with meaning so as to go on living.' Even in the works of lesser writers this effect can occur, 'especially in autobiography':

> On they plod with their narrative and nothing happens, on they go, on we stumble, one thing follows another; then for no reason they present us with a scene, all of a sudden, and the scene begins to swell and to move and to float and to expand and is never afterwards to be forgotten, though by knocking about it has mixed itself up with so much else that one would be sorry ever again to compare it with the original.

The narrator then continues to tell – from 'memory' – the telescope story. The telescope, turned upon the earth, picks up hills, clouds, sheep, the leaves of trees, a church steeple, an old farm house, windows, and

> suddenly the disc of light fell upon two faces – a man and a woman, within that ring of perfect clearness, they were held fast . . . they kissed . . . There was life, there was love, there was passion. Sweeping the telescope aside, Henry crammed his hat on his head, rushed down stairs out onto the road, out into the world – and so became in time – was it Sir Henry Taylor of the Colonial Office?

In her framing of the telescope scene, Woolf was, it would seem, puzzling over the impact that the brief passage in Henry's Taylor autobiography had had on her, and made it stand for other 'scenes' which imprint themselves upon the reader's mind. She implied that the dull Victorian autobiography, like history, gives us one damn thing after another. But then we are brought to a halt by 'a scene' that is so resonant that it becomes a permanent dimension of the reader's experience. The autobiographer transcribes it, however, 'for no reason', Woolf suggests, as if the scene's very lack of narrative and subjective motivation, the unthinking quality of its presentation, were part of the condition for its transmission to another's subjectivity.

Woolf's phrase the 'unfurling of the scene' recalls Lily Briscoe's thoughts about Mr and Mrs Ramsay – 'She was not inventing; she was only trying to smooth out something she had been given years ago folded up; something she had seen.'[17] The liquid imagery – 'the scene begins to swell and to move and to float and to expand' – also echoes the most memorable scene of memory and scene-making in modern literature: Proust's recalling of his past in the cup of tea, and his analogizing of the act of memory in the unfurling and expansion of the little Japanese pieces of paper which become 'flowers or houses or people, solid and recognisable', once put into water.[18] Proust's analogy is also an allegory, as John Coyle suggests, 'of the transmutation of imaginative insight into fictional creation, and of the movement from solipsism to a populated world'.[19] Both the transmutation and the movement are echoed in Woolf's relationship to, and reconstruction of, 'the telescope story', as she turns the borrowed scene into fictional forms and represents the ways in which solipsism – that of the boy alone in his tower – is transformed into relationship through the focus on the world outside and his perceiving of life, love and passion. The sexual dimensions of Woolf's scene-making – the 'humming' and the 'mysterious throbbing' – are inextricably linked to the question of creativity and literary genesis: they are also to be found in her account (written in a letter to Roger Fry) of reading Proust in 1922, in which she described the extraordinary ways in which *A la Recherche du Temps Perdu* 'titillates my own desire for expression ... such is the astonishing vibration and saturation and intensification that he procures – theres something sexual in it – that I feel I *can* write like that, and seize my pen and then I *can't* write like that. Scarcely anyone so stimulates the nerves of language in me: it becomes an obsession.'[20]

Woolf used the Proustian image in *Jacob's Room*, when she described the fashion for putting 'little paper flowers' in finger-bowls; in the telescope story draft, however, it seems to raise more complex and unresolved questions of memory and of what it might mean to take on as one's own another person's memory. The scene becomes, in the liquid imagery of the story's opening, a 'floating incident' of the kind Woolf was to describe in her own autobiography *Sketch of the Past*, in which she also wrote of the ways in which the 'moments of being' she recalls always included 'a circle of the

scene which they cut out: and all surrounded by a vast space – that is a rough
visual description of childhood. This is how I shape it.'[21] Memory and
scene-making are thus shaped in the form of the telescopic or photographic
optic – 'in the circle of the lens' – as well as through the image of the self as 'a
porous vessel afloat on sensation'.

The drafts of the telescope story appear to be connected to Woolf's self-
representations and to the question of scene-making – her natural way, she
writes, in *Sketch of the Past*, of 'marking the past':

> A scene always comes to the top; arranged, representative. This confirms me
> in my instinctive notion – it is irrational, it will not stand argument, that we
> are sealed vessels afloat upon what it is convenient to call reality; at some
> moments, without a reason, without an effort, the sealing matter cracks; in
> floods reality; that is a scene – for they would not survive entire so many
> ruinous years unless they were made of something permanent; that is a proof
> of their 'reality'.[22]

The telescope scene survives entire, but, as Woolf suggests in her drafts, it
'mixes itself up with so much else'. What are the components of this
mixing? Increasingly, Woolf began to write the scene into Freshwater,
where her great-aunt Julia Margaret Cameron lived and took photographs
of 'famous men and fair women'. Henry Taylor was her guest and one of her
photographic subjects, and certainly one of the bearded sages to whom
Roger Fry alluded in the edition of the photographs he prefaced and edited
with Woolf: 'In that protected garden of culture women grew to strange
beauty, and the men – how lush and rank are their growths. How they
abound in the sense of their own personalities.'[23] The actress Ellen Terry –
married at the age of sixteen to the painter G.F. Watts and photographed at
this time by Cameron, most famously in an image entitled 'Sadness' –
entered Woolf's narrative frame. In the draft titled 'A Scene from the Past'
(with its marked echoes of *Sketch of the Past*) the motivation for the
narration of the telescope scene (for which Woolf was always searching)
became Terry's confession to Sir Henry Taylor, with whom she is walking
on Freshwater Down, of an illicit kiss in the garden the previous evening –
'He kissed me' – while the rooks call over Farringford Woods 'Maud,
Maud, Maud'. This leads Henry Taylor to tell Terry the telescope story,
of himself as a young man in his tower seeing 'A man kissing a woman'. The
narrative now revolves around two scenes of kissing.[24]

Henry Taylor recovers the past within a narrative whose own distance
from the past of its narration is insisted upon throughout: 'The scene was
Freshwater; the date 1860; the month June ... Everything there was different from what it is today.'[25] From the 'platform' (the term Woolf used in

Sketch of the Past) of 1860, we are returned to Henry Taylor's boyhood. As he 'brought before her the stamp of a horse in the stables; the clink of a bucket on the stones; moss on ruined sheds, and himself, a boy', Ellen Terry 'saw what he saw'. Memories can be transferred, in and through the mind's eye, and their transmission, within the frame of the story, from Henry Taylor to Ellen Terry models that of their transmission from writer to reader, exemplified in the transference of the original scene from Taylor's autobiography to Woolf.

In 'A Scene from the Past', Henry Taylor reproduces mimetically the gestures of that lost time as he narrates the scene from the past:

> One June day, he said, he mounted to his tower alone. And seizing the telescope – it was her arm he seized – he turned it – so – down onto the earth.
> Here he cast his eyes down on to the earth. Her's [sic] followed his. And she saw what he saw. Not turf, not daisies, but moors flowing and great trees. Rooks were rising and falling, and in the clearing of a wood she saw an old gabled house. And then – what then?
> He was silent. The climb to the top of the down was steep. Pressing her dove grey glove upon his arm she urged him: 'Tell me, tell me – what did you seen then?'
> He drew himself erect. His eyes flashed. And in a voice of thunder that drowned the cawing of the rooks he shouted: 'A man kissing a woman.'[26]

As in a film, one landscape, or backdrop, is replaced by another, a trope used by Woolf in *The Years*.[27] Woolf's narrative also conjures up the cinema in its representation of the close-up kiss, a central image and narrative device in film from the 1890s onwards, and the topic of numerous critiques, as the final kiss or 'clinch' became a standard way in which to close a scene or an entire film. The 1929 version of Woolf's story, 'What the Telescope Discovered', has, moreover, marked echoes of the titles of early films which, employing subjective point-of-view shots, often pointed up the 'voyeuristic' dimensions of their perspectives: G.A. Smith's 'As Seen Through a Telescope', in which a middle-aged man focuses his telescope on the ankle of a young woman bicyclist, which the spectator also views in the circle of his lens, was an influential model in the new medium. Its title would seem to be echoed by Woolf, who also hints at the voyeurism and the sexual dimensions of the scene she recreates, in her account of the 'mysterious throbbing' which leads the young Henry Taylor to turn his telescope from sky to earth, and the flush on the face of the boy whom he sees through his lens. In the 1930 version, 'Inaccurate Memories', the framing of the embracing couple is markedly filmic. As the boy focuses and lowers the telescope:

He could count the tiles, see the blue green pigeons waddling along the gutters, then the windows with their blinds blowing from the edge, and still lowering, it, suddenly the disc of light fell upon two faces, a mans and a womans; within that ring of perfect clearness they were held fast. They An extraordinary expression was on their faces; they closed together; they kissed. It was miles away; but the shock was like a blow on his own shoulder. There was life, there was love, there was passion.

Woolf seems, in certain drafts of the story, to be drawing attention to the cliché of the 'clinch'. The ironic distance she adopts is also at one with the suggestion that there is a very 'Victorian' bathos to 'the scene': 'I never knew a mother's love', she has Sir Henry Taylor pronounce in one version of the narrative.[28] Woolf's choices of an appropriate mode in which to tell the tale, and of the degree of irony to adopt, often seem uncertain and unstable: this undoubtedly contributed to her multiple writings and rewritings.

There would appear to be, however, more than an ironic intention at work in the proto-cinematographic focus on 'the kiss' as seen through the telescope and its exploration of its impact on the viewing subject. Suggestive connections emerge between Woolf's narrative and Walter Benjamin's project, described in a letter to his friend Werner Kraft in 1935, of 'pointing my telescope through the bloody mist at a mirage of the nineteenth century that I am attempting to reproduce based on the characteristics it will manifest in a future state of the world, liberated from magic'.[29] As Jan Holmberg argues, Benjamin's use of the trope of the telescope to overcome the distance between his own time and the nineteenth century expresses the 'ambiguous tension between distance and proximity' as a specifically modern experience, articulated most fully in his essay 'The Work of Art in the Age of Mechanical Reproduction'.[30] Holmberg suggests that this tension is 'aptly captured by the seemingly paradoxical concept of de-distancing' (Martin Heidegger's *Entfernung*), understood as 'the distanciation of distance', or, in Jacques Derrida's phrase, as a 'remote proximity',[31] and represented in cinema in the 'figure of closing in', in instances in which 'gaining knowledge is correlated with closing in' and in the use of extreme close-ups.[32] In early cinema, the frequent use of telescopes 'seems to underscore dimension of near and far' while, more generally, camera motion was described by early commentators as an interplay between emotional, spatial and temporal distance and proximity. As the film critic Eric Elliott wrote in 1928: 'Size may alter even as we watch the scene, that is, by *camera locomotion*. We, as spectators, draw near to a subject, may become intimate with a distant object or emotion; conversely, we may depart from the object or emotion, become more and more separated from it, until (if necessary) it becomes absolutely final and past.'[33]

The 'near and far' with which Woolf is concerned, and the interplay between distance and proximity, are profoundly linked to her relationship with the Victorian past and, as I have suggested, to the question of her own 'genesis'. In this sense, the 'telescope story' takes its place alongside *To the Lighthouse*, written at a time in which Woolf was writing about both Victorian photography and the cinema. In the novel, ways of seeing associated with optical technologies – telescope, photograph, film – become the media of memory and of the 'passage' between present and past, past and present.

Woolf's mother and father can also be glimpsed in the circle of the lens of the 'telescope story'. In biographical terms they both had family or professional connections to Henry Taylor, and Leslie Stephen wrote Taylor's *Dictionary of National Biography* (*DNB*) entry, making no mention of the scene in the tower, while detailing his literary career and his career in the Colonial Office. The *DNB* indeed figures in a number of the story's drafts, as a text which 'remains intact' during the war's destruction, while 'the book in which this story [the telescope story] is told, and the album in which you could see him [Henry Taylor] draped in a shawl posed as King Arthur were destroyed only the other day by enemy action'.[34]

In some versions of the story Woolf suggests that she is narrating what Leslie Stephen (in the 'person' of the *DNB*) excluded, though she represents the depredations of war taking their revenge, leaving only the official account. There is a strongly gendered dimension to these questions of historical writing: what is selected and what omitted, what is preserved and what lost or destroyed. Woolf's concern with gendered inscriptions and reinscriptions can also be seen in the ways in which she renders the telescope scene itself as a reworking of Tennyson's poem 'The Lady of Shallot'. In Woolf's versions, there is a man, not a woman, in a tower; the mirror has become a telescope; and looking, with desire, at the world outside and at human forms, is an invitation to life, and not to death. But, Woolf suggests, Henry Taylor ran towards the Colonial Office, and away from the scene, or the moment, or the perception, that might have marked him out for a different life-course. This is perhaps why Woolf wanted the scene for herself and why she keeps on retelling and remaking it. She did not so much steal the scene, it could be said, as rescue it.

Woolf's play *Freshwater*, written in 1923 and then fully revised in 1935, when it was performed by members of the Bloomsbury group, was also intertwined with the history of the composition of the 'telescope story'. The play was to be 'a skit upon our great aunts', as she wrote to Desmond MacCarthy: 'The idea is to have masses of Cameron photographs, shawls,

cameos, peg-top trousers, laurel trees, laureates and all the rest'.[35] Julia
Margaret Cameron was played by her great-niece Vanessa Bell, Woolf's sister,
opening up the question, always absorbing to Woolf, of how we might
'become' our ancestors: an imagining which also lies at the heart of
Orlando. The figure of Ellen Terry became, however, as or more prominent
than that of Cameron in both versions of the play, many of whose components overlap with the various drafts of the telescope story, though Henry
Taylor is not a presence in *Freshwater.* There are many reasons why the figure
of Ellen Terry should have fascinated Woolf, but one of them was clearly that
her life, for a short time, was so intertwined with those of Woolf's 'great
aunts'. They offered patronage to Watts, and strongly encouraged his marriage to Ellen Terry, who was thirty years younger than Watts: a marriage
which, she claimed in her memoir, 'delighted' her parents as much as it did
her young self: 'I was happy, because my face was the type which the great
artist who married me loved to paint.'[36] A year later, there was a complete
separation, 'which was arranged for me in much the same way as my marriage
had been'.[37] Woolf's great-aunts and uncles were clearly instrumental in
arranging both the marriage and the separation, playing a shaping, and, it
could be argued, shameful part in her story.

Freshwater, for all its farce and facetiousness, makes a serious point in
representing Terry as a victim of Victorian idealizations of female beauty
and passivity, and in this Julia Margaret Cameron is seen to be as complicit
as the male poets and painters, Tennyson and Watts, as she dresses Terry in
a turkey's wings to pose for the figure of the Muse. 'I longed to arrest all
beauty that came before me, and at length the longing has been satisfied',
Cameron wrote of her photographic art.[38] Recent critics and photographic
historians have pointed to the radical nature of many of her images and
techniques, including and especially her diminishing of precise and definite
focus. Woolf, however, in *Freshwater* in particular, represented Cameron's
art, and her obsession with 'beauty', as a very Victorian 'arrest' (in the sense
of making static) of the energy and movement that characterized the young
Ellen Terry and, as Woolf would later present it, of her own mutable,
changeable, 'sketch'-like art of theatre: 'Every night when the curtain goes
down the beautiful coloured canvas is rubbed out.'[39]

In the play, Terry escapes from Freshwater, and its group of Victorian
aesthetes and eccentrics, eloping with a young man who has no artistic
pretensions, and heading for a Bloomsbury address which had indeed
been the Stephens' own home. Through a contraction of time which
also characterizes the shift from the Victorian to the post-war in *To the
Lighthouse,* Woolf, in her comic play, thus had Terry enact a version of the

Stephens' children's own 'escape' from Victorian Kensington to the more
Bohemian Bloomsbury when their father died in 1904.

   Woolf's fascination with the figure of Terry culminated in a late essay on
the actress in which she drew upon Terry's memoirs, *The Story of My Life* (first
published in 1908 and revised in 1932), the correspondence between Terry and
George Bernard Shaw, published posthumously in 1931, as well as the theatre
director Edward Gordon Craig's account of his mother, *Ellen Terry and Her
Secret Self*. Woolf's essay was written in the autumn of 1940 and published in
February 1941: its composition overlapped with that of *Between the Acts*, in
which Terry's daughter Edith Craig and the Barn Theatre undoubtedly
provided models for Miss La Trobe and her staging of the village pageant.
A draft page of *Between the Acts* (part of the eighteenth-century act of the
village pageant) is backed by a quotation from Terry's memoir and part of a
passage from a letter to Shaw, both quotations describing the circumstances of
Terry's brief marriage to G.F. Watts. In her memoir, Terry wrote of the
period in which she became indifferent to her acting: 'I was just dreaming of
and aspiring after another world, a world full of pictures and music and gentle,
artistic people with quiet voices and elegant manners. The reality of such a
world was Little Holland House, the home of Mr. Watts.'[40] To Shaw, Terry
had written, in a letter dated 7 November 1896 (only part of which is
reproduced in the collection edited by Christopher St. John), of the significance of 'kissing' and of 'my first kiss': 'I made myself such a donkey over it,
and always laugh now when I remember.'[41] Woolf begins the transcription of
the passage from the sentence that followed, omitting the bracketed portion:

> Mr Watts kissed me in the studio one day, but sweetly and gently [all
> tenderness and kindness, and then I was what was called 'engaged' to him
> and all the rest of it, and my people hated it,] and I was in Heaven, for I knew
> I was to live with those pictures. 'Always,' I thought, and to sit to that gentle
> Mr. W. and clean his brushes, and play my idiotic piano to him, and sit with
> him there in wonderland (the Studio).[42]

As in the Henry Taylor 'telescope' scene, 'the kiss' changes the course of
a life.

   Woolf drew directly on Terry's words in her published essay on the
actress, in which she played on the concept of the 'sketch' as something both
written and drawn: in her letters and memoirs, she suggested, Terry

> dashed off a sketch for a portrait – here a nose, here an arm, here a foot, and
> there a mere scribble in the margin. The sketches done in different moods, in
> different angles, sometimes contradict each other. The nose cannot belong to
> the eyes; the arm is out of all proportion to the foot. It is difficult to assemble
> them. And there are blank pages too.[43]

Picking up on Edward Gordon Craig's account of his mother's 'secret self', Woolf's essay pointed to Terry's multiple selves which are schematized by 'the two Ellen Terry's – Ellen the mother, and Ellen the actress'. She also used Terry's account, in her letter to Shaw, of looking at a 'very beautiful' old chair – 'rush-bottomed, sturdy-legged and wavy-backed' – to emblematize the ways in which the world of the stage could be readily displaced by Terry's intense, painterly perception of reality.[44] Perhaps, Woolf implies, Terry could have been a painter rather than a painter's Muse.

For a time, Ellen Terry's life touched closely upon that of Woolf's mother, despite the radical differences in their class and background. Born within a year of each other, Ellen Terry and Julia Jackson were both beautiful young women who, in the early 1860s, were 'presented' at Little Holland House (where artists and writers met at the home of Woolf's great-aunt and uncle Prinsep) and photographed by Julia Margaret Cameron. In 'Sketch of the Past', Woolf wrote:

> How easy it is to fill in the picture with set pieces that I have gathered from memoirs – to bring in Tennyson in his wideawake; Watts in his smock frock; Ellen Terry dressed as a boy; Garibaldi in his red shirt – and Henry Taylor turned from him to my mother – 'the face of one fair girl was more to me' – so he says in a poem. But if I turn to my mother, how difficult it is to single her out as she really was.[45]

Woolf's fascination with Terry's mercurial qualities, and her 'secret self', begins to bear on what she saw as her mother's two lives, evidenced in her two very different marriages: the first to Herbert Duckworth, and the second, after Duckworth's shocking sudden death in the first years of the marriage, to the widowed Leslie Stephen. The attenuation of the relationship between the half-siblings – the Stephen children and the Duckworth children – after Leslie Stephen's death would seem to confirm the absoluteness of the difference between the two men and the two marriages and, by extension, Julia Stephen's 'two selves'.

The central connection between 'the telescope story' in all its variants and those writings of Woolf with which these versions intersected in the space and time of composition – *To the Lighthouse*, *Freshwater*, 'Ellen Terry', 'A Sketch of the Past', *Between the Acts* – is the question of origins. We might imagine a version of the story in which a child looks through the telescope at the figures of the parents – 'a man's head, a woman's head' – as in Rachel's view from the ground, in *The Voyage Out*, as she sees the figures of her lover Terence and her aunt Helen kissing above her.[46] We might also be reminded of the

photograph taken at St. Ives, in which we see Virginia as a child, in the corner
of the room, looking at her parents reading on the sofa, as well as the haunting
image of the mother in *To the Lighthouse*: 'faint and flickering, like a yellow
beam or the circle at the end of the telescope, a lady in a grey cloak, stooping
over her flowers, went wandering over the bedroom wall, up the dressing-
table, across the wash-stand, as Mrs. McNab hobbled and ambled, dusting,
straightening.'[47] Such images are, as I have suggested, framed in and by the
relation between distance and proximity (including and especially the relationship between modernity and the Victorian past) which lies at the heart of
so much of Woolf's writing, and is so often viewed through the lenses of the
technologies of vision.

The published version of the story – 'The Searchlight' – occludes,
through a fiction-making marked by the theatricality of its performance,
the markers of the story's own genesis. Sir Henry Taylor and Woolf's own
'Victorian' family are absorbed into Mrs Ivimey and her drama of her
origins. Vanessa Bell commented on the curious name Woolf had chosen
for the protagonist of the story, at the same time noting that she felt very
drawn to illustrate it, but perplexed as to the choice of visual image she
might make for so multifarious a narrative. It could be argued, however,
that Woolf was able to complete 'The Searchlight' precisely because, in
contrast to the other variants of 'the telescope story', it possessed the self-
containment of the overtly fictional artefact and had not (in the words
Woolf used to describe the processes by which a 'scene' is transmitted and
incorporated) 'mixe[d] itself up with so much else'. The variants of the
'telescope story', provisional and sketchy as many of them are, provide
windows onto the components of this 'mixing' and onto the ways in which
the 'telescope scene' came to function as a 'primal scene' or 'ur-scene'. It
allowed Woolf to explore the genesis of 'scene-making' – the basis of her art
and writing – as intertwined, in complex and overdetermined ways, with
the issue of her own cultural and biological origins and 'making'.

Notes

1 Virginia Woolf, *The Diary of Virginia Woolf*, edited by Anne Olivier Bell with
  Andrew McNeillie, vol. 5 (London: Hogarth Press, 1984), p. 204.
2 J. W. Graham, 'The Drafts of Virginia Woolf's "The Searchlight"', *Twentieth-
  Century Literature* 22, no. 4 (December 1976): 379–393, 385.
3 Jane de Gay, 'An Unfinished Story: The Freshwater Drafts of "The Searchlight"',
  in *Virginia Woolf: Turning the Centuries: Selected Papers from the Ninth Annual
  Conference on Virginia Woolf*, edited by Ann Ardis and Bonnie Kime Scott (New
  York: Pace University Press, 2000), pp. 207–215, 209.

4 Graham Falconer, 'Genetic Criticism', in *Encyclopedia of Contemporary Literary Theory: Approaches, Scholars, Terms*, edited by Irene Rima Mabaryk (University of Toronto Press, 1993), p. 71.

5 Henry Taylor, *Autobiography of Henry Taylor, 1880–1875*. 2 vols. (London: Longmans Green, 1885), vol. 1, p. 45.

6 Graham, 'The Drafts', p. 383.

7 Thomas Hardy, *Two on a Tower* (1882/1895) (London: Macmillan and Co., 1920), p. v.

8 Andrew Radford, Review of Pamela Gossin, *Thomas Hardy's Novel Universe: Astronomy, Cosmology and Gender in the Post-Darwinian World* (Aldershot: Ashgate, 2007). Review section, *The British Society for Literature and Science*, http://www.arts.gla.ac.uk/bsls/.

9 Virginia Woolf, 'The Searchlight', in *The Complete Shorter Fiction of Virginia Woolf*, edited by Susan Dick (London: Grafton, 1991), pp. 269–272, 271.

10 Holly Henry, *Virginia Woolf and the Discourse of Science: The Aesthetics of Astronomy* (Cambridge: Cambridge University Press, 2003), pp. 54–55.

11 Julia Briggs, *Reading Virginia Woolf* (Edinburgh University Press, 2006), p. 52.

12 Henry, *Virginia Woolf and the Discourse of Science*, p. 52.

13 Ibid., p. 51.

14 The significant works in these contexts include, from the mid–late 1920s, 'The Cinema' (1926), *To the Lighthouse* (1927), Woolf's introduction to the Hogarth Press edition of Julia Margaret Cameron photographs, *Victorian Photographs of Famous Men and Fair Women* (1926), the first version of *Freshwater* (1923), the first version of 'The Searchlight' (1929) and *A Room of One's Own* (1929). Works from the mid–late 1930s include the second version of *Freshwater* (1935), *Between the Acts* (1941), 'Ellen Terry' (1940), later draft versions of 'the telescope story' and 'A Sketch of the Past' (1939).

15 Virginia Woolf, 'What the Telescope Discovered'. Ts. MH/B9j, pp. 1–5, Monk's House Papers, University of Sussex, England.

16 Virginia Woolf, 'Inaccurate/Incongruous Memories', Ts. MH/B9k, pp. 1–5, Monk's House Papers, University of Sussex, England.

17 Virginia Woolf, *To the Lighthouse* (1927) (London: Penguin, 1992), p. 215.

18 Marcel Proust, *In Search of Lost Time*, vol. 1, *Swann's Way*, translated by C. K. Scott Montcrieff and Terence Kilmartin, revised D. J. Enright (London: Chatto and Windus, 1992), p. 55.

19 John Coyle, 'Pulp Fiction: Or, Proust and Joyce's Rhetorical Flourishes', 2006, p. 3. http://www.arts.gla.ac.uk/STELLA/COMET/glasgrev/issue3/coyle.htm.

20 Virginia Woolf, *The Question of Things Happening: The Letters of Virginia Woolf 1912–1922*, edited by Nigel Nicolson (London: Chatto and Windus, 1976), p. 525.

21 Virginia Woolf, 'Sketch of the Past', in *Moments of Being: Autobiographical Writings* (London: Hogarth Press, 2002), p. 91. Woolf used the image of the circle in her essay 'A Glance at Turgenev' (1921) as, in Nena Skrbic's words, 'a supreme symbol of wholeness and unity, a wholeness and unity constantly

threatened by the chaos outside it' (Nena Skrbic, 'Crossing Cultural Boundaries', in *Trespassing Boundaries: Virginia Woolf's Short Fiction*, edited by Kathryn N. Benzel and Ruth Hoberman (New York and Basingstoke: Macmillan Palgrave, 2004), p. 33). In the essay Woolf wrote of Turgenev's 'Russian' melancholy: 'Beyond the circle of his scene seems to lie a great space, which flows in at the window, presses upon people, isolates them, makes them incapable of action, indifferent to effect, sincere, and open-minded. Some background of that sort is common to much of Russian literature': *The Essays of Virginia Woolf*, vol. 3, ed. Andrew McNeillie (London: Hogarth Press, 1988), p. 316.

22 Woolf, *Moments of Being*, p. 145.

23 Roger Fry, 'Mrs. Cameron's Photographs', in *Victorian Photographs of Famous Men and Fair Women* (1926) (London: Chatto and Windus, 1973), pp. 24–25.

24 Woolf wrote the draft entitled 'A Scene from the Past', or 'Scene from the Past', in at least five versions. The longest version, from which these quotes are taken, is 'A Scene from the Past', Ts. MH/B10e, pp. 1–25, Monk's House Papers, University of Sussex, England.

25 Woolf, 'A Scene from the Past', p. 1.

26 Ibid., p. 4.

27 In the final part of *The Years*, 'Present Day', Woolf has North, at the family party, 'looking at a couple at the farther end of the room. Both were young; both were silent; they seemed held still in that position by some powerful emotion. As he looked at them, some emotion about himself, about his own life, came over him, and he arranged another background for them or from himself – not the mantelpiece and the bookcase, but cataracts roaring, clouds racing, and they stood on a cliff above a torrent . . .': Virginia Woolf, *The Years* (Harmondsworth: Penguin, 1968), p. 203.

28 Woolf, 'A Scene from the Past', p. 3.

29 Walter Benjamin, Letter to Werner Kraft, [date], *The Correspondence of Walter Benjamin 1910–1940*, edited by Gershom Sholem and Theodor W. Adorno, translated by Manfred R. Jacobson and Evelyn M. Jacobson (Chicago: University of Chicago Press, 1994), 28 October 1935, p. 516.

30 Jan Holmberg, 'Closing In: Telescopes, Early Cinema, and the Technological Conditions of De-distancing', in *Moving Images: From Edison to the Webcam*, edited by John Fullerton and Astrid Söderbergh Widding (Sydney: John Libbey, 2000), pp. 83–90, 85.

31 Jacques Derrida, *Spurs: Nietzsche's Styles*, translated by Barbara Harlow (Chicago: Chicago University Press, 1979), pp. 50–51.

32 Holmberg, 'Closing In', p. 84.

33 Eric Elliott, *Anatomy of Motion Picture Art* (Territet, Switzerland: POOL, 1928), p. 67, italics in original.

34 Ibid., 24–25.

35 Virginia Woolf, *A Change of Perspective: The Letters of Virginia Woolf 1923–1928*. Edited by Nigel Nicolson (London: Chatto and Windus, 1977), pp.72–73.

36 Ellen Terry, *The Story of My Life* (London: Hutchinson, 1908), p. 53.

37 Ibid., p. 59.
38 Julia Margaret Cameron, 'Annals of my Glass House', *Photo Beacon* (Chicago) 2, 1890, pp. 157–160. Reprinted in Beaumont Newhall, ed., *Photography, Essays and Images* (New York: Museum of Modern Art; Boston: New York Graphic Society, 1980, pp. 135–139; here p. 135. Online at http://macaulay.cuny.edu/ eportfolios/lklichfall13/files/2013/08/Cameron-Annals-of-My-Glass-House.pdf.
39 Virginia Woolf, 'Ellen Terry' (1941), in *The Essays of Virginia Woolf*, vol. 6, pp. 285–292, p. 286
40 Terry, *The Story of My Life*, p. 48.
41 Christopher St. John, *Ellen Terry and Bernard Shaw: A Correspondence* (1931) (London: Reinhardt and Evans, 1949), p. iii.
42 Virginia Woolf, MH/B5a. Monk's House Papers, University of Sussex, England.
43 Woolf, 'Ellen Terry', p. 286
44 Ibid., p. 289.
45 Woolf, *Moments of Being*, p. 98.
46 Woolf, *The Voyage Out*.
47 Woolf, *To the Lighthouse*, p. 149. The draft version of this passage shows Woolf rendering the optic less that of the telescope than of early projected film.

CHAPTER 12

Virginia Woolf and the Art of the Novel

In the last months of her life, Virginia Woolf was working on a writing project to which she gave the title 'Reading at Random'. The first of her notes for this work is dated 18 September 1940. The book was to have an historical orientation – as Woolf wrote in the first entry, 'Keep to time sequence'. But, she added, there should be 'No "periods": No text book'. In a later note she wrote:

> The 19th Cent. to consist of outlines of people.
> Skip present day.
> A Chapter on the future.[1]

'Reading at Random' bears similarities to Woolf's work, nearly two decades earlier, on the essays which became the two volumes of *The Common Reader*, Woolf's working title for which was 'Reading'. In the first reference to what would become *The Common Reader*, first series, Woolf wrote in her diary (23 May 1921): 'I'm wondering how to shape my Reading book.'[2] Two years later (11 May 1923), she described 'edg[ing] in a little time every now & then at Reading. I am at the Greek chapter (in reading). Shall I read a little Greek? ... Or shall I plunge into early Elizabethans, of whom I am appallingly ignorant? What happened between Chaucer & Shakespeare. I think that attracts me as a basis'.[3] The entry is interesting in part because it suggests a more linear model of literary history than *The Common Reader* in fact offers, in anticipation of 'Reading at Random'.

In August 1923, Woolf set out in detail the shape of the 'reading' volume:

> The question I want to debate here is the question of my essays; & how to make them into a book. The brilliant idea has just come to me of embedding them in Otway conversation. The main advantage would be that I could then comment, & add what I had had to leave out, or failed to get in ... Also to have a setting for each would 'make a book'; & the collection of essays is in my view an inartistic method. But then this might be too artistic: it might run away with me; it will take time. Nevertheless I should very much enjoy it ... The first thing to do is to get ready a certain number of essays ... No doubt fiction is the prevailing theme. Anyway the book shd end with modern lit.[4]

The two lists she made in this diary entry – one of writers and topics as they would appear in the volume, the other 'in order of time' – suggest a need both to respect chronology and to disrupt it. Not all the chapters Woolf planned were included in the final version, but 'How It Strikes a Contemporary' retained its place as the final essay in the planning and the execution.

Woolf's reference to 'Otway conversation' evoked her recently published review, in the *Nation and Atheneum*, of a group of Conrad novels, entitled 'Mr Conrad: a Conversation', in which one Penelope Otway discusses Conrad with her old friend David Lowe. Penelope, 'a small dark woman turned forty . . . had always, since the age of seven, been engaged in reading the classics' and had had the freedom of her father's library, 'a method of education which, since it spared his purse, deserved his benediction'.[5] In the course of the conversation about Conrad, Penelope persuades the initially sceptical David that Conrad is 'a great writer', 'many and complex'. In fact, David takes rather little persuasion and Woolf's 'dialogue on Conrad',[6] though its form recalls Henry James's *Daniel Deronda: A Conversation* (1873), functions without James's ironies at the expense of both Eliot's text and his dramatized readers. In her diary for 5 September 1923 (two weeks after her plans for the extension of 'Otway conversation' into the entire Reading volume, now named as *The Common Reader*) Woolf noted: 'I am slightly dashed by the reception of my Conrad conversation, which has been purely negative – No one has mentioned it.'[7] She implied that this had changed her mind about the ways in which *The Common Reader* would be written: 'I shall really investigate literature with a view to answering certain questions about ourselves – Characters are to be merely views: personality must be avoided at all costs. I'm sure my Conrad adventure taught me this. Directly you specify hair, age &c [*sic*] something frivolous, or irrelevant, gets into the book – Dinner!'[8]

Woolf did include an essay on Conrad in *The Common Reader*, but it was the appreciation she wrote for *The Times Literary Supplement* on the occasion of Conrad's death and not 'Mr Conrad: a Conversation'. Her decision to abandon the plan for 'Otway conversation' as the framework for the essay volume was, I think most readers would agree, well judged. The initial impulse, however, is a telling one. 'The reader' would have been dramatized (in the person of Penelope Otway) as a woman whose passion for literature had been shaped in and by the freedom of the library and not the training of school or university. More broadly, the appeal of the dialogue may have arisen from the difficulties and doubts that arose about the writing of literary history and literary criticism, and the related desire to create a more dialogical method of airing critical judgements. It was also an attempt to reawaken classical aesthetic discourse, and in particular the Platonic or Socratic dialogue, a mode to which Woolf would indeed return some years later in her long essay 'Walter Sickert: A Conversation' (1934).

An experiment with dialogue comparable to Woolf's in the first versions of *The Common Reader* can be found in one of Georg Lukács's early essays, written in 1909 (part of a grouping which would be published as *Soul and Form*), entitled 'Richness, Chaos and Form: A Dialogue Concerning Tristram Shandy'. As in James's *Daniel Deronda: A Conversation*, there are in fact three people involved. James gives us two women, Theodora and Pulcharia, and a man, Constantius, in debate about Eliot's novel. Lukács constructs the argument about *Tristram Shandy* as an argument about form and formlessness that is also a competition between two young men, Vincent and Joachim, for the affections of a young woman, a fellow student, who has not read Sterne's text and for whom, at the essay's close, Joachim's kiss comes as 'the thing for which the whole argument was only a highly unnecessary preparation'.[9] In his 1962 Preface to *The Theory of the Novel* (written during 1914–1915), Lukács (who later disowned this early work, an exploration of the relationship between literary form and the philosophy of history) noted that it was at first

> meant to take the form of a series of dialogues: a group of young people withdraw from the war psychosis of their environment, just as the story-tellers of the *Decameron* had withdrawn from the plague; they try to understand themselves and one another by means of conversations which gradually lead to the problems discussed in the book – the outlook on a Dostoevskian world. On closer consideration I dropped this plan and wrote the book as it stands today.[10]

The dialogue form thus becomes constructed as a utopian space outside the terms of historical exigencies, but one ultimately, like Woolf's 'conversations', abandoned.

Yet we might continue to think of the essay form, as Lukács intimates in his 1910 essay 'On the Nature and Form of the Essay', as an inherently dialogical mode and as a conversation with the reader in which the essayist becomes a mediating figure between reader and author, present and past. The tenor of 'the conversation' and the figure of 'the reader' continued to be at the heart of *The Common Reader*, as Woolf took up Dr Johnson's figure of 'the common reader', who differs, as she noted, from the critic and the scholar: 'he is guided by an instinct to create for himself, out of whatever odds and ends he can come by, some kind of whole – a portrait of a man, a sketch of an age, a theory of the art of writing'.[11] A number of the essays in *The Common Reader* have a strongly reflexive relationship to this model of creation. The essay on Montaigne, for example, points to the exceptional nature of his self-portraiture and to the complexities, and the self-contradictions, of his concepts of the good life: 'Movement and change', Woolf glosses Montaigne, 'are the essence of our being; rigidity is death; conformity is death; let us say what comes into our heads, repeat ourselves, contradict ourselves, fling out the wildest nonsense, and follow the most fantastic fancies without caring what the world does or thinks or says. For nothing matters except life; and, of course, order'.[12] This call for 'order', seemingly at odds with the call for absolute freedom of thought and action, is explained by Woolf through the importance Montaigne placed on the guidance of 'un patron au dedans', which she defined, in post-Freudian terms, as 'an invisible censor within . . . this is the censor who will help us to achieve that order which is the grace of a well-born soul'.[13] We might extend this model of selfhood to writing, and, more specifically, to the genre of the essay itself: digression (*parekbasis*, excursion) and the following 'of the most fantastic fancies' is a departure followed by a return, to the place where a topic, or a self, is (provisionally) grounded.[14]

In his essay 'On Books' Montaigne wrote that it was only 'chance' which put order into his writings: 'As my thoughts come into my head, so I pile them up . . . Even if I have strayed from the road I would have everyone see my natural and ordinary pace. I let myself go forward as I am.'[15] His discussions of literature, Montaigne added, 'are not matters about which it is wrong to be ignorant, or to speak casually and at random'.[16] Woolf's essay 'On Reading', or 'Reading', written in 1919 and published posthumously, spoke back to Montaigne's 'On Books'. An immersion in books leads both to a form of time travel – the past comes alive as the narrating 'I' reads the Elizabethans and traces a lineage of English literature – and to the creation of a continuum between book and world. The essay, like *To the Lighthouse*, is formed of three parts, in which the central section is a 'passage', interlude, interval or excursion. The middle, in 'On Reading', is also an eruption of autobiographical memory into the critical essay, conjuring up a childhood experience (an actual excursion) of a nocturnal moth-hunt. The world of the night, Woolf seems to suggest in both texts, is an interruption of the diurnal world, breaching the familiar surfaces of dailiness, disrupting linear time, and opening up a rent in the fabric of being.

This three-part structure is also at work in the first essay in *The Common Reader*, 'The Pastons and Chaucer', though it also acts as an inversion of 'On Reading', as we move from 'life' to 'the scene of reading' and back to 'life'. The middle section (entered into as Sir John Paston, a transitional figure in a transitional age, turns away from his daily activities and, in the inward turn which structures Woolf's history of reading, begins to read Chaucer), uses the collective pronouns: 'we' and 'us'. The act of reading creates a community of readers which crosses boundaries of time and space – 'a common mind', as Woolf wrote elsewhere. The essays in *The Common Reader*, in their various ways, explore both this commonality and the recognition of radical differences, of culture and period, as in 'On Not Knowing Greek' and 'The Russian Point of View'. 'Rambling Round Evelyn' comes back repeatedly to the terms of similarity and difference and of our likeness or unlikeness to figures from the past: implicit in all of the essays is a history of subjectivity as well as a history of literature.

The terms of difference and resemblance are writ large in the final essay, 'How It Strikes a Contemporary' (slightly revised from the original version published in the *Times Literary Supplement*, 5 April 1923). Taken in the context of *The Common Reader* as a whole, and as its concluding essay, its address to the question of engaging with the present rather than turning back to the literary past becomes particularly charged. 'There is something about the present', Woolf writes, 'which we would not exchange, though we were offered a choice of all past ages to live in.'[17] 'Modern literature', she continues, 'with all its imperfections, has the same hold on us and the same fascination. It has the same endearing quality of being that which we are, that which we have made, that in which we live, instead of being something, however, august, alien to ourselves and beheld from the outside.'[18] The reader as time traveller is returned to his or her own moment.

This concluding essay also seems to bear the imprint of an originary dialogue, conversation or argument, as it veers between opposing positions: 'everybody is talking at once and it is time to be going', Woolf writes towards the essay's close.[19] It is a performative piece of writing, which enacts the very absence of critical certainties which it takes as its central topic. Its internal contradictions, and its vacillating or veering between one position and another, play out the contradictory, ambivalent, fragmentary conditions of the present, defined by Woolf as by so many of her contemporaries, as a transitional age.

The essay begins as a lament for the age of the great critics: 'Reviewers we have but no critic; a million competent and incorruptible policemen but no judge'.[20] It moves to suggest that the first two decades of the twentieth century have produced little that is substantial in the literary field – there are fragments, but no great works. Then Woolf turns around her own argument. Life in the moment – 'on one of the first fine days of spring' – 'is not altogether lacking in colour'.[21] The present, Woolf seems to suggest, is more present, more alive, to her contemporaries than the present of past generations was to them. This seems to be the result of her age's radical break with the past – 'We are sharply cut off from our predecessors'[22] – brought about by the war, by shifts in the social structure (we are reminded of Woolf's claim, in her essay 'Character in Fiction', that 'on or about December 1910 human character changed', as evidenced by changes in 'human relations' and 'in the character of one's cook').[23] There is 'widespread originality', she notes in 'How It Strikes a Contemporary', in the work of her contemporaries, stemming from the desire to express differences from the past and not resemblances to it. But, contemporary literature continues to disappoint: 'Book after book leaves us with the same sense of promise unachieved, of intellectual poverty, of brilliance which has been snatched from life but not transmuted into literature'.[24]

So we vacillate in 'How It Strikes a Contemporary' – between enthusiasm and pessimism. The critics will not serve us. Turning back to the texts of the past, we find in them 'an unabashed tranquility' and a refusal 'to gratify those senses which are stimulated so briskly by the moderns; the sense of sight, of sound, of touch – above all the sense of the human being, his depth and the variety of his perceptions, his complexity, his confusion, his self, in short'.[25] 'Yet' (the favoured connective in this essay) in the texts of the past, we also find an escape 'from the cramp and confinement of personality'.[26] The recommendation is to take the longer view: 'The storm and the drenching are on the surface; continuity and calm are in the depths'.[27] The essay appears to end with a model of tradition – or, at least, with a sense of a continuum. But there is also an exhortation to the critics to follow the example of Lady Hester Stanhope, 'who kept a milk-white horse in her stable in readiness for the Messiah and was for ever [*sic*] scanning the mountain tops, impatiently but with confidence, for signs of his approach': the critics should 'scan the horizon; see the past in relation to the future; and so prepare the way for masterpieces to come'.[28]

We could at this point use Woolf's invocation of Messianic time to connect her essay on the contemporary to that of Georgio Agamben, in which Messianic time becomes exemplary of the division within the temporal moment, putting 'the present' in relation to past and future time, or to the work of Walter Benjamin.[29] The sceptic, on the other hand, might see Woolf's conclusion to her essay as a 'mere' rhetorical flourish, opening up no particularly complex philosophy of time for us to pursue. The writer and critic Edgell Rickword, reviewing *The Common Reader* in 1925 in the short-lived magazine which he edited, the *Calendar*, wrote of Woolf's exhortation to the critic-reader: 'This is advice which the middle-aged will perhaps welcome; but we doubt if these studious evangelists are of much use as path-straighteners for the Messiah. If the past is any guide, he will come with none of the signs of grace and perhaps attempt to borrow five pounds from the ladies and gentlemen scanning the horizon.'[30] Rickword was engaged by *The Common Reader* and by Woolf's exploration of 'the relation of artist and audience'[31] (particularly in 'The Pastons and Chaucer'), though his review expressed a contempt for the general state of literary criticism in the present age.

In her invocation of the figure of Lady Hester Stanhope, Woolf was repeating material from two of her earlier essays. In 'The Eccentrics' (1919) she wrote:

> Lady Hester indeed kept her white horse perpetually in readiness for the Messiah in her stable. How often, sitting alone in her castle at the top of Mount Lebanon . . . did she not see herself riding into Jerusalem by the side of the Lord and enjoy in fancy the consternation with which Lord Palmerston and Queen Victoria received the news![32]

The quality which marks all true eccentrics, Woolf notes in the essay, 'is that they never for a moment believe themselves to be eccentric', but that it is the rest of the world 'who are cramped and malformed and spiritually decrepit'.[33] The out-of-centre, we could say, finds itself to be the centre, and this reversal suggests the transfer of values which Woolf would locate and promote in women's writing. 'The Eccentrics' also borrowed from an 1910 review by Woolf, 'Lady Hester Stanhope', in which she outlined the great woman's life and travels: 'With what expectations she set sail for the East we know not, but she emerged in Syria, astride her horse, in the trousers of a Turkish gentleman . . . the natives thought her neither man nor woman, but a being apart'.[34] This figure would become central to Woolf's *Orlando*, informing the episodes in Constantinople in particular. It also suggests that the significance of the call to follow the example of Lady Hester Stanhope, in scanning the horizon for the future of the novel, might be related less to any image of Messianic time (the future contained in the present, rendering the present ex-centric to itself) than to an imagining of an androgynous fiction ('neither man nor woman') to come, anticipating the 'utopian' dimensions of *A Room of One's Own*.

Woolf repeated the image of a figure scanning the horizon for a glimpse of the future in a companion essay to 'How It Strikes a Contemporary'. 'Poetry, Fiction and the Future' was published in two parts in the *New York Herald Tribune* in 1927: it had its origins in a talk Woolf gave to the Oxford University English Club. In the essay, Woolf defined the modern age, and the 'modern mind', as being characterized by contradiction and conflict, 'contrast and collision': 'Beauty is part ugliness; amusement part disgust; pleasure part pain. Emotions which used to enter the mind whole are now broken up on the threshold.'[35] Prose rather than poetry is the form of literature, she suggests, that is most suited to the expression of such complexities. Yet the future of fiction lies in its taking on some of 'the attributes of poetry', which it can do once freed 'from the beast of burden work which so many novelists necessarily lay upon it of carrying loads of detail, bushels of fact'.[36] The essay argues that the future of fiction lies in its turning towards 'impersonality – poetry and the 'soliloquy in solitude'[37] – and in these tenets it seems to lay the groundwork for the writing of *The Waves*.

Woolf opened the essay with the assertion that 'Far the greater number of critics turn their back upon the present and gaze steadily into the past.'[38] They leave 'comment upon what is actually written at the moment' to 'the race of reviewers whose very title seems to imply transiency in themselves and in the objects they survey'.[39] But, Woolf writes,

> one has sometimes asked oneself, must the duty of the critic always be to the past, must his gaze always be fixed backward? Could he not sometimes turn around and, shading his eyes in the manner of Robinson Crusoe on the desert island, look into the future and trace on its mist the faint lines of the land which some day perhaps we may reach?[40]

While Robinson Crusoe would seem to work as a parallel figure to that of Lady Hester Stanhope, a different set of determinants are in fact in play. A year prior to 'Poetry, Fiction and the Future' Woolf had published a review of a new edition of Defoe's novel, with an introduction by the journalist and critic Charles Whibley (who had given The Leslie Stephen Lecture at Cambridge in 1917 on the topic of Jonathan Swift). In the review essay, Woolf took issue with various critical approaches to literary texts, including the biographical approach and such high-ways and by-ways as 'The Rise and Development of the Novel' and 'the spirit of the age': 'It is not detail that we want, but perspective':[41]

> All alone we must climb upon the novelist's shoulders and gaze through his eyes, until we, too, understand in what order he ranges the large common objects upon which novelists are fated to gaze – man and men, Nature, and, behind or above, the power which is conveniently called God ... simple in themselves, these objects can be made monstrous, strange, and indeed unrecognisable by the manner in which they are related to each other. People who live cheek by jowl and breathe the same air yet see trees very large and human beings very small, or the other way about, man vast and trees in miniature. Writers who live at the same moment yet see nothing the same size.[42]

Here time would seem to give way to space – what is contemporary is in fact divided by the difference in perspective (the 'difference of view', as Woolf would define it in the context of women's writing). This has significant implications for the writing of literary criticism, and must trouble the concept of 'literary history', of 'periodization' (always linked for Woolf with 'text-book') and of the 'Zeitgeist'. It also bears on the notion of the contemporary and contemporary writing – space, perspective and relative size seem to shatter the temporal/historical continuum from within.

In her discussion of *Robinson Crusoe*, Woolf perhaps overstates the extent to which material reality pushes out spiritual enquiry in the novel – it is surely not the case that 'God does not exist' in Crusoe's world, and indeed his story is to some extent one of spiritual conversion. Her broad point, however, is that it is the fact, the material reality, the 'solid object' around which we orientate ourselves as readers of Defoe's novel.[43] 'De Foe, reiterating that nothing but a plain earthenware pot stands in the foreground, and that to its plainness and earthiness everything else must give way, finally ropes the whole universe into harmony.'[44]

As in her earlier discussion in the essay of objects rendered 'strange and monstrous', Woolf's terms echo those she used in writing of Tolstoy. As she observed in 'The Russian Point of View' (an essay written for *The Common Reader* series one):

> Even in a translation we feel that we have been set on a mountain-top and had a telescope put into our hands. Everything is astonishingly clear and absolutely sharp. Then, suddenly, just as we are exulting, breathing deep, feeling at once braced and purified, some detail – perhaps the head of a man – comes at us out of the picture in an alarming way, as if extruded by the very intensity of its life.[45]

Woolf brings together the question of optics (the view through the telescope) with the estrangement produced by the enlarged and 'alarming' detail. I use the term 'estrangement' here to evoke the work of Victor Shklovsky, whose theory of '*ostranenie*' (making strange) was indeed a theory of perception, with its origins in the analysis of Tolstoy's realist aesthetics, 'his method of seeing things out of their normal contexts'.[46] 'Simple in themselves', we have seen Woolf write, 'these objects can be made monstrous, strange, and indeed unrecognisable by the manner in which they are related to each other'.[47] 'The purpose of art', Shklovsky wrote, 'is to impart the sensation of things as they are perceived and not as they are known. The technique of art is to make objects "unfamiliar," to make forms difficult, to increase the difficulty and length of perception because the process of perception is an aesthetic end in itself and must be prolonged'.[48] Here the question of temporality – as prolongation – is inseparable from that of space and distance.

There is no evidence that Woolf had any direct knowledge of Shklovsky's writings. The coincidence of their similar terms, however, does suggest that Woolf was reaching for models of literary history, or literary relationship, which could incorporate the new modes of perception associated with modernist art and literature. She brings in, as did Shklovsky and Proust, optical metaphors as ways of representing the changes to perception which art brings into being. The networks of association in her essays of the mid-1920s – so many of which foregrounded aspects such as perspective, perception, distance, viewpoint, and vantage point – informed, in crucial ways, her writings about literature. They also shaped the writing of *To the Lighthouse*, the novel in which so much depends upon distance, and in which time is profoundly imbricated with space and perspective.

Woolf's connections with the writings of the Soviet avant-garde on art and literature must remain as a question of simultaneous discovery. We are on firmer (if more conventional) ground if we put Woolf's writings on the novel and on literary history in relation to those of her British and American contemporaries. The majority of Woolf's essays on the art of fiction as well as her planned book on the novel *Phases of Fiction* were written in the 1920s. The decade also saw the publication of a number of influential studies on the novel as a genre, including Percy Lubbock's *The Craft of Fiction* (1921) and E.M. Forster's *Aspects of the Novel* (1927). Less familiar, perhaps, is the poet, critic and translator Edwin Muir's *The Structure of the Novel* (published by Hogarth Press in 1928, two years after the Press had published his book on contemporary writers, *Transitions*). John Carruthers' (the pseudonym of the Hume scholar and editor J.Y.T. Greig) short study *Scheherezade: Or the Future of the English Novel* was published in 1928 in Routledge's 'To-Day and To-Morrow' series. A further study, Clayton Hamilton's *The Materials and Methods of Fiction*, was reviewed very critically by Woolf in 1919, and discussed by Forster in *Aspects of the Novel*. Most of these texts were in dialogue – usually implicit rather than explicit – with Aristotle's *Poetics:* the driving motive of such early twentieth-century studies of fiction was to construct or delineate a set of aesthetic and formal categories for the novel which would enable this 'youngest' of literary genres to enter the arena of the higher arts occupied by poetry and drama.

Issues and concepts of time and temporality in their various manifestations – as history, sequence and development – were both negotiated and avoided by these early theorists of the novel. Questions of the contemporary – introduced, for the most part, through the issue of the contemporary novel – troubled the formal, typological and universalistic principles which most of the critics constructed in their accounts of the art, or craft, of fiction. Eschewing for the most part – as Woolf does in 'Phases of Fiction' – a developmental account of the novel, there was nonetheless a felt need to give an account of the novel of the present and the future, and hence to engage with the question of present and future time. Yet this had to be squared with the view that the novel as a genre could be understood outside temporal or historical categories. For E.M. Forster this was in a part a pragmatic question – what we might call a strategic synchronism. He was not, he suggested, a scholar or a philosopher able to 'contemplate the river of time' and hence to explore the novel in its chronological development,[49] and he did not wish to act in this context as a pseudo-scholar, referring literature back to the history of its time or to some 'tendency'.[50] Linear models of temporality, it would seem, were problematic both because they demanded an historical account and because time itself had become such a marked subject of conceptual enquiry in the time-philosophies of the period, with the existence of 'the present' placed under particular scrutiny. Better, Forster suggested (and here we have echoes of Eliot's 'Tradition and the Individual Talent'), to imagine 'all the novelists writing their novels at once . . . in a circular room'.[51] Woolf seems to have been largely sympathetic to a model of simultaneous creation – as she wrote in 'Modern Fiction':

> We do not come to write better; all that we can be said to do is to keep moving, now a little in this direction, now in that, but with a circular tendency should the whole course of the track be viewed from a sufficiently lofty pinnacle. It need scarcely be said that we make no claim to stand, even momentarily, upon that vantage ground.[52]

Yet she would use Forster's image of the 'circular room' (and, by extension, Eliot's 'tradition') rather differently in *A Room of One's Own*, in which the round reading room of the British Library comes to stand for the patriarchy.

Edwin Muir's *The Structure of the Novel* used the Aristotelian distinction between the 'universal' and the 'particular' to define the differences between 'the chronicle' (instanced by *War and Peace* but defined by Muir more generally as the 'the ruling convention of the novel at present') and 'the period novel' (which Muir describes as 'already outmoded').[53] For the terms of his argument, he turned to the French critic M. Ramon Fernandez and his recently translated volume of essays *Messages*. Here (in an essay on Balzac) Fernandez drew a distinction between the novel and the *récit* (which his translator renders as 'recital'): '*The novel is the representation of events which take place in time . . . The recital is the presentation of events which have taken place*.[54] The distinction appears to draw on that made by Aristotle (in the *Poetics*) between history and poetry: 'the one says what has happened, the other the kind of thing that would happen. For this reason poetry is more philosophical and more serious than history. Poetry tends to express universals, and history particulars'.[55] Muir extends such distinctions to define the work of Wells and Galsworthy, for whom 'society is there full grown as an idea at the beginning; it is not created by the characters, rather it creates them . . . the period novel is really a spurious kind of history which occasionally breaks into fiction'.[56] 'The bondage of the novel to period has naturally degraded it', Muir writes, and he instances Bennett's and Wells's descriptions of the 'devices which have changed modern life'.[57]

The temporal paradox contained in Muir's account is that 'the period novel' is both confined to its own present (linked, as in Woolf's 'How It Strikes a Contemporary', to journalism and 'fashion') and (as *récit*) records that present as past and completed action. The contemporary novels which he contrasts with 'the period novel', and which he views as a reaction against it, include works by Proust, Joyce, Woolf (*Mrs Dalloway*) and Huxley; *Ulysses* and *Mrs Dalloway* are defined as novels of character and of space rather than time: 'their vision is of scenes rather than sequences'.[58] They are, Muir suggests, 'devious returns to the pure imaginative convention' and, as such, are 'more in the pure aesthetic tradition of prose fiction than the work of the preceding generation, the generation of the period novel'.[59] To this extent, Muir posits a continuum between the past of the novel and these new 'experiments', with the work of the 'period novelist' viewed as extraneous to the aesthetics of fiction. The 'period novel' is, moreover, viewed by Muir (as by Woolf, as she articulated it in 'Modern Fiction') as having skewed the development of the novel:

> A great number of the wilder experiments in form recently must have sprung from a hopeless contemplation of the mediocrity of the conventions which the novel has observed for twenty years or so. If it could be proved that these conventions are not traditional but merely fashionable, the reaction against them might be more effective as well as less violent.[60]

In his book *Transition*, Muir had engaged specifically with the literature of the present (including the work of Joyce, Lawrence, Woolf, Huxley and Eliot), though he defined his period as an 'age of transition' amongst others. His study (which bears the imprint of the self-taught Muir's education in philosophy through Nietzsche and through Orage's journal *The New Age*) defined the *Zeit Geist* in agonistic terms:

A man who apprehends the power of the age will regard himself as its
enemy . . . This hostility is in certain writers inevitable; it is in effect a testing
of the age by itself, an assaying process from which, its deceptions and
fashions burned away, the age emerges in greater purity . . . Without this
hostility against itself the spirit of no age could come to realization; it would
remain undifferentiated and unawakened; it could never be objectified, for
all objectification implies separation.[61]

The terms echo those of Nietzsche in 'The Use and Abuse of History for
Life', in which Nietzsche argues that it is the anachronism of his work in
classical philology that renders it effective by reason of its 'inappropriateness
for the times, that is, in opposition to the age, thus working on the age, and,
we hope for the benefit of a coming time'.[62] 'The good writer', Muir asserts,

is not concerned with the things which in literature have been proved
permanent, but rather with the things in his age and his experience which
have not been so probed, to which by realizing and objectifying them he may
give them permanence. What we recognize as the Zeit Geist of a past age is
that part of it which in this way has been objectified. What we feel as the
contemporary Zeit Geist, on the other hand, is a raw potentiality whose
crystallizations in art are less clearly recognizable by us the more completely
we are under the influence of that potentiality.[63]

'Fashion' is for Muir the enemy of both permanence and potentiality (he
defines Huxley as 'our best example of the fashionable writer').[64] It bears for
him none of the temporal complexity which it was granted by Walter
Benjamin and, to an extent, by Woolf, for whom (as in her reference to
'the romance' of the telephone in 'How It Strikes a Contemporary'[65]) 'the
devices which had changed modern life' also had their particular fascination.
The terms of the immanent and the permanent do, however, have their
echoes in Woolf's writings on art and aesthetics, as in 'Life and the
Novelist': 'there emerges from the mist something stark, formidable and
enduring, the bone and substance upon which our rush of indiscriminating
emotion was founded'.[66]

Woolf's conceptions of fictional form and shape also resonate with the
arguments of Percy Lubbock in *The Craft of Fiction*, which Woolf discussed
in detail in her essay 'On Re-Reading Novels' (1922). She adopted a critical
distance from Lubbock's discussion, arguing (rather curiously, given how
important the art theories of Clive Bell and Roger Fry would be for her
aesthetics) that his use of the word 'form' in discussing the novel was too close
to the language of the visual arts.[67] Nonetheless, she was almost certainly
more sympathetic to Lubbock's book than to many other contemporary
studies of the novel, using, in her essay 'Phases of Fiction', language very

close to Lubbock's in relation to fictional form and shape: 'As the pages are turned, something is built up which is not the story itself.'[68] She also addressed, in 'On Re-Reading Novels', the issue of constructing a developmental model of the novel as genre. Drawing the comparison with drama, honed as a genre by centuries of audience response, Woolf suggested that the novel, in its relative newness, was still an almost uncharted terrain, a situation exacerbated by its multiplicity and multifariousness. 'Let us look', she enjoined, in her attempt to take a 'general view' of the genre, 'not at each story separately, but at the method of telling stories as a whole, and its development from generation to generation.'[69]

Throughout Woolf's essays we find her exploring the question of 'development' in literary history and of the relationship of the past to the present. In 'How Should One Read a Book?' (1926), biographers and memoirists are associated by acquaintance, and, in reading them, 'we have passed from one end of English literature to another and wake to find ourselves here again in the present, if we can so differentiate this moment from all that have gone before'.[70] 'The poet is always our contemporary', she writes in the same essay: 'we may be sure that the newness of new poetry and fiction is its most superficial quality and that we have only to alter slightly, not to recast, the standards by which we have judged the old'.[71] In 'Reading' (1919), she writes of the moment in which 'We want what is timeless and contemporary.'[72] In 'Hours in a Library' (1916) she had written of the appeal of 'reading our contemporaries', which grows as we grow older: 'the old hunger to know what the immortals thought has given place to a far more tolerant curiosity to know what our own generation is thinking'.[73] Here she asserts the radical difference between past and present which 'How Should One Read a Book?' would posit as merely superficial. 'No age of literature', she states in 'Hours in a Library', 'is so little submissive to authority as ours, so free from the dominion of the great; none seems so wayward with its gift of reverence, or so volatile in its experiments ... whenever there is life in them they will be casting their net out over some unknown abyss to snare new shapes'.[74] The various, at times contradictory, answers she provides to questions of history, change, development, past and present do seem to suggest that these were areas in which she perceived particular complexities. This would then shape the ways in which she would approach the question of 'literary history' and of the history and the art of fiction in particular.

As I have suggested, Woolf avoided a model of 'development' in 'Phases of Fiction', the essay version of the proposed book on fiction on which she worked intermittently through the mid-1920s, and which was intended for a Hogarth Press series, planned by Leonard Woolf and George [Dadie]

Rylands, to be called 'Hogarth Lectures on Literature'. 'Phases of Fiction' was, she wrote, an

> attempt to record the impressions made upon the mind by reading a certain number of novels in succession . . . It was allowed to read what it liked. It was not, that is to say, asked to read historically, nor was it asked to read critically . . . It went its way, therefore, independent of time and reputation . . . making itself a dwelling-place in accordance with its own appetites.[75]

The language of 'appetite' seems chosen to differentiate her approach from that of the despised furred and gowned professors of literature: she appears to have read a good many studies of fiction in preparation for her own, and to have found most of them wanting.

'Prose perhaps is the instrument best fitted to the complexity and difficulty of modern life', Virginia Woolf wrote at the close of 'Phases of Fiction'.[76] She took her examples not only from English fiction, but also from the literatures of Scotland (Scott, Stevenson), America (Melville, James), Russia (Tolstoy, Dostoevsky) and France (Flaubert, Maupassant, Proust). She divided the field into a number of categories in 'Phases of Fiction' – 'The Truth-tellers', 'The Romantics', 'The Character-mongers and Comedians', 'The Psychologists', 'The Satirists and Fantastics', 'The Poets'. These traverse historical periods, though there is significance, recalling the essay 'Poetry, Fiction and the Future' and its invocation of the novel's future conjoining with poetry, in Woolf's closing with 'The Poets'.

Woolf's letters and diary entries written between 1925 and 1928 reveal something of her progress, or lack of it, in the composition of 'Phases of Fiction'. She outlined her plans for the book in a diary entry, written at the close of 1925, in terms which anticipate the terms she would use in her essay on *Robinson Crusoe*.

> I am reading The Passage to India; but will not expatiate here, as I must elsewhere. This book for the H.P.: I think I will find some theory about fiction. I shall read six novels, & start some hares. The one I have in view, is about *perspective*. But I do not know . . . . I don't think it is a matter of 'development' but something to do with prose & poetry, in novels. For instance Defoe at one end: E. Brontë at the other. Reality something they put at different distances. One would have to go into conventions; real life; & so on. It might last me – this theory – but I should have to support it with other things. And death – as I always feel – hurrying near. 43: how many more books?[77]

By October of the following year, the planned book had become 'that intolerable dull Fiction'. As she wrote to Vita Sackville-West on 9 October 1927:

Yesterday morning I was in despair: You know that bloody book which Dadie and Leonard extort, drop by drop from my breast? Fiction, or some title to that effect. I couldn't screw a word from me; and at last dropped my head in my hands: dipped my pen in the ink, and wrote these words, as if automatically, on a clean sheet: Orlando: A Biography. No sooner had I done this than my body was flooded with rapture and my brain with ideas. I wrote rapidly till 12. Then I did an hour to Romance. So every morning I am going to write fiction (my own fiction) till 12; and Romance till 1.[78]

In representing the origins of *Orlando*, Woolf contrasted the instantaneous conception of the fiction with the sterile planning of the critical work. Yet we could see *Orlando* as to some extent continuous with *Fiction* (Woolf's working title for her critical study). *Orlando* is also, of course, a literary history of a kind, and indeed a more linear one than 'Phases of Fiction', though historicism (in this instance the division of the historical continuum into discrete periods, marked by the boundaries of the centuries) is itself one of the targets of her satire. *Orlando*'s representations of present time, as well as the lengthy final section of *The Years*, 'Present Day' and the 'present day' sequences in the pageant of *Between the Acts*, also foreground the complexities and the fascination of writing the present, of writing in and of the now.

I return, in closing, to Woolf's final planned work of literary history – 'Reading at Random': 'Skip present day. A chapter on the future'. There is no way of knowing how that text would have been written, and from what vantage point – in the absence of 'present day' – 'the future' could have been imagined. The desire to 'skip present day', to reach towards a future, in the context of World War is, of course, wholly comprehensible. The determination or aspiration is part of its historical moment. It may also, however, tell us something more general about the asynchronicities contained with present time and the time of the contemporary, and about the uses and abuses of literary history for life.

Notes

1 Virginia Woolf, '"Anon" and "The Reader": Virginia Woolf's Last Essays', edited by Brenda Silver, *Twentieth Century Literature* 25 (1979): 356–441, 375.

2 Virginia Woolf, *The Diary of Virginia Woolf: Volume 2 1920–24*, edited by Anne Olivier Bell (London: Hogarth Press, 1978), p. 120.

3 Ibid., p. 242.

4 Ibid., p. 261.

5 Virginia Woolf, 'Mr Conrad: a Conversation', in *The Essays of Virginia Woolf: Volume 3, 1919–1924*, edited by Andrew McNeillie (London: Hogarth Press, 1988), p. 376.

6 Woolf, *Diary* vol. 2, p. 259.
7 Ibid., p. 265.
8 Ibid.
9 Georg Lukács, *Soul and Form*, edited by John T. Sanders and Katie Terezakis (New York: Columbia University Press, 2010), p. 174.
10 Georg Lukács, *Theory of the Novel*, translated by Anna Bostock (London: Merlin Press, 1971), pp. 11–12.
11 Virginia Woolf, 'The Common Reader', *The Essays of Virginia Woolf: Volume 4, 1925–1928*, edited by Andrew McNeillie (London: Hogarth Press, 1994), p. 19.
12 Ibid., p. 75.
13 Ibid.
14 Ibid.
15 Michel de Montaigne, *Essays*, translated by J. M. Cohen (Harmondsworth: Penguin, 1958), p. 160.
16 Ibid.
17 Woolf, *Essays* vol. 4, p. 238.
18 Ibid.
19 Ibid., p. 241.
20 Ibid., p. 236.
21 Ibid., p. 237.
22 Ibid., p. 238.
23 Woolf, 'Character in Fiction', in *Essays* vol. 3, pp. 421–422.
24 Woolf, 'How It Strikes a Contemporary', in *Essays* vol. 4, p. 238.
25 Ibid., p. 239.
26 Ibid., p. 240.
27 Ibid., p. 241.
28 Ibid.
29 See Georgio Agamben, 'What is the Contemporary?', in *What Is an Apparatus? and Other Essays*, translated by David Kishik and Stefan Pedatella (Stanford: Stanford University Press, 2009), pp. 39–54; and Walter Benjamin, 'Theses on the Philosophy of History', in *Illuminations*, translated by Harry Zohn (New York: Harcourt, Brace and World, 1968), pp. 253–264.
30 R. Majumdar and A. McLaurin, *Virginia Woolf: The Critical Heritage* (London: Routledge, 1975), p. 154.
31 Ibid., p. 153.
32 Woolf, 'The Eccentrics', in *Essays* vol. 3, p. 40.
33 Ibid., p. 38.
34 Virginia Woolf, 'Lady Hester Stanhope', in *The Essays of Virginia Woolf: Volume 1, 1904–1912*, edited by Andrew McNeillie (London: Hogarth Press, 1986), p. 327.
35 Woolf, 'Poetry, Fiction and the Future', in *Essays* vol. 4, p. 433.
36 Ibid., p. 438.
37 Ibid., p. 435.
38 Ibid., p. 428.
39 Ibid., p. 429

40 Ibid., p. 429.
41 Woolf, 'Robinson Crusoe', *Essays* vol. 4, p. 332.
42 Ibid., p. 332.
43 Ibid., p. 333.
44 Ibid., p. 335.
45 Woolf, 'The Russian Point of View', in *Essays* vol. 4, p. 188.
46 Viktor Shklovsky, 'Art as Technique', in *Russian Formalist Criticism: Four Essays*, edited by Lee T. Lemon and Marion J. Reiss (Lincoln: University of Nebraska Press, 1965), pp. 3 24, 17.
47 Woolf, 'Robinson Crusoe', *Essays* vol. 4., p. 332.
48 Shklovsky, 'Art as Technique', p.
49 E. M. Forster, *Aspects of the Novel* (1927) (Harmondsworth: Penguin, 1990), p. 28.
50 Ibid., p. 31.
51 Ibid.
52 Woolf, 'Modern Fiction', *Essays* vol. 4, p. 157.
53 Edwin Muir, *The Structure of the Novel* (London: Hogarth Press, 1928), p. 119.
54 Ramon Fernandez, *Messages*, translated by Montgomery Belgion (London: Jonathan Cape, 1927), italics in original, p. 63.
55 Aristotle, *Poetics*, translated by Malcolm Heath (Harmondsworth: Penguin, 1996), p. 16.
56 Muir, *Structure of the Novel*, p. 123.
57 Ibid., p. 118.
58 Ibid., p. 132.
59 Ibid., p. 133.
60 Ibid., p. 151.
61 Edwin Muir, *Transition: Essays on Contemporary Literature* (London: Hogarth Press, 1926), pp. 4–5.
62 Friedrich Nietzsche, *The Use and Abuse of History for Life*, translated by Adrian Collins (New York: Macmillan, 1985), p. 8.
63 Muir, *Transition*, p. 8.
64 Ibid., p. 14.
65 Woolf, 'How It Strikes a Contemporary', in *Essays* vol. 4, p. 237.
66 Woolf, 'Life and the Novelist', in *Essays* vol. 4, p. 401.
67 Woolf, 'On Re-Reading Novels', in *Essays* vol. 3, p. 339.
68 Virginia Woolf, 'Phases of Fiction', in *The Essays of Virginia Woolf: Volume 5, 1929–1932*, edited by Stuart N. Clarke (London: Hogarth Press, 2009), p. 83.
69 Woolf, 'On Re-Reading Novels', in *Essays* vol. 3, p. 343.
70 Woolf, 'How Should One Read a Book?' in *Essays* vol. 4, p. 597.
71 Ibid., p. 578.
72 Woolf, 'Reading', in *Essays* vol. 3, p. 153.
73 Virginia Woolf, 'Hours in a Library', in *The Essays of Virginia Woolf: Volume 2, 1912–1918*, edited by Andrew McNeillie (London: Hogarth Press, 1987), p. 58.
74 Ibid., p. 59.
75 Woolf, 'Phases of Fiction', in *Essays* vol. 5, p. 40–41.

76 Ibid., p. 84.
77 Virginia Woolf, *The Diary of Virginia Woolf: Volume 3 1925–30*, edited by Anne Olivier Bell (London: Hogarth Press, 1980), pp. 50–51.
78 Virginia Woolf, letter to Vita Sackville-West (9 October 1927), in *A Change of Perspective: The Letters of Virginia Woolf 1923–1928*, edited by Nigel Nicolson (London: Chatto and Windus, 1977), pp. 428–429.

Index